The Cure of Poetry in an Age of Prose

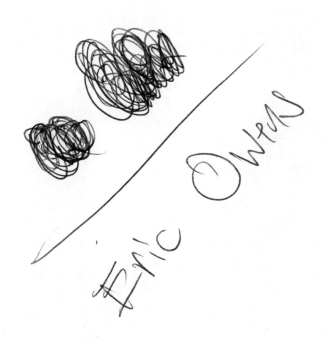

The Cure of Poetry in an Age of Prose

*Moral Essays on the
Poet's Calling*

Mary Kinzie

The University of Chicago Press
Chicago and London

Mary Kinzie, director of the creative writing program at
Northwestern University, is the author of four volumes of poetry (most
recently *Autumn Eros*) and of criticism and reviews of the work of
more than one hundred poets.

The University of Chicago Press, Chicago 60637
The University of Chicago Press, Ltd., London
© 1993 by The University of Chicago
All rights reserved. Published 1993
Printed in the United States of America

02 01 00 99 98 97 96 95 94 93   1 2 3 4 5

ISBN: 0–226–43735-3 (cloth)
0–226–43736-1 (paper)

Library of Congress Cataloging-in-Publication Data

Kinzie, Mary.
    The cure of poetry in an age of prose : moral essays on the poet's
calling / Mary Kinzie.
      p.   cm.
    Includes index.
    1. Poetry—History and criticism.   2. Criticism.   I. Title.
PN1031.K494   1993
809.1—dc20   92-43870
                                                                  CIP

Contents

Acknowledgments

"The Rhapsodic Fallacy" originally appeared in *Salmagundi* (Fall 1984); material has been added on Gary Snyder from "Pictures from Borges," *American Poetry Review* (hereafter *APR*) (November/December 1983); on James Wright from "Through the Looking-Glass: The Romance of the Perceptual in Contemporary Poetry," *Ploughshares* (Spring 1979); on idiomatic usage from "Idiom and Error," *APR* (September/October 1984); on Jorie Graham also from "Pictures from Borges."

"The Romance of the Perceptual" originally appeared as "Through the Looking-Glass: The Romance of the Perceptual in Contemporary Poetry," *Ploughshares* (Spring 1979); material has been added on A. R. Ammons from "Haunting," *APR* (September/October 1982); on Louise Glück, also from "Haunting"; on Ted Hughes from "Idiom and Error"; on Robert Pinsky, also from "Idiom and Error" and from "Meaning in Place: A Moral Essay," *APR* (January/February 1991); on Ben Belitt from "A Servant's Cenotaph," *Salmagundi* (Summer 1990).

"Three Essays on Confession" contain previously published material as follows: (1) "Pure Feeling" is based on "Two Lives" (on Bogan and Roethke), *APR* (March/April 1981); (2) "Pure Pain" makes use of "The Prophet is a Fool: On *Waking Early Sunday Morning*," *Salmagundi* (Spring 1977); (3) "Applied Poetry" uses a reduced version of the essay by that name which appeared in *Poetry* (June 1989).

"A New Sweetness: Randall Jarrell and Elizabeth Bishop" draws on "The Man Who Painted Bulls" (on Randall Jarrell), *Southern Review* (Fall 1980); and "Her Revery" (on Elizabeth Bishop), *Kenyon Review* (Winter 1984).

"The Signatures of Things: On Howard Nemerov" appeared in *Parnassus* (Fall/Winter 1977–78); and the last section appeared as "The Judge Is Rue" in *Poetry* (September 1981).

"Deeper Than Declared: On Seamus Heaney" appeared in *Salmagundi* (Fall 1988).

" 'Irreference': On John Ashbery" appeared as " 'Irreference': The Poetic Diction of John Ashbery" in *Modern Philology* (February and May 1987).

"The Cure of Poetry" appeared in *Southwest Review* (Fall 1991).

"The Poet's Calling: On a New Model of Literary Apprenticeship" contains work previously published as follows: from "Letter on the Poet's

Responsibility," *APR* (May/June 1984); from "Learning to Speak: On a New Model of Literary Apprenticeship," *Salmagundi* (Summer 1985); and on Edgar Wind from "The Overdefinition of the Now," *APR* (March/April 1982).

I would like to express my thanks to the journals of original publication and their editors for engaging me to write the essays that form the core of this book. I am especially appreciative of the encouragement of Robert Boyers, editor-in-chief of *Salmagundi,* and of David Bonanno, co-editor of *American Poetry Review.* I am grateful to the President's Fund for the Humanities at Northwestern University for awarding me a research grant for a year of leave in 1990–91, during which I recast many of the essays and composed the title essay. I am also indebted to Patricia and Martin J. Koldyke for sponsoring the teaching award that provided me during the past two years with word-processing equipment as well as the help of two research assistants, Mark Gobel and Kate Lovelady. I would also like to thank Mark Alsop, who retyped the essays for me.

For intellectual community and friendship during the period when thought and word were surfacing, I would like to thank my colleagues at Northwestern University. Several long-distance colleagues also deserve mention—Mary Etta Knapp, John Koethe, Ruth Limmer, and Eleanor Wilner. These are a few among many to whom I owe debts of insight and attention difficult to measure. There is no doubt that I have been unusually fortunate in the teachers I have had and the poets I have known. Over time, the two roles intertwine.

Mary Kinzie

Evanston, Illinois
May 1, 1992

Introduction: The Level of Words

Being Seen Through

The Cure of Poetry in an Age of Prose is a collection of essays in which I take as given the poet's deliberate seizure of language from the generality of prose. That effort is a restorative one; the poet aims to restore to poetry the universality and aboriginality that over time have mistakenly been reassigned to prose. Poetry is the preconditional state of language, not its late and shiftless offspring. The essays that ensue share a preoccupation with the multiplicity and breadth of which poetry has been and may yet again be capable. Poetry was once the queen of literature, not its poor cousin. At various junctures drama was written in it; so were letters. Once the medium of songs as of satire, of philosophical meditations and allegory, of civic as well as private praise and lament, poetic verse periodically could do anything a thoughtful or unruly bard wished it to do. It was the very expanse of possibility in which literary structure was secured. I subscribe to the notion that, if language can be thought of as a pyramid, its base is poetry, not prose. Poetry is the ground—the ground of resemblance, controlled in time—from which literature of all kinds takes shape.

"Poetry" is thus the inclusive term for literature broadly and complexly construed; when so applied it brings back to mind the traits often only latent in the more attenuated written arts, namely, technical concentration and moral truth. Poetry is language carried to the highest expressive power commensurate with clarity of representation. This definition reflects the demand that a novel, poem, play, or artful meditation reply to the need for coherence in human life while reflecting the facts of experiential complexity, and that literary work must speak memorably about our great anxieties—affliction, injustice, death.

As a result I believe that one cannot dictate to artists—or to readers as they study artists—that one or another ideological grid must lie behind the genesis of a work. Tendentious ideology, which would insert its programmatic if well-meaning bias into a reading of all human behavior, can produce only bad art—and bad criticism, too—"bad" in the sense of being naïve on the one hand, stunted and corrupt on the other. But even at its most benign, reading by ideology assumes that the artist must share with laborer, clerk, and scientist an unavoidable and often unwitting cultural placement—a condition of embeddedness in historical particularity that prompts those preoccupied with its identification to overstress its role (that is, its inevitability) in literary creation while neglecting the more demanding and subtle concept of the poet's calling.

There is a poem by Rilke that suggests a more positive course for the poet and critic alike. It is a sonnet praising an archaic stone torso of Apollo, the god of poetry (from Rilke's *New Poems: Second Part,* 1908). Despite the fact that the figure has no head—hence no eyes—the entire torso, says Rilke, still glows, when we see it in our day, like a candelabra, as if the eyes were shining everywhere in its flesh. Apollos' gaze has actually been diffused across the entire muscular play of his body. This is why one is blinded by the flexure of the chest and why, as the onlooker traces the lithe composure of sinew and limb, one imagines a smile forming: Because the "consciousness" that radiates from the sculpted body is so intense, it suggests the locale of those most human of gestures, smiling and intelligent gazing—namely, the cranium and the face. And then comes the famous close of the poem:

> *denn da ist keine Stelle*
> *die dich nicht sieht. Du musst dein Leben ändern.*

> for his body has no single place
> that fails to see you. You must change your life.

This statue sees you. Even headless, Apollo compels you with his observation. If you are doing it right, rather than your watching it, art sees and changes *you.* Rather than an exclusive interpretive movement backward from the audience to the work, with all the opportunities for distortion and projection which that return might underscore, what if one imagined the work itself to be announcing its demeanor, and soliciting and modifying our scrutiny by its own?

I have frequently experienced the sensation that to study a work, a painting or poem, was to be studied in return, until studying, listening, or reading became also a process of being studied, of being read. It may well put us closer to the truth of art to wait rather than interpret. It may be that if we could restrain our chronic urge to reduce art to something else, we might perceive truths we could not have predicted. Perhaps the insistence of interpretive schemes diminishes the light of poetry in the same way urban glare obscures the light of stars at night. I, for one, would be curious to see how the intellectual environment might grow less obscuring, where art is concerned, if a number of readers were to entertain a posture of readiness and even need for guidance from the works of artists. In this way we might reacquaint ourselves with the human and curative powers of creation. To experience art would mean to be scrutinized by the creative intelligence that worked through it in its growth, and to be, at the very least, alerted to these emanations from the Other when not actually ennobled, crushed, and transformed by them.

Of course, what might transform readers in the act of appreciating art is increased manyfold in the experience of making a work like a poem: It is at once a contract with self-scrutiny, and a state of being illuminated or seen through by it. The poem you are writing sees you, sees (in both senses) through you: It shows you up, and it requires your humble cooperation. In the process, of course, one undertakes the stages of a rigorous emotional discipline—as a means, as the novelist Pavese once suggested, to achieve possession over one's own past, one's own pulse, and one's own untoward and surprising predilections. Rather than canceling the individual person or obviating self-knowledge, the disciplines required by art return to us perfected command over what is most fruitfully idiosyncratic.

To cure poetry would thus be to redefine it for others while composing out of inner conviction that one is oneself being taught, indeed renovated, by the endeavor. The poet seeks to purify the language of the tribe (as Eliot suggested), but by the most intimate and emptying of encounters. In this ambiguous fulfillment, at once impersonally stylized and deeply self-interested, the poet struggles to identify in words, and *at the level of words* to unearth the means of embodying, clear and specific ideals of personhood and integrity. The poet who emerges from the twisted passages realizes how valuable is the true poem in proportion to its rarity, not to mention its humbling human cost. The boon of eloquent exactitude is a prize pure to the point of extinction—for even in amplitude and extensiveness the poet's means must be rigorously approved. So although the goal is universality, the poem's arena of achievement is necessarily strictly contained and the poet's attitude one of precarious transparency. Good poetry thus produced is cleansed of dross, falsehood, and everything extraneous to the representation of the poet's primary subject, inevitably an affirmation of the ideals in question. "Good" applied to poetry in this sense points to its moral significance, which coordinates the poet's psychological need with an aesthetic aim in the interest of creations that exceed a narrow construction of either. The cure of poetry is the achievement of the poem's rescue from an accumulation of prosaic impulses that stanch the spring of feeling and idea.

In another sense the idea of cure is one of redemption by the very uncompromising excellence of the poetic medium itself. In an age of prose like our own, poetry offers the more satisfying imaginative resolve, holding out before the apprentice writer the promise of what in the Middle Ages was entailed by courtly *hohe Minne*—dedicated service and erotic awe. Because the service of poetry magisterially summons the writer, makes demands, and designates the ways of approach to itself, it is appropriate to speak of the poet's *calling*.

It is not accidental that I invoke some terms more familiar in religious circles than literary ones. For the task of the poet in the world is to act as seer while embodying in her own development the confrontation with affliction, or fate, that may approach transcendence.[1] Furthermore, the critic, too, must acknowledge the quasi-religious strength of this calling. I call these deliberations "Moral Essays" both to respond to my sense that the job of the critic lies in recognizing the lineaments of individual struggle toward transformation in the act of creation, and at the same time to accommodate my sense that the poet is engaged in a series of similar recognitions. From the perspective of critic as well as poet, making and meaning in poetry are moral in origin, as well as moral in the pattern of obligations—which are more than technical and linguistic ones—between the poem's auditory and linguistic orders and its essential saying. Syntax and semantics properly construed by the practicing artist might provide terms broad enough to imply this concerted, moral work of imagination; but in a climate of intellectual reduction it is difficult to suppose that many readers would associate a category like "syntax" with spiritual or even mental work. Furthermore, I am not trying to promulgate laws abstracted from the practice of poetry. As far as I have been able to see, there is no theory apart from practice in the task of soul-making to which the poet is called.

Curing the Critic

The critic is inevitably involved in the cure of poetry to the extent that the act of criticism reflects not only by pondering but more subtly by paralleling the poet's work. And because the moral engagement of the poet with her material is necessarily one that occurs in myriad small and local movements, not just in the preliminary or climatic ones, this relation presupposes an awareness of the limitations that enable the poetic tradition. Here, too, the spirit of Rilke's poem is in command of our knowledge, determining how it shall be communicated and how we shall prepare to take it in. And the result is that we are asked to see *slowly*. In these more deliberate rhythms we are more apt to receive the inexorable pedagogy of the muse. Responding to such a vision, in order to make a poem that stems from and embodies acts of moral imagination and redemptive yearning, the cloth the poet makes must be whole. That is to say, it must be woven, carefully, out of thread. Just so, for the critic, it must be small stitches that generate the larger weave. The veritable texture of the work does not come into view unless one's vantage is also very close. One can work one's way through a poem only at the level of words. Thus I would defend the process of the many close readings of individual poets in the ensuing studies. From the belief that the poet's struggle to craft a cure and follow a high calling occurs, obsessively and repetitively, at the verbal level, it necessarily follows that the critical method of demonstration is one of exemplification and sifting. That is the approach of these essays.

Critics cannot elect *not* to read slowly and closely unless they are to be resigned to irrelevance. There is no viable interpretation that does not (like the path through the forest in the fairy tales) lead through the thicket of reading word for word. When critics chronically or prematurely become distracted from that path, they mistake the poem's method. Still, critics of such critics may demur: The reader authentically attuned to poetry is by that fact equipped to discriminate what is art from what is folk or commerce or therapy or revolution, because such a reader has followed the poet's path, becoming an apprentice to the tradition as well as a disciple to its artists. Emerging from an apprenticeship not unlike the poet's own, the ideal reader is better able to articulate the inner workings of the artist's calling so as to estimate that threshold where variegated culture stops and the implacable demand of depth begins.

This demand is an appalling one. True artists live under a ban, a compulsion, with a pressing, incomplete *assignment* hanging over their heads. Whatever the poet discovers as an answer to the need for human significance will, in its distillation, be colored with a certain constraint, as well as a certain sadness; but it is a sadness poetry strives (monumentally strives) to lighten. Poetry subjects the indefiniteness of yearning—the yearning by which each person is encouraged to fill the void created by living in time—to the maximum rigor, and it is rigor that makes light. It is this lightness without irony, fully embraced and believed even as the heart is breaking, that makes perfect poems like Ovid's *Metamorphoses,* Buson's haiku, and many of the lyrics of Christina Rossetti, Louise Bogan, Edwin Muir, Elizabeth Bishop, and Janet Lewis feel redemptive. Many another exemplary list could be constructed: Lightness similarly irradiates the gloom in the Psalms, Herbert, Traherne, Swift, Coleridge, John Clare, Dickinson, Wallace Stevens, Marianne Moore, F. T. Prince, Geoffrey Hill, Julia Randall, and Sandra MacPherson; the point is that it is not merely the lyrical mode that fosters the archetypical emotions of poetry but all types in which the artifices of the given period are subdued. For it is this lightness of perfected flexibility that distances sentimentality and despair, while acknowledging the pertinence of pity and outrage in the personal realm.

To meet such a criterion, paradoxically, poetry must spring from the soul of an individual living in time, somebody replete with unique contingency. Then we may discern how, in the work, the poet retains the inflection of individuality even as the spirit sails on before. Above all, such characterizations cannot remain true only of the poet. For the conduct of criticism, too, techniques of clear and eloquent response must similarly spring from a foundation in a fully *formed* and sentient individual; neither good critic nor good poet will emerge if the inertia of the sedulously formalist tradition or (yet more accidentally) theory is the only school of insight and feeling.

At present theory and tradition construed pejoratively are mutually exclusive; formal tradition would appear to be what theory wanted to topple—and essentially has toppled, for today how many aspiring writers, creative or analytic, bother to learn the rudiments of literary art? Literature, with poetry at its base, has only intermittent contact with either theoretical discourse or tradition in its role as straw man. Overhearing their dissensions from her inner room (her eye bewitched by the pen moving over the page), poetry remains aloof from the wrangle. She is intent on some act of aboriginal imagination liberated by a form; the poet need not debate form's place, only know it so well she can bend it to her purposes. The devices of the tradition enable humanly expressive functions; theory may elect to overlook these, but the poet and critic do not. For it is the form's rhetorical, analogical, and auditory techniques with their aesthetic interrelations (all of them living variants of inherited devices) that reflect and make eloquent this crucially solitary, individual writer's quest—a quest at once ontological and aesthetic. The critic must follow her toward this uncertain inner place.

Crippling Requirements

The reflection of meaning by method occurs there, within—painfully, but also efficiently. If poetry is the best mode of literary art for conveying feeling, and for conveying thinking *about* feeling, it is because poetry constitutes a species of spirituality that is *übergeistlich,* working on a plane of superlogic, or razory cognition—and because, by a twin compulsion, poetry is the product of torment that feeds on itself; in short, it is haywire, unmannerly, perverse. If we diagnosed true art by our experience of it, we would point to the formative recurrent sensation that, through the bright net of art, we glimpsed the inchoate deep casting up flecks of foam, and in this experience we would know with an instant knowledge that that foam was poison, that sea death. The artist is enjoined against any mode of travel other than by this sea, and that injunction is her bane.

Her response is thus all the more remarkable, since it is that of adjusting the body against pain. This means training the body to accommodate it until they seem magnetically aligned. The most prominent motive in poetry, which is to say the poet's desire to re-create insight into a truth experienced as absolute and apodictic, launches itself in spirited recoil against (but therefore along the same axis with) the fact of mutability; and, in the resultant flooding-in of yearning, which she flees before, the poet designs something to outlast, a little, the plague of fragmentation. Yet chronic contact with the theme strengthens its pertinence, until, rather than recurring as thematic genre or stylistic mode, an elegiac tenor is everywhere dispersed in poetry since the romantics, saturating the medium and conditioning both language and response.

Moreover, this heritage—the heritage of a creature aflame with meaning, will, sympathy, and desire—encounters the ironic impediment, indifference. What is, I believe, more frustrating to the natural unfolding of any poet's authentic mission than the difficulty of the mission is that the poet must endure the scrutiny of a world not of her making, and one that disdains the authority true poetry must naturally command from all who hear her. Poetry lives her own creative life, yet as she lifts her head from the desk, she catches sight of the gargoyle at the edge of her field of vision. It makes a minatory gesture, that of a new theory bent on reducing or restricting language (including the language of art) to unpredictable exchanges of momentary illusions about meanings. One such supposed "illusion" is that an author might intend and create these meanings. How can a real poet take the deep divination of poetry to be illusory? It is, said Goethe, only the attitude of belief that is fertile for the writer—even if one is compelled to skepticism by the age in which one lives.

Not only is the world indifferent to the poet, not only are the medium of poems and the soul-searching proper to them painfully hard to take on, but the task of writing is also one of chronic returns to incompletion. Even after producing a precarious magic out of words, the good writer is obliged to return to the start, begin again with her ordeal of witnessing that uncovers the harrowing clockworks of existence and consciousness. And she must not merely repeat her ordeal, but behold it with a newly flayed, profoundly raw obedience.

This crucial return to a posture of obedience before life's material unfoldings involves both experience as commonly understood and the distinctive *artistic* experience (of summoning and arranging words about experience so as to heighten her consciousness of its enormity). There is no pure poetry without referents; the most dispassionate self-deprecation in experimental literary art can never entirely elude the forming, about the transparent phrases, of a sort of temperamental weather. (One might think of Hart Crane with his sensibility so electric and so identifiably different from cool Marianne Moore's.) The handling of formal materials sends messages about the presentation of the artist's person that we can also correlate with successful, inventive, and proper (or unsuccessful, repetitive, and incoherent) formal technique. For good artists reinvent their working principles from work to work, and in the absence of such discernible principes the work is chaos, however inspired.

Moral Essays and Judgment

> I am not writing about aesthetics but about the ethics which are altogether less visible in a poetic tradition. Who the poet is, what he or she nominates as the proper theme for poetry, what self they discover and confirm through this subject matter—all of this involves an ethical choice.[2]

I am conscious that I use terms denoting value that stand at the juncture of moral and artistic judgment—"good poetry," or more crucially, "the good writer," "good artists," "the true poet." It is the mission of the book that follows to become familiar with the determinants of this goodness and this truth attaching not solely to works but equally to the persons of its makers during a period when poetry has been particularly susceptible to prose. Although the boundaries between prose and poem as localized genres necessarily shift and, on occasion, fuse, it is still the obligation of the good writer to be answerable to standards of serious human response and "to express [these] with humanly significant fullness," as Philip Wheelwright says of radically symbolic language.[3] Even with a great admixture of contingent peculiarity, dilation, overemphasis, principled evasion, and in general an unavoidable hobbling by the poets' own temperaments, I believe this obligation is met by the way that some poets address reality, but not others. One can reach conclusions worth reaching only by considering the example of individual writers. In poetry, as distinct from theory, only actual successful practice provides a profitable adumbration of an ideal.

Furthermore, until a writer has dared to extend a verse-kind beyond itself, we as readers do not know what is actually possible in art. There is always something chancy, potentially misguided, about the new turning. This is why the critic must labor to be as closely in sympathy with answerable style as it is possible for a mere critic to be. On the other hand, while honest diagnosis of flawed work inevitably seems too caustic, if it *is* honest and intelligent, the critic's careful treatment of failures prepares the ground for regeneration. And even when it seems harsh to some, good criticism is not proscription. Proscription is irrelevant to genuine innovation and its recognition.

Discipline, however, which seems to many proscriptive, is hardly irrelevant to the idea of an artist's apprenticeship. This is one area of thought about art and art theory that has been slighted in the past twenty years—during a time of unaccountable acquiescence in the widespread abdication of standards in the award and patronage systems that support art. Too little thought is given, in the literary marketplaces of publishing houses and (remarkable this) even in university writing programs, to the training of the competent writer let alone of the gifted artist. What constitutes a proper threshold of training in literary art? What is it we want any writer to be able to *do* before deciding among literature's major career paths (assuming, that is, that poetry might be considered a career path)? There is no theoretico-cultural trend that I know of that attempts to school the literary apprentice in any of the techniques that promote flexibility of choice, fluency of technique, and integrity of execution.

In examining the work of poetry primarily during the past twenty to thirty years, I have been concerned to preserve the image and presence of the person, as Allen Grossman eloquently urges us to do.[4] It seems important to keep the image of the person at the center of the thought of poetry for the sake not merely of the poetry but also of the criticism we produce and the teaching we conduct. My assumption throughout is that the work of literature requires an author, not merely as a cultural fiction but as an act of personal commitment. The commitment extends itself to teaching and criticism as well. Hence, again, the pertinence of the term "moral" to these essays—a term at odds with the ways of understanding art when art is taken politically. "Moral essays" are required because art cannot be produced in the absence of the person creating it, or understood other than humanly at the level of words.

Five of the pieces that follow treat these necessities and some of the work (at times commendable) formed in reaction to them. Four longer studies of individual writers trace the ingenious compromises of Randall Jarrell and Elizabeth Bishop, and of John Ashbery, Howard Nemerov, and Seamus Heaney by means of which they avert debasement in the present age of prose. A departure essay, "The Cure of Poetry," links the calling of the novelist to that of the poet. A conclusion adumbrates a new model for the apprenticeship of writers of prose *or* verse.

The first of the general essays, "The Rhapsodic Fallacy," contains a study of the invasion of the poem by prose in contemporary verse (despite its nominal ideal of liberated subjectivity). The goal of rhapsodic outpouring is shown to be ill served by the gestures and attitudes of prose and prosaic cliché. After a brief sketch of the evolution since the romantic period of extruded (nonstanzaic) forms and the paradox of the continuing, parallel requirement of thematic "depth," I examine some works by Jorie

Graham, James Wright, and Gary Snyder that distort the ethical categories they invoke. If on occasion these poets insist on the authentication by broken speech, they simultaneously remove from the poets' own control the *ordonnances* of style by which creators might forge *un*broken meanings. The line of inheritance is then more predictable from broken speech to random and bland traits in contemporary verse and versification, despite its continuing insistence on rhapsodic postures and claims.

The next studies, "Three Essays on Confession," examine a specific literary-historical nexus of rhapsodic assumptions. In the first of these, "Pure Feeling," I adumbrate competing models for purity of feeling in verse. The controversy is illustrated in the lives and careers of Louise Bogan and Theodore Roethke. In the second piece, "Pure Pain," confessionalism is linked to the shrinking of modes of self-expression. On this view, primacy is accorded to movements of regression, wish fulfillment, anger, exhibition. Disturbance becomes a laudable life-path in the exemplary confessional poet, Robert Lowell. This study presents an extended look at Lowell's poem "Waking Early Sunday Morning." The third study in this series, from a review essay called "Applied Poetry," explores the relation between formal and thematic excess, and the ethos of the amateur. However hard poets like Anne Sexton labor to make a virtue of necessity, there are certain dismaying consequences of the failure to command the basic verbal and rhythmic techniques that enable one to tamper successfully with the norm. The case of Anne Sexton only warrants the slipshod; Sandra Gilbert can also be seen in this light. I include in this version the instructive exceptions in the poems of Jim Powell and John N. Morris, because their books, however arbitrarily cast up in the same batch of review copies, and however little known, illustrate two essential modes of the many that can be imagined in resistance to cant and exhausted conventions.

The study of Randall Jarrell and Elizabeth Bishop naturally follows from the sequence on confessional poets and confessionalism. Intimately acquainted with Robert Lowell, both Jarrell and Bishop take the tangent of naïveté, adopting the child's angle of vision in recoil from pain and complex modern experience. The child's vision authenticates purity of feeling, as well as depth of reverberation—despite the want of systematic evolution by the categorically immature self. The example of Marianne Moore is brought in to highlight the style of overemphasis and understatement on the part of both Jarrell and his follower, Bishop.

The romance of the child is followed by an extended look at some of the modes of the perceptual sublime. Chapter 5, "The Romance of the Perceptual: The Legacy of Wallace Stevens," proposes the overarching example of Stevens as a point of reference for examining the varieties of bareness and exaltation that predominate when many contemporary poets engage visual perception. Perceptual poetry thus often crosses over into superstitious awe, beginning with the Stevensian use of landscapes as self-projections. Examples in this essay are closely read interpretations of the work of A. R. Ammons, Mark Strand and the "lyric school," Louise Glück, Ted Hughes, Robert Pinsky, and Ben Belitt.

A monograph-length study on Howard Nemerov charts the emergence of mastery and the evolution of spiritual transparency in the career of perhaps the greatest postwar conversational and meditative poet. A long essay on Seamus Heaney studies the subtleties of political anxiety on the part of this celebrated inventor. A major stress is placed on the flexible juggling of dichotomies in style as well as theme—Latin formalism, for example, as a counter to Celtic wildness. A third monograph-length essay, on John Ashbery, traces this masterful and evasive poet's accommodations of radical syntactic, semantic, and prosodic experiment to recognizable thematic organizations. Maintaining the constant tonal irony of implied cliché enables Ashbery to experiment with the very elaborations of feeling he resists adopting. Although all three poets practice feints and evasions, they belong to different cultural moments and indulge divergent impulses. They are brought together with a double purpose: in order to demonstrate the virtue, for interpretive clarity and even economy, of extensive exemplification within an individual poet's oeuvre, and to suggest how such a method of criticism merges with the method of the poet. For as the critic moves at the level of words across the terrain of several such complex and idiosyncratic poets' imaginations, it is hoped that the critical enterprise can itself be perceived to mirror the interplay, in any true poetic work, between critical and creative faculties.

In the essay that gives the collection its title, "The Cure of Poetry," I meditate on the discipline of word and spirit in conditions of dryness, suggesting a sympathetic bond between the mission of the poet as Louise Bogan exemplifies it and that of the great contemporary parabolic novelist, J. M. Coetzee.

The concluding essay, "The Poet's Calling," answers some of my critics and proposes a new model of literary apprenticeship that would train writers and readers of prose as well. Such an apprenticeship, aimed at inculcating openness to an expressive ideal, would entail two major and distinct preliminary stages, learning to speak and learning to wait. Here the apprentice must pause for some time at the level of words before touching the threshold of song.

1

The Rhapsodic Fallacy

Contemporary poetry suffers from dryness, prosaism, and imaginative commonplace, but these are hardly its worst features. Rather, the stylistic dullness is disagreeably coarsened and made the more decadent by being a brotherly symptom of, and in fact a technical support for, the assumption (which has only strengthened in the past 150 years) that the aim of poetry is apotheosis, an ecstatic and unmediated self-consumption in the moment of perception and feeling. The flat style is thought of as a kind of private charm that protects the writer against falsehood, insuring sincerity. But it has tended to take for granted the real content of the inner life, affecting the mannerisms of sincerity without the coherent values which that sincerity might express. The poetic has thus made an odd marriage with the prosaic, and it is this parasitic weakening of the subjective idea by an aimless prosaic experimentalism that we see in much new verse. Subjective experience is expressed as objectively derived, in a diction that is indifferent, reductive, even, on occasion, somewhat dull-witted. To judge from their practice, many poets have assumed that complexity would work against the freshness of perception. Hence, although emotion is the overriding topic, paradoxically it is not immediacy but diffuseness in diction, syntax, and argument that has manifested itself as the overriding style. To see why our culture has so confounded the poetic with the prosaic, let us review.

Most critics agree that a major begetter of a rhapsodic theory of poetry is Edgar Allan Poe (with two essays in particular, the defense of "The Raven" called "The Philosophy of Composition" in 1846, and "The Poetic Principle," published the year after Poe's death, in 1850). In Poe, we find articulated two modern tendencies. First, a desire for intense brevity—a desire that carries with it the belief that intensity can be achieved only in spontaneous, fragmented utterance.[1] The second tendency adumbrated in Poe (less in the critical work than in his own practice) is the contradictory belief that the mental epic is viable. Poe has bequeathed us the long skein of excited prose about the origins and ends of the universe, which he thought of as a poem, called *Eureka* (1848),

the very title of which bespeaks Poe's seizure by the drama of his own
insights. The text itself lives up to Poe's claim that coherent argument is
irrelevant. It proceeds by fiat and elegy to portray the coming dissolution
of the cosmos as emanating from the yearning of all things to return to
their union in God. Like Swedenborg a century earlier, Poe believed that
all matter shared one rationale; in *Eureka* the projection from man to
atom is dressed as scientific procedure in the service of the Divine, and
the prose, in gorgeous surges and retards, bathes the thinker in the ebbing
of his thoughts, the artist in the ecstasy that warrants his art. In fact, the
thinker *is* the artist, and conversely, the artist the only philosopher. The
aesthetic or poetic artifact thus fades before the experience into which the
artist can plunge.

Beginning with Charles Baudelaire in 1852, the writers who took up
Poe's theories and poses in the nineteenth century, or those who, like Mill
and Arnold, independently corroborated Poe's opinion that the long
poem on public themes was a contradiction in terms, were in fact participating in a process that not only involved weeding out the stunted and
unworthy genres like civic poems and didactic verses.[2] They were also
continuing the major felling of giant oak and elm from the forests of our
literature. "One after another," as A. D. Hope says, "the great forms
disappear; the remaining forms proliferate and hypertrophy and display
increasing eccentricity and lack of centre."[3] The following poem expresses
something of the current attitude:

> I like it when
> Achilles
> Gets killed
> And even his buddy Patroclus—
> And that hothead Hector—
> And the whole Greek and Trojan
> *Jeunesse dorée*
> Is more or less
> Expertly slaughtered
> So there's finally
> Peace and quiet
> (The gods having momentarily
> Shut up)
> One can hear
> A bird sing
> And a daughter ask her mother
> Whether she can go to the well
> And of course she can
> By that lovely little path
> That winds through
> The olive orchard.[4]

The poet breaks the proscenium, first to accommodate a Holden Caulfield type of vernacular ("I like it when" something or other happens; "his buddy Patroclus"; "hothead Hector"), then to allow himself to assemble counterproofs of his own cleverness (*"Jeunesse dorée"*; the fastidious adverb "expertly" for the rugged "slaughtered"; the self-congratulatory deftness of the indirect discourse, "And of course she can"); and finally the proscenium of the major tradition of literary action is broken to permit the child to enter, and with it, the nameless, the sentimental, the unheroic, and the everyday.

We have now eliminated from the available repertory of literary responses not only those forms associated with the eighteenth century— formal satire, familiar epistle, georgic, and pastoral—but also those associated with the Middle Ages and the Renaissance—allegory, philosophical poem, epic, and verse drama and tragedy—until nothing is left for us but a kind of low lyrical shrub whose roots are quickforming, but shallow. This ecological metaphor is beautifully developed by A. D. Hope in the essay from which I quoted, "The Discursive Mode," where he describes as follows "the sparse and monotonous vegetation of the arid steppe: little poems of reflection, brief comments, interior monologues, sharp critical barks and hisses, songs that never become articulate; earnestness that lacks the enchantment of truth, and frivolity that disgusts by its absence of charm."[5]

Another critic reminds us that in cutting away all but this meager foliage of the immediate, descriptive-rhapsodic cameo, the nineteenth- and twentieth-century poets were in effect not only erasing their own literary past: They were making themselves over into types of untaught, innocent children again. What the nineteenth-century poets achieved for us, says Geoffrey Tillotson, was a language in which we could address the startlingly individual quality of each unique moment. But while a certain freshness is not to be gainsaid, what was increasingly missing in their practice was any sense of hierarchy, propriety, literary order.[6] So today, form, trope, and diction have been democratized, leveled, subjected to the mechanism of the lowest common denominator—which is to say that rhetoric has been flattened to the standard of idle conversation in an era in which the art of conversation has been scrubbed clean of art and gentleness.[7]

Free verse has been the great equalizer and democratizer of poetic speech, liberating it to utter the small impression in homely language, but at the same time creating its own built-in obstacle to the registering of leisurely and complex idea, the ad hoc proscription on rhythm—the requirement that prosody and the arguments that the prosody might bear need to be re-created spontaneously and energetically at every point.

Furthermore, free verse marks the last stop before verse proceeds into the flatlands of prose. But prose is not practiced today with anything like the sophistication of Bacon, Browne, and Johnson. The current generations of writers in America have less command over, because less acquaintance with, the reasoning, the rhetoric, and the distinctions that were basic equipment for poets in the great ages of prose, the seventeenth and eighteenth centuries. We are even beginning to lose sight of the differences between high style and low style. As a result, to ask as Ezra Pound did that poetry be at least as well written as prose is no longer to insist on the excellence of either kind of writing.

We must also recognize that the reduction of poetic possibility to the brief compass of the free-verse lyric entails the loss (and I mean the literary *and* cultural loss) of the very keystone of logic, namely, the art of making the transition—the art of inference and connection, the art of modulation and (hence) surprise. When poems not only set themselves at a uniform pitch, but also contract themselves to recurrent, predictable five- or ten-line climaxes, pretty soon the surprises do not surprise us any more. The new prosaic-lyrical effusion is organized to get us into and out of the poem with extraordinary rapidity and no lasting effects.

Behind this enormous literary leveling that began in the early nineteenth century was also the shift away from the notion that art was supposed to reflect the truth, whether the truth of nature, in which case we are dealing with one or another of the mimetic theories of poetry; or the truth of beliefs, in which case the poem was a pragmatic tool toward engendering belief in the reader. Instead of the idea that poetry was supposed to imitate reality in nature or in the ethical realm, there emerged the idea that poetry was supposed to express idea, feeling, and the inmost being of the poet.[8]

William Wordsworth was the most eloquent and influential of the expressive theorists before Poe. It was Wordsworth who called the proper ground of the poem "the spontaneous overflow of powerful feelings," thus elevating the expressive criterion from the periphery of the poem into its center. Feeling was no longer result, but origin of the work of poetic art. The reader would be given not nature and the world, but the poet's responses to them. The "growth of a poet's mind," as Wordsworth subtitled *The Prelude* (1805), is a series of striking moments during which the poet-speaker stands (usually in the open air) *transfixed* by his insights—insights, we should add, that he owed in part to the landscapes to which he has imaginatively returned. Since "feeling overflows into words," as Meyer Abrams points out, expressive theorists from Wordsworth to I. A. Richards tend "to give to the nature and standards of poetic diction, or 'language,' the systematic priority which earlier critics had given to plot, character, and considerations of form." "Truth to nature," Abrams concludes, "has been replaced by sincerity," or "the *air* of truth."[9]

In their exclusive and proprietary relation to language, expressive theorists have helped promote the paradox of modern letters, facilitating the double treatment of words as both ordinary *and* mysterious, clear *and* turbid. Words are at once more transparent to experience than ever before, because less prepossessing and ornate, as in the work of the imagists, and simultaneously far more dense than any of the verbal ornaments devised by Lyly or Pope, because in the work of some influential modern poets words are reverenced as powers in an almost magical way; consider the curious fact that, although unrelated on every other conceivable dimension, Gertrude Stein and Gerard Manley Hopkins resemble one another in their tendency to make words obstreperous, stubborn in the mouth, thinglike in the mind.

Between these two word-habits in our century, the treating of words as transparent, and as dense, the orphic attitude on the one hand and the hermetic on the other,[10] or, one could say, between the utilization of words subjectively and objectively, modern art has arranged a peculiar interdependency. Some poets, like Wallace Stevens, may begin in whimsy and wordplay early in their careers, and end behind the most transparent of linguistic veils. Others, like T. S. Eliot, base their aesthetic upon a continual oscillation, within the given poem, between the two attitudes, the orphic or transparent taking turns with the hermetic or self-conscious. Eliot also brings into the modern poem the language of the lie—the dullness of the clerk, the hot shabbiness of office and *Stube,* the broken ends of distracted conversation in several languages. It is in *The Waste Land* (1922) that the little typist assesses her lovemaking in these starkly unembellished syllables, "Well now that's done: and I'm glad its over." This transparent realism stands out against the heavily brocaded ground of literary and religious lament.

A third poet, William Carlos Williams, comes to the task of expression in language with a single-minded fervor. He praises Gertrude Stein for "disinfecting" literature: "It's the words, the words we need to get back to, words washed clean."[11] And in Williams's own poems we frequently glimpse the scrubbed haloes shining about the words themselves:

BETWEEN WALLS

the back wings
of the

hospital where
nothing

will grow lie
cinders

in which shine
the broken

pieces of a green
bottle[12]

The abruptness of this poem has an extraordinarily pleasing finish, the word (*and* the thing) made shiny, plain, whole, and absolute, all the while significance hums in the background ("the back wings of the hospital where nothing will grow")—where, in other words, our social order's health cases are deposited like empties; where our discards languish. Carlos Williams gives a shifting transparency to the linguistic "thing" that he has made so preternaturally dense. To phrase this paradox another way, Williams objectifies words, and hence baffles his impulse to make them transparent and get rid of them entirely.

After disinfecting literature, Williams busily sets to, adorning words with color and moral opinion again. The green bottle, the red wheelbarrow, the sheet of brown paper, the plums in the icebox, the hind paw in the empty flowerpot, the fleshpale smoke from the yellow chimney, and the red brick monastery beside the polluted stream are all images that have been stamped twice into the wax of memory—once, visually, owing to the exactness of Williams's diction, and next, formally, owing to the kind and amount of white space that isolates word from word. Williams bequeathed to Denise Levertov and Robert Creeley something of his outstanding genius for breaking the short free-verse line. But in later poets the trick has, I think, been exhausted. What began in brio ends in mechanization. The concreteness of William Carlos Williams degenerates into the stolid, dull, and, above all, repetitious materialism of Marvin Bell.

Now that we have come down with a thump to the present time, we might look at some examples of current earnestness and frivolity with a clearer sense of origins and of the sheer weight of the "tradition" that impresses itself on poetic practice. For it's not as if the myriad composers of poetry in this country had conspired in their own dullness without the considerable tutelage and support of the readers and critics and teachers of poetry. The rhapsodic fallacy is committed by writers only with the consent of those who read literature, which is to say, with the consent of that cultural environment that includes and excludes material from works according to shared expectations about the good poem's contours. Although the rhapsodic fallacy holds strong emotion to be the overriding human bond and index of striving, it also permits the poet to keep this material peripheral, promissory, in reserve. So widespread is the assumption that "melancholy, nostalgia, puzzled yearning, and the like"[13] are central issues that one need only, it would appear, nod to these emotions as one passes through the poem. Meaning is thereby alluded to in a fashion that suggests both conventionality and enciphering.

Under the general convention of the prosaic-rhapsodic, we can distinguish three main contemporary substyles. In some sense, these three substyles are permeable to each other, and the modulations between them automatic. I take the objective style to be the easiest to recognize, if not to master.[14] Next comes the more sophisticated voice-play involved in the mixed ironic style. Finally, I would recognize an adjustment of the objective style to reveal the demonic or surreal; this technique of adjustment we can call the innocuous surreal style.

The objective style is determined by the cumulative effect of a string of brief, bland declarative sentences. The speaker is frequently solitary; the ambience an empty landscape or interior; and the mood sought after one of nondescript anxiety:

AUBADE

The pool remains clear.
The bedside glass holds water as warm as the room.
It will taste too sweet, the mouth
accounts for that. The light
insinuates, you know nothing of sleep,
you know nothing. If you wait it will dim.
Think of the margin of the sky.
Too distant for rain, the fingering clouds.
Good paper before the water and brush.
The sheets are stiff
with expectation. The raveled horizon
comes round again.[15]

Many of these statements suggest alternatives. That the pool *remains* clear suggests that we had expected it *not* to remain clear, hence the fact that it does so must constitute a little victory of some sort. This aura of victory-contrary-to-expectations spills over into the second line ("The bedside glass holds water as warm as the room"); although no alternatives are hinted at here, the warmth is a sympathetic value, betokening an almost intentional thermal transfer between water and room. But in the third line, the water is rejected as a beverage, not because it is too warm, but because its tepidity releases flavors (that sweetness) less perceptible when the water was cold.

We know from the title that the speaker is thirsty, and finally that there is some revulsion in the speaker's response to the sweetness imputed to the water: "the mouth / accounts for that. The light / insinuates, you know nothing of sleep, / you know nothing." Here we are suddenly struck by how the legal language of casuist proof and counterclaim is daubed in (as the drawing metaphor also emerges) over the literal details. Furthermore, the painter-plaintiff is the external world; it is the *light* which insinuates. Nevertheless, the trope of personification is as little explored and justified as is the hint of neurotic projection (is this a speaker who would impute "insinuation," consciousness, or malice to the very woodwork?). But no, there is neither obvious personification nor projection here.

Nor is the kind of metaphoricity we find in the objective style derived from abstraction or cognitive statement; this is not a poetry of concepts. Although "Aubade" is neither specific nor particular, it is not general, either. Or rather, the poem is a generalization of deliberately eccentric perception, whereby the poet ascribes to the world the limited faculties of immediate emotion and daydream. The poem before us insinuates anxiety, yes; some recognition that the routine of nature herself is weary, again yes; and some sort of communal disappointment at the communal expectations that stiffen the sheets, animate clouds, and hold the water clear in its volume, very well. But there is neither social nor mental relation to sharpen the focus of "Aubade"more than this. The history-less immediacy of perception as well as the limitation placed on experience are well served by the way the declarative sentences nudge each other aside in effortless non sequitur. No particular point is being made about the world's aesthetic intentions, nor is anything asserted or implied about the relation of the speaker to place; there is merely the gesture of objectless ennui as "The raveled horizon / comes round again."

The tools of the objective style—juxtaposition, portent, non sequitur, and passivity—can be endlessly manipulated. Here is an example of the realistic approach:

> Czechoslovakia, the smell
> of turned earth, the house
> at field's edge.
> I know these things.
> There was diphtheria,
> a child lost. The small grave
> is circled with small white stones.
> The osprey inhabits the marshes,
> the stork is common, portentous.
> The forests go on forever.
> There will be men killed there.[16]

The noncommittal passivity of the objective style claims for itself a kind of repertorial honesty ("I know these things"), and, in the context of reportage or guidebook writing, the non sequiturs tease up deeper implications, so that the smell of the earth and the death of the child and the ospreys in the marshes seem causally connected to each other and to the greater adult deaths in an Eastern Communist state. The loose method of inference here, however, seems as dubious as the methods of the unmentioned regime, and the remote omen of the deaths to come gains no authority from the argument of the poem, which falls into deadened hearsay and melodrama.

Where the blurred realism of the objective-rhapsodic is concerned, two writers in particular, both in the tradition of William Carlos Williams, have exercised enormous influence. In the work of James Wright we find not just simple seeing, not just descriptions of scenes, but also an attitude of proprietorship about the terrain covered, as if to say: This is mine, because I lived it. "I am what is around me," Wallace Stevens finds it possible to assert, then weaves the delicate permeability of this idea into a metaphysical pattern.[17] But the formula many other poets use for getting this proprietary exercise down on paper resembles a set of working notes. All the items, characters, stage props, weather conditions, etc., are made note of . . . and then the metaphor is appended or allowed to emerge. William Wordsworth was one of the first to write whole poems as conscious disgressions; William Carlos Williams was not to be the last. "St. Francis Einstein of the Daffodils" (even its title would serve) is a good example of a poetic method based on meandering, on a theme that twists contingent being into a necessity. To the extent that he pays homage to the primary anecdote, the telling event in one's past, the memory one can't forget, Williams is in the accepted sense "confessional." The physical and personal, which for most people does *not* yield very easily to the visionary, is pommeled into submission. The confessional program says in effect: It is good if I look upon it; what is opposite is joined by my regard. The title poem of James Wright's *To a Blossoming Pear Tree*[18] is a case in point. The poet addresses the flowering tree, admires it, admits it is from a realm where beauty is second nature, then decides to tell it "Something human." The "human" anecdote Wright settles on is an intentionally jarring encounter with an old queer:

> He was so near death
> He was willing to take
> Any love he could get,
> Even at the risk
> Of some mocking policeman
> Or some cute young wiseacre
> Smashing his dentures,

> Perhaps leading him on
> To a dark place and there
> Kicking him in his dead groin
> Just for the fun of it.

Wright's speaker knows that the blossoming pear tree isn't engineered to "Worry or bother or care" about such encounters in winter in Minneapolis. Nor, in Williams's "St. Francis Einstein of the Daffodils," do the daffodils or Einstein, who is "tall as a blossoming peartree," care about

> the old negro
> with white hair who hides
> poisoned fish-heads
> here and there
> where stray cats find them[19]

The point of both poems is the sheer juxtaposition of the pure and lovely with the bitter and unsavory, and Wright, for one, sides with the latter. There is no moment of tentative hovering between realms, no teetering between the right and wrong sides of the looking-glass—in other words, no *satori* joining butterfly to beast. James Wright can be pretty straightforward, when he wants to, about everybody staying in his place:

> Young tree, unburdened
> By anything but your beautiful natural blossoms
> And dew, the dark
> Blood in my body drags me
> Down with my brother.

This is not very definitive poetry. It is slightly flowery prose. The opposition between the pear tree with its "little mist of fallen starlight" and the old man with a "singe of white / Beard on his face" occurs by the instrument of analogy-in-difference, the small dislocation of an obvious but all the same ineradicable private association. That the *singe* of white beard and the *mist* of starlight join in the logic of language as well as in the poet's mind is all Wright asks of the lyric.

The problem with this method of the private launched into the public sphere is that, if you are to be a true confessional poet, you have to be interesting in off-moments. You are hobbled by the sorts of things that idly and inadvertently occur to you. And when the confessional, anecdotal method of poetic thought is paired with a studious avoidance of standard poetic means—prosody, controlled diction, conventional checks on the behavior of metaphors—you cannot always insure that the poems will come off at all. There is a tendency in much anecdotal poetry toward buffoonery and self-pity. When there are no formal checks, fakery and sentimentality infect the simple statement as well as the complex. Wright's "Redwings" begins:

> It turns out
> You can kill them.
> It turns out
> You can make the earth absolutely clean.

We are, unfortunately, used to this kind of irony. Someone is to blame for the fact that redwings are so easy to kill, but who? The members of the rifle clubs? Industrial pollution? The silly birds themselves? Man's own resinous heart? You can, if you are such a beast or such an average American, clear the earth of gentle, lovely creatures. But the poet is safe in his rhetoric: He is, after all, the canary in the mine.

Although the lines that result from the romance of simplicity (no ideas but in things) initially sound very different from the lines of the autodidact who also speaks to us in Wright and Williams, there is something uncomfortably similar in the tones of voice, as if Williams's saxifrage and not the rose had become the ultimate particular:

> Some crumbling of igneous
> Far off in the coverts
> Of my orplidean country,
> Where tall men
> Are faintly bearded
> Pines, now, the slow stalagmon
> Gathers downward
> Stone, milk of mineral
> Below my graying face.
> This is another river
> I can still see flow by.
> ("One Last Look at the Adige: Verona in the Rain")

The river to which Wright refers in the first nine lines of the poem (with a geological pedantry far exceeding Williams's—or even Auden's) is the Ohio near Steubenville; the river in the last two, the Adige, near Verona. The one is hellish, the second beautiful, although of course the poet's imagination is more obsessively connected to the "black Crust" of Steubenville, the "shallow hell" of America "where evil / Is an easy joke, forgotten / In a week." Except that Wright, then dying of throat cancer, cannot forget. His attachment to Verona and the Adige is moving and sweet, but finally a bit unreal: "My moving jewel, the last / Pure vein left to me." His real connection is not to the place in which he is but to the place of dirt and wrong that is his fate.

In Wright's poems, the sense of appetite is overwhelming: Meaning *will be drawn* from the anecdotes whether the reader is made to care about the anecdotes or not. The poet, in these moods, swallows the world whole. "On a Phrase from Southern Ohio" is about the poet and six other white boys beating up two black boys in a wasteland of strip-mined hills, dirty rivers, and wild, mutant vegetation. The Janus-face of Williams is resurrected, so that we slide without warning or logic between the portentously naked, reduced, and simple to the equally portentous spasm of excess:

> Then from the bottom
> Of that absolutely
> Smooth dead
> Face
>
> We
> Climbed
> Straight up
> And white
>
> To a garden of bloodroots, tangled there, a vicious secret
> Of trilliums, the dark purple silk sliding its hands deep down
> In the gorges of those savage flowers, the only
> Beauty we found, outraged in that naked hell.
>
> Well, we found two black boys up there . . .

The poem is not tactful. It juxtaposes a sentimental "clarity" with an equally sentimental pose of "instinctive" erudition and passionate remorse. There is no formal structure by which the *kind* of expression can be controlled, and eventually both voices, the overly plain and the overly elaborated, sound merely approximate, played-at, and, for all the enormity of the theme of racial conflict, poetically vacuous. It belongs with a thronging category of the confessional, anecdotal poem that accumulates stubborn details to which a metaphor is pinned; as in the last poem quoted, there is a tendency in James Wright to use two voices, one sedulously plain—the bedrock voice—the other educated, elevated, and "inspired," to navigate between the often disjointed vehicle of certifiable evidence and the tenor of inexpressible feeling.

Formally as well, materials divergent in theme are forced together by the fiat of the free-verse line. In James Wright's "Redwings," "One Last Look at the Adige," and "To a Blossoming Pear Tree," the lines and the simplified grammar coincide. At most there can occur a twist from one moment to another, but no qualification; *all* experience, such a form implies, is equal. Many of the poems by Wright ask that we stop at every word, forget natural cadences, and restrict ourselves to tiny compounds of words, lifted from their natural framework, that lack not only syntax but perhaps even denotation. Even if the principal vanity of the tapeworm poem is its precision vis-à-vis things, the cutting off of word from word often makes the whole enterprise tediously abstract. All the poets who follow Wright and Carlos Williams (including even A. R. Ammons) must confront this relation of the abbreviated free-verse line to a thematics short-circuited (therefore set to explode) by compression.

Gary Snyder provides a different example of pared-down simplicity. The aura, if not always the attitudes, of *disciplina* shines about him, owing in part to the quests from which he has returned, but also to a decision about keeping mere personality out of his poems. Snyder, whose work is also full of visual delight, goes about description quite differently from Wright, despite their nominal similarity of simplified means. Most striking is the fact that Snyder avoids the sort of metaphor in which two realms of conjunction, frequently one physical and the other spiritual, mix on the surface in such a way that the depths beneath will beckon, until *any* surface glancingly has something of depth in it. Contrary to that principle of steady sympathetic evocation, Snyder gives us *only* the surface and expects us *not* to expect it to ripple down to the depths beneath:

> soaked drooping bamboo groves
> swaying heavy in the drizzle,
> and perfectly straight lines of rice plants
> glittering orderly mirrors of water,
> dark grove of straight young Sugi trees
> thick at the base of the hill . . .
> ("Delicate Criss-Crossing Beetle Trails Left in the Sand")[20]

Even the title of the poem alerts us to the presence of a devoted nominalist, perhaps of an oriental persuasion—a suggestion made by the details (beetle, bamboo, rice, rain) and corroborated by the implied disciplines of composure, composition, linearity, and crystalline geometric design ("glittering orderly mirrors of water"). But implication is only casual. The rich nominalism of this fine description is not perfected in the service of any larger pattern. There is no sure link between the smooth, wet, attractively rectilinear scene and an answering order in the psyche. Rather, the "heavy" description floats uneasily in a medium of "light," chatty realism. This happens to be the Japanese village the poet's wife Masa comes from, although even this fact seems to pull the poem away from rather than toward its center:

> Walking out on the beach, why I know this!
> rode down through these pines once
> with Anja and John

> And watch bugs in their own tiny dunes.
>> from memory to memory,
>> bed to bed and meal to meal,
>> all on this road in the sand

Beds and meals are of equal weight with memories—in fact they are pretty much all the memory this poet of the present moment manifests. Whoever Anja and John may be, they belong with the troupe of chums named Steven and Mike and Wendell and Tanya and Ron and Bill and Cindy and Rod and Patty who move through Snyder's recitals with their earnest but illusory circumstantiality. These rural familiars, who have shrugged off their surnames, are also an aspect of the author's new domestication, part of the cultural baggage taken on in an attempt, in middle age, to steal a little back from time, to settle down without compromising the basic orientation of the wanderer, the taster and trier, the genial and honest vagabond of the spirit. Snyder's mode of jotting—appearing to record pretty casually the undifferentiated stream of minor events, which suggests a method of indifferently taking in all that is done by and in the speaker's consciousness at a given moment—worked better when Snyder was out in the woods, for then place, as it were, kept coherent a kind of thought process that cannot monitor itself.

What is unpleasant in Snyder's work comes about from his refusal to distinguish the poetic from the nonpoetic in his writing. Many of the pieces in this volume raise no resistance to the jargon of causes; Snyder does not try to render or place the clichés of ecological activism and California zen ("biome," "biomass," "ecosystem," "petrochemical complex," "joyful interpenetration"), which he has taken into himself as equably as he'd done earlier with the languages of primitive myth, monasticism, logging, and the merchant marine: He simply blurts the phrases out. His poem on breasts is at once offensive and hilarious (his is not a world for women, except in their function as squaws):

> But the breast is a filter—
> The poison stays there, in the flesh.
> Heavy metals in traces
>> deadly molecules hooked up in strings
>> that men dreamed of;
> Never found in the world til today.
>> (in your bosom
>> petrochemical complex
>> astray)

These lines show the validity of an old truth: how little help to the poem is the conventional worthiness of its sentiments. There is even a question for me, here, whether putting "petrochemical complex" and "bosom" side by side is not the sign of deep failure in integrity. Both phrases sound flimsy and borrowed; hence the combination is slovenly, sentimental—qualities repeated in the eccentric spelling, the coy mysterium-style ("that men dreamed of"), and the outworn and overdramatized rhyme ("today/astray"). Snyder might take a lesson from the poisons he abhors in his physical world and realize that poetry cannot continue unharmed on a steady diet of buzzwords, archaisms, and banalities.

Snyder has a real knack for the seasonal, geographical haiku, brief, rapid, spontaneous, and striking in its reticence. On a trip to a large aborigine reservation in central Australia, the speaker of one such haiku blends/falls so effortlessly into the land and culture, it would appear he had no shedding of civilized traits to perform. That is the kindest one can say of this:

> Sit in the dust
>> take the clothes off. feel it on the skin
>> lay down. roll around
>> run sand through your hair.
>> nap an hour
>>
>> bird calls through dreams
>>> now
>> you're clean.
>
> sitting on red sand ground with a dog.
> breeze blowing, full moon,
> women singing over there—
> men clapping sticks and singing here
>
>> eating meaty bone,
>> hold the dog off with one foot
>>
>> stickers & prickles in the sand—
>
> clacking the boomerang beat,
>> a long walk
>> singing the land.
>
> ("Uluru Wild Fig Song")

One might try to elevate such writing by arguing that the speaker's mundane consciousness has been excluded and the actor in the piece is entirely but not effusively given over to the habits and emanations round about. It's crucial that the quality of his attention be both flexibly aimless and disciplined by nonverbal awareness. By withholding all responses but the obvious physical ones—feeling clean, getting full, hearing accurately, stepping on thistles—Snyder makes factual rather than arbitrary the problematic dream-bird's call and the origin of the final song. There is calling, there is singing, and there is, throughout the fig grove, the awareness of these, not necessarily ascribable to the subjective individual. But such a reading works only on paper. The poem itself remains savorless and brain-dead.

I would like to be better persuaded than I am by Thom Gunn's essay on Snyder's method of firing up the merely perceptual into a fully conscious and even celebratory poem.[21] The means of transition is a careful retardation as the items of notice separate themselves out from the myriad-teeming visual field. Yet the poems move not from sleep to vision, or from dullness to sparkle; the descriptive poem at which Snyder is adept is an always open general field in which perceptions "overtake each other and accrete" by virtue of a sensibility already, and throughout his work, "imbedded in time." Gary Snyder's small gift shows best in poems of coolly excited physical well-being, in his strange combination of country ease and monastic stubbornness, in restraint of ego that is like and unlike T. S. Eliot's doctrine of impersonality. Snyder's impersonality does not bring with it the mannerisms of restraint, only the clarities of openness and humility. This poetry is the product of control that does not yet suppress or reject what is produced by energies and motives unlike its own. And this is the difference between real impersonality and Eliot's kind of decorum.

Snyder's identity is not bound up with style. The logical and experiential upshot of this state of mind is that the poem dims while the experience grows. At its most logical (or most extreme) this attitude sidesteps art and subsides into a state of soul. At times—however, by no means consistently—the poem that dims out into life can present sounds, contours of phrase, and aptness of image and illustration that move and delight. Consider, from one of Snyder's tool-and-work poems, these lines about trying to split waterlogged oak for firewood:

> Lifting quarters of rounds
>   covered with ants,
>   "a living glove of ants upon my hand"
> the poll of the sledge a pit peened over
> so the wedge springs off and tumbles
>   ringing like high-pitched bells
>   into the complex duff of twigs
>   poison oak, bark, sawdust,
>   shards of logs . . .

Here is physical pleasure both in the activity of labor and in the selection and arrangement of words and the deft choice of the analogy, "ringing like high-pitched bells": For a moment or two the auditory sense echoes above the intensely local visual details. But the result is categorically minor.

To write a poem in the second of the prosaic-rhapsodic substyles, namely, the mixed ironic style, one selects the electronic chip that programs into the work a stylistic agitation that at first feels rich, sensitive, conscious, attentive to response. But in fact the mixed ironic style is conscious only of its own circuitry; immediacy and confidentiality are themselves disguises. The work of one poet in particular exploits an almost obsessive promiscuity of styles and attitudes:

> The first year was like icing.
> Then the cake started to show through.
> Which was fine, too, except you forget the direction you're taking.
> Suddenly you are interested in some new thing
> And can't tell how you got here. Then there is confusion
> Even out of happiness, like a smoke—
> The words get heavy, some topple over, you break others.
> And outlines disappear once again.
>
> Heck, it's anybody's story . . .

Thus John Ashbery, in "More Pleasant Adventures,"[22] avidly works into the poem the jargon of a composite, hypothetical character who might have gone to high school in the late 1940s:

> Heck, it's anybody's story,
> A sentimental journey—"gonna take a sentimental journey,"
> And we do, but you wake up under the table of a dream:
> You are that dream, and it is the seventh layer of you.

Reading Ashbery, one could imagine that one is listening to a ceaseless patter almost out of earshot; the message comes back distorted, the predicates blurred, some nouns exchanged, so that only the fossil impressions of the intensives and temporal adverbs and the adversatives still stand out. His art is at once sprightly and depressing; he has subjected the hopelessly prosaic to his uncanny radioactive energy, while at the same time he undermines feeling by an irony so tight and dispassionate that it, too, is nightmarish. This is T. S. Eliot's "extinction of personality" carried out in the service not of a great literary heritage, but of a tawdry and dangerously sterile commercial commonplace. Ashbery is the passive bard of a period in which the insipid has turned into the heavily toxic.

This congress between the toxic and the insipid makes one, first, feel badly for the many poets who seem to be written by their own manner-

isms. Consider the desire shown in so many contemporary poems to leap
from objective detail to moral rapture, to express the perceptual in ethical
terms, and to make an inadvertent memory universal and prescriptive.
Meditative, discursive, and comradely urges were never more in need of
help from, which is also to say self-censorship from, older models of
literary decorum. Imagine what Samuel Johnson would say about the
following case of self-indulgence, with its specious emotive buildup of
landscape items as if they *produced* the memory of the father whipping the
sister, and with its fatuous pun on "sawing":

> These mornings in green mountains
> When the air burned off blue
> . . . .
>   Mornings I can imagine the men
>   still go out along the Blue Ridge
>   to handcut trees—summer and winter,
>
> hickory and oak, sycamore and maple.
>   Nineteen forty-something-or-other.
>   I still see my father
>   sawing on my sister with a whip.
> Virginia green. Sometimes when you love someone
>   You think of pain—how to forgive
>   what is almost past memory.
>   All you can remember is the name,
>   some place you have in mind
> where all the blue smoke, all the ghost water collects.[23]

Surely, if at first we pity such posturing, our next immediate impulse is
to condemn it, for this is poetry that fibs about its purposes and origins,
which are purely self-congratulatory (note the fussy portentousness of the
list of trees) and tell us nothing whatever about what it means to forgive.
Such lines make us wonder at the writer's understanding of the term, and
I, for one, would rather not find myself in a position to be forgiven by
such a human being, since the gesture has no moral contour except that
of an autocratic will. Yet despite the unwholesome insinuations masked
by the speaker's blandness, the excerpt above, with its tarnished halo of
ethical concern, represents a central type of contemporary ironic memoir.

The irony is equally provisional in the hands of poets like Jorie Graham.
Eager to flog her team across the wild rivers of outraged innocence, she
is baffled by the frailty of the bridges; the categories of ethical judgment
seem to have eroded. The very language of good and evil has been irretrievably coarsened, as a selection of phrases and claims from Graham's
poems makes clear.[24] Beauty is said to emerge from hurt, or from hurt
held in: "contained damage makes for beauty." Ethical terms are wrenched

out of context: Wasp nests are "a dark grey freedom." Good and ill are as little distinguishable and their difference as little burdensome as flickering light and shade: "right and wrong like pools of shadow"; "the architecture of grief, its dark and light"; "the light keeps stroking them as if it were love." Various oxymora confuse rather than adumbrate the contrasting terms: "that good injustice," "good lengths of privacy," "the shape of the mess, its beautiful bone." Exaggeration undermines some phrases: "terrible insufficiencies of matter," "harsh fecundity," "lush righteousness"; while shrillness and periphrasis work against others: "the loss of uselessness," "sunshine's zealotry," "horribly better," crime's "wrongest beauty, coherent refusals." And finally, that disturbing habit of equation between all available abstract nouns: "that measuring, that love"; "that love. That deep delay"; "How far into the earth can vision go and still be love?"; "one lust . . . one long chord of justice."

Most of the assertions in this mixed ironic oeuvre from which I have quoted are so ambiguous it is hard to clear them up; but there are some maxims like the following that are simply and outrageously false: "There isn't a price that won't live forever"; "You have to hate one thing and hate it deep and well"; "We are defined by what we will not take into ourselves"—this last, a fairly taxing hypothesis to prove, as it constrains the researcher to list the universe. And when the speaker of a poem on the Viennese painter Gustav Klimt asserts, "I think I would weep for the moral nature of this world," myriad queries arise. Why "would weep" and not "could weep"? Indeed, why not "*do* weep"? Why only "think" she would weep—is certainty impossible even in something so basic? What is "moral nature," when there is no allowance made for the discernment, let alone castigation, of wrong, falsehood, sin, malice, or evil? Would not "the *immoral* nature of this world" better prepare the way for the horrors with which the poet proceeds to decorate this poem?

These discontinuities between cause and effect are in part owing to theme. *Erosion* is a profane gnostic text, devoted to the cult of victims who have suffered violence and to the painters and poets who have rendered violence, and to the religious and historical forces who have performed it. But sometimes rendering involves complicity in the deed. The poems here illustrate the complicity unwittingly, being often the working out of a generalized prurience about torture, as is also true in some of the work of Adrienne Rich and Sharon Olds, the poems' energy directed toward the soothing of an entirely self-evolved itch, the fascination with torment, decay, and wounded tissue. But in Graham these are reflexively juxtaposed with beautiful and sleek and unmarred creatures. While Jorie Graham tries to enlist our support by declaring how much she is touched by others' pain, it is she, after all, who decided to focus upon these excruciating moments (a rape, a castration, a murder, an exhumation, the torture of St. Francis, Signorelli's aesthetic autopsy on his son, and so forth). Furthermore, all blame is withheld; responsibility for actions is never demanded; malice is treated as if it were accident; and indeed the connections between one act and another, or between an act and concomitant, pleasant, realistic detail are purely arbitrary. The poet's usual response is a half-shrug of wonderment at how awful the world is, and a satisfied reiteration of exuberant perceptual "sensitivity":

> Far in the woods
> in a faded photograph
> in 1942 the man with his own
> genitalia in his mouth and hundreds of
> slow holes
> a pitchfork has opened
> over his face
> grows beautiful.

Surely this is the wrong rhetoric to use under the circumstances. Even if the prettifying is intended as irony, where is the confident and forcefully invoked convention that tells us of ironical devices to display indignation? In the absence of such a context, the terms *slow, Grows,* and *beautiful* are offensive gushing. They are on a par with the gratuitously sweetened-up natural details that come next: "The ferns and deepwood lilies catch the eye. . . . The feathers of the shade touch every inch of skin."

Related to such sentimental sleights with diction and rhetoric in Graham is a rather prominent device of rhapsodic authorization, which is to keep emphasizing the personal balking-points of the speakers of the poems and the circumstantiality of the occasion, even when these mannerisms detract from the credibility of the claims:

> we stitch the earth, it seems to me, each time we die
>
> *
>
> We live a harsh fecundity, it seems to me.
>
> *
>
> for such a night is this, I think.
>
> *
>
> When I look at her I think Rapunzel.
>
> *
>
> If I have a faith it is something like this.
>
> *
>
> I would not want, I think, a higher intelligence.
>
> *
>
> The dead would give anything I'm sure, to step again
>   onto the leafrot.
>
> *

I think I would weep for the moral nature of this world.

*

But this too is a garden I'd say, with its architecture of
    grief, its dark and light in folds.

*

I want to say to them, Take your faces out of your hands.

*

It's beautiful . . . And yet I thought it was freedom.

*

I think the world is a desperate element.

The last sentence might raise the first of many questions: Why not say,
"the world is a desperate element" and dispense with "I think"? The poet
makes it clear, however, that she is less interested in the world than in
the artifice of her own responses. Of course, one might say this of many
artists: Not the world, but the world through me. But this artist differs
from others like Keats, Herzog, Signorelli, Klimt, Goya, Masaccio, and
Piero della Francesca (all of whom she uses for analogical purposes) in
the way the stimuli of Graham's experience fail to fit the distortion in
response they were supposed to have caused.

In a further direction taken by the mixed ironic style, other poets, using
a more experimental form of discursiveness, suspend the moral in a web
of innocent nonsense:

LANDFALL

The sun rises on an uncertain shore;
loons float off to port.
This morning I'll take my new palaver out
and try it on the pilgrims.

Failing that, there's always the rum and concertina.
Some way can be found, a frame that clips nicely.
A baby cries, child of sea and storm.
The passage is all that it knows.
In my contract the terms are plain as paste,
and the chart speaks not only to the wise.
We go, always and ever,
in an expensive circlet homeward.[25]

One can see why Ashbery, who chose this poem for a portfolio of younger
poets in a magazine, should have found the experiment appealing: He
himself might have been the originator of that jazzy and self-conscious
cool in phrases like "my new palaver," "a frame that clips nicely," "plain
as paste," and "an expensive circlet" (which I keep reading as *expansive*

circle—a mistake the poem encourages because it has used metaphors of shores, maps, and a spatial geography rather than money and jewelry). Although geographical setting is at work here, it is not realistic and does not ground the speaker temperamentally or verbally. In other words, the factual layer of the poem can be violated at will.

In the final extension of the rhapsodic fallacy into innocuous, whimsical surrealism, the factual surface can be violated as often and as abruptly as there are brief inconsequential declarative sentences to tinker with. Some surreal prosaists depend on relentless shock, as in this excerpt from a dramatic monologue spoken by the virgin martyr St. Lucy:

> I think the erotic
> is not sexual, only when you're lucky.
> That's where the path forks. It's not the riddle
> of desire that interests me; it is the riddle
> of good hands, chervil in a windowbox,
> the white pages of a book, someone says
> I'm tired, someone turning on the light.
> . . . .
> Emptiness
> is strict; that pleases me. I do cry out.
> Like everyone else, I thrash, am splayed.
> Oh, oh, oh, oh. Eyes full of wonder.
> Guernica. Ulysses on the beach.
> . . . .
> I'd rather walk the city in the rain.
> Dog shit, traffic accidents. Whatever God
> there is dismembered in his Chevy.
> A different order of religious awe:
> agony & meat, everything plain afterwards.[26]

The violation of this poem's realistic surface is accomplished by further intrusions of exaggerated and rapid-fire realism, not unlike Eliot's method in *The Waste Land*. But the pronouncements, made in the pouting manner of a child, are distinctively postmodern, as are the curt, fragmented style and the ever-potent claims: *this interests me; that pleases me.*

This may be the point to explore briefly the implications of idiom and its derailment. We find a deliberate *rejection* of linguistic perfection in many of the oeuvres studied in this chapter and later on. Perhaps the most characteristic gesture of poetry in this century is to reject the jeweled Tennysonian line with its aureate diction and rhetoric of sublimated awe. While doing so, poets nearer to us in time aim for a different purity, closer to what Williams called "disinfected," but which highlights a new kind of blemish, the want of modes of expressing ease. The "dog shit

[and] traffic accidents" idiom displays a deliberate want of smoothness that is not (quite) idiomatic. Idiom usually involves some notion of error, but error agreed upon. Idioms are once-aberrant conventions that are fueled and defined by mainstream language as well as by the mainstream attitudes toward convention. Most languages in fact make provision for dissent, until in time the aberrant is finally encoded in the central tongue. Idiom is always tending toward a standard of correctness; tame use of the idiomatic is already conventional.

Although there is nothing necessarily to admire in the idiom of province or neighborhood, let alone in the recitals of certain individuals, we frequently take pleasure in hearing these peculiarities rendered back to us, selected and revised, by masters of caricature like Sterne, Gogol, and Dickens. And while linguists like Chomsky argue that there is nothing good or bad in the use of language, but only success or failure in being understood, still we can deem some second-order renderings of idiom better than others to the extent that they accurately give back the heft and lilt of some familiar phrasing. Here, then, is a second sense in which idiom may suggest error. Attempts to reproduce the idiomatic may fail. The desire to sound authentic to some region (whether geographical, racial, or intellectual) may not succeed. Or, once successful, the attempt to render an idiomatic usage may have no function; it may even, in a poem based on non sequitur and irrelevancy, be the wrong irrelevancy for the occasion, or too pale a one. To the extent that an idiomatic style is mimetic (a reflection of tone, rhythm, lexicon, and/or phrasing which themselves have something wrong with them), the style may in places or as a whole strike us as inept, failing to catch just that shade of wrongness in its snare.

To adapt some of the categories supplied by Marjorie Perloff in her exposition of "language poetry,"[27] accuracy of portrayal where idiom is concerned assumes language to be, in part, its own evidence or object, and not merely the medium for objects or ideas that lie outside it, except insofar as language in vitro mimics language in vivo. A further complication is that poetic practice has disdained the "fetish of commodity," as well as the "conduit theory of communication," without (as the "language poets" appear to do) dismissing the qualities of personal voice.

The contemporary poem tends to be spoken by a great Shadow-I, one of whose problems (whatever else may occur in the poem) is that it must worry-out and worry-through the way it sounds. This worrying of the style in and through which the voice progresses is, however, more a necessity of personality than of intellect—and even at that rate more compelling for technical reasons than psychological ones (although we should not discount the almost theurgic superstition with which contemporary writers set out to tamper with words). On the other hand, unlike many a

nineteenth-century writer, surer of the individual's relation to literary convention, the Shadow-I of the present must invent a language that sounds
at once indebted to other speakers *in general* (hence the blurred or shadow
quality) and thoroughly orthogonal to the norm, with a snap eccentric to
his or her style (hence the function of the retrograde ego in the enterprise).
In this way the contemporary writer is almost compelled to work at cross-
purposes with subject and materials.

Yet a third way in which error combines with idiom is, therefore, in
excusing the broken subject of the poem as a necessary product of its
style, and thus excusing the halting style as the pattern and key to its
subject. So the Shadow-I who speaks the poem may risk or even induce
clumsiness, fragmentation of thought (as well as expression), and strait-
ened provisionality of outcome. These hobblings warrant the genuineness
of the problem (the problem of finding simultaneously a self, a theme,
and a language) as they testify to the sincerity of the one who so ruefully
and, it may be, misguidedly, tries to cope. If the Shadow-I stumbles or
temporizes or breaks off, it is because these acts are the preconditions for
the kind of breakthrough in which the world and the ego merge into one
interpretive terrain. Distractions of consciousness presumably diagnose
the uneven rhythms and sudden adjustments of external matter and objective fate to laws of their own. Weakness is the poet's very armor as the
error-ridden, incomplete, uncertain verbal hero forays out into a chaos of
possibilities, a paradise of imperfections.

This last approach to necessary error and imperfection, however, can-
cels out or overrides the second, so that the critic is almost automatically
held back from judging the success of any poetry of provisionality. It is
as if incomplete divinings were by definition successful and praiseworthy,
and as if any idiom, no matter how heterogeneous or flavorless, were
above either systematic commendation or reproach. Clearly, such a stale-
mate will be short-lived. It will never be enough, in estimating a poet's
achievement, merely to categorize the poet by thematic and formal allegiance. The work must be *judged,* the idiom related to norms, its use to
pertinence, its lack of pertinence to the virtues of surprise, surprise in turn
to coherence. However, sympathetic, the critic must stay awake.

"It is an old story," says another poet, who has specialized in the muted
innocuous surreal, "the way it happens / sometimes in winter, sometimes
not." Contemporary surrealists are uncomfortably tied to the idea of landscape and season; externals are partially internalized but, again, with the
selective gauge we noticed in the objective style, whereby things and
gestures are frozen, arrested (just as the shadowy narrative selves are arrested) prior to the completion of their significance. The poet of the "old

story" goes on: "the misfortunes come . . . their wooden wings bruising the air."[28] The world of the surrealists today would seem to be populated by enormous installations of heroic statuary; huge caryatids of doom and oblivion; winged, acephalous bodies; great three-dimensional volumes of oppressive loss whose medium is the fluidity, blankness, and paralysis of the dormant state:

> All night, though dead, they stir.
> All night toward an unknown invitation
> The children reach, like boats
> Toward open sea, but are moored against it.
> They test their tethers. They rock
> And rock in a bloodless sleep.
> . . . .
> All night we seem to hear their breathings
> and longings, a shattered colonnade around us.[29]

Or, again in sleep, the adults share with these limbo children a hypnagogic flattening of experience, language, and particularity; the woman of the next excerpt sleepwalks heavy, nay, monumental, toward the logical end of the rhapsodic-prosaic style:

> The stars madden, and satellites hum silently
> Where no sound can awaken a sleeper. She dreams
> A language which cannot trouble her, a vocabulary
>
> Without voice. She has forgotten the ugly grammar,
> The deformed sentences. She has forgotten
> The irregularities of memory, the unknown knowns,
>
> The can-no-longer-remembers, the slow impeachment
> Of experience. She rises, stunned and serene,
> Toward the promise of nothing.[30]

The brooding melancholy and trance of inwardness, which Edgar Allan Poe urged his countrymen to substitute for didactic verses, have been explored with sedulous abandon in American poetry. The "promise of nothing" is the logical end of the rhapsodic program, nor are its plodding rehearsals particularly unpleasant; they affect one rather like the sounds of someone working away at three low notes on a bass viol.

But there may be one last worse type in store for us—the comic surreal, where absurdity is embraced and then forgotten.

> Stuffed against the coat
> her breasts want to be naked.
> They bloom there
> as though they lived in the tropics.

In some other life she traveled light.
In some other life she slipped away at dawn
scarcely disturbing the thick branches.[31]

The most disturbing feature of this stanza is perhaps that it was clearly devised as a kind of technically neutral, unrigorous experiment with manner that the literary decorum of the day allows. It is neither sufficiently manic nor sufficiently purged of romantic narrative elements to be "authentic" surrealism, yet it was not intended to be funny and is deaf to its own fatuity.

The great difficulty, finally, with the rhapsodic fallacy is precisely that it nourishes such aimlessness, such provisionality, such nonsense. It has no standards to impose, no goals to hold out before the writer, not even the goal of rapturous utterance, inasmuch as the effusive does not need to be thorough or even central to be assumed operative in the poem. Neither does the fallacy permit the poet to evaluate or improve, because it denies the validity or possibility of shared standards of judgment, and holds subjective effusion preeminent. This illogic at last imprisons both poet and critic, who have come to circle each other like dead stars, and the novice writer as well, who learns from their empty orbiting very little about good literature. For although they may present no significant barriers to genius, neither do the assumptions and techniques that cooperate in the kind of monotonic poetry examined here do anything to encourage, or positively enable, great thought or great poetry.

2

Three Essays on Confession

The first essay below, "Pure Feeling" studies the lyric achievement of Louise Bogan in light of her reticence—particularly in contrast to the work and career of Theodore Roethke. The second essay, "Pure Pain," looks at the work of suffering in Robert Lowell. In the third piece, "Applied Poetry," the essentially minor work of Anne Sexton raises some issues about the formal implications of an ethos of disturbance.

I. Pure Feeling

It will be clear from the foregoing chapter that one characteristic impulse of contemporary poetry is the attempt to evolve imagery for that habit or turn of mind when the mind is engaged not so much actively with experience as nonspecifically with itself. However, the poets on whom I have concentrated are concerned not with mind in the sense of knowledge but rather with the emotions of temperamental drift, thought as daydream. The individual perceiver's psychology becomes the measure of interest. Even when suppressed, this pressure to break rhapsodically out in pity and self-pity guides the maneuvers of the voices and the choice of imagery. For this reason, James Wright is as much a confessional poet as Robert Lowell.

A distinction is also to be drawn between poems of feeling and poems of confession. The issue of reticence is primary to this distinction. For example, when one places side by side the poems of two poets like Louise Bogan and Theodore Roethke who were influenced by the same writers (e.g., Yeats) and upheld the same goals for lyric, one sees how chronically the one recoiled from while the other encouraged the light of interpretation-by-personality:

> My truths are all foreknown,
> This anguish self-revealed.
> I'm naked to the bone,
> With nakedness my shield.
> Myself is what I wear:
> I keep the spirit spare.

27

Thus Roethke attempts to make a poem out of attitudes in "Open House" (1941).[1] Although the lines above appear as the second published stanza of the poem, the author is here still only in the forecourt of a poem, making notes about what the poem is to treat, still not at the stage where he can brave the transition between writing *for* the poem and writing the poem. Roethke is someone who in the main body of his lyrics leaves behind the versified record of his earnestness in approaching but not reaching the right word—or the right rhythm (see the discussion below of "Song for a Lyre," a poem by Bogan also in trimeter stanzas); Roethke's trimeters are cadentially plodding, whereas it's fair to say that Bogan is a poet who has left behind, in her poems, almost nothing but the perfected poems. When she writes in "Zone" (1941),

> We have struck the regions wherein we are keel or reef.
> The wind breaks over us,
> And against high sharp angles almost splits into words,
> And these are of fear or grief,[2]

we realize we are in the presence of a sensibility of great psychological insight as well as poetic eloquence. It is a sensibility impaled (without whimpering) on a memory whose painfulness is obscure, complicated, and surprising. Although helpless in their destructive passions, the protagonists are also the aggressors: In order that one be the reef the other must be the keel; thus even passivity has the rigid inexorability of coming shipwreck. Compared to this, the wind's chronic rages are benign. Not for Bogan the Roethkean glibness of analysis: The shield of nakedness is more hers than his, but only to the extent that she does not proclaim it. And since their oeuvres diverge so strikingly on this issue of reticence, it may be useful to compare their public and epistolary selves.

Theodore Roethke's notebooks and the journals of Louise Bogan are, I think, illuminating for anyone who cares about poetry.[3] These two poets, who figured importantly in each other's lives in the middle 1930s, reveal themselves clearly in these two volumes. Roethke's character impresses one as coy, undisciplined, and predatory. Bogan's biographer, Elizabeth Frank, describes him wonderfully:

> At twenty-six [when their affair begins—Bogan was thirty-eight] Roethke was physically overwhelming and emotionally gargantuan, a floating continent of exquisite sensitivity, towering despair, insatiable appetite, and howling self-ignorance.[4]

While Bogan's character is vivid, direct, and passionate, she is someone able to speak and write her mind. One can see how the flash, excess, and plaintiveness of Roethke's poetry are mutually related, and how that mutual relation is a function of his appetitive poetic temperament. In the same way, the piercing beauty and slight quantity of Bogan's poetry are related to one another, and to the circumspection of their author, by an equivalent if rather less obvious mechanism. It is revealing that, although both honored some of the same models (not only Yeats but the Elizabethan and cavalier poets, also Rilke), Bogan triumphed over her influences while Roethke was trapped, for much of his writing life, by his. The difference between Roethke and Bogan has, also, to do with how they educated themselves and how they approached the career of poet.

As Ruth Limmer's chronology in *Journey Around My Room* reminds us, Louise Bogan was born in Maine in 1897, lived in little (and very poor) towns in New Hampshire and Massachusetts until the family moved to Boston in 1909. Bogan started to write poetry in 1910.

> The life-saving process then began. By the age of 18 I had a thick pile of manuscript, in a drawer in the dining room—and had learned every essential of my trade.

After her first year at Boston University, Bogan married her first husband and in 1917 in the Panama Canal Zone gave birth to her daughter and only child, Maidie. In 1919, back on the East Coast, Bogan separated from her husband and from then until 1924 (except for a six-month stay in Vienna, studying piano on her husband's army pension—he died in 1920), Louise Bogan worked at odd jobs, clerking at Brentano's, cataloguing for Columbia sociologists, working at branches of the New York Public Library. From 1923 until 1934 she lived with the writer and editor Raymond Holden (they married in 1925). During this decade she published her first two books of poems (in 1923 and 1929) and her first magazine reviews. Her first breakdown followed the loss of their house in Columbia County (N.Y.) by fire; her second, in 1933, followed another trip to Europe and a maritally disastrous homecoming.

In 1934 Holden and Bogan separate; her affair with Theodore Roethke begins in 1935. From 1934 until her death in 1970, Louise Bogan lives with Maidie or alone, writing for the *New Yorker* (she was their poetry reviewer from 1931 to 1969), translating (Renard, Valéry, Jünger, Goethe), doing the infrequent teaching stint (several times at the University of Washington while Roethke was on leave), giving occasional lectures, and working for a month each year at the MacDowell Colony. Half of 1965 is again spent in institutions after a breakdown.

Bogan won awards and at least twice applied for grants, but although she shared the Bollingen Award in 1955 with Léonie Adams and served as Consultant in Poetry to the Library of Congress in 1945, she was recognized far less than she should have been—or *could* have been, had

she used the influence that was hers. A further point about foundation
and committee support to Bogan is that it seems to have been spread over
five- to ten-year intervals. She never won the Pulitzer.

Theodore Roethke's life follows a different rhythm, at least outwardly
more secure and stable. (The dates are taken from Ralph J. Mills's edition
of his letters.)[5] Roethke was born in 1908 in Saginaw, Michigan, where
his father had built a massive network of greenhouses and nurseries (there
was even a swamp for harvesting moss). Roethke graduated with a B.A.
from the University of Michigan in 1929, did graduate work at Harvard
from 1930 to 1931, taught at Lafayette College (Easton, Pa.) from 1931
to 1935, had his first breakdown in the fall of 1935, returned to the
University of Michigan to take an M.A. in 1936, taught at Pennsylvania
State College from 1936 to 1943, at Bennington College from 1943 to
1946, and at the University of Washington in Seattle from 1946 to his
death in 1963.

In 1953 Roethke marries Beatrice O'Connell (age twenty-six) and visits
Europe for the first time. He is forty-four. His first book has been published in 1941, when he is thirty-three; his second in 1948, from which
point on he will have a book out every two or three years. He receives
numerous Guggenheim and Ford Foundation grants, wins the Pulitzer
(1954), the Bollingen and the National Book Award (1958), records a
half-hour program with the BBC, and is even filmed (*In a Dark Time,*
1963). In the middle and late 1950s and during the last three years of his
life, Roethke is periodically hospitalized for physical and nervous dis-
orders.

Several points should be made about these two lives, each in its way
compulsive and touching. Bogan married early, Roethke late. Bogan had
no settled existence until the age of twelve; Roethke was born and reared
in the same Michigan town. The great presence in Bogan's early life was
her mother, whose departures were a source of nightmare.

> The curved lid of the trunk is thrown back, and my mother is bending over
> the trunk, and packing things into it. She is crying and she screams. My
> father, somewhere in the shadows, groans as though he has been hurt. It is
> a scene of the utmost terror.

The great presence in Roethke's early life was his father, whom he mythi-
cizes as the son of the former *Hauptförster* of Bismarck:

> His hand could fit into a woman's glove,
> And in a wood he knew whatever moved;
> Once when he saw two poachers on his land,
> He threw his rifle over with one hand;

> Dry bark flew in their faces from his shot,—
> He always knew what he was aiming at.[6]

Bogan supports herself and her child at times menially, at first haphaz-ardly, is even evicted once in the mid-1930s, but she never appeals; and from the age of thirty-three on she writes prose to deadlines. Roethke supported himself by endless appeals—teaching, reading his poems to audiences, *talking;* he had a monstrous problem writing even the briefest pieces of prose for publication. Bogan goes to Europe early (Vienna in 1922); Roethke explores the Continent late (with every emollient— Auden lent him the Ischia house; John Lehmann and the Sitwells lionized him in London; and his letters home to friends in 1953 are full of dealing, name-dropping, arrangements for strategic magazine publication, and bragging over the large advance he had "bullied" out of Doubleday). Bogan struggled not to use her charm in the wrong way, which meant not using it at all:

> My decision that I, too, must go to the P.E.N. dinner looking as regal as possible is, of course, a childish and ignoble idea. My life and hopes cannot be in that direction. So I'll turn it down. The world is not for me and can never be—I have not been trained to it and my approach to it is too easy, too false. I can assume too cleverly all the ignoble trappings that others assume with effort, and by the fey lightness and ease of my assumptions I am self-mocked and self-betrayed.
>
> (Journey, p. 95)

A glance at the collected letters of the two is also telling. Roethke's are, in a double sense, public documents. They concern his public stature almost exclusively, and they have in them little that is friendly, little that is adjusted to the people he is writing to. Roethke's *Selected Letters* begins with a request to Harriet Monroe in 1931 that she personally read (and, it may be, reject) the poems Roethke encloses. The first letter in *What the Woman Lived: Selected Letters of Louise Bogan*[7] is a request to William Carlos Williams (who had published an obscure defense of John Coffey) that he write to Coffey directly in the insane asylum. Bogan does not mention that she is a twenty-three-year-old poet, nor is her approach to Williams ever followed up or manipulated; she is simply trying to help the young Irish Thoreau whose political thefts had been punished as madness.

The substance and quantity of Bogan's letters testify to the fact that her correspondents valued and saved what she wrote to them. Morton Dauwen Zabel (whom Bogan came to know when he worked at *Poetry*) had a special "Bogan Box" for her letters, and incurred her fierce and unabashed rage when, on a visit to Zabel at Chicago in 1941, Bogan discovered he had no intention of letting her have them back, or even see them.

> I have finally come to realize that you are not treating the letters as a gay correspondence between friends, but as a *collection*. In other words, everything I write to you is being put into a kind of coffin, and kept there. I am being treated like a character out of some memoirs; I am being put in cold storage while still alive. This realization must, of course, break my correspondence with you. I am a live, growing object; and I'll thank people to treat me as such.

Being the collector and recorder that he was, Zabel kept this letter, too.

Bogan's letters to editors (like John Hall Wheelock at Scribner's) are decorous, principled, and to the point. She did not think books of verse should contain more than thirty poems and refused to pad hers out; she refused to republish many poems that had appeared in magazines like *Poetry* and the *New Yorker;* she was even a hard critic of work she had allowed to appear in her first two volumes, and kept the long poem "The Flume" out of her *Selected Poems* (1953) and *The Blue Estuaries* (1968).

When Bogan first lived in New York, she met and became friends with people we think of as august—Edmund Wilson, Léonie Adams, Margaret Mead, Ruth Benedict, Rolfe Humphries. These were not, however, potentates whom Bogan courted, but people of intelligence and mettle who went on to make their work known. Her letters to them in the twenties and thirties are valuable reading. With Humphries she talked often about craft; with Wilson about literary and aesthetic values; with Benedict about place and mood. And with all her correspondents, Bogan not only spoke her mind about the work she and they were doing: She tried to amuse, to inform, to craft without falsehood or self-consciousness.

Roethke's letters, even to those like Rolfe Humphries and Louise Bogan, with whom he was acquainted before the exchanges began, are grimly and exclusively about himself. No doubt piqued by people, as time went on, about his ego, Roethke began to refer to his self-references as "I-love-me-items," but kept on shamelessly writing them. To John Ciardi in 1949, then assembling manuscript for *Mid-Century American Poets* (1950), Roethke gives a list of the poems of his he thinks would wear well in the anthology, and after each poem, indicates which of the critics had liked which:

> "The Cycle" Cunningham, Winters, etc.
> . . . .
> "The Heron" Cal Lowell, Winters, Cowley, etc.
> . . . .

"The Adamant" Winters said "One of the best things in the book and in recent poetry" in *Kenyon*. I nearly fell dead.

. . . .

"Night Journey" Winters, Kunitz, Cunningham, etc.

He sent a poem to John Crowe Ransom in 1947, saying that it had been "typed by Master Robert Lowell." To Kenneth Burke (whom Roethke addressed as "Pa," who explicated and supported Roethke's work, and to whom Roethke wrote more often and fully than to anyone else) the poet sedulously reports every success, every rumor flattering to himself:

> I get some very fancy talk from characters as diverse as the Shapiro's (Evalyn and Karl) and S[eldon] Rodman, etc. about what a pisser of a poet I am; how "The Lost Son" already has an underground reputation, etc. etc. Well, at the ripe age of 39 I could stand a few hosannahs. . . . Auden says he is going to write Eliot to see whether Faber would want to publish the book.

In the famous letter to Babette Deutsch in 1948, explicating the poems that were to form the fourth section of *The Lost Son and Other Poems* (1948), Roethke not only quotes an extravagantly flattering review in *Poetry*, but after the flat-footed interpretation of his own symbols, also returns to blatant tub-thumping:

> I've read almost no psychology. Several people have made the point that [this groups of poems is] at once a personal history and a history of the race itself. (That sounds high falutin'; but that's what they said.) I can make no claim, of course, one way or the other. They *are* written to be heard; and they were written out of suffering, and are mine, by God. What gives me a kick is the dent they seem to make in people who don't care for poetry often.

Roethke competed with T. S. Eliot both covertly (as above) and overtly, as he did with Dylan Thomas, braving the likeness he and others discerned, and hoping, often suggesting, that he was going them one better. When he confesses, in his letters to Dylan Thomas, that the latter's new work has made him jealous, Roethke was only incidentally expressing his approval.

In his letters to Louise Bogan, Roethke tends to whine about his fame and his poetic merit, seeking her praise, irritated by her advice. In her letters to him, Bogan is fearless and sympathetic. "Stop forcing things," she wrote him in 1937:

> Stop trying to get a certain number of things taken, this year, just because you had a certain number of things taken, last year. Forget your score, and let yourself dam up a little, inside. Perhaps you're all sluiced out, for a while.

In 1941, during a heat wave, Bogan resolves to answer Roethke's "moaning letter" (about his mother's illness—and whether people really liked his poetry). She passes along to him what she knew would be welcome praise from W. H. Auden, as well as unwelcome tonic:

> Auden respects and likes you thoroughly, I should say. He wrote that review, you must realize, against all his decisions not to review contemporaries. He thinks you a good poet, a good teacher, and a fine person generally; but we both agreed that you should GROW UP, and stop pretending that your childish side is melancholy, WHICH IT ISN'T. Now, worry over that one!

One is struck by the subtlety with which Bogan leavens the flattery coming from such a high place—by mentioning the broken pledge Auden had made to himself, and then the communal chaffing of Roethke's posturings.

Whatever one may think of Louise Bogan and Theodore Roethke as poets—and surely there is room in American poetry for the genius of both "Cassandra" and "The Lost Son," for "Night" (source of the phrase "the blue estuaries") as well as "The Far Field"—it is clear that their genius operated in different ways. So much of Roethke's energy was siphoned off into teaching that little, it appears, remained for those exercises in tact, comfort, explanation, and clarification that result in the letter, the memoir, the leisurely essay, or the meditation—those quiet and residual forms of discourse. Furthermore, Roethke was a dependent and product of the American university. He wrote his first poetry in college, was encouraged by his teachers, began submitting to magazines, and began to see his work published—all within a very few years. He was allowed, in other words, to grow up in public. In his case, it was a very pampering public. For him the measures of worth were magazine acceptance, book publication, coterie fame, prizes, and finally his success at, and appetite for, the poetry reading. He had written, from the 1940s on, poetry that "read well," occasionally to the disadvantage of the honesty of the poems. But then he also began to write poems *for* the poetry reading. Roethke thus seems to me a case of the poet with no innerness—whose impulse is so constantly directed toward the gaining and maintaining of an audience (if indeed the same arts that did gain a power must it maintain) that in consequence he overacts—"sluices himself out," to use Bogan's phrase.

Louise Bogan devoted a great deal of her energy to prose, to be sure; but the discipline to see and write clearly and succinctly taught her lessons from which all her readers may benefit. If there were exertions that impeded her poetry, they were the exertions of feeling. But she never wore her rages and depressions as a badge. Bogan's achievement, stunningly documented by the mosaic Ruth Limmer has assembled, is to have become continuous with herself. In 1961 she writes:

Now, in my later years, I have no hatred or resentment left. But I still cannot describe some of the nightmares lived through, with love. So I shan't try to describe them at all. Finished. Over. The door is open, and I see the ringed hand on the pillow: I weep by the hotel window as she goes down the street, with *another;* I stare at the dots which make up the newspaper photograph (which makes me realize that I then had not yet learned to read). The chambermaid tells me to stop crying. How do we survive such things? But it is long over. And forgiven.

To pardon her mother, Bogan must draw herself back into the moment of the betrayal. I know few transitions more heartbreaking than this moment, when the open door, which promised release, becomes the path into the labyrinth: "Finished. Over. The door is open, and I see the ringed hand on the pillow . . . " That is superb writing, because feeling guides it.

Few writers in any age manage to do themselves justice. For too many, the tour de force is the top of their bent—that scintillation toward which all the effects are contrived. These flourishings can cancel complexity. Theodore Roethke craved these tours de force, marshaling everything else in his life (friends, musings in solitude, his past, his readings, his envies) to the end of that burning occasion. His notebooks display his crooked efforts to sound like the great ones in their greatest moments; and he seems to have lacked two talents crucial to anyone with a poetic gift—self-censorship and a sense of interlude.

Louise Bogan comes from a much older and saner tradition than Roethke, the world of letters. *Journey Around My Room* reflects a sensibility both passionate and civilized. Bogan's merit as a poet—and she was one of our greatest lyric poets—should not prevent us from seeing that the volumes of her journals and occasional writings do not at all depend on prior devotion to Bogan's *Blue Estuaries* (as Roethke's notebooks could interest only those who adore him for other reasons). For those weary of the humorless indulgences of American writers, the title story in the autobiography, "Journey Around My Room," will prove fresh and disturbing. Those who despair of lyrical wit may read Bogan's prose meditation on "Coming Out," which begins, "Going in is like this." For any who doubt the dramatic potential of ordinary scenes, I would point to Louise Bogan's commemoration of the French marigold. And for all poets, *Journey Around My Room* offers a charm against costly adolescent display: It is the record of an independent soul.

When one turns from Bogan's journals and criticism and public demeanor to her poems, one senses how much that independence may have cost her. The poetry is a blending, or more, a burning together of the least like traits—those of the ballad, and those of the reflective image, of folk poetry at its deepest and most wrenching, and the poetry of reflective breadth, of the unmediated, and the humanistic. Bogan spiritedly lists among her favorite authors "Mallarmé and Yeats and whoever wrote 'Johnny I hardly knew yeh.'"[8] One can feel both motives—and feel their fiery and fruitful antagonism in the soul—in a poem like "Song for a Lyre," three stanzas long; here is the first:

> The landscape where I lie
> Again from boughs sets free
> Summer; all night must fly
> In wind's obscurity
> The thick, green leaves that made
> Heavy the August shade.
>
> (*The Sleeping Fury*, 1937)

The obeisance to tradition occurs on a number of levels: Locally and prosodically there is the complex tug of an elaborated and postponed syntax against the brief trimeter line; this technique is reminiscent of Yeats—cf. "To a Friend Whose Work Has Come to Nothing."[9] The themes are also familiar; autumn disperses the qualities of summer that have the greatest density and heat. We can look to both Keats and Shakespeare for other occasions of ripe mournfulness. So, too, the obscure wind of change, the seasons of man, and the western wind of winter separation have an ages-old poignancy. One also sees how the great conflicts in the western lyric tradition are addressed:

> Soon, in the pictured night,
> Returns—as in a dream
> Left after sleep's delight—
> The shallow autumn stream;
> Softly awake, its sound
> Poured on the chilly ground.

The conflicts of absolute feeling with mediated image and of ballad mystery with the reflective tradition have been remarked by both Edwin Muir and Thom Gunn.[10] Muir writes of the former type as stronger, and Scots, the latter, as weaker, and English. Gunn considers the reflective, elaborated lyric a natural development from the ballads guided by economy, omissions, and unstated motives. In the true ballad, says Muir, there is "nothing but passion, terror, instinct, action: the states in which soul and body alike live most intensely" (Muir, p. 19). Whatever reflection there is in them is

... a mighty reflection, or rather something more than a reflection, [that] is implied in the very spirit of the ballads, a reflection on supreme issues which is unerring and absolute and *has come to an end;* a reflection ... not concerned with this or that episode ... or ... quality, moral or immoral, or with the practicality or impracticality of life but of life itself, finally and greatly; a reflection which is a living vision of life seen against eternity; the final reflection beyond which it is impossible for the human spirit to go. (My emphasis)[11]

Rather than morality or immorality, Muir claims that the ballads function on a more intense level, "as a vision of sin, tremendous, fleeting, always the same and always to be the same, set against some unchangeable thing." Muir then suggests the monolithic and universal quality of the pity, passion, terror, and sin apprehended by the ballad makers: There "life and death have the greatness and simplicity of things comprehended in a tremendously spacious horizon."

Without wishing to demur from the eloquent appeal on behalf of the Scottish ballads, it does seem that Bogan's stanzas suggest those same less evolved "things," which the ballads "comprehended in a tremendously spacious horizon." Not an ample horizon, not merely large, but (as Muir's adverb "tremendously" implies) final: "all night must fly / In wind's obscurity / The thick, green leaves"—the leaves in "Song for a Lyre" are being driven into death; "Softly awake, its sound / Poured on the chilly ground"—the shallow stream is thinning to little more than a sound as its moisture is absorbed by the hardening, "chilly" ground. Bogan's evocations, admittedly the products both of reflectiveness and of the image,[12] nevertheless occur under an horizon of enormity and utter finality. The resolution and celebration many see in this poem—which even the poet herself did[13]—is enacted against a countermovement of yielding to death. But for a moment it is still awake, "Softly awake" she describes it, permitting herself the kind of adverb she had learned to eschew, making it work by transferred affect (the stream is certifiably awake because it is making a soft sound). And still awake, her passionate sensibility acknowledges itself in an environment of aggressive change:

> Soon fly the leaves in throngs;
> O love, though once I lay
> Far from its sound, to weep,
> When night divides my sleep,
> When stars, the autumn stream,
> Stillness, divide my dream,
> Night to your voice belongs.

With the relinquishment of possibility comes the possession—the poetic possession—of a self-knowledge supple enough to permit a grand assertion. As it happens, the addressee is Theodore Roethke, with whom her affair is forecast as ending even as it proceeds. In another sense, Bogan is bidding farewell to the complication and pain of involvement by accepting the memory of having loved, and putting it into a foregone time. In the biography, Elizabeth Frank conjectures that the feeling produced by romantic attachments was unwelcome to the extent that it "would lead . . . to the need to write poetry, and poetry, if it was to be what Bogan took for poetry, inevitably exacted some form of emotional violence toward the attachment."[14]

Around this time Bogan mentions to Morton Dauwen Zabel in a letter some sentences by Thomas Mann

> concerning the heightening which comes to the artist when he acquires the habit of regarding life as mythical and typical. That's only another way of saying that when one lets go, and *recognizes* the stream on which we move as the same stream which moves us within—that it is time and the earth floating our blood and flesh, floating its own child—and stops fighting against the kinship, the light flows in; peace arrives.[15]

Thirty years later, Louise Bogan again used the image of the stream as an emblem of passion—this time the reduced passional life of a once-handsome woman, which in later life has "nothing on which it can be dissipated":

> For the energy once expended on delight . . . is like a river which has made a broad bed for itself, but now has dwindled into a tiny stream that makes hardly any show among the wide sweep of pebbles that show the boundaries of its former strength.[16]

It takes no great leap of association to see this dwindled river as cognate with the "shallow autumn stream" of "Song for a Lyre": That poured-out quality the poet evokes in "Song for a Lyre" suggests not only relinquishment to the "floating" of our "blood and flesh" upon the earth, as Bogan wrote to Zabel—a soothing and suspension of care in a state of willing immersion—but also a diminution in an environment that dwarfs the human speaker with memories of former potency. Along with the sweetness of consummation, the emptying into extinction also obtains. And all of this dense web of heartbroken implication is suggested in verse as serene and perfected and memorable as any American poet has produced: pure feeling of loss, transmuted into pure achievement of verse.

II. Pure Pain

How unlike are the poems of pure feeling of Louise Bogan and the work of professed pain we have come to label "confessional," the poems of Sylvia Plath and Robert Lowell in particular, but also those of Roethke, Schwartz, Rich, Snodgrass, and Sexton. Of these, the poet who did most to define the ethos of neurotic and irresponsible suffering was Robert Lowell. (Plath I believe to be a poet of a more daedal, less therapeutically indulgent variety.) A study like Alan Williamson's,[17] which is essentially forbearing toward Lowell's personal voracity (in *The Dolphin* [1973], particularly), subtly but unmistakably makes it impossible to distinguish a good confessional poem from a failed or flawed one. Although Williamson tries in advance to counter this circularity of revelation and aesthetic depth that helpfully warrant each other, his provisos about the possibility of "wrong turnings . . . into self-deceptions" (p. 10), and his generally strong, even riveting readings of texts by Plath and Lowell cannot withstand the objection one might raise that a writer like Lowell seems remarkably self-deluded, about art, about the interest of his own turmoil to his art.

Williamson's casuistry (like Lowell's) is winning, however. Even someone who is only a moderately good reader, Williamson claims, will feel that Robert Lowell's "error" both "aesthetic and ethical" persuades us

> —with fear, and a certain joy—now [Lowell] cannot step outside either the immediacy of the present or the accumulated bearing, and the limitations, of his history and mental structures. In turning on himself, he casts himself into the round.
>
> *(Introspection, p. 23)*

I believe this assessment to be accurate; what I question is whether it is valuable or productive of better poems than those in which the poet permitted himself fewer "errors." Mr. Williamson would answer that the quest for the contours of the self was a reaction against excessive knowledge, the want of mystery produced by the too-vivid spotlight of New Criticism. Poets fled away from foreordained impersonal authority into a demonic, numinous landscape characterized by self-doubt and primal dissociations. Again, it appears to be a quest that cannot guarantee the poetry of the results.

Let me counter the psychoanalytic readings provided by Williamson with a more archaic kind of parable, about the dreams of various types of personality. Sir Thomas Elyot in his *Castle of Health* (1534) wrote about the kinds of dreams the four complexion types usually had. (The types are the sanguine, the melancholic, the choleric, and the phlegmatic.)[18] The sanguine man, who sleeps a great deal, dreams of red colors and pleasant things. The sanguine mind has always seemed to me particularly suited to metaphysics or first philosophy because of the rapidity with which emotion is forgotten, and because of the merry abstractions into which this type consistently retires. Among poets, the sanguine type can be represented by Marianne Moore and Wallace Stevens.

The choleric man dreams of thunder and of bright, dangerous things. As far as bad temper and a violent disposition are concerned, the choleric man might be Robert Frost. But I am not wholly pleased with this assignment. Frost, despite his excellent ear for song, is balked in his faculty of praise or celebration that the bright, dangerous things of which he dreams imply. I would assign the oneiric or poetic part of this complexion to poets like Louise Bogan and Geoffrey Hill.

The phlegmatic man dreams of watery things or of fish. In the phlegmatic temperament are some aspects of Robert Lowell's themes and of his sensibility (his New England horror of the ocean and death by water; his intellectual battery of responses like repulsion and disgust). But nature and the watery and fishy are analogical in Lowell's work. The only American poet who is phlegmatic by disposition and not by analogy must of course be Theodore Roethke.

It is now obvious what complexion one may divine for Robert Lowell—the melancholic man, who is such a bad sleeper and hence infrequent dreamer that the fearfulness of the dreams he does have are apt to be indistinguishable from the funks and fretting that dog him by day. The melancholic is the one whom sleep seldom visits, and who has therefore no benefit from other realms. The self is the only realm this poet has.

This parable of the humors may help to illustrate the special, massive irritability of Robert Lowell's poetic voice. While Lowell's religious conversion is the most documented of any poet since Eliot, to judge from the poetry there has been little relief or access of hope as a result. Lowell is fundamentally someone who needs to argue with God. Yet he stands in a special relation to the Faith, similar in bitterness to that of the apostate, and complicated by the oddity of religious diction to our pursuits. As is evident in "Waking Early Sunday Morning,"[19] the political and cultural ambience he confronts as a poet is conceived in terms of religious faithlessness. Lowell's verse is importantly that of a prophet on an a priori fruitless mission to a damned culture. It may be that he resents us for being unsalvageable as much as he despairs of himself for being displaced among us. Lowell's stance is thus much like the prophet Hosea's: "The prophet is a fool, the man of the spirit is mad, because of your great iniquity and great hatred" (Hosea 9:7).

As the self who aspires but who falls into reckless moods, Robert Lowell is a particularly hard poet for most of us to write about. He has been the teacher of several generations of poets and critics (Sylvia Plath and James Atlas the best known in each group), but one must consider, too, his mentoring of poets of such intellectual reach as Anne Winters and Alan Williamson. Indeed, it is hard to conceive of the current literary scene without Lowell's pedagogy. Still, in the very extent of Lowell's authority we find mixed his quality of radical flamboyance. As one feels about a parent, then, who chronically becomes selfish or irretrievably emotional, Lowell's excesses in feeling and diction from *Lord Weary's Castle* to *History* elicit from us an embarrassment that is frankly difficult. His accommodation to our fallen level hasn't helped. The looser, clever sounds of an after-generation make his voice oddly brittle, as does the shabbiness of current issues. Lowell is perhaps the most important of our poets to have made being adrift in a world without cause or subject his chief poetic cause and subject.

The filial metaphor seems the more apt for our bond to Lowell in proportion as he, too, embodies the filial revolt against a somewhat stricter parentage. He revolted, perhaps as part of conversion, against his own intellectual gifts, so that we are always as dazzled by his poems as we are shocked by the unselective explosions of his prideful verbal skill. He consistently manifests a downhill kind of modesty, like that of the delinquent prodigy whose gifts it exhausts in shallowness.[20] The jumble of the perceived world, as well as the cluttered solitude of the perceiving intelligence, are his subject as well as his way.

"Waking Early Sunday Morning" reveals the clutter, the anger, the intelligence, and the perverse carelessness which I take to be indicative of the aggressively delinquent posture from which Lowell writes his poems. It starts from that marvelous hypothesis which poets have often made use of: that they are sitting down to record their dreams, lying awake at night, meditating, making entries in journals, drowsing abed. The frame is loose, like the novel's, and whatever the mind's angle of vision discloses is meet and just. It's exciting to begin to read such an *essai,* and to test the play of another's daydreaming against one's own.

Like many another contest between harmony and invention, "Waking Early Sunday Morning" begins with great freshness and promise, the poet conscious of his own enormous tensile strength and of the treasure of time tumbled out before him. It begins ("O to break loose") with a chinook salmon leaping up and bruising itself against the rocky falls, then clearing the top "alive enough to spawn and die." The poem ends with this planet a joyless cinder, a ghost orbiting "in our monotonous sublime." One could of course point out that the negative element was there from the beginning (as I suppose it always is for Lowell), in the frantic necrophilia of the salmon. But the first two stanzas, whatever else might creep in, are about his joy in the feeling of possibility:

> Stop, back off. The salmon breaks
> water, and now my body wakes
> to feel the unpolluted joy
> and criminal leisure of a boy—
> no rainbow smashing a dry fly
> in the white run is free as I,
> here squatting like a dragon on
> time's hoard before the day's begun!
>
> (stanza two)

Despite the pattern of definition-by-negation in the description of a joy which is "unpolluted" and leisure which is "criminal," there is still no way for us to second-guess Lowell about the course the poem will take; all we are prepared to do is await the *turn*.

There will be something, probably emanating from within, which will ruin the recitation, blot the gorgeous page. We may be dealing with a developmental pattern similar to that in "Tintern Abbey," where that young man's growth from blood to heart to purer mind finds echo here in the waking of the body in the second stanza, then in stanza four, the "Fierce, fireless *mind,* running downhill," and then, in stanzas five and six, the introduction of the religious spirit. Our perceptual behaviorism differs so little from its eighteenth-century forebear that the gradual awakening of the self from the kinesthetic level (awareness of physical balance and interior borders) to mere affect and finally to intellectual or spiritual consciousness is as available to us as a metaphor for ontogenetic development as it was to Wordsworth. The chief difference in Lowell's application of the schema lies in the diminution of happiness and power as the mention of spirit—and its exercise—nears.[21]

The breaking loose of the first line is a strong kinesthetic theme echoed in various downhill runs, wanderings, "obsessive, casual" all-night motions, and in pointless impulses to energy (which are, as Lowell twice says, expended "anywhere, but somewhere else!"). The theme is finally capped by the perpetual motion of the lifeless star earth has become.

The ghost/spirit theme in the last stanza ("the earth, a ghost / orbiting forever lost / in our monotonous sublime") can also be traced back through the poem from, here at the end, the death of spirit in an offhand or casual war, to the "ghost-written rhetoric" of that rough and doggy pol, President Lyndon Baines Johnson, in stanza twelve; the vague spiritual angst that manifests itself in random movement and the piling up of abstractions (restlessness, sanity, caution, deception) in stanza eleven; the vanishing of the emblems of God in stanza nine; and the emptiness of biblical histories and Hebraic credos, which promise "little redemption" (stanza ten). Borrowing Paul's image of a world without love in Corinthians, these biblical patterns are "old lumber banished from the Temple . . . the wordless sign, the tinkling cymbal."

The intermediate body-empty-of-soul metaphor is implicit in those tinkling cymbals and wordless signs of stanza eight, in the wordless hymns of stanza seven which are heard but not read and from which the soul is lucky to escape, and in the images of stanza six where the soul is "tinged" and "tarnished" by its "strain" (song, bent, tendency, or *ingenium*), just as the water glass in stanza five is silvery and neutral in its skyey reflections until a "shift, or change [in] mood" intrudes a dark wood-grained background. Here Lowell conflates the looking-glass/reflector idea with the idea of the holy vessel (man is what God puts it in him to become). The skewing comes because not God but man does all the putting, displacing, and mood changing.

"Waking Early Sunday Morning" thus arranges to cover important ground about Sunday, and Lowell's (or the speaker's—I don't think it matters which) recollections and present attitudes toward personal redemption and social religious forms. The transitions between ideas and metaphors are fantastically abrupt, and one must suspect that Lowell is drawing on some mental formulas—some prearranged poetic signals in his thought—which propel him across terrain that is indicated by map but, for us, at the moment, invisible.

Certain easy linkages we can make. The association of Sundays with something slightly criminal occurs in the poem "Law" (*For the Union Dead*). Practically asleep within four-line stanzas of irregular one- to five-measure lines, Lowell reaches for capsule images of frozen violence. On Sunday mornings as a boy the poet had gone "bass-plugging out of season on / the posted reservoirs."

> Outside the law.
> At every bend I saw
> only the looping shore
> of nature's monotonous backlash.

It may be the same procedure whereby consciousness of wrongdoing heightens and more deeply impresses on the wrongdoer the majesty or exactitude of the adventure. Because Lowell's boyhood self had been poaching, his imagination was the more primed for the special fixation upon double rehearsals from which singular beauty comes. Because Wordsworth was either stealing a boat or rifling a nest for eggs or decimating the nut tree, the power of majestic otherness went more deeply into his mind. In Lowell's case, I think the special condition of breaking the Sabbath, by eliciting more associations and greater contrition, outweighed any other infraction.

One of the Sabbath associations for the boy in "Law" is with periods of historic conflict as represented in ritual form by the "battlefield" (the Civil War, or possibly where Puritans fought Indians) and by the Norman landscape. The ritual or quasi-religious aspect of wars, whether in Europe or America, was often the subject of Lowell's earlier verse. The old man in Lowell's "Falling Asleep Over the Aeneid" (*Mills of the Kavanaughs*) not only breaks the law by missing church, but also finds himself involved in two funerals, one from the classical past, and one from his boyhood, both of which, along with his own death, are circumstantially connected to profaning the Holy Day. Like Lowell, the old man is at the end of a long line of glorious and strong-willed Puritans. He recollects meekly saying to his boyhood self, "It is I," while the bust of Augustus, Vergil's patron, is blankly reflected in his glasses. He is sedentary and impressionable while his cultural and religious forebears were active and convinced. This is a scenario that occurs frequently in all of Lowell's books, although in his last years the ancestors tended to be more human and life-size.

The Protestant hymn "Faith of our Fathers" which plays in stanza six of "Waking Early Sunday Morning" is thus doubly meaningful in terms of the Lowell canon, where not only do fathers in the form of Devereauxs, Lowells, and Winslows abound, but holy wars and satanic temptations also have been fiercely chronicled. In one of the two stanzas Lowell revised for the poem's appearance in *Near the Ocean*, the particular anomie of his late-born condition is evident:

> Empty, irresolute, ashamed,
> when the sacred texts are named,
> I lie here on my bed apart,
> and when I look into my heart,
> I discover none of the great
> subjects: death, friendship, love and hate—
> only old china doorknobs, sad,
> slight, useless things to calm the mad.[22]

When he rewrote this stanza, Lowell wanted to make clear that his deep personal anomie was not just a secular habit but part of a religious *crise*. (So that its context is obvious, I give the new ninth stanza preceded by the eighth.)

> No, put old clothes on, and explore
> the corners of the woodshed for

its dregs and dreck: tools with no handle,
ten candle-ends not worth a candle,
old lumber banished from the Temple,
damned by Paul's precept and example,
cast from the kingdom, banned in Israel,
the wordless sign, the tinkling cymbal.

When will we see Him face to face?
Each day, He shines through darker glass.
In this small town where everything
is known, I see His vanishing
emblems, His white spire and flag-
pole sticking out above the fog,
like old white china doorknobs, sad,
slight, useless things to calm the mad.

The command to "put old clothes on" is in patent defiance of Sunday habiliment. The search for "dregs and dreck" and "old lumber," on the other hand, is so often enforced as a motif in "Waking Early Sunday Morning" that the storeroom where discards are kept becomes a metaphor for the poet's sentimentality. The junk of the "year's output, a dead wood of dry verse" (from the rejected stanza three), like the "old china doorknobs" found in his heart where love and hate should be (a ligature removed from stanza nine), are the caked and random residues of a life misspent in a particular way, and they lead to the frantic remorse we are so flayed by in reading Lowell. The particular way in which the poet's failings dog him becomes the more evident in the revisions, where the "dead wood" of poems becomes the "dark nook" where mice roll marbles, and the woodwork where termites sleep:

> listen, the creatures of the night
> obsessive, casual sure of foot,
> go on grinding, while the sun's
> daily remorseful blackout dawns.
>
> (stanza three)

As there are no great actions, he will sing of frogs and mice. Not the poet's detritus as in the original verses, but now a house undermined and inhabited by primitive smallfry who portion out the uneasy hours of the night. And the house, by implication, is hollow, decayed, and termite-ridden. The substitutions in stanza nine also emphasize the similarity between a hollow house and the equally hollow spirit within, since the ragtag junk and china doorknobs are neither household detail nor emblems of family shame but domestications of public architectural detail—

the spire and pole-knob of a New England town's church. These emblems of worshipful belief then vanish in the general, dirty fog.[23]

This double balance between his own spirit and its leavings on the one hand, and between the world's "wake of refuse" (stanza four) and his own sympathetic harboring of dead and sundered objects on the other, creates a Janus-posture from which Lowell's peculiar invective is launched in "Waking Early Sunday Morning." Derision of self and derision of society go hand in hand where faith has been scrapped and shredded. Unlike the conduct of business under an edenic covenant in Psalm 107, going down to the sea in ships in 1965 does not enable men to see the works of the Lord and his wonders in the deep, but only "refuse, dacron rope," and the messy trails of pleasure yachts. There are "No weekends for the gods now. Wars / flicker"—and President Johnson's compulsive, indecorous press conferences and the Vietnam "incidents" that cloaked destruction in euphemism are given an odd turn by Lowell. He compares our "action" in Southeast Asia with David's destruction of the Philistines. Both nations in each epoch, ours and David's, suffered. Both, by implication, were destroyed by the businesslike conduct of war. And, in a madly ugly phrase ("when that kingdom hit the crash: / a million foreskins stacked like trash"), the mutually binding death-to-the-spirit of Israelite and Philistine alike is rendered ambiguously (David was notorious, like Saul, for collecting foreskins from every tribe he defeated). Such verbal aggression is doubtless designed to plant the Great Society under the Philistine label, and in order that our period's dreck and its empty edifices, as well as the poet's own pottage of scraps, can be seen in the rubble. But the diction and the image are still nasty rather than tremendous, and something small lingers about the attempt of the whole.

The world of many Lowell poems, so full of dead foliage and scrubby, "frizzled" trees, gradually grows tattered and burned-out.[24] This would be of secondary interest were it not for the infusion of emotion which makes the junk and cinders emblems of a deep and horrifying remorse. One example: "The Public Garden" in *For the Union Dead* is a place of dead leaves and the season's wreckage, as well as the wreckage of the passion David had for Bathsheba. Once, they drowned

> in Eden, while Jehovah's grass-green lyre
> was rustling all about us in the leaves
> that gurgled by us, turning upside down . . .

but this is very much a vision *in illo tempore* and has nothing but negative links to the present time, when the waters of the fountain "fail." In the last line Lowell avers that "Nothing catches fire" because the sin (the murder of Uriah, infidelity) broods and hectically burns like an ember that is almost spent. The last stanza of "Waking Early Sunday Morning" calls upon us to

> Pity the planet, all joy gone
> from this sweet volcanic cone;
> peace to our children when they fall
> in small war on the heels of small
> war—until the end of time
> to police to earth, a ghost
> orbiting forever lost
> in our monotonous sublime.[25]

(stanza fourteen)

Neither Shelley's "intense inane" nor Stevens's "perverse marine" (because the former was a borrowed and floundering expression of his theme, and because the latter was a phrase never intended to be important in its place) possesses the satisfactory and conclusive flourish of Lowell's resonant adjective nomination, "monotonous sublime." Embraced here are the final end both of hymns and belligerent racket, drawn down alike into a monotone; the "resolution" of faith into a ridiculous sublimity; and the reduction of trial and error into a final tablet, on which is written, "that which is done is irrevocable."

Perhaps there is nothing more frightening for a consciousness impelled by remorse than the closing of the book of the recording angel. By an interesting psychological reversal, the idea of death, like a veil, is taken down from the drafty corridor before which it hangs and is wound about the figure of our living act, so that we can no longer move, or work our way out of an evil turbulence, or redeem what we've done by stepping into what we might do. We become a mummified vestige of fallible intentions. Marlowe's Faustus may be the last and best exemplar of the allegory of the eleventh hour (we do not find the same kind of terror in Goethe). To posit other planes, afterlives, ways of going on, is another sublimination of the fear and places the veil only further down amid dim colonnades. Lowell wrote in "Jonathan Edwards in Western Massachusetts," "We know how the world will end, but where is paradise?"

In "Waking Early," the awareness of finality (punishment and holocaust) looms on the horizon in the world's emblem as a "sweet volcanic cone"—which refers to origins as well as ends, as Lowell's etiologies tend to do. Even the Divinity was finished before He began:

> I suppose even God was born
> too late to trust the old religion—
> all those settings out
> that never left the ground,
> beginning in wisdom, dying in doubt.

This is from the last stanza of "Tenth Muse" (*For the Union Dead*), a poem about Sloth who comes to the speaker's bed and, strangely enough, does not take him over, cushion him, or seduce him, but reminds him of what she is *not*. And she is no fun at all; she is only that which he ought to be doing, like opening his mail, or remembering Moses, who made the effort and lugged down from Sinai the heavy stones of the old law. He should make, receive, or at least abide by law. Due to Lowell's naturally patristic[26] turn of mind, Acedia's pleasures, like God's trust in Himself, are barely given time to breathe before doubt and vexations draw the cord.

Lowell's brave yet virulent fascination with late Rome possibly has its meaning here. Caligula's depravity was not simple, easy, or merely bad and promiscuous, but grotesquely anguished. Certainly, to ascribe to Caligula even psychotic masochism would be a kindness, given how repellent he was on every human level. But in Lowell's attention to him there is an assumption of complicity between them which is not entirely due to self-effacement or sheer, outrageous irony. Lowell claims for them both "the lawlessness of something simple that has lost its law" ("Caligula," *For the Union Dead*). Not only is this a splendid capsule of what psychology has always claimed about our illnesses, but it's an important position statement for Lowell as well: The world, and he as its unemployed prophet, are simple at root, but it is a simplicity neither will ever see face to face. In place of such simplicity, there is the exercise of a conscience that is pained and even wrongheaded. There is thus no probity except, by accident, among the meek and vaguely memorious—those who suspect how desire may once have been fitted to belief. There is much anguish in conscience, the more for an intelligent and learned poet who wrestles with the perversity of will and anarchic detours on the part of lives and minds (including his own) which are probably, on their best face, rather uninteresting, *simple*. Such intimations of the character of a simple, conscience-less self are supremely withering: Even with all our meanness and self-consciousness aside, none of us would exist very much.

"Waking Early Sunday Morning" is a bleak, irritating, and stunning poem. By its form it is a black parody of the elegance of Marvell's "The Garden." Once the form draws us to the text, we find a parody of substance as well. Within the rich and almost merry closure of an engaged belief (I would call Marvell a sanguine temperament), metaphoric and imaginative conceits blossom and dodge, retreating and amplifying themselves. Marvell's aesthetic ebullience invents quite broadly, but on themes that are hardly doubted. Because there is no harmony among Lowell's beliefs, or much clarity to his predication as a whole except in attesting to ragged states of mind, there cannot be the same contract for invention.

He crosshatches his verse with allusions because he must try to reinstate the recorded world each time he writes, and cull from the ruins the pieces that seem intuitively important for the building of some new, minor harmony. To this end, he culls from himself as well, and much of the text of "Waking Early Sunday Morning" has about it the air of critical apparatus.

There is a sense in which most poets write one poem all the time, however much they change. There is also a closet full of "tics" which form a permanent wardrobe—speech tics, image tics, even moral ones. Among those "tics" of Lowell's which I can see here, I am most interested in the ones that seem to have leaped out of the private into a fully public dimension. From among the former sort, I have already singled out a few of the many images of things burned-out and used up: dead wood, the volcanic cone, old lumber, the "Bible chopped and crucified," doorknobs, candle-ends. A subclass presents itself, that of *wood* which can't be used any more; the pattern will culminate in the tree of life which is being disposed of in stanza eleven. "Where the Rainbow Ends" from the end of *Lord Weary's Castle* convenes similar images:

> The torn tree waits
> Its victim and tonight
> The worms will eat the deadwood to the foot
> Of Ararat: the scythers, Time and Death,
> Helmed locusts, move upon the tree of breath;
> The wild ingrafted olive and the root
>
> Are withered . . .

The "tree of breath" (*spiritus* = breath, life), the thorn tree of the Passion, and the deadwood on Ararat, as emblems of Adam, Christ, and Noah, present the analogical discipline of finding types of Christ in a characteristic Lowell skewing: They are being eaten by worms, defoliated by locusts, or made into cruel crowns. Nothing much flourishes in Lowell's Holy Land. There remains, however, something further or deeper about Lowell's fondness for the dead branch and the sickly stand of pines that I cannot locate, and which I must ascribe, reductively, to a habitual swerve in the poet's memory.

An example of another sort of "tic" which rises to metaphor is related to this indicated (but not fully visible) pattern of dying out, obsolescence, the tree of breath and the dead wood of dry verse, and to the diminishment of an irreligious present even (because pointedly disjointed from us) by a religious past. But naming and listing will never quite prepare one for the end of stanza eleven. As a further codicil, I should also say that when Robert Boyers asked me to write about a Lowell poem for *Salmagundi* some years ago, I chose "Waking Early Sunday Morning" because of this stanza, and because I see in it the kind of personal nightmare about the public world which is absolutely embodied and absolutely unforgettable:

> No weekends for the gods now. Wars
> flicker, earth licks its open sores,
> fresh breakage, fresh promotions, chance
> assassinations, no advance.
> Only man thinning out his kind
> sounds through the Sabbath noon, the blind
> swipe of the pruner and his knife
> busy about the tree of life . . .

This is a suddenly quiet moment "sounding" in a poem otherwise full of conflicting song, ruckus, chimes, "stiff quatrains," tinkling cymbals. It is a dreadful, sinister hiatus which reminds me of the moment when Sir Gawain came to that turning in the dark ravine: Suddenly an ear-splitting noise burst upon the air, and Gawain knew he was near to the heart of the mystery—that the Green Knight was *there,* grinding his scissors and knives. I am also reminded of another great moment in literature, when Anna Karenina looked up to the platform from the wheels of the train that was crushing her, saw the old peasant doing something with metal and muttering, and realized what her recurrent nightmare about that peasant had finally meant. Tolstoy has given us here one of those terrible moments of truth when our triviality and our worst fate become indistinguishable: Somewhere in their bond is the final modern horror.

The trivial is seldom far distant from the lethal in the verse we have been considering; but wretched death and the shallowness of our personal mystery are never so well bonded into true horror as when, having raised himself from a bad night into a quickly extinguishing joy, Robert Lowell picks his way through the babble and lost hope of centuries to see what the trouble could be. And after stumbling through four lines of substantives which mirror the rhetoric of the evil they denote, and skirting small war and open sore, he comes to the clearing where it's only man, working at something—"the pruner and his knife / busy about the tree of life." In language and symbols perfectly tuned to the poem's whole context, yet totally in the grip of an inspired private vision, Lowell meets the only kind of creature whose act and belief are in concord. And that is the Killer. The same eerie, tawdry figure who, with "the scythers, Time and Death," has managed to turn ploughshares back into spears. The tree of life, our dead wood, is his whetstone.

The prophet may be a fool, but the hatred and iniquity are commandingly perverse. This grim hypothesis, unlike the resounding imprecations in Hosea, Jeremiah, and Isaiah, creates in Lowell's work a psychic deadlock, for there is no God to whom one might sacrifice one's anger, or any countermood in the embrace of which it is possible to attain mildness, mercy, or peace of mind.

III. Applied Poetry

One of Auden's epigrams comes back to me as I reflect on the work of Anne Sexton, and it sheds a chastening but forgiving light on an oeuvre otherwise undeniably hobbled by unwitting self-parody: "Poetry is not magic," the saying goes; "In so far as poetry, or any other of the arts, can be said to have an ulterior purpose, it is, by telling the truth, to disenchant and disintoxicate."[27] In light of such a mission, Anne Sexton is under a serious misapprehension as to the nature of art. When I began to study the posthumous edition of her *Selected Poems*,[28] what struck me as most characteristic of her work were the passages in which the mechanism that might ordinarily censor the material had been radically disconnected. In its absence, nightmare, wish fulfillment, and self-destructive urgency—all the agents of toxic untruth—coil and tumble onto the page, as in "Flee on Your Donkey":

> Soon I will raise my face for a white flag,
> and when God enters the fort,
> I won't spit or gag on his finger.
> I will eat it like a white flower.

The writer of these lines clearly wants to shock us, perhaps as a way to reproduce in herself the sensation of atrocity that accompanied her illness. She gives us a metaphor comparing her contested body to a fortification, her anguished face to the white flag of surrender, and the power over her life and sanity—a power she identifies with God—to an enemy who takes command of and extracts humiliations from the vanquished persona until she is tempted to gag. But one looks in vain for the connection between *finger* that goes in the mouth and *flower* that is eaten. Although each may lead back to the floating hint of medication that may be on its way to her room in the clinic (to which she had just voluntarily recommitted herself), in close succession the references to flower and finger of God only disturb each other's associations, not least because gagging on a finger is an inducement for vomiting, as if God were trying to purge her rather than initiate her into a divine cannibalism as the patient consumes this part of Him. But these hypotheses can be neither proved nor disproved. The flesh of God and the lotus-flower of forgetfulness may separately return to the oblivion of chemical treatment, but only in overriding their relation to one another.

Readers who admire the work of Anne Sexton have claimed that she is delving into the dark earth of the unconscious and bringing up painful psychic matter to the light. This may well be true, but the matter is still chaotic; the key is often missing by which we might estimate the necessary consanguinity of one item with the next—let alone the pertinence of Sexton's setting them down in these abrupt orderings.

> It is not that I am cattle to be eaten.
> It is not that I am some sort of street.
> But your hands found me like an architect.

Can it possibly help matters to know that the speaker of these lines is a woman's breast? It seems instead that the overwrought dramatic situation intrudes an unintentional comic element into the non sequiturs of "The Breast." This observation reminds us, in turn, of the many efforts in the volume where the hand of the clever or outrageous (at least, self-conscious) rearranger of words is evident:

> That is what poems are:
> with mercy
> for the greedy
> they are the tongue's wrangle,
> the world's pottage, the rat's star.
> ("With Mercy for the Greedy")

Under these wildly disjunctive images of extremity of soul, the writer is only toying with her rough and fitful rhetoric. One can feel the great difference between such exercises and that range of her work that suggests a sensibility truly deranged. There are fathoms of unimaginable suffering separating them. The poem about Judas Iscariot, for example, is a mad work that stands apart from literature that draws upon derangement, like that of Céline, Djuna Barnes, Dickinson, Baudelaire, and Sylvia Plath— writers who wrestled their demons with words. Instead, here is someone in torment trying, with her flotsam of cleverness, to disguise the unmistakable leer of the void:

> Of course
> the New Testament is very small.
> Its mouth opens four times—
> as out-of-date as a prehistoric monster,
> yet somehow man-made,
> held together by pullies
> like the stone jaw of a back-hoe.
> It gouges out the Judaic ground,
> taking its own backyard
> like a virgin daughter.
> ("The Legend of the One-Eyed Man")

About other poems of "hallucinatory flux," the editors of this volume have the following to say:

> What organizes the hallucinatory flux in these "spiritual" last poems is confidence in the power of words in sequence to *carry* sense, beyond the mind's power to *make* sense. No matter how florid or irrational the simile a mind may form, Spirit resides there: in the architecture of syntax, the irreducible intelligence of metaphor.

Like the poetry it glosses, this comment suggests nothing more profound than the nerve to try to get away with writing it, for such distinctions about the poetic mind are nonsense. In their own obscure way the authors appeal, just as they say Sexton does, to some ghostly shaping authority outside language. But if metaphors had an "intelligence" regardless of their content, and if syntax always provided a reliable "architecture," surely a great many poems would be more coherent and persuasive than they are.

Not that Anne Sexton is incapable of being interesting. Anyone who goes at writing for more than a couple of years has a fair chance of occasionally getting something right in words. Bright phrases—and true recognitions—do appear. "Once I was beautiful. Now I am myself." "I have come back / but disorder is not what it was." In relation to her beloved's wife, whose style is heavy and sculptural, Sexton is a wispier artist: "I am a watercolor, / I wash off." Before surgery, "I turn in my bin like a shorn lamb." Protestants are "the people that sing / when they aren't quite / sure." Suicides are "Like carpenters[,] they want to know *which tools. / They never ask why build*." But alongside the lucky hits loom the wastes of what can only be called juvenility and misjudgment. For me, despite the attempt to reckon the tally otherwise, the blunders preponderate: "Once I thought the Bunny Rabbit was special." "Life is a trick, life is a kitten in a sack." "[T]he important lungs." "I want to say [to her daughter] there is nothing in your body that lies." "His penis [Jesus' as it happens] sang like a dog." "You are singing like a school girl" ("In Celebration of My Uterus"). One even hears her falling, with a kind of wooden defiance, into the style of Ogden Nash: "the sea has turned into a pond of urine. / There is no place to wash and no marine beings to stir in." This desperate brazening-it-out seems to fuel her in poem after poem.

> Disgusted, mother put me
> on the potty. She was good at this.
> My father was fat on scotch.
> It leaked from every orifice.
>
> Oh the enemas of childhood,
> reeking of outhouses and shame!

> Yet you rock me in your arms
> and whisper my nickname.

("Cripples and Other Stories" is addressed to her doctor.)

On the other side of the ledger is the undeniable fact of Anne Sexton's enormous reputation as a victim-seer. What does it suggest about the Zeitgeist that she remains admired despite the patently therapeutic impulse, the ill-absorbed mental suffering that grimaces from the interior, and above all the wasteful dishonesty of the machinery she sets in motion? For there can be no doubt that, as the lore surrounding her suggests, Sexton's work has "helped" numbers of women (what people believe helps them is often inversely related to merit). Yet if she represents the plight of the mid-century American female in transition from a dark age of heels and martinis to a new world loud with vituperation of the past (in all its guises), neither can there be any question whether this has much to do with immortal song. For that matter, anger is a curiously overvalued enterprise; it is surprising that so many people should be proud of exhibiting it. (Although it cannot provide the same personal *frisson*, a zeal for justice is more to be trusted.) In the absence of other warrants for greatness, in any event, the premise of the extreme personal state cannot take a poet very far at all.

Hence there are two problems that solicit our attention. The first is that in Sexton we have a writer who collars us like the Ancient Mariner but whose mask of compulsive confidentiality we are asked to admire; whose literary judgment we are never invited to test; whose style—abrasive, hieratic, even fatuous—is often obscure, even when she veers toward the sentimental; and who cannot coordinate a poetic utterance of longer than eight lines—and a writer about whom all of that can be said is a virtual amateur. Thus her own standards are one issue. The second is the critical discrimination of her public. It is not just Sexton herself who dismantles the censoring device, but a powerful middle-class consumer industry that has cooperated in esteeming the result. A *persona* extrinsic to the making of poetry has been mistaken all the way around for an excellent *poem*. The intermediate steps by which insight and imagination can be said to be *embodied* have been abrogated.

Now some waggish interpreters may claim that the very lack of norms and forms must make the efforts of recent poets like Sexton more subtle because more anxious, so that the resulting "art" becomes more compelling than what is produced in periods when the modes are understood and shared. But such historical fatalism makes nonsense of the evidence of our senses, which shows us, in a certain range of contemporary poems, a lack of control bordering on automatism. Moreover, although it is true that in our literary culture modes are not shared—understood and generally valued—many poets still make use of their inheritance without becoming victims of their conventions. And one may read poets like John Morris and Jim Powell in the books below without detecting any slavish adherence to tradition, rather a flexible and fruitful conversation with the whole available language of poetry. Elsewhere we may be witnessing a situation in which poetry has begun to embrace its own shadows, trying to shed its substance in favor of ghostly comforts of self-help, healthy "realizations," and exposures of "honesty," which literary politics would make unassailable. One wonders whether work like Anne Sexton's ought not more profitably be placed in a category extraneous to poetry entirely.

In an entertaining yet severe essay on "Drab Age Verse" in his Oxford history of *English Literature in the Sixteenth Century* (Oxford University Press, 1954), C. S. Lewis coins a distinction pertinent to the casual intensities and antiformalist driftings in Sexton's poems and those of many others. The distinction comes about during a discussion of the native plain style (Drab Verse), with its rough-hewn character, epigrammatically ingrown and even "loutish" in its recoil from dignity and deftness. As the age, which began fairly strongly with Wyatt, progresses, "Drab" gets worse, falling into dilutions that stem from extraliterary interests. Lewis considers the *Mirror for Magistrates,* for example, to "appeal to an historical, not to a purely literary taste. . . . It is to be judged as applied poetry." Not only in such chronicle poems but also in almanac verse, the impulse toward application grows. Thomas Tusser's *Hundred Good Points of Husbandry,* though "they are scarcely art," nevertheless teach us, says Lewis, "that very minor talents should stick to 'applied' poetry and avoid the pure. The Eighteenth Century was quite right in recommending to them such subjects as the Mediterranean and the Barometer."

The "pure" poetry to which "applied" formed a codicil was clearly poetry that used the line without clunky inversion or crowding; it used trope commensurate with an illustrative or expressive end; its syntax ranged across the whole keyboard of the instrument, stretching easily to the grammar of hypothesis and contrary-to-fact; and pure poetry articulated a view of life based on insight, dignity, and depth of feeling. In this reconstruction of Lewis's notion of "purity" in poetry, the ends are high without being lofty (so some unromantic standard of decorum is implied), but above all means (matters of style) are always referred to ends (so the moral being is engaged).

In our period, it would seem that, unlike earlier chronicle poems, or those about farming, botany, and the tides, "applied" poems are no longer produced to convey useful information in plain dress. What is lacking is at once a sense of range and variety—and a recognition that some verse should assume an ancillary posture. Instead, "applied" poems today seek to supplant other notions and kinds of poetry with an exclusivity of thera- peutic discovery. In this they resemble nothing so much as poems of the rhapsodic demeanor momentarily slumming in the prosaic mode. For this poetry is made not to be read but (like all too much criticism *about* it) to be written, and for the sake of the "mysterious" processes of writing (which readers can pick up fairly fast because they need encounter no resistance from inherited norms or forms). Unlike an applied poem in the past, with its minor ambition to clear a small corner of the field, carrying rocks out of the way and setting out a row or two of seed, our applied poems set themselves up as major. They know only a little, yet they behave (justifiably, as it turns out) as though the entire intellectual pasture be- longed to them to plough or ruin as they saw fit. Those who congratulate the modern age on ridding us of classical baggage and outmoded notions like decorum and euphony are of course delighted by this new care- lessness, the chance to go hungry and let the soil waste for a while. One wonders, though, about the weak, scruffy things the ground is able to force up.

Anne Sexton was arguably part of the tide that turned from pure to applied preoccupations. The legacy of this turn is not only much bad verse but also the production, even in good writers, of uncertainty. Even when poems today are very good indeed, the false sparkle of application flickers around them, so strong is the drive of the emotional shortcut in an age of applied art. By chance it is the women writers in this essay's purview who are working furthest from pure poetry, as if in struggling against inherited forms of organization and formerly adumbrated themes they were misled to broaden their reach into applied poetry—applied both in the arbitrariness of insight and justment, and in the decay of prosody, whether metrical *or* free. Even if, at times, others of these volumes show the hand of an "applicant," it is still hard to resist the conclusion that it is the volumes by Sexton and Sandra Gilbert that fall into inexorable patterns: rambling through a formless brevity of time during which some speaker is aroused by a few scraps of life study or folklore. Information ("insight"), though invariably presented as difficult in the getting, is not only bland, but also instantaneous. There is a frozen quality in the experi- ence of recognition, a hush of reverence surrounding a stricken or ecstatic tableau. The diction of "breaking through" some barrier or obstacle is the more passionately promulgated as the syntactic and rhythmical evidence subversively whispers that there is nothing but level ground in view, and that the prisons were emptied long ago. For the poet/self, suffering is still an explosive and liberating drama; for the poem, it is mannered and rigidifying.

This I would call the final paradox of applied poetry: that the content is extravagantly emotional but the formal embodiments are loose, flaccid, inert. Everything about the applied poem points to the little worm at the core: that it was easy for the writer to write. (Anne Sexton's *Complete Poems* comprise more than 600 pages.) That such products should be required to give nothing beyond the authors' assurances (again, merely stipulated) that they reflect the intensest being of their composers is surely evidence of a widespread rhapsodic fallacy. Yet ease, automatism, and resultant *bulk* have consolidated themselves as the warrants of intensity.

In some poets, the evidence is venial. In the work of Sandra M. Gilbert it is mortal weight.[29] Gilbert carries to an extreme a syntax to which she can give spine only by cataloguing items and textures, asyndeton and parataxis chronically overfreighted:

> You strip away your silky blouse, your
> frilly bark, soft armor.
> Nude as a peeled tree, you stare
> at your pink-white body: swollen,
> female, pulpy where it should be rough,
> damp where it should be dry,
> open where it should be closed . . .

Except for the violent verb "strip," there is no action. Instead, the writer indulges the anxious habit of paraphrase, as if no *one* of the ideas were quite in focus. Thus the speaker's consciousness is blurred because the language is not choice nor are the symbols attended to. I miss the precision of good metaphor (recall "Daphne with her thighs in bark"), also the magical sense of that world of true poetry in which the expression is always the *right* one. Or open Sylvia Plath almost anywhere to find not only more mobile syntax but also a sense (even with her leaps) of a coherent poetic intelligence:

> It is easy to blame the dark: the mouth of a door,
> The cellar's belly. They've blown my sparkler out.
> A black-sharded lady keeps me in a parrot cage.
> What large eyes the dead have!
> I am intimate with a hairy spirit.
> Smoke wheels from the beak of this empty jar.
>
> ("Witch Burning")

Now return to the second stanza of the anti-Daphne poem by Gilbert to see how desperate must be her machinery of rescue from her own approximations:

> That's what he hates the most!
> More than the mushy breasts, the tender belly,

> He hates that swamp inside you,
> that moist cleft where flowers quiver,
> and darker things, night birds who call from
> heavy branches, nests of speckled eggs, small
> leaves warm with the weight of the sunset.
>
> ("What He Hates/What He Loves")

Can so many emblems crowd without irony into that one moist cleft? When we come to the "night birds," the hint of self-parody broadens. The aggressive *you*-locution (often substituted for *I* in contrast to *him*, the forbidding yet attractive male) I connect with Gilbert's other techniques of hilarity and high contrast. Her writing can be quick and jolly, like impromptu patter-singing, lest it appear she is too much concerned with "high art."

But the sleight is easy to detect, for she does surely wish to install herself in the pantheon with Sexton and Plath. That is why there is so much of the rhetoric of archetypes in her poems. It strikes me that for her, as for Sexton, the dependence on myth and folktale results in a manufactured darkness. "Frost is growing like mold / in your armpits," she says (with unintentional bathos), to an adversarial male. In another poem, reading a book on classical Greece in an airplane where she is served wine as she broods over a friend who doesn't love her former lover any more, the writer suggests that an ancient, cold, blue sky out of the Oresteia is freezing the windowpanes of the 747. Just as one starts to squirm at all this trivial *situating,* the context is comically inflated: "O Clytemnestra," she says—and one winces to hear the friend compared to the slayer of Agamemnon and Cassandra—

> O Clytemnestra,
>
> why are you so honest, how
> are you so clear, so true?
> When I hear you say
>
> "I don't love him,"
> I pass through the window
> into ancient cold,
>
> and I want to find out what love is.
>
> ("'But I Don't Love Him'")

With myths, says Calvino, one should not be in a hurry. In much of her thinking about myth, this writer begins too soon. Before sedimentation has taken place, an interpretation is already on her lips. In consequence, after making poems shallow individually, the goad of haste raises a fever of opportunism: The writer wants myth to spawn myth—to show the way to the next or the opposing role until she has "done" the whole family, thereby converting one small turn into a series of them. Thus we have not one poem about Andersen's Snow Queen, but a notebook full. In addition to the mandatory poem about the frog king (both she and Sexton have one), there is a series of poems, at once bland and diffuse, which echo other of the Grimm tales like "The Three Brothers," "Rapunzel," and "The Princesses Who Danced Their Slippers to Pieces." In the poem in which Clytemnestra is the model of clarity, the poet vaults over to a featureless Aphrodite, as if the allusion-making engine could straighten out the poem's lameness. But to the goddess of love she can only mutter, "I want to learn / what you bring." Not a hint here of the ancient eye-glitter of divinity, or of the throat aflash with strands of light—let alone of the turned eyes and the open mouth of love.

Finally, we have the Procrustean frame of the household tale clamped onto the early life of Phaeton ("You clench small fists . . . you want to rip out those stiffened manes / the way a gardener / uproots furious platoons of goldenrod"), or onto the late life of the great composer ("Beethoven's waiting, / he's waited all night, his enormous / thicket of hair is wet, But he smiles . . . and recites / / the single diminished / seventh / of his own death"). Needless to say, the reductions are orthogonal to their models, and one sees no further into the worlds from which these figures come.

Jim Powell is a better technician than Gilbert, better grounded in a tradition *that he understands,* and more tenaciously inventive within his unique unrhymed five-line stanza.[30] But I wonder whether he is re-readable. There is a hardness in him that he never directs at himself. He is self-scrutinizing, but only to approve what he sees. This can leave him vulnerable to pomposity (it saturates the poem about his cold-war childhood) and to unintentionally comic *sententiae:*

> close friends around a table, good dope,
> talk shared till dawn in a kitchen over wine
> after the party's left, can last awhile
> making a place to rest beside the stove
> that outburns every dark and cold . . .
>
> ("Revisting the Haight")

Something in every poet should balk when the word "sharing" strikes the page—especially in the neighborhood of "talk" or "thoughts."

That said, there is much in Jim Powell's current volume, which is his first, that gives pleasure: intelligence, exactness, calm, an ability to discriminate appetites (a relief from the monotonous mythifications of Sexton and Gilbert). And Powell also carries his work through. In his longer poems, in fact, he is obsessively thorough, rather like the creature in Kafka's "Burrow," tracking down associations, patching them back into the mainstays of the whole, worrying over the daubing, peering at his mental grid of invisible corridors, until Powell's long verse epistles become anxieties of surveillance.

Determination also informs the shorter poems in *It Was Fever That Made the World*, binding up (but less arduously) the layers of association from which his superbly expressive metaphors are made. His title burns away everywhere in the volume, in the fevers of eros, divination, memory, destruction, and grief. As befits the translator of the passionate Latin elegy in which Cynthia's ghost denounces her former lover, Propertius, Powell is not afraid of deepening his work by the grand and subtle technique of allusion. In "Fire Signs," two friends camp in the Southwest near a rock painting propitiating the theriomorphic gods. It is May, the sky suffused with significant light from the live and dead planets. The friends build a bonfire. Then the speaker watches while the other boy dances naked, swinging two burning planks above his head,

> the lit ends spitting fir sap, flames torching out
> on the wind you made, long sparks spilling off them
>
> into the night. I still have
> the photographs you took and printed in negative.
> I can still make out
> his horns, his fading temples, though you've been
> seven years now among the sightless dead.

The quaint classical epithet "sightless" comes out raw or sharp, like a thistle in the mouth. The speaker has not forgiven that loss, even in the face of all his sublime examples of influence poured into our world from those processions in the heavens.

Another poem broods more lingeringly over its mythic allusions to the fate and behavior of the dead as Powell's poet-speaker and other surviving friends bury the young photographer, dead at twenty-nine:

> Now in the tight trench you go
> down beyond shadow at noonday, footsteps
>   lost where the long slope
> quickens you downward, shouldered on
> through the swarming dank and mute trampling
>   down where the bloodless press close,
> bone white dice in the massive cold and formal hysteria
> where forgetfulness rules the Death Lord's gaze,
> his sunken island and iron horns,
>   his eyeless bride,

you go down
to be lost in a waste of burning cities,
        Dresden, Gomorrah, Dis:
there, haze gnaws at the rust air and communion ends—
there, still pools cast no light back to be lost.

                                        ("Time and Light")

In the absence of the elaborate architectonics possible in an inflected
tongue like Latin or Greek, note how Powell interweaves and even muscu-
larizes his English with adverbial extenders—phrases and clauses of direction, downward drive, perseveration, placement (slippage), tempo, and
cessation. But it is not merely the grammar of an archaic tongue that is
rendered flexible and faintly electric in these relentlessly moving lines: it
is the terrible pathos of the dead in Homer crowding around Odysseus
in the Cimmerian gloom and aching to drink of the living blood he has
poured out to draw them near. This Powell makes "modern," immediate,
universal. Personal grief is entirely transformed into poetry of a very general tenor of irretrievable sorrow, without ceasing to be strictly individual.
It is that specific gravity which gives the short catalogue of holocaust cities
such a chilling efficacy, exceeding Auden's in the twelfth sonnet of *In
Time of War*.

    Page for page, there is more sheer fine, clear, yet syntactically subtle
and metaphorically gorgeous writing in Powell than one ordinarily sees.
At moments, I do not like his sensibility, but even then, say at the end of
one of his long and patronizing epistles, I can find myself enormously
moved, as when he chooses for an image of the soul

        a statue called *The Venus at Arles*—just
        as she stands, twenty feet from one high wall
        in the enormous public space of the Salle
        des Cariatides at the Louvre, gazing
        reflectively down at a marble mirror
        broken away a thousand years ago,
        only its handle left in her grip.

                                        ("Inscriptions")

What is fine is the speed with which we are stripped of illusion—that
iridescent shimmer of life that broke from the cold body, to no particular
fanfare, centuries ago.

    Now that we have turned from the authors who capitulate, in whole
or in part, to therapeutic or ideological "application," we can relish the real
work of a poet: embodying the imagination in graceful and memorable
language. A primary benefit of a tradition that can produce two such
temperamentally opposed writers as Jim Powell and John N. Morris is

that certain weaknesses of insight or failures of nerve will inevitably be exposed. And if clarity and dignity are the poet's touchstones, failures cannot long go ignored. Thus it is that the classical plain style (a later meditative variant of the native plain style) teases mercilessly out into the open whatever arrogance may be there in the writer to start with. (In Morris there is no arrogance whatever.) But this style also, over the long haul, betrays any lack of sharpness, perspicuity, and breadth. It is this apparent threat which John Morris turns to advantage.[31] For if one discerned any flaw in him, it would be what used to be called fondness, a weakness in the will that produces unreasoning tenderness toward some object unworthy or harmful. Except that in this poet the object is ordinary life. Wistfully, patiently, he beholds the ragged patterns of our ways to pass the time. While the time passes, the trivial deepens.

> For an hour now you can assign each tree
> Its place in the forest, things you did not know
> You knew pouring out like a confession.
>
> This is a kind of forgetting
> It all into the absorbing paper.

Thus caution the examiners before our test. What we thought was the false light of an entertainment becomes with closer acquaintance the loose cage of our lives. For it is wonderfully true that the composition of an answer is a kind of fluent forgetting into the paper.

> One by one the early finishers drift away.
> Empty-headed you arise
> From the sleep of concentration.
> In black and white the hour is on the wall.
> Now you must leave the past behind you.
> Though you hope you have composed
> Some sort of explanation
> Of the events we hold you responsible for . . .
>
> ("A Word from the Examiners")

This was a history exam, of sorts. Spread over years, it exposes our drone-like quality—never originating our own thought; scarcely able to summon up anybody else's—and our feeling of being coerced is also implied here, along with our fecklessness and compliancy, so that, though we've scratched in some kind of explanation, "At the end you write *Time!* because there is none." What differentiates John Morris from Howard Nemerov, Auden, or Daryl Hine, all of whom share a round quality of punning play, is that Morris is also writing close observation of the poor students at their desks, not sacrificing them to an examination of our lives. No little restraint is required to resist the intellectualizing bent, and treat as tenor what others would take as vehicle. That is why the fit between them is so seamless. However, what Morris shares with these writers is also well to note: It is that gift of disengaged seriousness, of dignified and yet exuberant play, that acts as a tenacious censor fending off overearnestness, sentimentality, and other forms of applied crudity.

One often suspects that Morris's work gives him a greater chance for pyrotechnics than he is willing to display. He elects a path tangential to the high road, as if he had to ponder something the resulting poem may never quite touch. Indeed, the poem only becomes the log of an intelligence at work on what it expresses to us, to the extent that this role does not deflect him from his deeper object. This swerving aside (or rooting around) is easiest to catch in poems that flirt with stalling, like "The Period Rooms," a poem about the life-size replicas of Victorian sitting rooms in museums where, "unimaginably like us, someone / After someone lived in hope and stepped / A last time from the door we glance through / And closed it in our unforeseeable faces." At last the poet can envision a time when all of the rooms of the past ("rooms" and "past" in double senses, like everything here) will be monotonously and untouchably restored, "Never again to be at last forgotten." There is weariness and rue in that resolution, also the ideal of existence as something that cannot be true unless it can ripen and decay, hence weariness at the way such "perfect" images rebuff the living.

In Morris's most extraordinary poems, the focusing and the perfect plainness of the style carry a burden of tremendous feeling:

> My dear, who are they years ago
> By that weedy river? He has lost
> Something and she
> Is helping him to find it.
> They are only a day
> Old together. They do not know
> The river flows. The time
> They will have lost
> Closes about them.
> . . . .
> We know we must leave them alone.
> For a time thus shall we protect them:
> For a time they are wandering there,
> Though they are lost to us,
> Us who are lost to us,
> Lost in recollection.

("The Unburied")

This poem has the curious admixture of sadness that makes its affection hard to face, recalling the detached, passionate lyrics of a poet roughly contemporary with Morris, David Ferry. Both poets, resisting the urge to shine, burn long in the memory. Like Ferry, Morris is both learned and eloquent. The poems on Chaucer and Shakespeare are finely quirky. "*Hamlet* at Sea" is one of the pleasantest poems on the bard I know, based as it is on several irreverent premises, (a) that the play is performed at sea off the coast of Africa in 1607 by the sailors on one English ship for the amusement of those on another; (b) that none of them take "all that havering about being" very seriously; while (c) the narrator (left as watch on the second ship) cannot even hear "that faroff palaver," yet "In snatches of the Good Quarto / What comes across the water is merriment."

A second but quieter poem also uses a great tragedy as a living image of, or palimpsest with, episodes in the life of an angry and troubled child: "Every evening the table is laid before him / In the presence of his enemies. / The terrors of the earth surround him" ("A Particular Child"). It is as if all these years now we had mistaken what was really important about the deep sense of that play. Only a close tact in the biblical allusions supporting a freshly considered, almost egoless vision of Lear could produce that effect.

Morris's closing poem is also about a "particular" child, who has spent his life alone, among all those wonderful books the nineteenth century produced, and who is welcoming the newcomer to "The Club of the Only Children." He puts a book kindly into the new child's hands, suggesting that the story may involve the departure of your ship

> away from a great wailing
> Forever toward the horizon, toward the island.
> There you will step ashore, and in the illustration
> The black sails will come up out of the dunnage.

Having helped this child commence the imaginative effort needed to enter the great upper rooms of pointed solitude, the poet's persona adds these words of comfort. I propose that they be read as a text about the pleasures many a reader has in store in the poems of John Morris:

> But for my part, and speaking for myself alone,
> I say we are happy here. We have ourselves
> And no one disturbs you. For company
> Open the book. Goodbye. I bid you welcome.

This is poetry that quietly admits its minor status, then proceeds to speak truly, cleanly, and sweetly about its small corner of the field.

3

A New Sweetness

Randall Jarrell and
Elizabeth Bishop

We learned from you so much about so many things
But never what we were; and yet you made us that.

Variousness and innovation are the traits that enable extraordinary poets
to resist major trends, or to make their niches somewhere between them.
Just as Randall Jarrell is the bridge between the great Freudian poetry of
the twenties and thirties (especially that of Allen Tate and W. H. Auden)
and the definitive movement in American poetry since the war, confessionalism (Lowell, Schwartz, Roethke, Berryman, and later Snodgrass, Plath,
and Sexton), Elizabeth Bishop is the bridge from the postwar group (up
to and including the work of Frank Bidart), back to their modernist
forebears, particularly Marianne Moore and Wallace Stevens. In order to
give Jarrell his due as a poet, one need only reread Allen Tate knowing
that Jarrell would write after him. In this light, Tate can seem as class-
conscious, time-bound, predictable, and outmoded as Tennyson. Or compare Robert Lowell with Jarrell, and he sounds in *Mills of the Kavanaughs*
aimlessly mad (as if imitating Dylan Thomas), and in *Life Studies* and
For the Union Dead a bit like a Browning character suddenly losing self-
confidence. So, too, the example of Bishop casts an unintentionally un-
flattering light on Moore, who then becomes one-dimensional and quaint,
while Bishop's imitators, Bidart or even, at one remove, Louise Glück,
have a difficult time finding an original way to incorporate her angle of
childlikeness.

In other words, the way in which Randall Jarrell and Elizabeth Bishop
act as watershed tends to make both their forebears and their successors
(not to mention their contemporaries) sound traditional, or flat. Surely
this is proof, or partial proof, of their peculiarity, their originality in
absorbing their evident influences. But it is the kind of rescue, the kind
of proof, that has not motivated large numbers of critics to return to

Jarrell for his own sake, namely, for the sake of what he did that was never to be copied, and has even deflected many critics from what might be his most interesting work (*not* the monologues by women, but those by children). While Elizabeth Bishop, far from remaining with the small cult following of the 1950s, has increased enormously in stature since the 1970s. The unevenness of their critical fortunes has made it the exception that their work should be studied in tandem. I would like, somewhat, to correct that imbalance and point to some of the astonishing resemblances in their nearly simultaneous poetic discovery of the child among its objects.

Randall Jarrell

As Jarrell admitted, he identified himself, in a way no one else ever quite has, "with something something's wrong with, with something human." Although he was not in combat, no other writer in our period has managed to write about war, technology, military nerves, the common soldier or pilot so that their fearful and mysterious awfulness was evident. He is, in addition, one of the great psychologists of childhood and dream. And after Pound and Eliot and before Berryman, Jarrell is the great twentieth-century master of the dramatic monologue. Nor, finally, do I know of any other writer who could, at his best, so inundate his characters with the commonest kinds of objects to form their immediate world, yet present them as more than the sum of these things.

As an experiment, compare the disembodied quality of the disadvantaged in Jarrell with the treatment of the poor we get in that Thomas Hobbes of verse, William Carlos Williams. As soon as one puts the two writers with their two realms side by side, bizarre things happen, and the paralysis we are so struck by in a Jarrell poem like "Lady Bates" seems paradisiacal next to that in *Paterson*. And at the same time, next to Williams, that arch-poet of bare things and bare places, Jarrell appears to have come from no place. Without Whitman's rhetorical exuberance, being from no place could not mean, for Jarrell, being from everyplace. He was simply somebody who fit in not anywhere in particular but pretty well everywhere in general. Williams fit in New Jersey, he chose it and suffered it, even though his deliberate classlessness would seem prima facie the opposite of, say, Robert Lowell's identification with New England aristocracy. Again, in Jarrell's light, both Lowell and Williams seem more placed than they otherwise would.[1]

When asked what strikes them first and last about Jarrell's poetry, many writers have answered and I would concur: his heart, his sentiment, even his sentimentality. *He was,* critics, admirers, eulogists say, *so*—something; so fair, so soft, so tender; or so mean, so unyielding, so brave, so cruel—

that he could not . . . (whatever it was they wanted him to have done). The adjectives in the second group, of course, apply to his criticism; those in the first to his poetry. Jarrell seemed to many to have split his imagination in two, reserving for the poetry the gentler emotions while plying the critical reviews with his dazzling and rebarbative genius. It is on account of his powerful visibility as a critic that so many writers have divided over his poetry. He has been a principal case for the exercise of polemic. About what other writer has there been ranged so much dismay, so much misgiving, so much regret? Is it, moreover, any accident that Jarrell did for magazine writing after the war what T. S. Eliot did for literary criticism before it? Or that Jarrell gave to *his* critics the weapon by which he would most be wounded—not to be slain by the exercise of an equally abrasive and humorous genius, but to be ignored?

In the ideal *History of Taste* that someone will write for our period, a small and interesting appendix will be affixed to explain the unfortunate way Jarrell's writing of criticism, or the writing of the often obstreperous *kind* of criticism he wrote, clouded judgment of his poems not only on the part of those he irritated but also among those who knew the criticism better than they knew the poetry—or who responded to it more readily. (Many of us have been wont to take arguments about art more seriously than we take art. By a nice irony, Jarrell himself frequently wrote *essays* on this problem.) And in this *History of Taste,* in addition to a history of the ways in which Randall Jarrell's criticism not only described but also perhaps partially created the conditions under which poetry like his own could be dismissed (that is, because his principles of praise and blame were eccentric, evaluative, and uncodified), we would have to be given another history: of the extent to which, after the publication of *The Seven-League Crutches* in 1951, Jarrell could be said to have substituted the writing of prose for the writing of poetry. Might the chroniclers, then, side here with Robert Boyers, who in *Modern Occasions* in the Fall of 1972 wrote that Jarrell's choice of poetry as a medium throughout his career appeared arbitrary: "Frequently we have the sense that he might well have written in some other medium and done as well, said as much, moved us as deeply"? Or with Helen Vendler, whose observation that Jarrell "put his genius into his criticism and his talent into his poetry" has sparked one of the most insightful contemporary essays on Jarrell—by Sven Birkerts, who says of the famous poem "Next Day," "My interest is compelled, but my engagement is blocked"?[2] Certainly the criticism, the novel *Pictures from an Institution* (1954), the children's tales, and the translations of Goethe (all of *Faust,* part 1), Rilke, Chekhov, Mörike, Grimm, Radauskas, and Corbière were other mediums through which he moved, and moved us.

But the work of the poet does not appear to me to blend with the tones and concerns of the prose-writer—that strong surface gaiety that can suddenly rise to exuberance, that broad but limiting urbanity—until *The Woman at the Washington Zoo* (1960). And even in this volume, half of which is translations, and where we find, among others, the long, garrulous, and unsuccessful poem "The End of the Rainbow" (an attempt to reproduce his successes in "The Night Before the Night Before Christmas"), we also find some of Jarrell's most stunning work: the title poem, the marvelous and sinister Donatello poem, "The Elementary Scene," "Windows," "Aging," and "A Ghost, a Real Ghost." I would argue that, however his prose may have deflected his or our interest away from his poetry, and however different the voices of Jarrell in his great scornful epistles and in his many touching poems about childhood, the fortunes of Jarrell's genius are perhaps more complex than a simple split between genres, or than the application of different kinds of energy or intellect to different forms of discourse. Like all half-truths, this one can get us over the subject, not into it. It may well be one of the truest things ever said about Jarrell, and very revealing for any who practice both criticism and verse, that he was

> a poet-critic. By this I mean that his approach to criticism, his way of responding, was to write a kind of poem of association around the subject in question. . . . The criticism is . . . a pretext, and this is what gives it its revolutionary character. It is not criticism at all, but poetry carried on by other means.
>
> (Birkerts, pp. 90, 93)

Jarrell would have been delighted by the insight about the criticism. But he would have known that the stricture against the poems does not follow.

All poets, artists, and thinkers are hobbled by their temperaments, by their opinions. It is when their opinions, these automatic predilections, balance most precariously and searchingly over certain kinds of issues in the imagination that we can look at the result and say: This was a representative mind. (With regard to the increasing amounts of prose in his poetry, the hobbling of one's temperament can become a kind of stylistic fate, one no longer precarious because of the ideas, but standardized and a bit hopeless of solution.) One might label the two sides of Jarrell's automatic or temperamental predicament in this shorthand form: He was a negative thinker, tending to nihilism, about the way of the world, who nevertheless had a huge reservoir of nostalgia, melancholy, wistfulness, and pity that he displayed toward the categorically innocent individual. In the most debased numerical sense, one might say this point of view resulted in the judgment that the collective was evil, the negligible integer good. I will also label his truly representative result—the peculiar form Jarrell's defense against these irreconcilables took—as a narcissism out of which was drawn an inordinate sympathy for others. I would like to discuss some of the ways these warring opposites appear in the poems, and explain my reasons for thinking that his poetry gives us one of those extraordinary simplifying ideas that represent us to ourselves.

Jarrell was, I believe, one of those narcissistic poets to whom, as to Wordsworth and Arnold in their periods, we owe one of the most important of the modern age's definitions of the self. For Jarrell, the self is what comes into being without our help, without our notice, and without our having been, at any point, able to alter what we have become:

> That is what happens to everyone.
> At first you get bigger, you know more,
> Then something goes wrong.
> You are, and you say: I am—
> And you were . . . I've been too long.

This is a paradoxical attitude for a good Freudian to hold, although commensurate with Freud's thought as I will try to show later, and equally paradoxical for a poet as characteristically attuned to children and to his own childhood as Jarrell was. With respect to childhood, in fact, Jarrell had the uncanny ability to think himself back to states of mind, attitudes of hope, dread, and tremulous expectancy that the combative passages of adolescence arrange to hide from most of us:

> We wept so? How well we all forget!
> One taste of memory (like Fafnir's blood)
> Makes all their language sensible, one's ears
> Burn with the child's peculiar gift for pain.[3]

This ability to think back was so highly defined—Jarrell's self as a child so distant from and hence attractive to his later self—that he was able to extend the principle to the minds of others. He was able to relinquish himself to those monologists who are aging, misplaced, bewildered, dying; to become those speakers caught in the dark wood of a fairy tale or dream; to mime those voices audible among the dead.

Now neither Wordsworth nor Arnold was especially good at this kind of transfer of allegiance from their own to the lives and minds of others. The scholar-gypsy and Empedocles were counters for Arnold's ego and desire, just as the leech gatherer and the old Cumberland beggar, half-erased transparencies that they were, were agreeable places for Wordsworth to project himself upon the landscape. It is part of Jarrell's great difference from them, and part of his suitability to his period, that his concept of self does not allow for projection; the self is not continuous. Jarrell cannot rehearse the *changes of state* from infant to child, child to adolescent, adolescent to adult. He can only record the sense of confusion *within a state* that has no clue as to how to get itself changed. This is the source of the trapped, bewildered pathos on the part of the child questioning the adult world, the sense of loss of the mature being looking back on the child, and of the dead looking back on the living. Often, Jarrell will insist that the two are one, the man the child, the living the dead.

Among so many pairs of opposites in the poems—men *versus* children, living *versus* dead, bad *versus* good, the masses *versus* the human soul— there is one recurring mediating state: the dream. It is this uncertain threshold to which Jarrell the poet tried to hold himself, sometimes unsteadily or too vaguely, sometimes tipping over into rivers of mythic blood (*Orestes at Tauris,* "Che Faro Senza Euridice," "The Märchen"), sometimes falling into Freudian bathos ("A Little Poem") or the Audenesque variant ("The Iceberg," "Love, in Its Separate Being . . ."), and sometimes dwelling too obsessively on detail ("The End of the Rainbow," the longer of the two poems entitled "Hope"). But even in poems I would call failed or strained, the main business is dream-work, which translates the experience of the childhood self into the language of the adult. Not that the poetry is literally the product, as some poetry can appear to be, of dreams the author may actually have had; Jarrell's program is a deliberate dreaming-back, a relatively conscious act. It is further significant that the realm of early years to which his poetic dreams recur is principally the period of latency, not the earlier precognitive period. It is as if the two great periods of libidinal and aggressive energy, infancy and adolescence, had been erased by their very violence, and what remained were the states among which Jarrell holds his dialogue, childhood and maturity, two periods of achieved quiescence that do not know their real histories or their real names:

> Today, the child lies wet and warm
> In his big mother; tomorrow, too, is dumb,
> The dry skull of the cold tomb. "Between?"
> Between I suffered.
>
> ("The Difficult Resolution")

Some of the characteristic exclamations and insistent questions in Jarrell's poems derive from this matching of mutually exclusive consciousnesses, as if each version, child and adult, of the self-in-arrest were asking about its dark, forgotten, torrential years, suspecting that there is a link, a point of passage, all the while it is unable to prove anything. The terminal convalescent in "The Long Vacation" in *Blood for a Stranger* (called "A Utopian Journey" in *Collected Poems*) asks of his experience, "*But what was it? What am I?*" In the dream of "The Night Before the Night Before Christmas" the girl's little brother learns that he is dying. He replies, "I didn't know," indicating a touching acceptance, while the girl whose dream it is cries out her unaccepting "I don't know, I don't know, I don't know!" The sick child in bed in "A Quilt Pattern" discovers, or nearly discovers, strange truths in his feverish hallucinations; he almost knows that the true witch is the house of gingerbread:

> the house of bread
> Calls to him in its slow singing voice:
> "Feed, feed! Are you fat now?
> Hold out your finger."
> The boy holds out the bone of the finger.
> It moves, but the house says, "No, you don't know.
> Eat a little longer."
> The taste of this house
> Is the taste of his—
> > "I don't know,"
> Thinks the boy, "No, I don't know!"

In Jarrell, one might say, the self defines itself by its desire to be unlike the eternal rule, the law of the masses, the voice that says, You too will die and be unimportant, or, Your very unimportance is the equivalent of your death. But still the self hopes to escape the law of large numbers, the force of history's evidence, by being . . . itself. Some early poems of Jarrell's close on the irrevocable fact of this bleak knowledge:

> I see at last that all the knowledge
>
> I wrung from the darkness—that the darkness flung me—
> Is worthless as ignorance: nothing comes from nothing,
> The darkness from the darkness. Pain comes from the darkness
> And we call it wisdom. It is pain.
>
> > ("90 North")

But increasingly throughout his poetic career Jarrell inserts the strange keynote following the characters' recognition that pain outstrips knowledge, and this keynote is the tenacious belief in *something,* something else, something more, something one hasn't thought of yet that must nevertheless be there, something that will make a more human sense out

of this haunting discomfort. Often these assertions of the necessary existence of the saving residue are called, simply, "something":

> *Say again*
> Say the voices, *say again*
> *That life is—what it is not;*
> *That, somewhere, there is—something, something;*
> *That we are waiting; that we are waiting.*

What I find chilling about those lines is the fact that they are spoken
by people who have died. And as the dead here implore, in "The Survivor
among Graves," so Jarrell's other characters persistently ask that life be—
what it is not. But when his people try the statement out, and turn "Life
is life" into "Like is not life," "it sounds the same." The simple contrary,
the insertion of the negative into one's belief, makes very little difference:

> In the great world everything is just the same
> Or just the opposite, we found (we never went).
>
> ("The Märchen")

This perverse, affronted, ambiguous mood, in which to say *Life is life*
amounts to the same thing as saying *It isn't*, is part of Jarrell's depressive,
neutered style, the undercurrent of nihilism, that runs through the verse.
In the original version of "The Memoirs of Glückel of Hameln" in *Blood
for a Stranger*, Jarrell addresses the memoirist with the dismissive conclusion that about her

> there is none to care.
> Glückel, Glückel, you tell indifferently
> To ears indifferent with Necessity
> The torments and obsessions of our life:
> Your pain seems only the useless echo
> Of all the evil we already know.

In a poem he did not publish, Jarrell makes the same sort of heavily
careless statement: "Life is—why, life: It is what all our evils have in
common." Such statements stem from this poet's melancholy determinism, especially evident in the first three volumes, according to which nothing the individual does will make a difference to the State that is conduct-
ing war with *his* life. "The Wide Prospect" in *Little Friend, Little Friend*
is an apt example of the Jarrell allegory of Trade fed by the bodies of
living men. In the same volume, guns practice against the thin body of a
soldier "pinned against the light." (Jarrell often envisions victims as frail
insects.) A tormented life is nothing more than the fly caught in "the
lying amber of the histories." "The Difficult Resolution" exhorts us to

realize that we have no way to exercise the will except in realizing that we cannot exercise it. The warrior dressed in an ancient name to fight a modern war in "Siegfried" chants over and over to himself that "It happens as it does because it does." The great thinkers of the dawn of the scientific age, Bruno, Galileo, and Newton, have at last taught us how "to understand but not to change." The world tells the dead child that it "will not be missed." What is left to us in this dreary program is but the "bare dilemma of the beast—to go on being."

But something rather remarkable happens when the poet's ire is directed—not against the modern state at war, not against the tawdry laws of destiny, not against the evil mass—but against the mechanisms of unavoidable suffering in the individual's soul. The same logical structure is also present in the world of highly eccentric and highly self-absorbed individuals with whom we have come to identify Jarrell's best poetry. This wishful structure is that of the logical contrary made into a tautology, one that makes changing and not changing the same thing. Just as Siegfried implores everything to "be the way it was. Let me not matter . . . Let me be what I was," the woman at the Washington Zoo cries to the god she sees behind the vulture, "You know what I was, / You see what I am: change me, change me!" The state wished for in either case is that of the infinite, integral world of the past.

A phenomenon related to that of changing and not changing—a dilemma that resolves itself into the *tertium quid* of desire to be a child again, to be what one was—is the easy transitive relation between the world and the human being. It is not only in derisory poems like "A Girl in a Library" that Jarrell is moved to say, of the confrontation of the individual with reality, that "they look alike already." In the more mysterious confrontation of the soul with its deathly double in "Hohensalzburg: Fantastic Variations on a Theme of Romantic Character" (a title that is, to say the least, a bit defensive), the homely German ghosts transform the clumsy wanderer-through-the-wood into chandeliers and china roses: "these German ghosts . . . only change / Men into things, things into things." Even in the poems where we find what is certainly Jarrell's prescription for the highest human art, say a poem like "The Old and the New Masters," which was meant as a penultimate answer to the view of art Jarrell considered most despicable, namely, Auden's in "Musée des Beaux Arts," each piece of matter takes on a signal majesty—not only in contributing to the whole (the old organic argument), but also in settling once and for all the place of the negligible small object in the plan of God as we can still perceive it in the fallen world. Under this paradigm, the place of all the celebrants in Georges de La Tour's *St. Sebastian Mourned by St. Irene* is that of beings who watch, and are, "the one thing in the world."[4] Although the topic is not quite so elevated in the poem that follows in *The Lost World*, "Field and Forest," the same transitive sympathy occurs between the forests-that-were before the farmer cleared them and the fields-that-are, and Jarrell makes clear that an identical transitive overflow informs the farmer's guilty recognition that his boyhood self and the fox he watched from his young, credulous, observant life so many years ago are the same double being (no longer in harmony but accuser and accused); thus the melancholy irony that "The trees can't tell the two of them apart."

Taken to a further extreme, the principle of interchangeability between the human observer and the observed world results in a reflex of identification between the very feeling of being and the items from which the person derives that feeling. This is a technique Bishop admired in Jarrell, as David Kalstone observes: "With an odd mixture of envy and irritation she remarked of Jarrell, 'Of course he has all the material in the world' "; although he identifies the protagonists as "description" and "narrative" (or "autobiography"), Kalstone correctly ascribes the gift of Bishop as well as what she liked in Jarrell to what I have called a "reflex of identification" between self and world.[5] What Bishop may have felt she needed to learn is handled successfully by Jarrell practically from the beginning of his career, so that even in the very early poem, "The Christmas Roses," the dying woman, the poles of whose thought are her coming death and the master leaver whom she loves, knows that if he touches her she will not die. Similarly, after the long rehearsal of all the details in Dürer's engraving of the knight, death, and the devil, the poet can affirm that the being of the knight defines itself in despite the exhaustively catalogued qualities of his two companions: "A man's look completes itself." The intention of the human beings is equated by Jarrell with the intention of the world. Because they have the world within them, these figures become it and, after a fashion, do not need it.

Given a slightly different twist, this notion of the self-sufficiency of the intent consciousness allows Jarrell to make a long, scathing judgment of Donatello's vain adolescent David, the bronze statue of the indifferent, callow young victor which, by putting between itself and the world "a shining / Line of delimitation," becomes a thing entire and apart: "The body mirrors itself." Although the bronze David is viewed from a perspective that is not merely celebratory but critical, while the poems on Dürer and de La Tour are written in a mood more clearly affirmative both of the artist and the subject, I think one can see how the tendency toward definition of the self in the transport of high aesthetic moments resembles the selves defined in moments of extremity, as in "The Christmas Roses" or "Burning the Letters." One comes down in the end to mere being.

Gertrude Johnson, the ungenerous novelist satirized in *Pictures from an Institution* (1954), is brought to her knees by the question she asks herself: "*Am I*—was she what?" and then Jarrell writes that the question turned into "*Am I? Am I?*" His final lines describing the Dürer knight read: "The face is its own face—*a man does what he must*— / And the body underneath it says: *I am.*"

In light of the recessive claim, the small *I am,* it would be a marvelous solution to all the problems Jarrell has raised if it were still possible to watch with reverence a great miracle, to become thereby the miracle. But "The Old and the New Masters" is about a vision in that other time when everything, even art, was better. The more apt definition of the youth in the landscape is to be found in the first poem of *The Seven-League Crutches,* "The Orient Express." The vivid, brief tableaux one sees from the train window appear, says Jarrell, almost as they would to a child. By day, it's all right, "but at evening . . . a questioning / Precariousness comes over everything." The precariousness is not the imminent dissolution of the real into the unreal, but the awful reverse, as the sick child to whom the narrator looked back observes the few "things from a primer" about his room, then

> Outside the window
> There were the chairs and tables of the world. . . .
> I saw that the world
> That had seemed to me the plain
> Gray mask of all that was strange
> Behind it—of all that *was*—was all.

No mask hiding mysteries, the world is the dreary front—and back, and interior—of all that it is and has to offer. The people with their lives and real gestures beyond the train window, like the fields on which they are silhouetted, and the paths one can see leading to a wood all full of lives, and the train

> Passing, after all unchangeable
> And not now ever to stop, like a heart—
> It is like any other work of art.
> It is and never can be changed.
> Behind everything there is always
> The unknown unwanted life.

Something extraordinary happens to the condensation of this poem after the syntactic break. The tempo shifts to a swifter and more inexorable kind of utterance, and the last four lines raise as many questions as they solve. Was this series of scenes through a train window a work of art then? Was the scene beyond the child's sickbed one also? Is it the prime talent of art to be and not be changed? Is it the fact that "it" is art that makes it shelter "the unknown unwanted life"? Or is it because "it" is like any other thing that the unwanted and somehow one-dimensional life resides behind it? Does Jarrell mean that art is window dressing for the unmysterious world we all sooner or later learn is there?

If we go a bit beyond the terms set by the narrator of "The Orient Express," these questions will not be difficult to answer. Let us rephrase them, in fact, so that it is neither art nor even memory that constitutes the "it" that "never can be changed," but rather the self. The rapidly changing scenes beyond the train window (says the long simile of the poem) are like the solidly unchanging things in the child's bedroom, which at a crucial moment of insight and growth are collapsed into the props of the greater world beyond: "the chairs and tables of the world." At some moment, random as far as any direct cause could be discerned by the subject, yet known and recorded by thinkers like Freud and Piaget, the world fixes itself in the subject's attention in such a way as to make everything at once solid and coherent, and *unto itself.* The experience of selfhood is couched in terms of the retreat of the nurturing world to the outside, the Other, although of course the real result is the individual's sense of separate being. This produces the angry melancholy of the Jarrell poem: Those scenes are unmade, unwanted by *me.* Even here, needless to say, there is a rapid transitive interchange between the observing self and the observed world, so that, in proportion as the obstinate exterior scene is unwanted, the self perceives its own unwantedness, its own dispensability for some other observer, not least of all, finally, for itself.

Before discussing the companion poem to "The Orient Express," a work paired with it both in *The Seven-League Crutches* (1951) and *Selected Poems* (1955), namely, "A Game at Salzburg," I would like to suggest very briefly the early poems one would look to in order to trace this experience of the separation of the young self from the solid world, and of the emergent self's first insight into its own integral separateness. I do this for several reasons. First, to counter the dismissive and not always thoroughly informed reviewers like John Simon who have so summarily consigned Jarrell again to the stacks.[6] In the second place, it may provide us with an additional means of assessing the originality of Elizabeth Bishop to see the poet she envied and admired presented with greater accuracy.

In *Blood for a Stranger* (1942), Jarrell treats the coming of the self to the self as a polarity between love for the world and a sense of betrayal by it. "A Little Poem" and "Love, in Its Separate Being . . . " give us two variants on the theme of betrayal; in the former, a child has been usurped by the arrival of an interloper, another child, to whom he speaks while the other is still in the womb; in the second poem the child is betrayed by the forces of history. In a third poem, "Fear," Jarrell articulates this abused estrangement of the child by suggesting that the little girl here is caught and compromised by being a cipher in the dreams of the adult world, and in a grim forecast of the willful retreat of the chairs and tables of the world in "The Orient Express," the child is encouraged by the statues, those substitute adults, to "be like us, absolute."

"The Iceberg" and "90 North" are children's adventure dreams of Arctic exploration and skin diving in which the outcome of the exuberant voyages is a fierce despair. The iceberg is a symbol of necessity in a poem where even air and water are malevolent. In "90 North," when the child decides (as the strange arbitrary power-shifts of dreams permit him to do) to leave the North Pole and go home,

> Turn as I please, my step is to the south.
> The world—my world spins on this final point
> Of cold and wretchedness: all lines, all winds
> End in this whirlpool I at last discover.
>
> And it is meaningless.

Although this voyage to the north had meaning for him as a child, now the speaker sees that (as we quoted earlier) the knowledge he thought he had gained was worthless, and that the pain he wrung from the darkness and called wisdom was really only pain.

On the other side of the picture we find ambiguous, painful dream poems in which love for the world and the state of being loved by it—the self's adventuresomeness rewarded—are emotions that the dream keeps curiously blocked or inflexible. In "The Lost Love" a dead woman (the mother as lover) returns to caress the dreaming child; when the child responds, something fearful is suggested: "When I touched you / My hand was cold." "The Skaters" is the early apotheosis of the adventure poem (and of the category of poems like "Fear," which are broodings on hidden losses when the self and the world dream together). But "The Skaters," like "The Lost Love," is also a poem of yearning that nearly becomes passion, a passion repressed by the eeriness of the rhythms of the dream; "How long we pled our love! / How thorough our embrace!" is followed by the two lovers' rout into

> The abyss where my deaf limbs forget
> The cold mouth's dumb assent;
> The skaters like swallows flicker
> Around us in the long descent.

The original love of the child and the mother finds its place here, in the pleading and thorough embraces of stanza six, just as the mother returns to the child in "The Lost Love"—and in many later poems ("2nd Air Force," where the mother, perhaps to his infinite aggravation, visits her son in basic training; "Mother, Said the Child," the first of the many *Kindertotenlieder* Jarrell was to write, among them "Come to the Stone . . . ," "Protocols," and "The State," in the same volume of which we are now speaking, *Little Friend, Little Friend,* 1945).

Many inflections are given to the central theme of the child's family struggle, which is also the struggle to import the child's flexible sense of adventure into the world of action without being haunted by sexuality. The escape to dream in "The Skaters" is linked to the poems in which the child escapes yet further from his life, and makes his family pay yet more dearly for his loss. The schoolboy's fantasy of his own disappearance in "A Story" in *Blood for a Stranger* (1942) is written in the same ingenuous, sorrowing mood as the later laments of those who are actually dead in *Little Friend, Little Friend* and in *Losses* (1948), "Lady Bates," "Jews at Haifa," and "In the Camp There Was One Alive." When these songs of the dead children in *Losses* are compared to the living child's bereavement at the loss of his father after his parents' divorce in "A Child of Courts" in the same volume (renamed "The Prince" in *Collected Poems*), it is clear what equivalences have been enforced between the living and the dead. The child construes loss not as the absence of the good but as the presence of the good turned into the bad, into the dead. Even the overassignment of roles has a childlike circularity—the child lies in an agony of fear, shrinking up like his pet rabbit, when he hears the father's hand like a rabbit's paw scraping at the dirt. Then, in a majestic act of courage and forgiveness, the boy "inch[es] my cold hand out to his cold hand." In the third stanza, after nothing has grasped his heroically offered hand, the boy throws his "furs" off, then hears a sentry calling.

> I start to weep because—because there are no ghosts;
> A man dies like a rabbit, for a use.
> What will they pay me, when I die, to die?

The transfer in the child's reason from the retreat of the parent to his own retreat in death is made here by the sudden additional knowledge, or recollection, that the child is grown, asleep in a barracks in wartime, that they have all long since really died—father, rabbit, many military cronies, many millions of Europeans—and that the smaller deaths were to be followed by the greater ones. Across the chasm of guilt abruptly opened as the child turns—before his own eyes as well as ours—into a grown man, the speaker has no opportunity to enact the desired retribution:

to make *them* pay for their "deaths" or disappearances by dramatically embracing his own death. When he does die, it will be for a small use, as a rabbit dies for a use, as a soldier dies in his numbers.

Losses contains several other poems in which a child wakes up in the war. The recuperating dreamers here all bear a strong resemblance to the regressing child of courts. The prisoner with a pet rabbit in "Stalag Luft" dreams an adventure dream about being an Indian brave ("The dappled mustangs graze / By the quills of the milky leggings"). The wounded pilot in "A Field Hospital" translates the remembered sound of an air battle into the report of a hunter's gun:

> "The great drake
> Flutters to the icy lake—
> The shotguns stammer in my head.
> I lie in my own bed,"
> He whispers, "dreaming"; and he thinks to wake.
> The old mistake.

The wounded men in "A Ward in the States" dream that they are still in the Pacific wishing they were home. And the wounded man of "In the Ward: The Sacred Wood" creates a more complex relation between the child's creation by things outside him and his own desire, or even ability, to "unmake" that which made him:

> The trees rise to me from the world
> That made me, I call to the grove
> That stretches inch on inch without one God:
> "I have unmade you now; but I must die."

In *Losses* we also find two of Jarrell's most famous war poems, "The Dead Wingman" and "Pilots, Man Your Planes," the latter a record of a long air engagement between American and Japanese planes that ends in the destruction of the aircraft carrier. These two poems, realistic rather than hallucinatory, both end in a way curiously complementary to the dreams: The pilots fall asleep. The one

> Knows, knows at last; he yawns the chattering yawn
> Of effort and anguish, of hurt hating helplessness—
> Yawns sobbingly, his head falls back, he sleeps.

The other, failing in his search for his wingman, keeps on

> Gliding above the cities' shells, a stubborn eye
> Among the embers of the nations, achingly
> Tracing the circles of that worn, unchanging *No*—
> The lives' long war, lost war—the pilot sleeps.

Clearly, these are the responses of utterly weary bodies; but equally clearly, the yawn "of effort and anguish, of hurt hating helplessness" makes the pilots kin to the helplessly dreaming wounded in the book, to the speaking dead who cannot yet bear to leave the earth, to the lives from which men try to wake as children again ("the old mistake").

I began by claiming that Jarrell influenced modern poetry through his definition of the self as something that got to be the way it is without the human's conscious ability to control what that self would become, or even to record the process of becoming. The dream seemed to me to be the mediating state in which Jarrell's children discover or combat the discovery of what they are becoming, and where his grown-ups become children by forgetting the same knowledge, or courting an earlier, less lethal form of it. Jarrell is a poet who proceeds in shadow language, as if to sketch the truth in a dream released him from the guilt of revealing it. The characteristic pleas, *Let me be what I was, Let nothing matter, Change me, change me!* resemble the characteristic questions, *But what was it, what am I?* and the brilliant exclamations, *I don't know, I don't know!* as well as the repeated assertions of belief in *Something, something,* because they all rehearse, after their fashions, the principles of avoidance and incredulity in the developing life. Thus the urgency on the part of things to turn into things, and on the part of men to turn into things or to share with things the bare property described in the statements *These are,* or *I am,* are solutions with a double edge. On the one hand, to feel that one *is* makes one the center of a reverently circumscribed world; but on the other hand, one shares that simple, dull, and unqualified extentional being with everything that lies beyond, sometimes only a short distance away, just as unknown, but also unwanted. In discussing "The Orient Express," and with a view toward returning to it and to its companion poem "A Game at Salzburg," I suggested that the dark pattern of being—life as what all our evils have in common; the conviction of our unimportance and the simultaneous knowledge of our death—was always balanced in Jarrell by the contrary impulse to affirmation, the light pattern, the unutterable love. I also suggested that both the light and dark patterns were adumbrated in the dream poem, and that the alternations between them illustrated the child's recurrent "family tragedy." It may have sounded casuist (although I do not think it is) to uphold a poem like "The Skaters" as a crucial scene in the family tragedy by virtue of its "happy ending"; that is, the flexible hope of the dreaming child is protected by the dream both from itself (his desire) and from his companion (the world). ("The Skaters" belongs to that plaintive group of Jarrell poems that treat of yearning in the human soul; I hope to place "The Black Swan" beside it in a moment.)

The sadder or more vicious counterparts to "The Skaters" in the child's family album, the little-child-lost poems, "The Child of Courts," and the *Kindertotenlieder,* are still visible in the background when we come to the large group of war poems in *Little Friend, Little Friend* and *Losses.*

One of the most remarkable features of Jarrell's style is his application of an essentially descriptive, cataloguing turn of mind, not to nature descriptions or to the households where his people find themselves (we see very little in a sure photographic sense), but to the psychological traits and the life-histories of his personae. When, as is the case in "Lady Bates," "The End of the Rainbow," or "The Next Day," the person's life is reputed to have been bound up with things—blackberries and washtubs, tubes of paint, grocery bags—we discover through these assemblages a bit about where and how these people lived. But the emphasis is on the wavering habits of selection, a sort of neurosis of choice, whereby the suburban matron, the old lady who paints watercolors in Laguna Beach, and the wife and mother visited by the eland/*Elend* in *"Seele im Raum,"* take from the real world only what is nearest for reflection in their inner worlds. At the same time, Jarrell is so anxious that we know the people he speaks of that he is not always judicious in letting them select. The reason may be that Jarrell needed to discover people through their things—even to discover his own thought through its accidental or contingent counters, for he uses the same catalogue system when he writes of his own childhood in "Children's Arms," "A Night with Lions," "A Street off Sunset," and "Thinking of the Lost World." Jarrell might have been speaking of this habit of desultory obsessiveness when he wrote, in "Children's Arms," that in his

> Talk with the world, in which it tells me what I know
> And I tell it, "I know"—how strange that I
> Know nothing, and yet it tells me what I know!

The most successful of the long life-portraits that Jarrell drew is "The Night Before the Night Before Christmas" in *The Seven-League Crutches* (1951). The young girl here is presented differently, with much more sympathy, than is "A Girl in a Library." We know more about the Christmas girl because she thinks more deeply about things than the Phys. Ed. major with glasses and braids and the legs of a Valkyrie. She is, in addition, more full of pathos because she is surrounded by pathos: Her little brother is perhaps dying; her mother is dead; the squirrel that she and her brother had fed in the park has gone away; her father is a distant and, one suspects, harried Rotarian with peppy slogans on his office wall. The young girl has a social conscience that she imposes somewhat stubbornly on friends and family—she is wrapping a copy of Engels for a Christmas gift, and her mind is full of workers' slogans, an enlightened atheism, Value, Power, the imagery of victimized ponies in the mines. But she is also fond of cosmetics and angora socks and full of vaguely romantic yearnings. Her world is also haunted by the residual talismans of a childhood she assumes she has left behind—the fairy tales on her bookshelf, the covering presence of the spirits of animals, the story of Hansel and Gretel, the dream of a galaxy webbed with the icy eyelashes of the squirrel.

The point of the poem, when we reach the end of its thirteen pages, *cannot* have been a life study or a grotesque (in Sherwood Anderson's sense). What is the point then? Simply that we assent to the realization that "they were all there together"? That is part of it. The rest is to be brought through the long emotional crescendo of the last five pages of the poem, not just to a sympathy with the essential being of the girl—her knowledge that her brother is dying, that she and he are suspended in an ambiguous universe together, and that she cannot help any of it—but to a manifestation of Jarrell's victory over his own limitations. Although he restricts the portrait to what he considers truest about the young girl, limiting himself to a narrative instead of a full-fledged dramatic monologue, still we do not feel he has either falsified or condescended to her. For the poet knows that the girl only plays with Marxism the way most middle-class Americans do, making it sentimental at a safe distance; he also knows that, even among those who play with moral and political structures they need not adopt, there is a craving for the good. He reflects this craving in the dramatic monologue's central trope—that of emotional transparency.

The great crisis of sympathy in Jarrell's portrait comes about when the sister "grows up" into her essential childlikeness. What come to matter are the facts that her brother is sick and that Friedrich Engels (in German the name means angel) represents a snowy presence, a Father Christmas, with no feast to celebrate: "There is not one thing that knows / It is almost Christmas." The poem's closing rush of sentiment, so characteristic of Jarrell's work, is thus a true "arrival" for this girl, and a much less cloying image than the one of her brother being sent down into the capitalists' mines: "She feels, in her hand, her brother's hand. / She is crying." We hear in these closing lines a muted reference to a more powerful plot in the poem—although Jarrell doesn't press the point but rather allows the long associative struggles of the sister to bring this last small clue to the surface: She had earlier seen how "At the side of the shepherds Hansel / Stands hand in hand with Gretel."

The pull of the fairy tale is particularly strong in *The Seven-League Crutches* (1951), doubtless Jarrell's best book. The parable of the two children who are turned into birds in "The Black Swan" presents the love of a girl for her sister, who has been turned into a black swan, as a willingness to follow the changed one into death. Both Sister Bernetta Quinn and Suzanne Ferguson have traced the fairy-tale sources in many of the poems. But no one in speaking of Jarrell's Grimm fixation has explained it as devastatingly as Karl Shapiro: "Germany is the preconscious of Europe, almost all—no, all—her geniuses are maniacs, Germany itself is a maniac, the bright dangerous offspring of the Western soul."[7] At the same time, I don't know that anyone in talking about Jarrell's use of Grimm has indicated the persistent divergence of the poet from the flexible spirit of these tales. Jarrell has imposed something closer to Hans Christian Andersen's conception of final metamorphosis, immutable change, and unabsolvable guilt upon the essentially restorable world of the Brothers Grimm. The maimings in the *Märchen* are fierce, bloody, and gratuitous, but in the end, really, no harm will come. The severed head is restored to the body; the hands that were cut off are put back; the bear turns back into the prince; the blind see; the foul are cleansed. In the other realm, although there is less bloodshed in the Andersen stories about the little mermaid, the red shoes, the snow queen, and little Inger, the girl who stepped on bread in order not to dirty her fine new clothes, the maimings and changes of state, when they do come, horrify the more because they are more lengthy and irrevocable. Consider the many long years during which little Inger must stand like a caryatid in the peristyle of hell until her heart is softened by her mother's tears. At last Inger is allowed to become a sparrow who gathers crumbs for the other birds to expiate her wastefulness. But she is never turned back into a girl. Whereas the seven swans or seven ravens into which a witch has transformed the princess's seven brothers in several Grimm tales are allowed to return to human shape after seven years of their sister's silence, and finally they are all human again, and they can all speak, and they have not grown in the meantime very much older.

In Jarrell's "Black Swan" the little sister wants to expiate some sin— perhaps that she has a "bad sister," as the child in "A Quilt Pattern" has a "Good Me" and a "Bad Me"—but the form of expiation is union with her sister, so that love and longing are indistinguishable from remorse and complicity. The poem tells us (and the little sister knows this, too) that the transformations into swans are only happening in a dream,

> But the swan my sister called, "Sleep at last, little sister,"
> And stroked all night, with a black wing, my wings.

In other words, the poem tells us that its experience is not real, but in a way it then retracts: We get no comfort from the proviso that it's only a dream. The little girl whose sister was turned into a swan, who yearned toward her in the center of the lake where she, too, was transformed into one, keeps on being a swan stroked by the black wings of the other. Although it is true, as Jarrell writes at the end of "The Märchen," that these tales are allegories of the human heart, and that the exercise of power in forming and delivering the wishes one is allowed to make is a version of the desire *to change, to change!* the spirit of this and other poems of Jarrell's tells us that the change we wish for is never the one that visits us.

More and more, in the later poems in *The Woman at the Washington Zoo* (1960) and *The Lost World* (1965), the world of the great fantasies, in which tales like "Hansel and Gretel" had figured, contracts. Consider the use of the tale in "A Quilt Pattern" from *The Seven-League Crutches* (1951)—

> Here a thousand stones
> Of the trail home shine from their strings
> Like just-brushed, just-lost teeth.
> All the birds of the forest
> Sit brooding, stuffed with crumbs.
> But at home, far, far away
> The white moon shines from the stones of the chimney,
> His white cat eats up his white pigeon.

—and then in "The Elementary Scene" from *The Woman at the Washington Zoo:*

> Looking back in my mind I can see
> The white sun like a tin plate
> Over the wooden turning of the weeds;
> The street jerking—a wet swing—
> To end by the wall the children sang.

It is interesting that "The Elementary Scene" rejects the child's point of view to speak from the adult's: "I float above the small limbs like their dream: / I, I, the future that mends everything."

Another poem from *The Woman at the Washington Zoo,* "A Ghost, a Real Ghost," in which the present time is just as dreary, dead, and removed, contains an equally harrowing formulation of the principle we have already found at work in so many of the poems: "The child is hopeful and unhappy in a world / Whose future is his recourse." But there is no future in this poem, only mournful retrospection:

> The first night I looked into the mirror
> And saw the room empty, I could not believe

> That it was possible to keep existing
> In such pain: I have existed.
> . . . .
> Am I dead? A ghost, a real ghost
> Has no need to die: what is he except
> A being without access to the universe
> That he has not yet managed to forget?

It is as if the girl in "The Night Before . . . Christmas" were speaking from the other side of maturity; as if the sister turned into a swan were addressing the world she loved from the vantage of her paralyzed, disenfranchised doom.

Jarrell had earlier written of the stubborn duality of the unwanted world and the "unknown unwanted" self in "The Orient Express." In "A Game at Salzburg" he lets the world speak its parallel poem of yearning toward humankind, for in proportion as the self and the world had only their flat contours in common in the one poem, in "A Game at Salzburg" they have in common their compatible need of the other in order to be:

> the sun comes out, and the sky
> Is for an instant the first rain-washed blue
> Of becoming: and my look falls
> Through circling leaves, through the statues'
> Broken, encircling arms
> To the lives of the withered grass,
> To the drops the sun drinks up like dew.
>
> In anguish, in expectant acceptance
> The world whispers: *Hier bin i'*.

One hears in this splendidly modulated poem even the rhymes that aren't there. By virtue of the sing-song peekaboo game of the Austrian children earlier in the poem (*Hier bin i', Da bist du*), and the appearance here of the word "dew" in the third from last line, we "hear" the speaker's response to this innocent, breathless, confidently quiet chant of the new-risen world, *Da bist du*, Yes, there you are. In his note to the poem in *Selected Poems* Jarrell wrote, "If there could be a conversation between the world and God, this would be it." Coming after the morose final stanza of "The Orient Express" ("Behind everything there is always / The unknown unwanted life"), the gentle hide-and-seek of Jarrell with the universe in "A Game at Salzburg" is welcome, and revealing. I suspect that we hear the two poems' closing statements as complements, neither of which is hard to resolve with the lines about the ghost who cannot touch the very world he cannot forget, or with the lines about the fighter pilot at the end of "Pilots, Man Your Planes": "He yawns the chattering yawn / Of effort and anguish, of hurt hating helplessness." Compare "In anguish, in expectant acceptance / The world whispers: *Hier bin i*'." Even if the outcomes of the war poem and the Salzburg poem are different, the direction of the language and the accumulation of the descriptive prepositional phrases that take all the weight of the emotion, while the verbs retreat from motion, are very like.

As a description of how Jarrell's imagination functions in the presence of his most tender and beleaguered subjects, these remarks about the expansion of the qualitative markers and the simultaneous retreat of the formative ones (prepositions and adjectives gaining strength over verbs) may provide a useful model for the way Jarrell's methods in the earlier poems extend to his work as a whole. His attentiveness to the qualities of things, to moods and feelings and secondary characteristics, is magnified, while the motion and strength of the world shrink to a small point. One of the most telling illustrations of such a method becoming a fate of style, a Weltanschauung, occurs in *The Animal Family* (1965), which is not only Jarrell's best children's book and the site of Maurice Sendak's wisest collaboration with Jarrell,[8] but also a work that can risk comparison with *Pictures from an Institution* (for example, with the passage near the end of the novel where Constance is trying to read "The Juniper Tree" in German and breaks into tears because the story is so touching and her life is so good and she perceives herself to be so stupid and so blessed). In the following excerpt from *The Animal Family,* what I would draw to your attention is the way the world seems, here at the close of this marvelous allegory of childhood, to have become dimmer, smaller, somehow weaker, while the heart is nevertheless moved to respond, *Da bist du,* once again:

> . . . the meadow was no different for the mermaid's tears or the hunter's knowledge; warm and soft and smelling of flowers, it ran out to the sunny beach, green to the shadowy forest, and the hunter and the mermaid sat there in it. Below them the white-on-green of the waves was lined along the white shore—out beyond, the green sea got bluer and bluer until at last it came to the far-off blue of the island. There were small seals on the seal rocks, and the little gray spot out above the waves was a big blue-and-white osprey waiting for fish. But no fish came, and it hung there motionless. Everything lay underneath them like something made for them; things got smaller and smaller in the distance, but managed, somehow, to fill the whole world. . . . The lynx started down through the meadow, and the hunter stood outside the door, half-listening to the story the mermaid was making up, and half-looking at—

> He didn't know what he was looking at. He stretched with his front
> legs, like the lynx: that is, he held out his arms and tightened his muscles
> and reached out as far as could reach, for nothing. The lynx was already
> small in the distance. . . . The boy looked and saw him and said laughing,
> "That's where he found ME!"[9]

The hunter was looking at . . . he didn't know what he was looking at.
The world. The things that get smaller and smaller and yet seemed to fill
the whole world. How characeristic is that break in the telling. One becomes the things one sees: a point of substance as well as a point of style.
Like the speaker of "A Man Meets a Woman in the Street" (*New Poems,*
1969), Jarrell believes about his hunter and his mermaid that they were
"so different from each other that it seemed to them, finally, that they were
exactly alike." And like the Salzburg peasants under siege in Gottfried
Rosenbaum's parable of the artist in *Pictures from an Institution,* who kept
painting new markings on their one remaining steer and leading it along
the ramparts to convince the enemy that they had an endless supply of
food, Jarrell was touchingly ingenious in the face he put on sameness.

Randall Jarrell was very much a poet of the homely horrors, for at
the back of every transcendent impulse he saw the doom of common
disappointment crouching in its lean and idle way behind the bolster. In
his brilliant essay on Jarrell's ideology, as much a tour de force as Jarrell's
essays on the stages in Auden's, Jerome Mazzaro (*Salmagundi,* Fall 1971)
suggests that Jarrell was done in by happiness, and that to have been
comforted and forgiven was equivalent to having been bereft of every
defense against his own accepting world: "The mechanisms by which
one's self has been defined, once withered away by forgiveness, leave one
nothing by which to define self—a fear implicit in any real skepticism
and here expressed 'in happiness.' " Jarrell's imagination followed Freud,
dwelling not on illness but rather on what Freud supposed to be our
common condition, human suffering and yearning. I therefore do not
intend to make Jarrell's art seem more neurotic than it is when I maintain
that he wrote about being trapped in the state of being that never changes:
the child under the thumb of mortality, the adult who cannot yet manage
to forget the loved earth. Critics of American verse would be well rewarded by better concentration on Jarrell's image of the self that "float[s]
above the small limbs like their dream" and on his deep impression upon
the poetic world of the mid-century above which he hovered, condemn-
ing, accepting, helpless, unable to leave:

> We learned from you so much about so many things
> But never what we were; and yet you made us that.
> We found in you the knowledge for a life

But not the will to use it in our lives
That were always, somehow, so different from the books'.
We learned from you to understand, but not to change.
                ("The Carnegie Library, Juvenile Division,"
                        Little Friend, Little Friend, 1945)

Elizabeth Bishop

Like Jarrell, the remarkable elegist of the child's feeling of paralysis and entrapment, Elizabeth Bishop tends to view the worlds of art, of social relations, and of family as if they were part of the world of objects—fixed, external, fated. While there are many poets (Louise Bogan, for one) who relish and admire the *ordonnances* of scrollwork and painted swags and profusion in human design, Bishop appears stalled at the threshold of art, more readily occupied by randomness than by symmetry, more enchanted—no, arrested—by the skewed than by the formed. In this, she is the comrade of her mentor Marianne Moore. One anecdote will illustrate the tendency. Accompanying Elizabeth Bishop's memoir of Marianne Moore, published posthumously in *Vanity Fair* in May of 1983, appears a photograph of Marianne Moore's writing desk. The array of small statues, *boîtes*, and paperweights is, one suspects, dense with personal anecdote, but there is one riddle that is plain to see. Above the book-ledge, on the wall, hang reproductions of three paintings by William Blake in which the naked bodies of God, man, and angel twine and tumble, the heavy articulation of each body's musculature repeated in the large sweeping arcs of massed shapes. The impression in both the large view and the small is of distinct, firm plaques of living matter nested side by side.

Then, below the book-ledge of Moore's desk, is something that, on reflection, appears to "answer" the stylization of Blake with distortions equally profound and equally whimsical. Directly in back of the leather portfolio that promises to contain working drafts of poems like "Apparition of Splendor" and "His Shield" is propped a postcard-sized reproduction of the famous Albrecht Dürer woodcut, *Rhinoceros*. With leopardlike spots on its horny rib-jacket, platelets on its flanks, coin-shaped depressions like rivets on its shoulderplates, and overlapping reptile scales on his legs, this exotic plated animal is replete with madly misapplied specifics, down to the conch-shell flap, like a gill, beneath the jaw, and exorbitant bristles under its rubbery padded beak and on its tail. One can easily imagine the gusto with which Moore savored Dürer's refined sense of the grotesque.

Clearly, however, the visual impression made by the Dürer woodcut is lethargic and rigid, while the impression made by Blake's paintings is swooning and fluid. So the resemblance between them, if there is one, cannot be based on the impression of shape or, equally unlikely, on subject matter or topic. If the two visions have a reciprocal relationship, it can emerge only under the light of language: It is only when we apply to Blake and Dürer alike such terms as *articulation, outline, border, shell, plating,* or *armor,* that we begin to see how analytic both artists are—or rather, how the wit of the poet might suspend their differences by the analytic thread.

It is this same wit by which Elizabeth Bishop aligns herself—her poetry, her style of perceiving the world—with that of her mentor, supporter, and friend, Marianne Moore. In addition to the stylistic traits they have in common (dry abstractions; jargon and cliché; repetition; trial-and-error revision; tropes often highlighted by alliteration and rhyme), Moore and Bishop share a method of daydream, or reverie. They place themselves before the objects most congenial to their temperament and muse about them through a controlled *loosening* of ordinary mental habit. Bishop elsewhere calls this procedure of creation "a self-forgetful, perfectly useless concentration."[10] Disinterestedness is crucial for the life of art; poetry is not based on utility or appetite or the flourish of ego, which Moore calls "throat"; rather, art is made by a faculty that is neutral to ends and blind to self-promotion, that is intense only in its means—*useless* concentration, but still *concentration*. Thus when, in interviews, Bishop admits to having wasted time—when she says, "I think I've been, oh, half-asleep all my life"[11]—she is explaining that quality of self-forgetfulness, which she connects with inutility and aimlessness, but not with unconsciousness. She has not been asleep, but "half-asleep," musing, drowsily inclined toward the world that has chosen her for its expression.[12]

The floating daydream on which her creation coasts, however, is not as sanguine as Bishop's charming remarks imply. The suspension and postponement of category are also to some extent the avoidance of it. David Kalstone conjectures that Bishop's poetry was itself still half-asleep until she moved to Brazil in 1951.

> [W]hat was missing in her Northern landscape poems . . . and what only became fully available to her in the stories of 1953 written after she'd settled in Brazil, was the remembered recuperative power of village life.[13]

"Recuperative" it may have been, but the Nova Scotian life of her earliest childhood, as she recovered it, also caused wounds as well as healing them. Like the crack in the teacup in Auden's poem, the recovery opened a lane to the land of the dead. When such presences are reawakened, balance is disturbed; tears are shed; suffering not understood at the time is undergone again in a different mode. Although Bishop did not elect the pitiful paralysis of Jarrell's children, helpless before their feelings, she is no less curiously helpless before her own. Thus, even when she resembles someone like Marianne Moore *most* in withholding anticipated connections, her motives inevitably feel more internally impelled.

But the immediate key—the key that opens at least the first door—to Elizabeth Bishop's metaphors, and to Marianne Moore's as well, is that they suspend the main and obvious differences among the things compared, choosing for comparison objects and ideas that frequently have few obvious similarities. Moore arranges her desk so that her gaze has to negotiate between a rhinoceros and the bodies of the celestials, between a fabulous beast and a transcendent physicality, between rigid and fluid suggestion; so do her poems constantly urge her out of the path of efficient logic and into the unmapped regions of metaphor. The jerboa makes no music, and is neither particularly lyrical in its movements nor (to most sensibilities) beautiful in its form, yet Moore's musical analogy is perfectly convincing: The desert rat moves across the sand "By fifths and sevenths, in leaps of two lengths, / like the uneven notes / of the Bedouin flute." The lonely melancholy of the flute ennobles and thus justifies the jerboa as a fit agent for the secret work of poetry. Ecstasy affords the occasion.

Elizabeth Bishop, describing unsavory beasts like vultures or the homely detail of street, factory, barnyard, or stable, skirts the unattractive—suspends it in a compelling, larger movement at once precise and elegiac—but without falsifying the tawdriness and dirt. In a factory district, the waterwagon comes by in the morning, "throwing its hissing, snowy fan across / peelings and newspapers."[14] The lyrical and the mundane move side by side. When the water dries, it looks "light-dry, dark-wet, the pattern / of the cool watermelon." She makes us aware of heat by suggesting the thirst the homely watermelon might quench. In fact, what melon and wagon refresh is the spirit itself. Elsewhere, buzzards circling over carrion drift down "like stirred-up flakes of sediment sinking through water."[15] Although the behavior is delicately languorous, the subject is bound to offal and silt. Similarly, at a soccer match in a small Brazilian village,

> Buzzards and delicate tissue-paper kites poise high overhead and the players in their brilliantly striped jerseys and brief shorts are running, running.
>   It is also a common sight to see the local washerwoman's line hung with the jerseys of one team, sweaters striped like wasps—a cheerful display—sometimes against the background of a city dump, with more buzzards and more paper kites hovering over it.[16]

This description is undeniably stamped with Elizabeth Bishop's signature, especially in the way items and qualities repeat at different distances and concentrations, from the close poetic phrasing of "running, running," to the somewhat less obvious redundancy of the striped jerseys, first on the men, then on the wash line, to the longer intervals before the da capo return (with a new and ironic weariness) to "more buzzards and more paper kites." The irony comes from the repeated bracketing together of the soaring toy with the carrion bird over areas, like the soccer field and the village dump, where only one of them properly belongs; they are like a mismatched couple in a pantomime. The sense of persons and personalities in the scene is further enhanced by the wasps, which the team jerseys resemble; their buzz of activity (which is twice insisted upon by the sound of the word "buzzards"), along with the activity of the players from afar, and the airy movement of buzzards and kites at various distances, condense and flex in the space of our attention, moving the eye, arresting our auditory imagination, and at last speaking softly and musingly to the emotions. Brazil more than any other locale had this soothing effect on the poet: It opened to her the experience, as she saw it, of an entire nation devoted to graceful, friendly absorption in its own paradoxes.

Bishop announces her presence as well in the graceful and poignant parenthetical phrase, "a cheerful display," which reminds us of the remarkable lexical feat she elsewhere performs with quite a commonplace vocabulary, calling up the child's responses while enlarging its grief or wonder, as in the conclusion of "The Bight" (the dredge "brings up a dripping jawful of marl . . . untidy activity . . . awful but cheerful"),[17] and at several critical moments in the story-memoir, "In the Village." This story, which first appeared in the New Yorker in 1953, was reprinted in Bishop's 1965 poetry volume, Questions of Travel, which many readers consider her best, but "In the Village" was not reprinted thereafter in a poetry volume.[18] This is a pity, as "In the Village" is a necessary codicil to the Nova Scotia poems, "Large Bad Picture," "Poem," "The Moose," "Sestina," "First Death in Nova Scotia," "At the Fishhouses," and "Cape Breton," and to the poem whose rendering of childhood has been so highly praised, "In the Waiting Room." I believe "In the Village" captures the hurrying shocks and transitions of the child as credibly, and more fully.

As in that poem, the shocks of self-recognition are precipitated by a scream or a series of screams; in the poem "In the Waiting Room," the scream comes from her foolish and cowardly aunt in the dentist's office; in the story "In the Village," the screams come from the child's mentally ill mother, still unable to get over her husband's death, who is back with her parents, sisters, and the five-year-old girl she had had to leave with the grandparents. By the end of the story, the mother has reentered the sanitarium for good; thus the little girl is at last effectively orphaned by the unfamiliar mother. The scream that has already sounded so horrifyingly is

still tingling in the hard blue sky and the cold stream water of the landscape that acts as palpable support to the speaker's reassembly of her
world.

On several occasions in "In the Village," she visits the blacksmith who
makes a fine and regular *clang* with his metals, a sound that mutes the
(for her) always audible and threatening scream, and that also, despite the
infernal nuance of the red-hot forge, substitutes for the church bells and
the subtle rural evangelical fever of which Bishop speaks both in this story
and an earlier one, "The Baptism." The blacksmith's is a holy nook, a
scene of what we might call the domestic esoteric. His shop is a temple
in which "The horseshoes sail through the dark like bloody little moons."
The shop is also a home, and the smith and the townsmen are avuncular
presences. Furthermore, like some of the other animals in Elizabeth
Bishop's work—for example, the fish, the moose, the owl, the seal, and the
little circus horse—this Nova Scotian dray-horse is the persona's magical
totem:

> Nate sings and pumps the bellows. . . . Two men stand watching, chewing
> or spitting tobacco . . . they are perfectly at home. The horse is the real
> guest, however. His harness hangs loose like a man's suspenders; they say
> pleasant things to him; one of his legs is doubled up in an improbable,
> affectedly polite way, and the bottom of his hoof is laid bare, but he doesn't
> seem to mind. Manure piles up behind him suddenly, neatly. He, too, is
> very much at home. He is enormous. His rump is like a brown, glossy globe
> of the whole brown world. His ears are secret entrances to the underworld.
> His nose is supposed to feel like velvet and does, with ink spots under milk
> all over its pink. Clear bright-green bits of stiffened froth, like glass, are
> stuck around his mouth. He wears medals on his chest, too, and one on his
> forehead, and simpler decorations—red and blue celluloid rings overlapping
> each other on leather straps. On each temple is a clear glass bulge, like an
> eyeball, but in them are the heads of two other little horses (his dreams?),
> brightly colored, real and raised, untouchable, alas, against backgrounds of
> silver blue. His trophies hang around him, and the cloud of his odor is a
> chariot in itself.
>
> At the end, all four feet are brushed with tar, and shine, and he expresses
> his satisfaction, rolling it from his nostrils like noisy smoke, as he backs into
> the shafts of his wagon.[19]

David Kalstone properly calls the milieu of this story "a radiant primal
world."[20] The pacing of syntax and metaphor conveys the patience of the
child's attention, alongside her quickening awe; particularly striking are
the comparisons having to do with the badges of secret office and the
carefully maintained suggestions of danger (the glasslike bits of stiffened
froth, the noisy smoke from the horse's nostrils) and taboo (the world-

globes of the buttocks and secret entrances to the underworld). But these metaphors are almost too daedal, too fixed, too majestic. Consequently, with these, Bishop interweaves the language of comfort, of reassurance, of home: "He, too, is very much at home"; "they say pleasant things to him;" the horse is patient and polite; "He doesn't seem to mind"; he is comfortable in his harness for "His trophies hang around him"; he at last positively "expresses his satisfaction." More than the denotations the words actually carry, this murmurous exchange of approval and pleasantry functions as a diction, a style, or tone of voice, to remind the child that all is well. Hers is a world whose mystery is so potent and whose turmoil, so palpable, as to require such gentling. The esoteric—large, eloquent, ominous—is checked by the gentle tethers of conversation.

Like the poems of Randall Jarrell, with their radiant childlike chatter, the works of Elizabeth Bishop address an earlier state of being with a later mind and resources. But adult ease only intensifies the illusion of young wonder and unmediated freshness, which, in turn, rescues the common-places, makes authentic (hence poetic) the self-evidential, approximate, halting, interrupted, and fussily circular utterances that pepper the style of both Jarrell and Bishop:

In my	What similarities . . . the
Talk with the world, in which it	family voice
tells me what I know	I felt in my throat, or even
And I tell it, "I know—" how	the *National Geographic*
strange that I	and those awful hanging breasts—
Know nothing, and yet it tells me	held us all together
what I know!	or made us all just one?
I appreciate the animals, who stand	How—I didn't know any
by	word for it—how "unlikely" . . .
Purring. Or else they sit and pant.	(Bishop, "In the Waiting
It's so—	Room")
So *agreeable*.	
(Jarrell, "Children's Arms")	
A farmer is separated from a	A specklike bird is flying to the
farmer	left.
By what farmers have in common:	Or is it a flyspeck looking like a
forests,	bird?
Those dark things—what the fields	
were to begin with.	Heavens, I recognize the place, I
. . . .	know it!
The boy stands looking at the fox	It's behind—I can almost
As if, if he looked long enough—	remember the farmer's name.
he looks at it.	. . . .

Or is it the fox that's looking at
    the boy?
The trees can't tell the two of them
    apart.
        (Jarrell, "Field and Forest")

art "copying from life" and life
    itself,
life and the memory of it so
    compressed
they've turned into each other.
    Which is which?
        (Bishop, "Poem")

Her thin feet, pointed neither out
    nor in
But straight before her, like an
    Indian's
And set upon the path, a detour of
    the path
Of righteousness; her
    unaccommodating eyes'
Flat blue, matt blue
Or grey, depending on the point
    of view—
On whether one looks from here
    or from New England—
All these go unobserved, are
    unobservable:
She is old enough to be invisible.
        (Jarrell, "The End of the
           Rainbow")

In the pink light
the small red sun goes rolling,
    rolling,
round and round and round at the
    same height
in perpetual sunset, comprehensive,
    consoling,

while the ships consider it
Apparently they have reached their
    destination.
It would be hard to say what
    brought them here,
Commerce or contemplation.
    (Bishop, "Large Bad Picture")

This hypothetical style is most pointed when there is some attitude- or rhythm-change on the part of the poem's speaker—when the fact that the poem *has* a speaker becomes salient or obtrusive. The hallmarks of this style are: *Declaration brought up short by doubt. Sincerity suggested by uncertainty—or more, by insecurity. A line of thought so fragile as to be nearly broken by the very act of following it through. Periodic "breakthroughs" to the right phrase. Slight or niggling revision that is formulaic or punning. Or sluggish repetitions massed in order to keep off the winds of distraction— to protect the thread of thought with sameness and cliché. At last, the redundancies remassed as tautologies*—and in this way, the protective vocabulary as it were threads its own fibers through the thought it was meant to protect against intrusions, thus thickening and defining it. With a stubborn air of clumsiness, world and perceiver are fused. Thought and method at once concentrate and cheer one another on.

Bishop's poem "At the Fishhouses" mutedly illustrates many of these stylistic hallmarks. With a saturnine absorption unusual for her, she collects and arranges her building blocks; it is a poem of nervously hushed, assiduous growth.[21] On the other hand, it is a poem of mastery and deep connection with the wellsprings of the psyche. Lorrie Goldensohn makes the electrifying suggestion that it is a poem fueled by erotic fear and love,[22] and I think the brimming up of strength and secret knowledge is responsible for the sense of visionary access. In the first movement, the building blocks have to do with textures of brilliance, shiny fish scales, glints, stains, sequins, skins of beast and ocean ("iridescent" is a key term). The old fisherman, encrusted with scales and worn (like his tools) to a kind of horny polish, is the genius of this inaugural movement of the poem—of shell, skin, and surfaces. In a kind of second movement, we pierce through the heavy swelling surface of the water to compass the depth, iciness, profundity, and hard rondure of the rock-bordered sea. Counteracting the intense upward flowing of libidinal energy is the gesture of *charm:* A charming seal, with typically curious demeanor, observes the speaker during her singing of Baptist hymns—both of them, observes the poet, believers in total immersion. But the childlike and the winsome corroborate and strengthen rather than entirely deflecting Bishop's excited fixation upon the world's cold energy. Not words alone, but word clusters, act to key the passage: "Cold dark deep and . . . clear," "clear gray icy," "the rounded gray and blue-gray stones," and so on. These clusters proceed seamlessly, without punctuation, as if indeed they had grown from the same tissue of the imagination, yoked in coldness as well as in an almost animal sympathy:

> Cold dark deep and absolutely clear,
> element bearable to no mortal.
> Cold dark deep and absolutely clear,
> the clear gray icy water
> . . . .
> The water seems suspended
> above the rounded gray and blue-gray stones.
> I have seen it over and over, the same sea, the same,
> slightly, indifferently swinging above the stones,
> icily free above the stones,
> above the stones and then the world.
> If you should dip your hand in,
> your wrist would ache immediately,
> your bones would begin to ache and your hand would burn . . .

The "swinging above the stones" bespeaks a mild projection of whimsicality, a childlikeness, upon the ocean, which the old fisherman and the seal at once provoke, by suggesting comradeship, and permit, by appearing noncommittal. Here, where the merging of sea and rock seems to begin, we have the catalyst: The speaker, her eyes still watering from the fierce ammonia smell of codfish, imagines that she invades the water with her hand, and out of the burning sensation produced on the skin by extreme cold, a small flame sprouts: "your bones would begin to ache and your hand would burn / as if the water were a transmutation of fire / that feeds on stones and burns with a dark gray flame." Finally, stone and sea *do* merge, in the phrase "cold hard mouth of the world," by which Bishop implies the rocks as breasts, saltwater as pap like an elixir:

> If you tasted it, it would first taste bitter,
> then briny, then surely burn your tongue.
> It is like what we imagine knowledge to be:
> dark, salt, clear, moving, utterly free,
> drawn from the cold hard mouth
> of the world, derived from the rocky breasts
> forever, flowing and drawn, and since
> our knowledge is historical, flowing, and flown.

In wonderment at her own insight that "knowledge," so supernal, so abstract, could be embraced by a set of experiences so intimate, Bishop dramatically revises her own lucid and preoccupied style; she punctuates the adjectives shared by both mind and sense with a recessional of commas, "dark, salt, clear, moving, utterly free," as the imagination moves backward into history, memory—the past—toward sources which (it turns out) are not "there" the way knowledge is, or, quite, the way immediate sensation is: Alas, it is no longer possible to drink from those breasts. We are orphaned from the world also; we can no longer live like a seal imbedded in it, drinking from it, bathed by it, freely dependent on it. Whatever sympathies join them, and although they are of the same blood, nature and humankind are as alien as if they belonged to different epochs.

Like at least a dozen of Bishop's best poems, "At the Fishhouses" builds itself up methodically, unspectacularly, using many of the attributes of the hypothetical-prosaic style that she shares with writers like Moore and Jarrell. The three writers have in common another curious quality: They write prose that in many respects sounds like their poetry; the genres, for each, do not really differ in the sort of rhetoric that is used. Rather, the poems tend to precipitate one device from the others in any given passage, also to use striking metaphors with greater frequency, and to enjoy the mild visual effect—the phrasing effect—of the free-verse lineation. But it is the prose quality, I think, which permits the prosodies of all three poets such lightness.[23] Unlike strict meters, which force the writer always toward a slightly overdramatized, verbal busyness, even when the poet wishes merely to mark time or prepare a transition, the proselike liberation of a "freed verse" like Bishop's encourages a precarious honesty in the thought. At the same time, slackness shows. It is easy to distinguish her standard poems from her good poems, for the mediocre ones are always *just* prose, yet with that false, poetical "aura" provided by line breaks. (I would place "The Man-Moth" here, despite its moist, waiflike fancy, also "Arrival at Santos," "Manuelzinho," and a poem collected in the 1983 volume for the first time, "Santarém.")

But when Bishop adjusts her prosody to one of the most interesting functions of prose, namely, its ability (perhaps its propensity) to reflect the mind at drift, she creates her modest masterpieces, "At the Fishhouses," "Over 2,000 Illustrations and a Complete Concordance," "Cape Breton" (all from *A Cold Spring,* 1955); "Brazil, January 1, 1502," "Questions of Travel," "The Riverman," and "Sestina" (1965); the extraordinary pair of poems from *Geography III* (1976), "Poem" and "Crusoe in England"; and the marvelous 1939 poem, discovered in manuscript, written in a loose version of elegiac couplet, "Pleasure Seas." Unlike Randall Jarrell, drawn to dramatic monologue and the poem of social commentary, and unlike Marianne Moore, drawn to meditation on the physical signs of virtue, bravery, and the kind of modesty that speaks aloud, Bishop's subjects are neither adjusted nor adjustable to categories. She tends to create the kinds of category that have as yet only the two members contained in the analogy. Such a new category, trembling with a sense of unmourned-for loss of innocence, is created in the poem that compares the young prostitute, dancing alone in the square, to a "feverish atom." A new partition has been placed upon the world when the child of "In the Village" takes her walking stick that stands beside the back door "clad in bark." The poet has set the wave rippling, by touching the surface with her metaphor, and its vibrations keep glinting in the distance.

There is a sense—giddy, provisional—of overflow, of slightly overfull reservoirs, which is as much an indication of Bishop's cast of thought as the hypothetical twists we examined earlier. Moreover, this delighted brimming-up to the limits of expressability, then spilling-over them, is augmented by the devices of the hypothetical style. Above all, it is the question—not the metaphysical question, but the idle and bemused question, mere quizzicality, useless wondering—that Bishop brings to bear on the pictures and sensations that form hazily and haphazardly before her. Bonnie Costello has devoted an essay to Bishop's interrogative mode, examining the work in terms of the dualism between travel and pause, uncertainty and rest, homelessness and coalescence, remarking on the poet's formation of symbols that ground the affections at the same time as they unmoor the self. Hence, says Costello, her fondness for "the sudden feeling of home."[24] To Costello's theses I would add only that Bishop's aesthetic is already thoroughly "grounded" in the very movement of unmooring, "useless concentration," reverie. Rather than certifying her homelessness over the earth, it is precisely the attitudes of traveling and querying, of coming in late, ill-informed and uninvolved, that warm Bishop up, permit her to begin the real work of alchemization of self into art. Her very uncertainty launches the poem out on those radial lines of trial and error which, as Gaston Bachelard suggests, make reverie possible, reflecting qualities of consciousness at once obsessive and meandering, awake and asleep.

Querying is the implied syntax of all reverie—the mildly suspenseful concentration upon an area, a mere patch, which, however attractive, is not yet reachable or ponderable. Ignorance is an essential tool, since the less you know, the more you are capable of making up—or making *back* up. For Bishop, and Jarrell along with her, are engaged in a twofold enterprise. First, they are attempting to remember what a nonadult consciousness felt like—how its smells, surprises, and longueurs settled themselves in the psyche. The brilliant children's writer-illustrator, Belgian-born Leo Lionni, believes that anyone who wishes to study literacy must go "back to the images that precede words *and to the feelings that precede both.*"[25] Elizabeth Bishop, too, is looking in another realm, another *time,* for the momentum that propels her as she casts herself adrift into disjointed reveries; for, in properly circular fashion (since art does not advance, it only accumulates), only in such a suspended state can she recapture the earliest tremblings of an insight. Lionni directs our attention to such an "initial feeling" that antedates even the image as the artist attempts to reembody the most powerful and crucial part of his or her past:

> Before an even rudimentary image, what is experienced is more like an internal gesture. . . . a presymbol, an *Urgestalt,* which like an embryo contains all the essential information necessary for its subsequent development.[26]

In her methodological digressiveness, Bishop bears out Lionni's pertinent observations about the stirrings of poetical idea. She resists premature assignment of signification, and in this she resembles nothing so much as the character in her story "In Prison," whose one desire was to be given a dull book on a foreign subject, "perhaps the second volume, if the first would familiarize me too well with the terms and purpose of the work. Then I shall be able to experience with a free conscience the pleasure . . . of interpreting it not at all according to its intent."[27]

This last suggestion—that the poet might court almost deliberate misinterpretation, getting it *wrong* in order thereby to get it *right*—is the corollary of the first intention. In order for Bishop and Jarrell to know the language of the heart, they must abjure the language of the mind, the *learned* tongue. They both would appear to follow T. S. Eliot in his wonderfully spirited and dotty claim that Dante can be understood (in Italian) before he can be read. Jarrell, too, preferred reading (and even translating) German without knowing it very well (although "Deutsch Durch Freud" with its punning title would suggest he knew it better than he knew). Elizabeth Bishop likewise blossoms in the very period when Lorrie Goldensohn believes her ignorance of Portuguese created "an opening for her own work with language to continue, unobserved, and unself-conscious," and in this way "her life drew strength from circumstances rooted somewhere beyond language."[28] Like the prisoner, Bishop reserves for herself the right to be irrelevant.

It is the child's right, and Bishop can annoy as oversensitive children can, by the very monotony of the fey and fantastic. But she can also afford long stretches of the purest delight. Here, in the posthumously discovered 1939 poem, "Pleasure Seas," she daydreams in the Florida keys:

> In the walled off swimming-pool the water is perfectly flat.
> The pink Seurat bathers are dipping themselves in and out
> Through a pane of bluish glass.
> The cloud reflections pass
> Huge amoeba-motions directly through
> The beds of bathing caps: white, lavender, and blue.
> . . . .
>   Love
> Sets out determinedly in a straight line,
> One of his burning ideas in mind.
> . . . .
> Happy the people in the swimming-pool and on the yacht,
> Happy the man in that airplane, like as not—
> And out there where the coral reef is a shelf
> The water runs at it, leaps, throws itself
> Lightly, lightly, whitening in the air:
> An acre of cold white spray is there
> Dancing happily by itself.

The close of "Pleasure Seas" may look forward to poor Crusoe's transparent companions, the waterspouts, "their heads in cloud, their feet in moving patches / of scuffed-up white," but even more than these beautiful ghosts, whom Crusoe calls "sacerdotal beings of glass," the water of "Pleasure Seas" that whitens across the sea's broad ballroom, "Dancing happily by itself," may remind us of another poet's lyric about reverie, in which we are given a glimpse of the young woman who will become a hurricane practicing "a thinker shuffle / Picked up on the street . / *Like a long-legged fly upon the stream / Her mind moves upon silence*." At the same time as

W. B. Yeats's verses on Helen deprecate their mythic reverberations, they also depend heavily on the large disturbances that were to emanate from that idle tinker shuffle. For Bishop's part, at the same time as she invokes with perfect and intelligent tact the great colorful canvases of the French fin de siècle, and the Renaissance climate of emblem and allegory (she and George Herbert are both wont to let "Love" speak), Bishop gently rejects her ease among the traditions that accompany her in the poems. For although her learning, her sprightliness, and her charm speak from almost every page, we may still frequently detect the strain she placed on description to render, in addition to the intensely accurate portrait, emotion, belief, and subtle and sustained thought.

4

The Romance of the Perceptual

The Legacy of Wallace Stevens

Six poets thought to share in a preoccupation elaborated and ennobled by Stevens are studied in the two sections below. In section I, "'I Am What Is Around Me,'" appear discussions of A. R. Ammons, Mark Strand and the "lyric school" of perceptual poets, and Louise Glück. Section II, "The Perceptual Sublime," addresses the work of Ted Hughes, Robert Pinsky (by way of John Ashbery), and Ben Belitt.

I. "I Am What Is Around Me"

Say that the palms are clear in a total blue,
Are clear and are obscure; that it is night;
That the moon shines.

I am what is around me.

(Wallace Stevens)

It will not have escaped the reader that many of the poems and poets discussed so far, both rhapsodic and reticent, occluded and openly child-like, have focused on landscapes or have visualizable settings whose eccentricity often warrants their reality. Vision is now the great literary cliché (just as it is undeniably the commanding sense of our physical being). Most of the poets encountered in contemporary poetry (since the Vietnam War) believe—nearly more strongly than they believe in anything else—in seeing. For the moment, I mean nothing more than their attachment to the visible, their looking around, their being on the scene. As topic and as vehicle for many of their central metaphors, seeing is considered a good in itself.

One distinction of what I am calling, "the romance of the perceptual" in contemporary poetry is that it transforms the passive into the active. The verb *to see* is not just a convenient way to get around saying *there is,* but renders acts of seizure and volition. If Josephine Miles were to up-date her tables in *Era and Modes in English Poetry*[1] to include statistical-frequency samples of word use in poets of the period 1970–90, we would

101

probably find that, after *to see* (a staple, after all, with George Herbert as much as with Wallace Stevens), the next most frequent verb would be *to hold, to take,* or *to pull.* To see is to grasp, conquer, and possess the phenomena. Beside every term of vision, whether *I see* or *it shines,* we are likely to find a companion-term of mastery. *Hand* attends *star; flesh* provides *light.* Even the use of *eye* in the context of *night* or *darkness* falls into this category of the passive made active—the eye as the active shedder-of-light, maker-of-meaning.

What is most surprising about "perceptual poetry" today is the decrease in negatives—nothing is ugly, or the ugly is no longer repellent—and the parallel increase in positives, those adjectives in which poets petition the phenomena, rather than recoiling from them. A list is easily compiled from the sampling of contemporary poets treated below with Mark Strand:

> clear, luminous, radiant, lucid, lustrous, streaming, *flowing,* shimmering, flashing, glazed, gleaming, glinting, blazing, rising, *long, open, widening, drifting, steep, high, tall,* transparent, translucent, *shifting, passing, lifting, single,* glaring, lightning, silver, white, bright, etc.

It is not simply that English is rich in visual nuance, this we knew, but that the italicized words are introduced from other senses and added to the available vocabulary of seeing. Wallace Stevens is responsible for the promotion of most of the italicized words to the visual realm, and in a passage from "Variations on a Summer Day" where he promotes yet another (the frequentative *dithering*), he also defends the new usage:

> Words add to the senses. The words for the dazzle
> Of mica, the dithering of grass,
> The Arachne integument of dead trees,
> Are the eye grown larger, more intense.[2]

James Wright merely moves Stevens's dictum a further step by speaking of a huge stone lifted by iron rods in "a dazzle of balance."

Similar to the list of favored adjectives is the list of favored metaphors. Stevens might not have approved of many of the metaphors, since they are often technological, yet what an elaborate and conscious array of visual technics: the lens, radar, the double exposure, the telescope, the palimpsest, focusing, the tunnel, the transparency, refraction in water, the veining of rock with bright minerals, the x-ray, efflorescence, the frontier between elements (as between water and air), the Gestalt language of figure versus ground—not to mention the mirror, fire, stars, the sun and moon, the lamp.

So far, none of these preferences is very surprising. But when we try to compile a list of pejoratives, we find that most of them are ambiguous, if not actually commendatory in their application:

> dark, night, black, obscure, vacant, solitary, desolate, wind, glass, ice, mist, cloud, secret, shadow, density, blurring, cold, snow, winter, etc.

The very words we would expect to be damaging to clarity of vision are turned back on themselves in a subtle refusal on the poets' part to give a pejorative value to anything that has intensity. Not only did Wallace Stevens rescue *cold* and *winter* from the proscribed camp, give to *glass* a grand new symbolic place (in "Asides on the Oboe" and "Chocorua to Its Neighbor," v and ix), and provide *darkness* and *night* with a new domestic, non-Byronic coloration; Stevens also redefined *desolation, vacancy, vanishing,* and *emptiness* as the crucial conditions for training the eye. Hence, the famous Stevens image of the reader, *solus,* reading the page by its (or his) own light.

In "The Man with the Blue Guitar," xxxii, Stevens enjoined poets to "Throw the light away"; "Nothing must stand / Between you and the shapes you take / When the crust of shape has been destroyed." Lack of external reference, an acute vanishing, erasure of the crust of shape, a transparency at the center—these are the "shapes" taken by Stevens's seer. *Taken* in both senses: as a thing, detached from us, is seized; and as a kinesthetic projection of self on world (as the taking of a measurement is to some extent the projection of the mind upon space). What Stevens required was that both kinds of *taking shape* occur simultaneously, the acquiring and the projecting; and this led to the strongest single *kind* of metaphor in Stevens, vision expressed in terms of kinesthesia (the body's sense of where it is in space and its ability to expand that sense). In other words, Stevens builds up the mythos of seeing in order, as it were, to see through it. When he says, "It is not an image. It is a feeling," it is not so that some other sense can take the place of the image, but so that vision itself can be entirely redefined, as an athletic passion of appropriation:

> It is not an image. It is a feeling.
> There is no image of the hero.
> There is a feeling as definition.
> How could there be an image, an outline,
> A design, a marble soiled by pigeons?
> The hero is a feeling, a man seen
> As if the eye was an emotion,
> As if in seeing we saw our feeling
> In the object seen . . .
>
> ("Examination of the Hero in a Time of War,"
> xii, *Parts of a World*)

Although Stevens dismisses the image of the hero as a model for emula-
tion, the hero is still a *seen* figure ("a man seen / As if the eye was an
emotion"). So also for description; it may at first appear to be able to make
things up, place palms at the end of the mind, scatter bright particulars
throughout the sky, but Stevens also demanded that the background to
thought stay stubbornly, really physical. Again, he makes his evanescent
perceptions work by expressing the visible in kinesthetic terms:

> Description is
> Composed of a sight indifferent to the eye.
>
> It is an expectation, a desire,
> A palm that rises up beyond the sea,
>
> A little different from reality:
> The difference that we make in what we see
>
> And our memorials of that difference,
> Sprinklings of bright particulars from the sky.
> . . . .
> The forms that are attentive in thin air.
> ("Description Without Place," v, *Transport to Summer* [1947])

Finally—and this will be my last point about Stevens as founder of "perceptual poetry"—the grave, methodical current of kinesthesia in his work
enables Stevens to make the world appear a little different *after* it is looked
at than it was before. The literal investment of places with the watching,
gazing self makes the face seen in the glass of air after all different from
one's own face. Someone, or Something, answers to the poet's regard:

> . . . he came back as one comes back from the sun
> To lie on one's bed in the dark, close to a face
> Without eyes or mouth, that looks at one and speaks.
> ("Yellow Afternoon," *Parts of a World*)

And from "An Ordinary Evening in New Haven," xxv (*The Auroras of
Autumn,* 1950), comes the eeriest version of the answering look:

> Life fixed him, wandering on the stair of glass,
> With its attentive eyes.
> . . . .
> There were looks that caught him out of empty air.

The "hidalgo," emblem of the permanent and the abstract, is "A hatching
that stared and demanded an answering look."
    Are we very far, in the looks that catch us out of empty air, in the
heavy scowl of the pediment of appearance, or in the eyes that open and
fix on us in every sky, from Stevens's firecat, who bristles in the way, or

from the sky that is full of bodies like wood, or from the deceptively amusing dictum that one looks at the sea as one improvises on the piano? Not really, since even in his best nonsense poems in *Harmonium* (1931) there is something rather uncanny. From the beginning, Stevens's world has about it something so solitary yet protean that we may find in his opus the most authentic indigenous version of the gnostic parable. As his obsession with perspectival volume should remind us, the narrowness is the way.

A. R. Ammons

Although a representative Ammons volume like his *Worldly Hopes* makes no overt announcement of a philosophical "system," this poet is clearly at ease with the jargon of logic and category.[3] Terms like "Augmentations," "Differentials," "Volitions," "Epistemology," and "Subsumption" occur in his titles, and the texts themselves throw off the occasional theoretical nubbin, "replications," "substance," "paradigms." Even more than in shop talk, however, the poems in Ammons's seventeenth volume announce their allegiance to metaphysics in arguing the relation of the poet to himself as pure being, to his creation as the embodiment of being, and to the world as the matter against which his creation is also the reaction or recoil. As in Stevens, images of the natural world are positive, of the human world negative; nature's substances, however dense and enveloping, allow the intangible to be seen, while human existence embrutes and clouds itself in the very exercise of its defining traits, speech and feeling. Thus Ammons's "Epistemology," a poem that treats emotion as an inevitable distortion of knowing, could just as well be entitled "Ontology," because it then links the distortion with the visible reality of the world. The poem is partitioned and argued much like William Blake's "Poison Tree," which begins, "I was angry with my friend; / I told my wrath, my wrath did end. / I was angry with my foe: / I told it not, my wrath did grow." Just as Blake's truism evolves a pictorial tree whose apple of suppressed wrath poisons the foe, Ammons's truism (the bit untold) grows into a "posture" so enormous it soon cannot be distinguished from everything that is the case:

EPISTEMOLOGY

A bit of
truth
told pops
its pip
and falls
small

into its
(if bitter)

consequence
but the bit
untold

avoided collects   solved or made
about it   to disappear &
networks   so by
bindings   recalcitrance &
of disguise &   complication
going   comes
around   to represent
till, an   the world
enormous posture   truly
it can't be   ours.
identified

As befits the topic of secrecy, the oral imagery is commanding: *bit* (bite), *told* (speak), *pip*[1] (peep, cheep, pipe), *pip*[2] (seed, apple, cf. pippin), and *pop* (therapeutic verbal explosion, cf. pop off). By echoing the sounds of *bit, bitter, its, pip,* and *pop,* the later alliterations of plosives and dentals and the short i's continue to echo the original failure of speech long after the result has obtained. The bit, "by / recalcitrance & / complication," at last matches up to the only world we can apprehend.

So much for the helpless results of psychology: It creates an unbreathably stuffed and stuffy atmosphere, cramming the world with objects of fear and aggressive inclination. Ammons responds to these impulses with what he phrases in his ars poetica, "Scribbles," "grievances of avoidance." His prevalent landscapes are those of emptiness, vacuity, and erasure, and the poet himself takes part in the housecleaning. "My endorsing song," he writes in "Calling," "blocks out / to blot out." The success of poesy is then measured not only by reduction to flattened negativity, but also by kinesthetic access or transport upward into another spiritual fabric: "my self-endorsing song, flattened, / snaking its way out, / reaching to weave into its rise." Like a huge protean macramé, the poetic creation imaged by Ammons weaves in order to unweave itself; in terms of aesthetic debate, the poem as artifact unravels before the gestures of the poet as singer and solitary perceiver.

In keeping with the reverence in which he holds occasion, the poet resolves many of his texts by consuming them. How often we meet images of combustion, inflammation, beating to airy thinness, rising up in a tangle of evanescent breath or smoke; efflorescence, exfoliation, evaporation, brightening and diffusing haze. These metaphors, in germ so close to the metaphysics of the imaginative sublime in Stevens, in context are stamped with Ammons's own unique signature, combining as they do a kind of heatedness and satyrlike ardor with an equal measure of cool gauzy abstraction. Undermining any wholehearted aesthetic of the sensuous,

Ammons is also attracted by the *via negativa* of the mystic, the hermit, the renouncer. Both of these temperaments, the manic and the entranced, work to define the religious spirit in this brief poem. Finally it is a matter of pacing that most differentiates him from Stevens:

PROVIDENCE

To stay
bright as
if just
thought of
earth requires
only that
nothing stay

The poet moderates the one extreme of erasure (the negative way, insubstantiality, vacancy) by bracketing it with the other extreme of invention (mental scintillation, metallic body). Another way to express this bracketing would emphasize how the writer here deromanticizes the creator's role by removing his props and toys and toils and *things*. Although, when thrown together, two such gestures—debunking the daedal and buffing up the ascetic—are at cross-purposes, either by itself would be off-kilter, whether over- or underexpressive of the truth. Thus the mentally brilliant vehicle (a shiny new thought world) has an organic tenor (it is *earth* who requires), a tenor that acts to soften and mystify those formerly clear-cut oppositions.

One would also note how Ammons's lineation of the poem reflects the play between divisiveness and mysterious hovering. The way the lines are broken is a very deliberate registering of the constant doubling that occurs in the *theme* of "Providence," by perching the tiny word-pairs together on the same rungs of their cage, regardless of their grammatical species. New, short-lived grammatical species are thereby produced. For example, *bright as* suggests a comparative noun to follow, *bright as X,* but in fact the syntax pulls *bright* back to line 1 ("To stay bright") while it casts *as* forward to its complement in lines 3 and 4 ("as if just thought of"). The split allegiance to syntax versus line creates the hovering counterpoint so crucial, as Charles O. Hartman has shown, to free verse.[4] "Epistemology," the first Ammons poem quoted above, illustrates a yet more extreme use of the free-verse line to truncate speech particles from each other. This truncation calls attention to the bracketing effect of the verse line, so that like briefly embraces unlike ("told pops," "till, an," "solved or made"), as well as calling attention to the "rhyming" effects that keep phrases whole or balance like with like ("and falls / small," "(if bitter," "but the bit").

On these narrow free-verse plateaus, Ammons convenes his subjects, from the frolicsome to the obscure; the lines at which he draws the knot tightest (one, repeated verbatim) are in italics:

> what's left
> from what I
> *was won't*
> turn my way
>
>   ("Lost & Found")

> My big round yew
> can stand a gust
> into a million
> presences: too
> many needles
> *to get through*
> *to get through*
> except drift through . . .
>
>   ("Night Chill")

And finally, a locution I can only just glimpse as it fades, about a droplet of water that after plashing down and racing the shallows is at last pleased

> to eddy aside, nothing
> of all but nothing's
> curl of motion spent.
>
>   ("Design")

In a poem like "Design," it seems to me that Ammons celebrates the lawfulness of nature (nothing has been spent) as he indulges his own delight in the intricately fashioned expression of what is fleeting. Unlike Robert Frost, whose sonnet "Design" posits a nature both ghoulish and fatal, Ammons has retracted his claws. But then there is his obeisance to the cosmic winter romantic transport, "Augmentations in Early March," which is characterized by the eerie cacophony of skreaking and cracking and freezing that one also finds in *The Prelude* I. 434 ff. (the ice-skating interlude), in "Mont Blanc," ll. 100–120, in Frost's "Birches," and in Howard Nemerov's late "Christmas Storm." Wallace Stevens's mournful jangle is audible here as well. In this tradition of a sublime that sets the teeth on edge, Ammons's trees are

> ice-corseted to the least
> twig and a breeze,
> sun-raised,
> squeaks the got-up skeletons
> limb against limb

with music frazzled
multiple as mist
settling or as treesful
of gritty grackles
on their way here now.

("Augmentation in Early March")

Despite the hint of the clique, it is easy to be charmed by that temporal
hitch that points up the imminent migrations of spring. In the vein of
influence I may prefer the more occasional *jeu* like "Rainy Morning,"
which, while it does not sustain as long as Stevens will the soaring of the
imagination, still rescues its small figure from the perceptual ground:

RAINY MORNING

Sometimes the ridge across
the way transluminous
emerges above the mist
and squares and detached rondures
of vapory ground with
dairy barns and old trees
break out afloat
separated in high lyings.

This is a poem strikingly American; I cannot imagine a poet of any other
nation reaching for just these effects: the casually domestic personification
that is yet not childish; the effortlessly lyrical neologism ("transluminous"); the quiet syntactic knotting of line 4 (at the first *and*); and the
marvelous substrate of diluvian suggestion. In making us by his sly clarities again mindful of our traditions and cognizant, as we read him, of the
skills of verbal attention, A. R. Ammons causes a new light to shine on
the perceptual romance.

Mark Strand and the "Lyric School"

He felt curious
Whether the water was black and lashed about
Or whether the ice still covered the lake.
        . . . If,
When he looked, the water ran up the air or grew white
Against the edge of the ice, the abstraction would
Be broken and winter would be broken and done,
And being would be being himself again,
Being, becoming seeing and feeling and self,
Black water breaking into reality.

(Wallace Stevens)

There is a surprising continuity, tending to monotony, in the metaphors and vocabulary of a group of poets who follow the example of
Wallace Stevens. Mark Strand is the best known of this "lyrical school"
of perceptual poets.[5] Consider Jane Shore's phrase, "that density / silence
roots the very / center of," and then consider the end of Peter Everwine's
"Distance": "Once more I find myself / standing as on a dark pier, holding / an enormous rope of silence." Then compare Mark Strand's poem
"White":

> As I walk, the darkness of
> my steps is also white,
> and my shadow blazes
> under me. In all seasons
> the *silence* where I find myself
> and what I make of nothing are white,
> the white of sorrow,
> the white of death.
>
>   (My emphasis)

There is good reason for Strand's repetitions of *white* and his application of the quality of whiteness even to things of opposite valence, like
darkness, just as there is good reason for Jane Shore to use *density* to join
touch to *silence* and for Peter Everwine to strike the solitary's pose on a
dark pier holding a *rope* of *silence*. These formulations continue the abstraction of symbolists like Eliot one step further away from experience, toward
thought. As in the quotation above from Stevens's "Extracts from Addresses to the Academy of Fine Ideas," the minimally concrete images by
which the verses are propelled—whether black water, density, rope of
silence, or a dark and blazing whiteness—must serve not just as representatives of the real world, but finally as representatives of the self's *replacement* of that world. We do not assume (the poetry under discussion,
including Stevens's, in fact prevents us from assuming) that the world is
being looked at. What is being looked at is the mind in its function as a
hoard of possibilities—as the landscape in which all kinds of events can
be replayed, in which all sorts of memories can be elaborated, but in
which, in certain moments, *nothing need happen* that is so deliberately
reminiscent of real life as recollected events and present meditations. What
the symbolist strain in contemporary poetry, as exemplified in Shore,
Everwine, and Strand in particular, tries to communicate is an imagery
for a habit or turn of mind when the mind is engaged not with experience
but with itself. To put the enterprise in its most extreme way: These poets
often give us the play of thought that for the present has no specific

content. The thought thus rendered is a condition that is all readiness, all habit, all emptiness.

The rich verbal enthusiasm that accompanies this emptiness is partial proof that our poets are hardly depressed, rather exhilarated, by observing their minds from a studiously peripheral angle. The frequency with which the vocabulary of whiteness, luminosity, and radiance is used is another indication of the real happiness they feel when liberated from the commonplace and the eventful. Consider Jane Shore's lines, "Waking in the dark the dark takes on / a kind of radiance"; Strand's phrases, the "brief luster of leaves" and the "luminous wind of morning"; Constance Urdang's equation between color and the act of adultery, "the street is luminous / with a sad rosy light." And here is Mark Strand again, in "Exiles":

> for when the air was silent
> and everything faded
> it meant only that
> exiles came
> into a country
> not their own,
> into a radiance
> without hope.

I doubt that Strand is talking about real refugees, or, even if he meant to do so, that he has described a bewilderment, phantasmagoria, or hopeless radiance any different from our own. His are exiles so faded from their wanderings and so bleached and indistinct from the tiresome and pointless knowledge that they do not belong that they are infinitely manipulable by the poet. In some faces, Strand's exiles even resemble dreamers:

> And when the trees
> and houses reappeared,
> they saw what they wanted:
> the return of their story
> to where it began.
> They saw it in the cold
> room under the roof
> chilled by moonlight.
> They lay in their beds
> and the shadows of the giant trees
> brushed darkly against the walls.

Again we are confronted by an intentional vagueness of outline that yields a restrained happiness, a sense of threshold and imminence, although the *content* of emotions and outcomes is still nondescript. This obsessive vacancy is a mood to which *any* content may be applied. The chill of the moonlight and the dark brushing of shadows against walls do not occur in the present time of the poem: They stand for the residues in the mind by which mental nothingness—the nothing that *is* there as distinguished from the nothing that is not—may be given a slight texture.

It is not only in the vagueness of setting and reference that many contemporary poets describe the rich nothingness of the image-making faculty: They also use more local devices for suspending words against the ordinary range of denotative meanings. Compare what Everwine says about the *rope of silence* and what Strand does with the word *white* with Jane Shore's suspension of the word *meteor* as it nears the literal surface of, say, the sky, the Constance Urdang's habit of separating part from whole in "Hands of Old Women":

> On the backs, loose skin
> and the pale, indecipherable messages of the veins
> . . . .
> She studies them, clasped in her lap
> . . . .
> the tips faintly blue
> scrolled with illegible writing
>
> It is the trail of the wind
> if she could read it, it would tell her
> where the wind blew
> when her great-grandfathers were born

In light of this metaphor of Urdang's (of the illegible message inscribed in the old hand's tangle of veins), consider Jane Shore's "If I hold my hand to the light, / the bright lattice of bones shines through," and Barry Goldensohn's "the eye / and vague self press / through each gate" of "The Inward City," and his description of famous lovers "raising the arm to glow against the light / naked within the habit of passion." Add to these images of light probing flesh and bone Mark Strand's version of the creation of Adam in the context of perception: "Even this late the bones of the body shine / And tomorrow's dust flares into breath," and also his description of the cold, true night,

> when the body's bones became light
> and the wound of the skull
> opened to receive
> the cold rays of the cosmos,
> and were, for an instant,
> themselves the cosmos

Just as radiance and luminosity tend to refer to conditions of emptiness of mind in which the possibilities of perception and insight are grown to huge capacity however little they actually contain, so in the habit of reading the script of the universe in the tangle of old veins, of throwing all the available weight of one's being onto the idea of light shining through the otherwise opaque bones and cranium, the knowledge gained and communicated by these poets is measurably small, but the feeling of power-to-knowledge immense. These images denote the pose of self-investment; the poet announces the risk he or she has taken with cells and marrow and a precarious consciousness in order that a general and ageless wisdom become dimly apparent. The sliding scale between the great world and the small differs from medieval cosmologies in allowing our human visionaries to become creators both of what is larger and what is more minuscule than they are.

It is interesting to note how easily the habit of linguistic dissociation and the bracketing of part from whole leads not only to little splinter worlds, as in Peter Everwine's "Night Letters" ("I wanted *salt* to be a woman again, / and *stone* to lose its stubbornness"), but also to the belief that each small world *is* the cosmos, the vines the trail of the wind, the bones the universe. And if the small can be the large, the reverse is equally possible. In these poems where the body is a world and the world a body, the poets rise from or dissolve into a landscape, river, ice floe, or cavernous night that are themselves mirrors of the self. Unlike Paul Breslin, who is interested in the way the "deep image" poets fasten on "stones and bones" in order to get at the primeval and archetypal, I am more struck by the feature in all of these poets of a Stevensian expansion or efflorescence of consciousness.[6] As many of the excerpts above indicate, the poets turn as Stevens does from the perceiving self *in* a place to the perceiving self *as* a place. Constance Urdang:

> Cushioning my bones
> from the bones of the hills
> my shawl of flesh
> a scarf of hair

Urdang in a wittier mood, here using the phallus as the light of the world:

> At nightfall, a man raises
> his 'little glass'
>
> In letters of fire, he reads in it
> that he is a man
>
> On the steep blue walls
> the mosaic of his life

Peter Everwine, shifting the whole landscape into a room:

> It was autumn,
> its iron gates darkening
> with smoke and oils
>
> The face of my village
> . . . which I was given for my own
> like an empty locket
> like a mirror in a locked room

In the same class with the excerpts from Everwine and Urdang, though more closely linked to the process of perception, Strand's own light-of-the-world assertion:

> And out of my waking
> the circle of light *widens,*
> it fills with trees, houses,
> stretches of ice.
> It reaches out. It rings
> the eye with white.
> All things are one.
> All things are joined
> even beyond the edge of sight.
>
> ("White," my emphasis)

Mark Strand is more clearly indebted to Stevens than any of the poets here. The *widening* of the circle of light in "White" is reminiscent of "A Primitive Like an Orb": "The breadth of an accelerando moves, / Captives the being, widens—and was there." Mark Strand's uses of *cold, high, blaze, desire,* and *particular* also have a distinctive Stevens ring. His use of the boat in "Where Are the Waters of Childhood"—

> Now you invent the boat of your flesh and set it upon the waters
> and drift in the gradual swell, in the laboring salt.
> Now you look down. The waters of childhood are there,

—is prettier, quieter, more "solved," but definitely less majestic than the same symbol in Stevens's "Prologues to What Is Possible":

> There was an ease of mind that was like being alone in a boat at sea
> . . . .
> The boat was built of stones that had lost their weight and being no
>   longer heavy
> Had left in them only brilliance, of unaccustomed origin,
> So that he that stood up in the boat leaning and looking before him
> Did not pass like someone voyaging out of and beyond the familiar.
> . . . .

As if all his hereditary light were suddenly increased
By an access of color, a new and unobserved, slight dithering . . .

And in "The Garden," Strand invokes some of Stevens' most famous phrases; the "it" in Strand is not identified, but we might safely read something like "memory" or "radiance":

And when my father bends
to whisper in her ear,
when they rise to leave
and the swallows dip and soar
and the moon and stars
have drifted off together, it shines.

Even as you lean over this page,
late and alone, it shines; even now
in the moment before it disappears.

Vanishing and vacancy—the whole ephemera of sight—are recognizable themes of Stevens. So is the image of the reader "late and alone":

The house was quiet and the world was calm.
The reader became the book . . .
. . . .
The quiet was part of the meaning, part of the mind:
The access of perfection to the page.

And the world was calm. The truth in a calm world,
In which there is no other meaning, itself

Is calm, itself is summer and night, itself
Is the reader leaning late and reading there.

Strand's "The Garden" uses the terms of leaning late and reading there, but the discipline of his poem is much more guarded than Stevens's, and has that tentative, terse use of careful particulars (with their lovely, surprising consonants, *brim, gravel, redwood, tangled, dip and soar, drifted, page*) that we find in Wallace Stevens's middle poems (see "The Reader," for example).

Now, the point of the comparison of Strand and Stevens is, I hope, not the invidious deflation of the one by the monumental example of the other, but the illustration of Stevens as one of the models whom recent poets can and have taken and made into a *manner*—a manner of expression, first of all, that is faintly hieratic in tone and mixed in diction. Where Strand is concerned, I think the borrowing of Stevens's expressive manner has been considerably softened and beautified and made to sound less mixed, as in "For Her" from *The Late Hour,* a far more elegant and less repetitive portrait of the eternal feminine than Stevens's Nanzia Nunzio:

> She will appear,
> looking like someone you knew:
> the friend who wasted her life,
>
> the girl who sat under the palm tree.
> Her bracelets will glitter,
> becoming the lights
>
> of a village you turned from years ago.

And at the same time that palm tree and the sweetly surprising conflation of bracelets with village lights are more purely haunting than Stevens's version in *Notes Toward a Supreme Fiction,* Strand's "For Her" is also a severely limited lyric when set against Stevens's "Farewell to Florida." Thus, even though Strand purifies his poetry of certain symbolist crudities, he deprives it of a possible range of tone that could lead to magnificence. Strand is too carefully uniform.

The second sort of *manner* in contemporary poets in which we can see the model of Stevens at work is the use of the older poet's habits of thought and perception, his characteristic analogies that turn the world into sight, transparency, "the vernacular of light," leading to the sharing of selfhood between mind and world. I would compare Stevens's idea that "In the wind, the voices / Have shapes that are not yet fully themselves" to Mark Strand's admonition in "The Man in the Tree" (*Reasons for Moving,* 1968) that "Things are not only themselves in this light." But where Stevens's lines are spoken from a point *within* the process of becoming, Strand's line, which takes up the manner of this subject, is spoken from *outside* it, as if he didn't grasp the problem yet admired and half seriously copied a certain spookiness and lightly worn, premonitory gloom vis-à-vis any other mode of being.

One is willing to grant poets their manners, to wait on them for what may come, and finally to give them credit for what they make that is their own. Strand has always *played with* nightmares, apparently testing the quality of the echo when his voice is set free of responsibilities. He very seldom makes mistakes, but that may be a fragile achievement.

Louise Glück

In thinking about the inwardness Strand and other bemused perceptualists suggest without embodying, one naturally turns to artists more adept at feeling their way past words into the worlds they project. One such artist is the Polish fabric sculptor Magdalena Abakanowicz (b. 1930). For a sense of her work one can view the photographs, published by Jonathan Brent in *TriQuarterly 53* (Winter 1982), of the seated "Backs" installed along the river Vistula near Warsaw, and of the "Heads" and the astounding round-ripe world of the "Embryology" assembly. Mary Jane Jacob, curator of the Museum of Contemporary Art in Chicago, credits Abakanowicz with having stimulated the enormous international experiment with fibers as a sculptural medium in the past two decades—all the more reason to attend to her haunting and seminal work.

As haunting for me are the prose vignettes, brief memoirs, and intense meditations in which Magdalena Abakanowicz projects her preoccupation with touch and explains her past: the mother who was at once stiff and soft, beautiful, clever, dissatisfied at having no son (she was to suffer horribly during the war); the father brave, aristocratic (part Russian, part Pole, part Tartar), historically haunted, distant; and Magdalena herself, fearful of being put under obligation by the adult world. She presents herself as a person to whom public behaviors, including speech as well as the decorum of music and graceful movement, were overbearing in their inscrutability. Characteristically, she responded to culture with subliminal offerings. She tells in one vignette how she brought her treasures collected from the woods, fields, and ponds inside their stone manor to constellate themselves before a dark mural of an armored knight with four horses. Slowly her objects came to life. "This took time . . . it turned into a dance. I was inside it." She communes with a natural world in which truths can be "accumulated without control, direction, or pattern."

> With a long pole, I pushed a wooden canoe into the reeds. Without a thought I became one with the murmurs of the time of day and with this whole world of movement and stillness, growth and decay. There I belonged. With concentration, for hours I looked at the grass and the water. I wanted to subordinate myself to them, so that I might understand the mysteries that separated me from them.

She collected twigs, bark, pebbles, threads, shriveled potatoes. Her dearest possession was a penknife. She was alone.

> Time was capacious, roomy; leaves grew slowly, and slowly changed their shape and color. Everything was immensely important. All was at one with me.
>
> The country was full of strange powers. Apparitions and inexplicable forces had their laws and spaces. I remember *Poludnice* [female ghosts said to appear on hot days at noon] and *Zytnie Baby* [rye hags]. Whether I had ever seen them, I cannot say; in the hamlet peasant women talked about them.

At another point in her *Portrait,* Abakanowicz actually remembers a little man the size of an acorn who scurries out from under a tussock. On another day, this secret and homely apparition:

> A transparent, large *Poludnica* was shimmering in the sun, in that terribly hot air in which it seems impossible to breathe. One could think about her, imagine her, but one must not look. With the whole body one felt the danger of being in the open fields at high noon.[7]

It becomes clear that the knowledge Magdalena Abakanowicz gained as a child was tactile, emotional, and cosmic—of a sort that retards and attenuates the values if not the skills associated with rational, categorical, and verbal development. Her superstitions are neither acquired nor chic. Her self-consciousness is transitive and pure. Her use of rhetoric is at once direct and lax, owing to her choice of another extensional realm for living out her thought about self, experience, and the tissue of being. She can and does exist *elsewhere* than in the literature she can create about herself—a fact we can acknowledge with pleasure only because she has happened to turn the light of words on moments like this (from the prose sketch also called "Embryology," printed entire in *TriQuarterly 53* with the photographs of the assembly by the same name):

> I was very little. Crouching over the edge of a marshy pond, I observed tadpoles. Enormous, about to be transformed into frogs. They were swarming by the bank. Through the fine membranes covering their distended stomachs one could clearly see the tangle of their guts. They were replete with the process of transformation, sluggish. They were tempting you to reach out for them. When they were pulled out with a stick onto the bank or inadvertently touched, their bulging bellies split and the contents leaked out in a confusion of knots. In a minute flies fell upon them. My heart was beating fast. I sat there shaken by what was happening.

One is instantly struck by the difference between Abakanowicz's early vision of "soft" (her word) and vulnerable fecundity and an essentially self-dramatizing vision like that in Seamus Heaney's "Death of a Naturalist" (1966), a poem about the ominous maturation of frog spawn into obscenely farting "great slime kings . . . gathered there for vengeance" against the boy who had stolen jars of the "warm thick slobber . . . of jellied specks" from the flax-dam. Heaney's poetic constructs are theatrically masculine, projecting as they do tableaux of confrontation and revenge in which the tropes of personification and a mythified allegory are prominent. As a vernacular Irishman fighting against English literary decorum, Heaney brandishes the devices studied at greater length in the chapter below—the kenning, accentual meters, a verbally replete world of textured particulars, and a self-consciously clabbering effect in his diction.

Whereas Heaney is undeniably influenced by his country boyhood, Abakanowicz is constantly being invaded anew by earth, childhood, the speechless passage of time in the cycles of the leaf, and the sluggish-transparent complexity of animal and plant tissue, of fluids and blood. Heaney writes about a nature so idiosyncratically textured by his description of it as to fade before the dazzling language in which it is realized. Abakanowicz, although not a poet, suggests an experience of nature closed to those who write, a nature that is prerational, prescientific, prelinguistic, which stands there shimmering with power, danger, and untouched, seducing form.

This is the nature Louise Glück aspires to enter, experience, and bring forward to us by allusion. It seems to me that Glück also wishes, like Magdalena Abakanowicz, to empty-out, take attention away from, words; at least the poet wishes to use this act of self-abnegation as a gesture and appearance in her work, which shines with the strain of refusal. To think of Louise Glück's poetry as the aesthetic-linguistic counterpart to the blunt, rapt, tongueless imagination of Abakanowicz moves me very far into Glück's poetry and permits a certain access of sympathy for the poet's deprived, harmed, stammering beings. For me, even the Polish sculptor's reverence for twigs, fibers, and stones, assembled so as to kindle into life their secret patterns, casts real illumination on the American poet's talismans. Glück writes of the sun's "cold plumage"; of the gods walking down the mountains "in their cloaks of feathers"; of the wool scarves of the drowned children; of their brilliantly colored overcoats; of the sexually exorbitant and enameled hues of flowers; of light and shade as intentionally woven fabrics; of her little dead sister's "head covered with black feathers." Glück toys in a grim way with the alien quality of one's own skin, so close to being fake fur, feathers, or hide, yet so near to the tender organs and conduits it shelters (heart, eye, genitals, veins.).

So at the same time that the personae of Louise Glück's poems are abstracted from their physical frame, they are peculiarly vulnerable to the slightest bruise from beyond. Her hints about the anorexia she may have endured as a child would emphasize both impulses, toward empty imperviousness and painful deterioration. This dichotomy of character and experience is in turn reflected in a dichotomy of language. The poet's diction is marked by an adjectival form whereby a Latinate, perhaps more dryly abstract term is yoked with a Germanic, more stubbornly concrete term. The now famous example is from "The Drowned Children," where a voice calls to the children from over Glück's shoulder:

> What are you waiting for
> come home, come home, lost
> in the waters, blue and permanent.

As in the larger descriptive milieu of many, many poems of hers, the combination of *blue* and *permanent* suggests a visual tableau of the frozen will, the iced-over and paralyzed libido. Glück clearly cultivates this intensely visual aspect in order to link the psychological interior with a quasi-natural externalized landscape; the link serves to relieve the inevitable claustrophobia of her theme, and to give her an ampler descriptive palette. The adjectives *blue* and *permanent* cut and nudge one another, neither by itself particularly resonant or evocative, but together creating an uneasily shifting compound of interreferential qualities that did not exist in isolation. This synergy between the two members is also at work even when etymology is not so divergent. "The Drowned Children" has two further examples of idiosyncratic descriptive doubling, "the pond lifts them in its *manifold dark* arms," "As though they had always been / *blind and weightless*" (my emphasis). It may not be merely a post hoc rationalization that would see in "manifold arms" alone a Shiva-like grotesquerie, which the addition of "dark" helps to soften.

In the second example, Glück has made explicit the current cultural-poetic dialect of sensibility in which blindness and airiness, vacancy and luminosity are equated. Soon enough, readers of poetry will look back at work like this and read the phrase "blind and weightless" as redundant. It is for this reason that she is studied as a fellow traveler with Strand and the lyrical school of perceptualists; for even if Glück has no immediate links with Stevens rhetorically or prosodically, she has established her aesthetics on a basis Stevens in part makes possible—that of the poetic seer who makes the world spring into relief, even (or, especially) in failing to maintain its contours for very long.

One saw earlier in Glück's 1975 volume *The House on Marshland* how the yoked-opposites method of description was gathering head, and how, in almost every case, a vulnerable attribute is brought next to a powerful one: There, the dead waited "lucid and helpless"; a "you" poised above the deer "wounded and dominant"; angels were called "burnished, literal"; the walls of a child's room were "spruce and silence"; and, continuing the noun variant of the yoke-idea, limbs aimed to be free of both "blossom and subterfuge." In the volume centrally featured here, *Descending Figure* (New York: Ecco Press, 1980), a quick selection of the trope shows a screened porch in youth filled with "a gold, magnetic light." Her little son now plays in cold weather among "the brown, degraded bushes"—a striking denigration. Finally, the sea of yearning and desire is said to be "false" like "all that is fluent and womanly." This last example reinforces the tension twice, first by pairing two words that are alike in rhythm and degree of softness but different in derivation (the Latinate *fluency* with the Germanic *womanly*), then by alliterating (a force for similitude and parallel) words of opposing sentiment and tone (*fluent* with *false*). Whereas the phrase "blind and weightless" might be thought predictable in the context of the poetry of the past two decades, Glück's *false* sounded against her womanly *fluent* is a case of her own more homegrown and ingrown obsession with ghostly lives. Here falsehood and fluency adjoin one another just as vulnerability alternates with oblivion and periods of hunger with those of coma.

The movements I imply from sin to absolution, deceit to candor, and hunger to death are in truth Louise Glück's own movements and implications. For her the preconditions of transcendence—and again Stevens can be imagined in the background, framing this aesthetics of relinquishment—are the denial, the flaw, the act of stepping outside the human community in promulgating defiantly aberrant perceptions. In the most powerful poetry of *Descending Figure,* the suite of "Lamentations," which Helen Vendler suggests are about the beginnings of religion, the poet appears to have raised to the level of cult her sense of being watched by the world she thinks. Of course poems like "The Logos" are part of the deliberate gnosticism and an organized profanation that powerfully distinguish Glück from the school of Stevens:

THE LOGOS

They were both still
the woman mournful, the man
branching into her body.

But God was watching

. . . .
Who knew what he wanted?
He was god, and a monster.
So they waited. And the world
filled with his radiance,
as though he wanted to be understood.
Far away, in the void that he had shaped,
he turned to his angels.

Does the deity turn to his angels to speak? to command, praise, or announce? Possibly. In every situation, familial or divine, the poet only shadows the relation of powerless to powerful—that frozen-tableau quality again. We do not, at any rate, hear what God might then have said. His *turn* functions, more characteristically, as a gesture both of denial (like the dangerous father who in other poems could hurt the daughter if he wanted to) and of sexual preference (this shadowy divinity turns aside to live with angels as Whitman planned to do with the creatures, in warm animality).

When I speculate about the emotion to which "The Logos" directs us, I am reminded how powerfully the language of rising and pooling is made to figure in the book. Here in part one of "Lamentations" the world has filled with radiance as if light were a fluid. In part two of "Lamentations," "A forest rose from the earth," and in part four God again "arose." Womanliness, as we saw earlier, is linked to fluency. The human body is often placed beside water, made analogous to vessels, pails, and pools. The human face is metonymy for the mirror in which it appears, floating up to the surface; in turn such a metonymy of face and eyes for mirrors points to a more interesting metonymic translation, of mirror into memory or consciousness. Glück's poem "Swans" is a crucial text for these gliding journeys from a physical element to a mental and emotional tissue. The narrative "I" addresses a married man, presumably craving his separation from his wife. Both wife and female speaker are transfixed by the mysterious dream image of the man summoning bridal swans to "settle on the scaled water"—"scaled" being the dream's term for the rigid, formalized frills of Glück's own postures, diction, and imagery. The wife is frozen before this scene of dread:

> I saw her motionless before your gift:
> always the swans glide unmenacing across
> the rigid blue of the Pacific Ocean, then rise
> in a single wave, pure white and devouring.

This grim denouement in which *rise* bespeaks the desire for a sweeping-away of her enemy, is stylized, as it were painted, hence oddly dwarfed in significance. Like a hawk mantling over its kill, the poet fans the symbolic wing of a cruel ascendancy over another: She summons that single curling wave. But the movement is smooth, oriental, balletic, and finally not very far removed from the verbal gestures in which Glück usually conveys hope, weariness, joy, or relief.

In "Swans," those tags of the stylized stillness of large waters (the odd peach color of the sky "from which the sea withdrew, bearing / its carved boats: your bodies were like that," "The horizon burned," and "The sea lay mild as a pool") resemble the poem "Happiness" in their noncommittal, clipped declarative fragmentation, their expression of visual impulse as somatic response, and their faint personifying transfers. In "Swans," "the sea lay mild," in "Happiness," the sunlight pools. Liquefaction is a quietly tenacious image source in each, and must cause us to think that, if this be happiness, it is in few ways preferable to dread:

> A man and woman lie on a white bed.
> It is morning. I think
> *Soon they will waken.*

On the bedside table is a vase
of lilies; sunlight
pools in their throats.
I watch him turn to her
as though to speak her name
but silently, deep in her mouth—
At the window ledge,
once, twice,
a bird calls.
And then she stirs; her body
fills with his breath.

("Happiness")

Following this first stanza, in which the fluid of breath and passion
rises in the lungs and throat to the mouth, Glück turns in the second to
her prevailing associations of liquid with pools at which the questing soul
leans to peer. Over the man's shoulder, an ominous Jacobean Sol pointedly keeps his distance from the lovers:

I open my eyes; you are watching me.
Almost over this room
the sun is gliding.
Look at your face, you say,
holding your own close to me
to make a mirror.
How calm you are. And the burning wheel
passes gently over us.

("Happiness")

At the muffled exclamation, "How calm you are," I imagine the eyes,
opened reflectors, to fill with tears, to glaze. The gliding and passing of
the sun on its effortless keel is cognate with the opening of the gaze, the
window/mirror magic between intimates, and the profound (*pools, deep,
fills*) physical reply. But the body and the consciousness are never at ease
in these offerings. Passion is always constrained, perception always something both passive and appalled, in the poetry of Glück. Her landscapes,
far from encouraging the emergence of some other spirit world, are tortu-
ous and haunting psychological projections—lunar landscapes both hopeless and furious. Louise Glück freely acknowledges the paralysis of will
from which her poetry can be said in both senses to *suffer:*

And pain, the free hand, changes almost nothing.
Like the winter wind, it leaves
settled forms in the snow. Known, identifiable—
except there are no uses for them.

("World Breaking Apart")

These are the words of someone who may not be able to continue in the same bleak vein without bowing to that uselessness and embracing hermetic silence. It is instructive that in her next two books, Glück would turn to Greek and Hebrew myth for a way out of this dire and intensely seen environment of bereavement.

II. The Perceptual Sublime

Ted Hughes

In contrast to the poets in the first perceptual group, whose images and preoccupations suggest a permeability between self and world, Ted Hughes is a poet whose boundaries are broad and definite. His poetry is full to bursting with textures and things for which he is the only true interpreter. Hence the issue of border and transgression and *struggle against* is raised in a way it seldom is by Ammons, Glück, or Strand. For all that, and although Ted Hughes does tend toward the cumulus method of composition—piling one metaphor, one impression, one quality on top of another—still he gives the impression relative to much contemporary poetry that a greater part of the keyboard available to the poet is being used. And, being British, he provides an opportunity for testing the pertinence of the concept of a perceptual sublime in a body of work in which Stevens will have exercised a less telling direct influence than has one of Stevens's shadow-forebears, Whitman. Even in the Hughes poems before the volume on which I shall concentrate, *River*[8] (when he begins to indent and drop lines—a practice that gives a new breathing room and dilation to the logical possibilities of lineation), Hughes is virtually incapable of writing tired free verse. His secret is, despite generally repeating grammatical structures (like a pattern of simple or, at most, compound declaration), to vary the armature of the individual phrase, so that even in one of the most programmatic poems in *River*, "An Eel," the lines seem fresher than the ideas give them leave to be:

> Eerie the eel's head.
> This full, plum-sleeked fruit of evolution.
> Beneath it, her snout's a squashed slipper-face,
> The mouth grin-long and perfunctory,
> Undershot predatory. And the iris, dirty gold
> Distilled only enough to be different
> From the olive lode of her body,
> The grained and woven blacks.

The sentence frame is minimal—noun fragment and pale copula—but the changing position of adjective relative to noun (which in turn affects the work done by metaphor), in addition to the place of the main noun relative to approaching or just-turned line boundary, and that flurry of logicizing adverbs ("only enough to"), give the set-piece unusual surface flexibility. When Hughes moves from such essay-poems-on-assigned-subjects (as he confesses the early "View of a Pig" to be) to the poems in which various speakers participate, he opens to a much more complex instrumentation.

I would not be misunderstood to praise the poet's use of familiar perso-nae, for he is still relatively young at the gentler tonalities that make for interesting conversational or meditative poetry. His real discoveries in the mode of personal lyric occur in *The Remains of Elmet* (1979), a far more subtle and attractive suite of poems than has been acknowledged. *River* is more monolithic in its subject and address, although in one clever exception the speaker contests the fishing rights of a cormorant and, clumsy, out-of-sorts, and empty-handed, makes this angrily decorous self-deprecation: "I . . . pray / With futuristic, archaic under-breath / So that some fish, telepathically overpowered, / Will attach its incomprehension / To the bauble I offer to space in general." The last three lines, with their airy displacements of quality and their skillful admission of lack of fishing skill, are as far removed as can be from the cumulus method of "An Eel," and serve as a stylistic measure of what we might expect in the way of range from the rest of the volume.

River is a collection in praise of the rivers where the poet/countryman/ farmer has fished. The descriptive flavor of the verse thus alters consider-ably as Hughes moves from the West Dart to the Dee and the Isle of Skye to an ominous river called the Gulkana in Alaska—and indeed the descriptive gift of Hughes is still a marvelous thing to see. On Skye, a little "clatterbrook" (referring at once to its sound and to his hurry across it) proves a stream so meager and shallow it doesn't even resemble water, instead "a hurry of shallow grey light so / distilled it looked like acid." These rivers, running as they do along the land, on occasion are described in terms of the life around them, as if the poet had set out to compose a geographical companion volume to the diaristic farm poems in *Moortown* (1979). The cattle come down to wade and "lift muzzles / That unspool the glair," their "Dark bodies dense with boiling light." When we cannot see cattle, lambs, and primroses, we catch sight of a landscape more famil-iar, as where a small channel crawls "Under / The mill-wall, with bicycle wheels, car-tyres, bottles / And sunk sheets of corrugated iron"; here a half-dead spawning salmon hangs in his tatters: "People walking their dogs trail their evening shadows across him. / If boys see him they will try to kill him" ("October Salmon").

There is a sort of mythic treatment that we identify with the galvanic harshness of this poet, the mode of *Crow* (1970) and *Cave Birds* (1978). Hughes mesmerizes his speakers, working them into a state of half-idle, horizonless trance, as if to enable himself and us to overhear the music made by the almost unearthly waterways. The primal power coursing through these rivers sometimes throws off a metal splinter or cold spark in the form of a salmon or trout. In many respects, the fish are the thoughts of the fisherman, just as the rivers are the medium of his thought, whether the stream of his consciousness or the flood of daydream that flushes and freshens consciousness from unconscious sources. In one of his broadcasts for children, the poet described fishing as a way of training the mind far more effective than going to school. The alchemical nuance at the end of this description is quite lovely, where the "living metal" (the poem) is raised like a fish out of darkness. He is arguing that fishing is anything but "drowsy":

> Your whole being rests lightly on your float, but not drowsily: very alert, so that the least twitch of the float arrives like an electric shock. And you are not only watching the float. You are aware, in a horizonless and slightly mesmerized way, like listening to the double bass in orchestral music, of the fish below there in the dark. At every moment your imagination is alarming itself with the size of the thing slowly leaving the weeds and approaching your bait. Or with the world of beauties down there, suspended in total ignorance of you. And the whole purpose of this concentrated excitement, in this arena of apprehension and unforeseeable events, is to bring up some lovely solid thing like living metal from a world where nothing exists but those inevitable facts which raise life out of nothing and return it to nothing.[9]

During the physically taxing fishing episodes of the *River* poems, the shock of a deeper colder current, not to mention the anticipated tug of a hidden heavy creature on the bait, come at once as a deepening of the consciousness, and as a wrenching of thought out of the ordinary round. These are journeys to a relentlessly foreign but inevitable interior world— for in the last pool, at the final hour, in an ultimate confrontation between the old and new selves, the speaker enters a Shelleyan penumbra of electrified Power. As a matter of fact, electricity and its cohort, manufacture, are curiously persistent sources of metaphor. For the boy raised in central England, where the mills of the Victorians scarred the hills as the steeples of their chapels pierced the skies, the metaphor of the "living metal" is bound to have an infernal appeal. Accordingly, there is nothing the least artificial, visually or ecologically, about the flowing water enfolded with the flint, iron, slag, magnets, corrugations, and currents of the giant trance of progress.

Quite naturally, the first poem in the book suggests that electrical-manufacturing nexus; the "core-flash" of the sun issues in a product—a "smelting"—which is in fact the liquid river. The surface of the water acts as a "mill" or "generator / Making the atoms dance." It makes a "magnetic descent" like a "mercury creature" whose "Flesh" is "Light" (as the title has it): Calmly, the living creatures and the metal turbine commune, for this is the river broken by the wading cattle, their "Dark bodies dense with boiling light." In a very fine descriptive poem, "Four March Watercolours," the blue river is seen as "a daze of bubbly fire" with an "intricate engine" revolving "full-bore" beneath its surface. Later in the same poem, echoing "Flesh of Light," a ewe lowers herself "To the power-coils / Of the river's bulge." Elsewhere the river is seen as the fish's life-support, the "peculiar engine / That made it and keeps it going" (reminiscent of the trout in *Wodwo* "thoroughly made of dew, lightning and granite").

The most majestic and sustained and eerie of all the poems about cosmic power pouring through the geological realm, and one that evokes the poetic energies of poems stretching as far back in Ted Hughes's career as "Wind" (1957), "Mayday on Holderness" and "Pike" (1960), and the *Wodwo* poem I quoted from above, "Stealing Trout on a May Morning" (1967), is "The Gulkana." The poem is set in a landscape (Alaska) so alien and upsetting that the speaker is almost literally driven out of his skin by the strange and lurid portents. The light is peculiarly colored, somewhere between rust and purple, and the photons seem constantly to jump and re-form. Pebbles are dislodged and the grinding shore scree alongside the Gulkana river disturbed by a "perpetual seismic tremor," and the sound of the water is horrible, "a deranging cry / From the wilderness" that "burst past us— / A stone voice that dragged at us." Fish too large to be eaten are "relaunched," "magnetized / Into the furnace boom of the Gulkana." These mating fish, like "seraphs of heavy ore" in this "hypnagogic" mineral landscape—and truly, one is enveloped by the mastery of the expression—are also weirdly possessed "By that voice in the river" which is accompanied by drumming and flutes from an unidentified source. With their "mulberry-dark torsos" and "gulping sooted mouths" and eyes like "glassy visors," "small, crazed, snake-like,"

> Bliss had fixed their eyes
> Like an anaesthetic
> . . . .
> And they rose and sank
> Like voices, like singers themselves
> In its volume

Later, these "drugged ritual victims" who were also "Aboriginal Americans," having reached their mating pools, would engage in a dance of utter body yet of ultimate disembodiment, their "Bellies riven open and poured empty / Into a gutter of pebbles,"

> The dance-orgy of being reborn
> From which the masks and regalia drift empty,
> Torn off—their very bodies,
> In the numbed, languorous frenzy, as obstacles,
> Torn off—
>   ecstasy dissolving
> In the mercy of water, at the star of the source,
> Devoured by revelation
>
> A thin wind off the peak of a mountain
>
> Every molecule drained, and counted, and healed
> Into that amethyst—
>
> I came back to myself

The narrative self comes back to the present, but only as a "spectre of fragments," sipping hot coffee in the plane en route home, thinking "a small boy held it, / Making its noise." In a very Laurentian finale, the profoundly shaken speaker relives the omens like someone who is "love-sick," for some reason fastening on the face of the Indian guide, at once utterly mysterious and utterly small and horrid, "his face / A whole bat, that glistened and stirred." Here "The Gulkana" ends. The poem, sinister and at times rambling and apparently unfocused, nevertheless as a whole moves and convinces, in part owing to the *successfully* provisional and unpolished jaggedness of its surfaces.

What is it the poem convinces us about? the "sincerity" of the speaker? the accuracy of the picture of the place? Yes, but these are less critical than the achieved impression of the landscape—its constant "bombard-ment / Of purplish emptiness." And with the visual and spiritual impres-sion of this inhuman, prehistoric place, Hughes has also set out to recap-ture something of a prehistoric sense of awe before earth and creature, without capitulating either to his own orgiastic vocabulary of egg-and-sperm or to any faked Jungian prattle, although each temptation makes itself felt. On the other hand, the sportsman's lexicon turns out to be the most expressive of helplessness and holy fear; their tackle merely "scratched the windows of the express torrent"—a metaphor that renders mechanical speed, glassiness, the blur of the river's headlong passing, also the unpleasant scrape of metal against glass, which is part of the sluggish ghoulishness to which their moods perversely vibrate: "We seemed under-powered. Whatever we hooked / Bent in air."

The least successful part of the 135-line "Gulkana" (145 if one counts dropped lines twice) is the most packed with information about the experience the narrator goes through. I can see good cause for something of this kind at this point in the poem without feeling obliged to approve or praise the 19-line nugget of explanations like "I felt hunted. / I tested my fear. It seemed to live in my neck. . . . And in my eye / That felt blind somehow to what I stared at / As if it stared at me . . . some disinherited being / And *Doppelgänger* other, unliving / Ever-living, a larva from prehistory . . . who watched me fiddling with my gear—the interloper, / The fool he had always hated," and so forth. Early on in "The Gulkana" he inveighs against "the stagnation toxins / Of a cultural vasectomy." Perhaps the poet does not believe anything will damage the credibility of his tale, but I find my own access to the world of the poem hindered by such garrulous tactics. Even in Hughes's brief poems, the hasty effects of skimover writing can be discerned.

The poet may have fallen victim to an enchantment endemic to the seer. His oracular program for living in the modern world becomes the measure of value for the poem, so that there is no longer any defense against his own demagoguery. Of course one can only speculate about the state of mind that permits such indulgence, yet I cannot help thinking there is something deludedly regal about it, as if a monarch were laboring to record for the people the text of his thought, inscribing the diaries of his passing moment. So bound up is his well-being with that of the land that he is duty-bound to remain continuously apprised of his own condition—to coincide verbally with himself.

Instead, therefore, of collections of poems crafted on different occasions with differing ends in view, the work of such a figure is more in the nature of one continuous poem in which repetitions are not only frequent, but also expected. Thus in *River* it is no surprise that metaphors of electrical energy and machine-power occur in a dozen settings, that the spawning fish is shown at least ten times in its lepercloths, jester's badges, and trailing regalia, "sacred with lichens," that a state of blank euphoria, ritual bliss, or fading consciousness is often climactic, and that the same rough liberties are taken over and over again with the same kinds of words and word-clusters (e.g., the use of "plasm" and "spasm" and "supple" as verbs; the accordion-pleating of double-epithet pairings). Not only does the regal self repeat, he also interrupts himself, follows a tangent and gets lost, forces information upon the text, or shrugs the enterprise casually aside, these being the prerogatives of someone who cannot err. Imperfection and provisionality are thus necessary signals, not merely of the misbehaving modernism of the work, but of the inevitable harmonies of informality— neither Hughes nor Wallace Stevens, after all, is writing either *paysage moralisé* or a nicely behaved descriptive-meditative lyric with proper landscapes. Hughes thus continues and extends the antitraditional approach by which, like Stevens, he hopes to obtain our assent to his role as accurate spiritual barometer in this oddly featured realm, and to our recognition of Hughes as something between a guide and a lightning rod receiving emanations from the world hidden from many but not from our self-appointed representative there.

Robert Pinsky

If the work of Robert Pinsky belongs to any "genre," it would be one that combines the processional and encyclopedic with the ecstatic and affirmative. Something visionary also fuels the whole. In these respects, he belongs squarely with the "Messianic Romantics" like Ben Belitt and Ted Hughes.[10] Perhaps this "genre" is a contemporary version of the romantic masque or triumph (which Shelley kept alive for Swinburne and T. S. Eliot). In Robert Pinsky's address to the "triumph" with its sabbath gathering of motley spirits from myth and time, however, we discover too the homemade ciphers of bittersweet joy, some flirtatious, others horrific, that make up part of this extraordinary poet's eccentric cast of mind. The blending of the parodic with the elegiac, of the commonplace with the lofty, which is to say the blending of high with low tonality that hypothetically characterizes the modernism of Pound, Eliot, and Stevens, appears in *History of My Heart* and *The Want Bone*[11] with a rightness and an urgency unmatched by any poet of Pinsky's generation, and with a naturalness and even a sweetness we never feel in any modernist poet but Stevens (and then, usually unmixed with the puckishness Stevens really left behind him after *Harmonium*). Robert Pinsky is more determined than Wallace Stevens ever was to maintain an exalted serenity while chafing against the infatuated circularities of the period of adolescence. Other poets have admired the whimsical; Pinsky takes the further risk of embracing the gauche.

But that formulation offends against the subtlety with which this poet concatenates the rhetorical web. For despite Pinsky's enamorment with farce and self-deprecation, he has, curiously and cannily in his aesthetic career, overcome the kinds of self-congratulation we might associate with such gleeful exposure of his own intellectual, sexual, and sentimental infatuations.

Pinsky himself offers the preliminary gloss on the genesis of his own practice in his excellent reflections on contemporary verse in *The Situation of Poetry*.[12] Here he makes an attractive argument for the virtues of prose in poetry. In fact the approximations and tentative maneuvers of writers like A. R. Ammons, Mark Strand, and Ted Hughes are accounted for and even extolled by Pinsky's embrace of the "prose freedom and prose inclusiveness" of the modernist tradition. The modernist poets he has in mind are T. S. Eliot, William Carlos Williams, and Wallace Stevens:

> I have in mind a range of passages in which the dull plains of description or the exactions of the "image" are not abandoned, but transcended: the poet claims the right to make an interesting remark or to speak of profundities, with all of the liberty given the newspaper editorial, a conversation, a philosopher, or any speaker whatever. (P. 27)

That is (to put it mildly) a wide range of idiom, from the undefined conversation to the highly delimited address of a philosopher—so wide that one might doubt the reach of the covering term. But modernism's democratic spirit makes little of the distinction between compressed and dilated forms. That all these prose possibilities could be part of one aesthetic mentality is anything but evident—until one supplies (as Robert Pinsky persistently does) the postromantic desire for transcendence over the contingent world. In the service of this ideal, many quite unideal tactics are permitted.

There is one poet who has been more successful than most at muddling through contingent and unideal landscapes with a copy of *Harmonium* in his pocket. Perhaps the scrappiest burrower, the most ingenious mingler of idioms, and the most elusive generally of the poets to inherit the glass cape of modernism is the shadowy John Ashbery.[13] I may be mistaken in believing that Robert Pinsky is haunted by John Ashbery; there is no mistaking that he is haunted by one of Ashbery's angels, Wallace Stevens. But then, it is ennobling to be drawn by Stevens's hypnotic and sacramental meditations on being, especially at a sufficient remove that one is always involved in one of those special gaps of time and sensibility of which Nabokov writes: "It is a question of focal adjustment, of a certain distance that the inner eye thrills to surmount, and a certain contrast that the mind perceives with a gasp of perverse delight."[14] It is just such a thrilling curtailment of scale between himself and Stevens, while maintaining the categorical interval between them, which Robert Pinsky explores in lines like these from *History of My Heart:*

> (a)   And Summer turns her head with its dark tangle
> All the way toward us; and the trees are heavy,
> With little sprays of limp green maple and linden
> Adhering after a rainstorm to the sidewalk
> Where yellow pollen dries in pools and runnels.
>
> ("Ralegh's Prizes")

(b)   The living, the unfallen lords of life,
      Move heavily through the dazzle
      Where all things shift, glitter or swim—

      As on a day at the beach, or under
      The stark, absolute blue of a snow morning,
      With concentric peals of brightness

      Ringing in the cold air.

                                          ("The Living")

Although more particulate and realistic than Stevens, the passages from Pinsky above personify, metaphysical-ize, indeed rhapsodize very much as Wallace Stevens does in "Large Red Man Reading," "Somnambulismo," "Page from a Tale," and in the poems excerpted below, alphabetically keyed to the passages above:

(a)   The bouquet of summer
      Turns blue and on its empty table
      It is stale and the water is discolored.
      True autumn stands then in the doorway.
                  ("Examination of the Hero in a Time of War," xvi)

(b)   The personae of summer play the characters
      Of an inhuman author. . . . He sees
      Them mottled, in the moodiest costumes,

      Of blue and yellow, sky, and sun, belted
      And knotted, sashed and seamed, half pales of red,
      Half pales of green, appropriate habit for
      The huge decorum, the manner of the time,
      Part of the mottled mood of summer's whole . . .
                                  ("Credences of Summer," x)

The end to which the metaphysical tends in Stevens is a definition of true being as it embraces self, weather, and (odd as this may seem) the seismic tremors of world event. Not merely the sum of impressions, the being derived from the world is rather an "organic centre of responses, / Naked of hindrance, a thousand crystals." Less ornamentally in a later poem, being is described as the "exactest poverty" of one's local element, as what one believes in. "What / One believes is what matters." Even if one were removed to another world where circumstances became alien and belief impossible, say to the moon, or (by implication) to a world at war (*Parts of a World* was published in 1942), one could still return at night, scourged of idea, "naked of any illusion," and be taken back into the truth:

> . . . returning from the moon, if one breathed
> The cold evening, without any scent or the shade
> Of any woman, watched the thinnest light
> And the most distant, single color, about to change,
> And naked of any illusion, in poverty,
> In the exactest poverty, if then
> One breathed the cold evening, the deepest inhalation
> Would come from that return to the subtle centre.
> ("Extracts from Addresses to the Academy of Fine Ideas," vii)

Between Pinsky and the Stevens of penetration and convergence there is a huge intellectual and temperamental difference. But one need only read the closing lines of Pinsky's title poem, "History of My Heart," to hear the broad rhetorical bond. The heart is described as

> Yearning further into giving itself into the air, breath
> Strained into song emptying the golden bell it comes from,
> The pure source poured altogether out and away.

Both passages express imaginative energy in somatic terms; even emotion-freshened affirmations like love and belief are brought into prominence with the action of breathing, as though Wallace Stevens could take in his deep and subtle knowledge with the very air, and as if Robert Pinsky could pour out his love by exhaling his musical celebration of it.

But the end to which the metaphysical serves in the younger poet's verse is un-Stevensian; Pinsky is more besotted with autobiography, to which he lends a lush and devious artifice. Through this latter trait, he brings us back to John Ashbery, who dominates his own blend of surrealism and parody with steely control and magisterial beauty in long poems like "Fragment," "The Wave," "The Skaters," "Self-Portrait in a Convex Mirror," and "Fantasia on 'The Nut-Brown Maid.'" If the surfaces of Ashbery's control are actually unreliable indicators of order and connectedness, they are nevertheless the wellsprings of its grace. The younger poet resembles him in devices of great verbal beauty that are several layers of nuance removed from coherent denotation, while elusively suggesting links to life and thought. Here is John Ashbery, followed by the extended finale of "History of My Heart."

> It would not be good to examine these ages
> Except for sun flecks, little, on the golden sand
> And coming to reappraisal of the distance.
> The welcoming stuns the heart, iron bells
> Crash through the transparent metal of the sky

Each day slowing the method of thought a little
Until oozing sap of touchable mortality, time lost and won.
. . . .
           Nothing is stationary
Nor yet uncertain; a rhythm óf standing still
Keeps us in continual equilibrium, like an arch
That frames swiftly receding clouds, never
Getting deeper. The shouts of children
Penetrate this motion toward, as a drop of water
Slides under a lens. Soon all is shining, mined,
Tears dissolving laughter, the isolated clouds spent.
                    ("Fragment," *The Double Dream of Spring,* 1976)

. . . Listen to *me,* the heart says in reprise until sometimes
In the course of giving itself it flows out of itself
All the way across the air, in a music piercing

As the kids at the beach calling from the water *Look,*
Look at me, to their mothers, but out of itself, into
The listener the way feeling pretty or full of erotic revery

Makes the one who feels seem beautiful to the beholder
Witnessing the idea of the giving of desire—nothing more wanted
Than the little singing notes of wanting—the heart

Yearning further into giving itself into the air, breath
Strained into song emptying the golden bell it comes from,
The pure source poured altogether out and away.
                              ("History of My Heart")

    The two poets have in common a drift toward auditory aspiration (the main reason, I suspect, for the word "altogether" in Pinsky, as for "rhythm" in Ashbery) placed against the clear dentals. Correlative with these auditory patterns is the faint tension between an imagery of release, efflorescence, disappearance, and airy dissolution on the one hand, and on the other the few weak counters that might have tied these floatings down (the promise of crashing and piercing—of real anecdote and locale). In both passages, the movement of consciousness is "out and away" from us toward a vaporous distance where shapes are formulated against the sky and summer is a band of children. A further support for the manifold dissolvings is the use of abstractions that sound almost like particulars. In Pinsky these are *the air, a music, the heart itself, the idea of the giving of desire, the notes of wanting, the golden bell, the . . . source,* and in Ashbery, *these ages, the distance, the welcoming, iron bells, the method of thought, a rhythm, this motion toward.* Furthermore, in at least two of these "abstract particulars," a double ambiguity is imbedded: Pinsky treats the gold bell of song and Ashbery the iron bells of welcoming as both real and analogical, the emotion suggested by each metaphor at once pressing toward embodied fact, and merely hovering over its ornamental status.

After a time this lexicon and these idioms come to look wispy and translucent, at least in Ashbery's work. W. H. Auden, in his introduction to Ashbery's *Some Trees* (Yale, 1956), reflected on the temptation to manufacture oddities "as if the subjectively sacred were necessarily and on all occasions odd." Pinsky also warns against "the horrible ease with which a stylish rhetoric can lead poetry unconsciously to abandon life itself." Thus, whatever impulse there is in Pinsky's own poems toward an Ashberian suspension of realia is balanced against a confessional urge, which he sometimes indulges with the happily ironic aplomb of Frank O'Hara, as when he recalls dancing with a girl in the back room of her parents' shop (what could be more reassuringly concrete?), with a pleased erection at the thought, *"She likes me, / She likes it,"* made happy "To see eyes 'melting' so I could think *This is it, / They're melting!"* The speaker's solipsism, however angular and unwieldy, is also crazily humorous.

Whereas in *History of My Heart* we often encounter rough mixtures of high and low, candor and artifice, self and world, *The Want Bone* produces an effect of greater concentration and intelligent ease. Ashbery would seem to be receding as an available comparison, while Stevens might be thought to come nearer. (One notes that Pinsky has long preferred Stevensian triplet stanzas.) "The Uncreation" proffers a good example of Robert Pinsky's method in his newly cleansed and pure processional mode. It is about song, its origin and its redemptive quality. But the poem is also about the narrowing encroachment of an apocalyptic time when we shall be no more and when no song shall be comprehensible. To some extent, this imminence of the song-less epoch is also a harking back to the time before life (hence the title, "Uncreation"). This idea leans with its own pathetic awe upon the heart, depressing us not only by the thought of our end, but even more so in the idea that the gods will preside over a world from which our extraordinary efforts have been removed:

> . . . after the flood the bland Immortals will come
> As holy tourists to our sunken world,
>
> To slide like sunbeams down shimmering layers of blue
> . . . .
> Until they find our books. The pages softened . . .
> Will rise at their touch in swelling plumes like smoke,
> . . . .
> And the golden beings shaping their mouths like bells
> Will impel their breath against the weight of ocean
> To sing us into the cold regard of water.
> . . . .

But the Gods will sing entirely, the towering spumes
Dissolving around their faces will be the incense
Of their old anonymity restored

In a choral blast audible in the clouds,
An immense vibration that presses the very fish,
So through her mighty grin the whale will sing

To keep from bursting, and the tingling krill
Will sing in her jaws, the whole cold salty world
Humming oblation to what our mouths once made.

                                        ("The Uncreation")

Who are these Immortals? Figures of the holocaust? Avengers of the
planet's misuse? Something at all events demonic hovers about them,
augmenting the majesty with which they command from the poet's language as from worldly creation the movements of obedient praise. Although many of Robert Pinsky's poems may begin as perceptual musings
("The Uncreation" ponders the music of quotidian inflection, "The little
tunes of begging, of coolness, of scolding"), the form he has discovered
for sending them forth in *The Want Bone* eludes the local motive in such
a way that we sense we are encountering something new—not merely in
the complete context of this poet's work, but also in contemporary poetry.
Pinsky is the manifestation of the possibility of self-dramatization without
confidentiality, and of cerebral ecstasy without abstraction. His work is
everywhere perceptually charged, utterly individual, but nowhere personal. He is eschatological but benign: Incapable of imagining cruelty, he
faces the appalling sanguinely, entertaining the archaic with an innocent
humor, or better, with the prophet's acquiescence.

Pinsky is also eager to incorporate the myths of the world's major
religions and images of the prehistoric without sacrificing any of his colloquial verve. Sometimes he fails to persuade us that the figures are authentic reformations of their models. However courageous as experi-
ments, *The Want Bone*'s "Jesus and Isolt," the inconclusive "Visions of
Daniel," and the apocryphal "Childhood of Jesus" strike one as webbed
or masked still—not yet unwound from their cloths. Of these the more
breathtaking "Jesus and Isolt" springs up after touching the lightning rod
of medieval vision literature in which the devout scribe imagines Christ
written into the indigenous mythology. Unlike the idea (we hear it in
Blake's little poem) that the feet of Christ once walked the local sward,
the attitude of Pinsky is that Christ can shed successive layers of his godhood, leaving a numinous gargoyle or ghastly metaphysical housepet for
the beautiful Isolt with her tragic and monumental passions. The poet is
fascinated by the threshold of dramaturgical identity: How much can one

change about a known character, before the essence also disappears? "I won't be bound by my own nature," Jesus had complained to his mother; so Pinsky hypothesizes that he "abandoned his divine form," altering, as he plunges down over the North Sea, into a ciclogriff: "Jesus felt the cold air split over his clenched beak, riffling through his fur, and the joyful pulse of risk and adventure was restored in him."

This extravagant parable is also another of Pinsky's attempts to meditate about the Jewish mentality, this time from the vantage of the one who lived as a marked outsider among outsiders, a god who is, furthermore, ostensibly weary of the Jews' factionalism and of the burdensomeness of their history, and wishes to discover in his new life with Tristan's Isolt "the movements and sensations of romantic love." Tristan also educates the Savior, particularly by his "bull-necked and scar-covered" exterior and precipitate physical courage: "One scar crossed his boyish face from his left temple to the corner of his mouth, and his body was a maze of puckered lines and pale indentations. In his arms was a blue harp." Both Christ and the reader are paralyzed anew with amazement at the ritualized brutality of knightly combat, with its "rules immutable as the musical scales," during which the combatants make "the ground slippery with blood" and thereafter escort one another to healing shrines. Yet for all the bizarrerie, Jesus recognizes a consanguinity between himself and the knight: "The Jewish soul of Jesus, pragmatic, ethical, logical, found in the passionate and self-defeating code of romantic love and knightly combat some of what he lacked in the jeweled pavillions of heaven." For his part,

> all that the ciclogriff told of the intrigues and sad abominations of Judea Tristan converted into poems of lofty and stylized combat. The intricate, subtle teachery of Herod Antipas, the hypocrisies bequeathed by Marc Antony to corrupt governors and wheedling catamites, perfected by rulers who as a matter of policy assassinated their sons and wives and mothers and grandmothers, Tristan took from the hooked beak of the ciclogriff and returned as highminded, repetitious lays and poems of preposterous beauty.
>
> ("Jesus and Isolt")

Clearly we are in the presence of a writer of astonishing rhetorical poise rather resembling that of García Márquez, not to mention one who has been similarly chosen for a new mode of literary achievement. Pinsky has been praised almost from his first appearance in book form as a notable poet-critic. In *The Want Bone* the critical intelligence has been absorbed and transmuted, at an earlier point in its emergence, into an imaginative elixir as bewildering as it is intoxicating.

Under its influence one registers the garrulous or familiar if no less devastating exactness of the poem called "Shirt," Pinsky's meditation on

the Triangle Shirtwaist Factory Fire that broods more generally on the
sadness of the working life and the inexorable mental enervation that
accompanies the labor of the hand. Beyond such tours de force, one
recognizes as well the blithe perfection of the waters of time flowing into
eternity in "At Pleasure Bay," the narrative of doomed love and the passage into the spirit world on the part of a police chief and a married
woman who commit their love to a suicide pact in 1927 in New Jersey
at a time when addled English aristocrats were slumming in a Berlin more
sinister and Nazi-fied each day. One of these pampered expatriots inspects
the well-furnished apartment she is about to requisition from two elderly
Jews (who eventually settle in Pleasure Bay). When the English enter the
war, this spoiled girl shoots herself, her life one that, like the lives of the
Americans Pinsky nostalgically rehearses (the Chief and Mrs. W.),
"passes / Into the lives of others or into a place." In all of these cases,
guilty or not, death metamorphoses neurosis, yearning, evil, in a dismem-
bering of its own:

> After you die
> You hover near the ceiling above your body
> And watch the mourners awhile. A few days more
> You float above the heads of the ones you knew
> And watch them through a twilight.
> . . . .
> On the other side, night air,
> Willows, the smell of the river, and a mass
> Of sleeping bodies all along the bank,
> A kind of singing from among the rushes
> . . . .
> You lie down and embrace one body, the limbs
> Heavy with sleep reach eagerly up around you
> And you make love until your soul brims up
> And burns free out of you and shifts and spills
> Down over into that other body, and you
> Forget the life you had and begin again
> On the same crossing—maybe as a child who passes
> Through the same place. But never the same way twice.
>
> ("At Pleasure Bay")

The effort to leave the earth is as mournful for the slovenly and ineffectual
as for the virtuous and active. In whatever state death finds one, Pinsky
suggests, the glowing image of love (and love-making) symbolizes the
enormity of unfulfilled and unfulfillable possibility—all one might have
been if opened out, although it would not have been the same if it were
possible to live through it again.

"At Pleasure Bay" is a poem in which the "influences" (of the American sublime; of conversation; of metaphysical lyricism; of individual inheritances like these from Stevens, Ashbery, and Whitman; and, not least, of Pinsky's tentative address to political consciousness) have been accommodated by the writer to the transformation of personal tics. Gone are the jokey demeanor and self-referentiality that keep distracting us in the earlier books. In their place is a rhetoric both sweet and serious, a thematics of longing, loss, and devotion, and an ethos of commitment, in a prosody and diction fluent as brookwater. "At Pleasure Bay" is a poem at least three poets I know confess they wish they had written. The truth that inheres in a text that commands that sort of regard will outlast any attribution of influence.

Ben Belitt

Like many of the "Messianic Romantics," but less wary of their rhetoric than either Robert Pinsky or Ted Hughes, Ben Belitt in his poems is an *isolato,* brooding over the world held at a distance, and (still at a distance) puzzling over its most attaching features. Like many romantics, he evolves a symbolism (that is, a hypertrophied preoccupation with, and stylization of, a visual and sensible pattern), which enables him to personalize and domesticate the landscape so miniaturized by removal. Belitt's most familiar and deep-seated symbol horde lies in the geological and metallurgical terminology with which he makes palpable and memorable a world in many respects outside social connection and clear of the crush of human life. Like Ted Hughes, he seems to choose the geological sublime in default of life above ground. There are precedents for this preoccupation in the poetry of continental polymaths like Goethe and Novalis; the work of Gerard Manley Hopkins naturally comes to mind; we are reminded, too, of Neruda's fondness for metallic and incendiary emblems. In fact, Belitt has remarked "Neruda's lifelong fascination with the telluric and the metallurgical."[15] But I think Belitt's fascination goes deeper, shows itself more singular and obsessive, and attaches itself to a more original and abrasive diction.

One significant difference between Belitt and either Hopkins *or* Neruda where "telluric and metallurgical" imagery is concerned is that Belitt cannot seem to shed the language of the foundry, quarry, and slagheap. This lexicon is familiar, and it is pervasive: *ash, tinder, cusp, caret, facet, magnesium, quartz, hexagon, sulphur, salt, solder, flint, hasp, trash, obsidian, helix, acidulous, wick, holocaust, glint, gelatin, disk, hive, pitchblende, boss, umber, gum, quicklime, plummet, iron, manganese, gunmetal, acetylene, steel, pewter, fuse, bitumen, brazier, pith, mica, brine, alkali, hearthbed, kin-*

dling, hod, brickdust, oil, emery, quarry, etc. Even a bog in Vermont, admittedly "uterine," soon glows metallic or trembles Vesuvian:

> . . . the disk of the pond glowed
> under the dragonfly's bosses, where a faulting
> of glaciers had left it—vaults of bog-rosemary,
> buckbean and Labrador tea, a dapple
> of leavening mosses soaking in ice-water, peat-wicks
> feeding their gas to the cranberry-braziers.[16]

Although much of the blame for the willfully skewed "reading" of the icy-wet as the molten-fiery must go to the metaphors themselves—the *gas* of *peat-wicks* being consumed in *cranberry-braziers*—still, some of the reneging from vegetal to mineral is committed by Belitt's diction (the alliteration hugely replicating itself in and distending the mouth, thereby suggesting the mastication of something substantial, even in the lighter parade of vowels: *dragon, bosses, faulting, vaults, bog, Labrador, mosses;* and indubitably imitating heavy matter in the pattern of the cognate plosive consonants *p/b: pond, bosses, bog, buckbean, Labrador, dapple, peat, cranberry, braziers*). The huge physical pleasure of saying the lines contributes to the alchemization of wet earth into mineral ornament.

If we can entertain for a moment the traditional association of the base metals with the sensuous world of unregenerate man,[17] we might conjecture that Belitt is more concerned with immanence, strife, concretion, and repetition than he is with transcendence, calm, abstraction, and unity. But in his singular "flexing" of the materials of the unregenerate world, Belitt is also attempting to bond higher to lower substance, to see toward the deep core from the surface, to witness the inner by way of the outer world. Thus, related to his tendency to "mineralize" is his typical pairing of metallic objects or properties with those that are wet, living, coursing with sap or blood. In an early poem he speaks of the "sweetness of metal: balsam and alkali" ("Departures, 5," *Wilderness Stair* [1955]); the sumac is a cobbling of contraries, dry "brickdust" jostling the wet swarm of "maggots": "a gargoyle of waxes and berries, / a cockscomb with its brickdust wattles / bared, like maggots swarming" ("Sumac," *Possessions* [1986]); a painter applies to her images of the "stainless steel" Alps "a plasm of oil" ("Brutto Tempo: Bellagio," ibid.); a "pulse" is "like a forge . . . that beats on the latent and makes the ambiguous bearable" ("Winter Pond: Lake Paran," *Nowhere But Light*); the bog is a "trampoline" of "sponge and bitumen" ("On Quaking Bog," ibid.); paper burns under a magnifying glass as under a stylus that writes in "carbon and gossamer" ("The Cremation: New Mexico," *The Enemy Joy* [1964]); a similar diad of "bitumen and nimbus" flares under another burning glass in "Battle Piece" (also from *The Enemy Joy*).[18] And in one of the most poignant examples of the conflation of dry and stony with sweet and fluid, Belitt recalls, at his mother's deathbed, a sensation from the womb:

> I heard a sound like the breaking of ash in a crater
> where once, in the watersheds
> binding my breath to your breast,
> knees to my chin,
> I slept under your heart.
>
> ("The Orphaning," *Nowhere But Light*)

Clearly, the imagery of furnace and holocaust ("the breaking of ash in a crater") has been domesticated to a context of nurturance and emotional release. Most poets (even the author of Job) work in the opposite direction, from inward to outward, soft to hard, and from an *explicandum* not of release but of disintegration. Belitt trades in a more appalling symbolism; there is, about his values, little of the cozy or *bürgerlich,* with their many inducements to melodrama. Whatever screens more "comfortable" humans hold between self and Other have here been dissolved.

One of Ben Belitt's finest poems, "Double Poem of the World's Burning,"[19] dissolves the filler between self and world in an even more shattering way. As the title of the volume in which it appears will attest, this poem from *The Double Witness* (1977) is concerned with the doubleness of the poet's attention—toward self and toward a "brute nature" that on scrutiny is not only eloquent but for Belitt actively pedagogical. Belitt's natural world is full of omens and signatures, which require a proper reading. But one finds that his central images are often obliquely "adjusted" by the somewhat contradictory ones drawn in their wake. For example, part 1 of "Double Poem of the World's Burning" is called "'Ah, Sunflower!'" This title refers us to the eight-line poem by William Blake (*Songs of Experience,* 1794), which, however elegiac, sheds at most a quaint, pastel light on the poem's main focus, the supersaturated colors and profoundly charged particularity (and equally profound and shattering premonitions of decay) of Van Gogh's sunflower canvases. Blake's evocation of cool melancholia in a blocked sensibility pining away with desire functions, fleetingly, in the margins of Belitt's poem, suggesting a troublesome, exigent likeness between dying by restraint of the libidinal self and dying by embracing it.

That "Double Poem of the World's Burning" is about sexual energy and transposed sexual desire is not, I think, open to doubt. What is more striking is that the shock of sexual recognition directed at Van Gogh's painting should be joined with a brand of folktale hyperbole, exotic, Rabelaisian, full of relish:

> Preparing for that presence, the pod
> chose a man's height, set its cleats in the leaves
> like a steeplejack, scribbled its target of ovals,
> and rose to eye level
> . . . .
>   a bull's eye
> of seeds with the pips pointing down into chain-metal, an obsidian
> disk bulging with roe like a carp . . .
>
> ("Double Poem," 1. "'Ah, Sunflower!'")

It is as if obliquity were at work even here to make the great painter coarse and cordial. In fact, the sexual "bulging" and hyperbolic brio in Belitt's lines mythify the painter's imagined world with a marked friendliness (the reverse of the elegiac distance that awaits us at the sunflower poem's conclusion). Van Gogh, creator of a furiously replete world of mingled menace, fruition, and loneliness, is now at the beginning of his most famous period, just after going to Provence in 1888 (he died in 1890); the many paintings of chrome-yellow suflowers "blaze forth," as he wrote in his letters from that time, "on various backgrounds—[all] blue, from the palest malachite green to royal blue"; "One of the decorations of sunflowers on royal blue ground has 'a halo,' that is to say each object is surrounded by a glow of the complementary color of the background against which it stands out." Not only do the sunflower pictures "have certain qualities of color," he wrote some months after their making, "they also express an idea *symbolizing 'gratitude'*" (my emphasis). Meyer Schapiro has conjectured about the curiously homely and domestic virtues Van Gogh was wont to attribute to the most tormented and exaggerated landscapes and still lifes, and their colors. He believes that Van Gogh was grateful to objects, and that he found certain rooms and landscapes restful and "sane," because they helped him resist disintegration by attaching himself to external reality:

> External reality is an object of strong desire or need, as a possession and potential means of fulfillment of the striving human being, and is therefore the necessary ground of art. . . . The loading of the pigment is in part a reflex of this attitude, a frantic effort to preserve in the image of things their tangible matter. . . . Personality itself is an object, since he is filled with an unquenchable love for the human being as a separate substance and another self.[20]

But this love of other selves and things yields to a helpless pathology in the self. To come back to Belitt's terms, the *first* witness, the one that looks without, anxious to render the available world in the firmest subsistent particularity, discovers that the *second* or inward witness will not sustain the untroubled perspective that makes dimension and proportion possible. Schapiro remarks that the late canvases of Van Gogh offer two contested lines of perspective, one lawful (the symmetry provided by the horizon), the other lawlessly reversed, distorted by Van Gogh's desire to bring the world toward himself. In the appalling late work, "Crows over the Wheat Field" (1890), the crows are apparently *falling out of the painting* toward the self, and the horizon has ominously doubled back over to engulf him. Belitt renders this perspectival betrayal (in a passage in which he reviews and links at least four of the famous late sequences by Van Gogh) as the consumption of matter by its own enormities:

> Then the terrible
> heaviness began—the failing of bronzes, the hasp at the sunflower's
> center breaking away, a fading of planets, eclipses, coronas,
> the falling and falling away of petals—
>
> Time's total weariness, the terrible weight in the sun—all
> that hammers at darkness and glows like the baize of the table Van Gogh
> saw at Arles, in the cornfields and candles: a madman painting the night till
> the sky was delivered again to the crows.
>   ("Double Poem of the World's Burning," 1. "'Ah, Sunflower!'")

In place of that homely relish with which (Belitt happily imagines) the painter projected himself upon a world where the human form with all its appetites could find itself repeated and received, Van Gogh crosses into an alien and intractable territory, gravity gone wrong, connections failed, and the one conviction that of the supremacy of the long-suspected divine Harrow.

The second part of "Double Poem" ("Glare: Atlacomulco"—another Mexican setting) traces a similar dramatic pattern, from increasing definition, visual fullness, and "resolution," to an overload, a straining at the boundaries, and a subsequent vault into destruction by the rapt hedonist and light of the world, Jesus Christ. In establishing the terms in which the repleteness of the senses are to be "read" in this part, Belitt alludes to the sonnet by Rainer Maria Rilke, "Archaic Torso of Apollo" (*New Poems: Second Part,* 1908). Not only is the sun-god Apollo apropos of the heliotropic flower in William Blake's little poem, of the chrome-yellow-flooded paintings of Van Gogh, of the dazzling burnished landscape of Atlacomulco, and also of the burning apparition of Christ, the Son of God, at the poem's close: More pertinent still is Rilke's coolly controlled appreciation of the erotic impact of this statue in the Louvre (from the theater at Miletus). Despite the fact that this statuary work has no head—hence *no eyes*—the entire torso glows still like a crown of lights in which the figure's gaze has been simply "turned down" or held back a bit.

This is why, Rilke writes, you are blinded by the flexure of the chest and why, when the loins lightly curve, a ripple that is curiously like a smile plays on that saddle of muscle that loops down to the groin. You will recall the famous close of the sonnet, quoted in the introduction to these essays:

> *denn da ist keine Stelle,*
> *die dich nicht sieht. Du musst dein Leben ändern.*
>
> for his body has no single place
> that fails to see you. You must change your life.

Rilke starts from the premise that sensual beauty is yet another manifestation of that godhood which is latent and attentive in the world lying just beyond us. Like Rilke, Belitt is drawn to the liminality and imminence of the Other; he, too, finds attractive the quality of just-beyond-ness in the space outside the self. This quality makes the extentional world, even in the direst mood, seem less a waste land, more vivid and mysterious. Unlike Rilke, however, Belitt is attempting to release a pent-up eroticism from the muted contexts in which it has heretofore been contained. Eros is the energy and the vertiginous icon that represent the imagination as it longingly surveys the urgent excess of the brute visible world.

> The invisible life that sleeps in the grossness of things
> and feeds on the bulk of the world
> bringing substance and weight and degree—
>
> the tumescence
> that traces a thread in the loins, to the swamp
> of our human duration
>
> and insists on the blood and the bone of our presence—
> shows the world's burning,
> turned low, like the flame in the bell of a lamp.
> ("Double Poem of the World's Burning," 2. "Glare: Atlacomulco")

Rilke's influence here produces a curious throwback-evocation of Blake: The world ("the grossness of things," "the bulk of the world") takes on the outlines of a male figure, whom Belitt views sexually. This mythic Albion, who reclines upon the landscape of our deepest imaginative core, has the look of something that wishes to be looked at. Put another way, the attractiveness that "sleeps" in the unpromising trappings of the real conceals—or begins to reveal—a nakedness that responds to us with longing. This longing response to the human consciousness (a response that is compact of gazing, burning, and sexual tumescence) is the way the world solicits our yet more passionate engagement in the

tasks of seeing and being. Such a "double burning" is as close as Belitt
ever comes to a theophany.

But "Glare: Atlacomulco" also insists, as does the first poem, "'Ah,
Sunflower!'" on a deteriorating balance between self and world. No
sooner has the "fullness of time" been achieved, and nothing left latent,
"withheld or unnameable," than there begins

> that burning away of the air, as the glowing erasure
> of limit begins: a glare
>
> on the claws and cusps of poinsettia
> tracing the heat's line with a solderer's iron, petal for petal—
> a talon of ash
>
> on a talon of smoking vermilion, forcing the fire at the center
> to bloom on the edges and smolder like metal
> . . . .
> blowing the coal of the world's
> calefaction till the unbinding of matter is done,
>
> the visible turns into the invisible . . .

In the first part of the poem, the genius of a world of saturated beauty
and terror is overtaken by madness. In the second, the poet/speaker's
belief in the "invisible life" with its constant subdued erotic flare burning
away at "the grossness of things" draws toward an unbearable fulfillment.
The "Light of the World," which is at once Christ and the perceptual light
by which the visible world is kindled, delivers itself up for destruction. If
the end of the inflamed and pellucidly visible is to "turn[] into the invisible," then the visible world of flesh, striving, indeed all human action will
be utterly unbound. In their place come the immolations of men who
believe themselves to be gods. Madness and extremity lie coiled at the end
of the furthest witnessing. If Belitt doesn't warn us off from this crisis, or
even take fright himself, it may be because he half-approves of the reassurance that the greatest beauty, seen most unflinchingly, is appalling. It
would also seem that he views as commensurate the aesthetic and messianic enactments of that recognition. Surely Belitt's oeuvre proves he has
earned the right to speculate on that abyss.

It may be evident what is unusually striking about the finest work of the
many fine poets discussed in this survey-chapter: At the top of their bent
they are all writing poems that are religious in nature without being able
to rely on the religious in structure. There are, accordingly, certain limits
just as there are dead-ends that baffle further progress. Writers like Strand
and Ammons in their ways parody their own hobbled situations; Pinsky,

Glück, and (to a degree) Ashbery elegize them, Hughes and Belitt "tragedify" the condition of belief without an object. None falls entirely back into the fairly retrograde genre explored in the three parts of the third chapter—that of confiding in the Self. But none, I think, yet approaches the scope of the attempts at resolution between the affections of the engaged self and the elusive, even repellent experiential world, on the part of Wallace Stevens and of the next writers discussed—Howard Nemerov, Seamus Heaney, and Ashbery himself.

5

The Signatures of Things

On Howard Nemerov

"Writing," as Howard Nemerov observed in 1959, "means trying to find out what the nature of things has to say about what you think you have to say." He was speaking of poetry but the principle of listening to the voice of the nature of things applies also to prose.[1] Nemerov himself was for about fifteen years one of the most interesting and reliable reviewers of poetry in the country, the author as well of thoughtful essays on novelists (the studies of Thomas Mann are little masterpieces), and on subjects as delicate and profound as the likeness between poems and jokes, how metaphor operates, what part belief plays in poetry, and even what part criticism plays in our understanding of literature and therefore of the world.[2]

There have been few poets whose essays can be read for information and instruction apart from what they provide in the way of apparatus to the poetry they write. I do not count here writers like Borges, Rilke, and Valéry, because their discourses about art stand at no great distance from their art. These authors have, I think, only one range of voice, and it does not accommodate itself to saying all the different things that must be said when works other than their own are at stake. Such writers have a greater or lesser command of knowledge, but only one kind of opinion about any piece of it. Between this group and the next, W. B. Yeats might be the bridge figure, half his attention on the inner world, half on the outer.

T. S. Eliot's criticism is idiosyncratic but perhaps for that reason historically crucial in having established the terms in which criticism in this century would go on to deal with tradition and doubt. Henry James's criticism, no less eccentric and "partial" (his term), illuminated the moral base of style in the nineteenth-century novel as few others could have done. Nemerov's criticism is less puckish and obsessive than either (although it is both at times); very cogent; and plain-spoken, however complex the insights. He most resembles Auden in this: even when he writes reviews and "treatments," he is also writing an *essay*, so that one has the impression the subject just came conveniently along to catalyze a number of lucid observations that had been generating for some time.

The comparable breadth and power of the essays of Auden and Nemerov may also make us wonder why there is such a sense of their difference, for Auden sounded, in both prose and poetry, as if he were writing for an audience; Nemerov seldom does, and indeed his *Collected Poems* came to a public that had noticed the publication of the nine volumes comprising it far less than they deserved. His prose pronouncements don't have the wallop of the "famous poet" behind them as, in an accidental or inherited, but undeniable way, Auden's do. Like most American men of letters, Nemerov sounds like a man who talks for his own edification.

Before discussing the poetry, a brief note on the fiction. One reason why Nemerov seems to me to fail as a fiction writer is that he thinks analogically and, as it were, alone. He is not adept at handling the social texture of the rather sophisticated characters he invents, nor on the other hand can he restrain himself from manipulating the symbolic texture as if he were writing a poem. An unwholesome little parable in *A Commodity of Dreams and Other Stories* (1959) called "The Sorcerers' Eye" is illustrative. In a castle with his parents lives a young man (wearing a golden spoon about his neck—"a family joke"). The father, a former army officer, had long ago lost a wager, the payment of which was to be handing over his wife for the night. The regiment expected him to kill himself, but instead he walked the streets, encountering the strange man who gave him the castle. (What the wife experienced that evening is never revealed.)

The son is in love with the strange magician's daughter. They want to run away together but first they must elude the sorcerer, who has one eye of flesh and blood with which he acts, another of glass with which he thinks. The pair plot to remove the glass eye, since, being the eye of knowledge, once he didn't have it he'd never know he'd lost it. By mistake, with that golden spoon, the young man scoops out the wrong eye, the eye of flesh and blood, and with the glass eye still intact the sorcerer howls, "I know you!" The boy swallows the jelly in the spoon and by the virtues of power and action becomes successful in the city, although he continues to hear the cry, "I know you," as he goes about his business. The castle vanished the instant the deed was done.

There is somehow little pleasure in recognizing the play of symbols in this tale. And the arrogant adolescent hero only stands in the way, making smart remarks to the gallery. But it is perhaps the very thing that mars this story that makes the poetry so powerful: the sense that the symbols are more magical than the people, and better represent them than they know.

Disputed Fields

One range of symbolism to which Nemerov returns in his verse and commentary is that of the four elements; in the story, for example, the real interest was the dichotomy between glass and flesh, wisdom and action. Nemerov's attraction to nature symbolism also extends to the tradition of its use, as in the remarkable essay comparing Wordsworth and Blake. He views *The Prelude*'s numerous mountain climbs and the visions the poet has atop the peaks as a transcending of earth only so far as the earthly paradise. Wordsworth's apotheosis takes place in the refined element of air,

> traditionally feminine (Blake calls it the region of Beulah) and traditionally representing the achievement of a purified natural reason. Further than this, the point at which Dante takes leave of Virgil and flies beyond the sun and stars, Wordsworth does not go: the sun, the fire, the father, remain unknown to him; his poem belongs to earth, water, air, to Nature as protecting mother, it is written under the auspices of the powers of the air, and its highest moment of vision—universal mind, "a majestic intellect" imaged by clouds imitating the forms of earth and sea—takes place not in the fiery sun but by the light of the full moon.
>
> ("Two Ways of the Imagination: Blake and Wordsworth")

Writing about his own poetry in similar terms, Nemerov discovers his tendency to oppose statues as symbols of the rigid domination of the past over present and future, and of "habitual idolatry" (in this, statuary is supported by the more recent oracles, newspapers and television) to the life of the imagination as represented by "a stream, a river, a waterfall, a fountain, or else [by] a still and deep reflecting pool":

> This image, of the form continuing in the changing material, belongs also to cloud and fire, and I once gave it a somewhat political shape in a despairing epigram: God loves (I said) the liberal thrice better than the conservative, for at the beginning he gave to the liberal the three realms of water, air, and fire, while to the conservative he gave only the earth.

After the full quotation of his marvelous poem "Painting a Mountain Stream," to which we will return later, Nemerov concludes:

> In this account I have stressed the liberal virtues and neglected the conservative ones, scorning the solids of this world to praise its liquids. That is not the whole truth, for how could you tell the stream but by its rocky bed, the rocks directing the water how to flow, the water—much more slowly— shaping the rocks according to its flow: But maybe I put the accent where I do against this world which so consistently in politics, religion, even in

art, even in science, worships the rocky monument achieved and scorns the
spring, the rain cloud, and the spark fallen among leaves.

("Attentiveness and Obedience")

Although Nemerov's poetry has changed over the forty years since *The
Image and the Law* was published—the very title of that first volume
indicating, in fact, the poems' tendency to see one kind of solid in terms
of another—he has remained unusually steadfast in his approach to the
elemental symbolism of the tradition.

In the earlier verse, conservative values were stressed. Europe appears
in two masks, as men dead in the war peopling a frozen city of the
damned, and as dead art and dead tradition from which no life emanates.
His accent falls on the rocky monument achieved. The paralysis of things
is duplicated in the blind stare of Europe's statues as well as in its corpses.
"Saint and demon blindly stare / From the risen stone." Saints who burned
and melted once upon their pilgrimage have now only the coldest sympathy for the kingdom they survey:

> Only the dead have an enduring city,
> Whose stone saints look coldly on a cold world
> With the compassion of pure form not flesh,
> They look upon the signatures of things
> Where clarity and singular radiance
> Display beholder and beheld. They see
> Only the clear reduplicated forms.
>
> ("The Situation Does Not Change")

Europe is the "Frozen City" where eyes stare "bright as broken glass."
The city "coruscates with eyes." "Glass Dialectic" warns us that once we
step through the looking-glass, there is no way to return:

> You have changed sides and cannot be recalled,
> From very hell your eyes reverse the world.

Coldness, radiance, and distance come together on the empty beach
and boardwalk of the shabby hotel in the "Elegy of Last Resort" as the
planet turns toward winter:

> This shoulder of the earth turns from the sun
> Into the great darkness, into the steep
> Valley of the stars, into the pit
> Of Cocytus . . .

And in that peculiar poem "The Place of Value" where MacLane, not
quite major man but representative of madness in these frozen climes, is

thrown off a bridge, we find these lines about the water where he fell: "Numberless stars, like snow / In Heaven, shine on the black / Water, so dancing and so still." "Advice from the Holy Tomb" rehearses these cold distances: "But glass, we are glass. Wherever we would stand / High noon will magnify light to a fault: / Doom will consume the land."

The magnifying glass of noon opposes, in some of its particulars but not in tone, the imagery of the Cave of Illusions where art is made in "Unscientific Postscript." The postscript is presumably appended to Stevens's poem "The Man with the Blue Guitar":

> There is the world, the dream, and the one law.
> The wish, the wisdom, and things as they are.
>
> Inside the cave the burning sunlight showed
> A shade and forms between the light and shade,
>
> Neither real nor false nor subject to belief:
> If unfleshed, boneless also, not for life
>
> Or death or clear idea. But as in life
> Reflexive, multiple, with the brilliance of
>
> The shining surface, an orchestral flare.

The joke here is multiple. There are fourteen lines as against the nearly four hundred lines of the Stevens poem and the five hundred pages of Kierkegaard's *Concluding Unscientific Postscript*. Taking the central theme of Stevens that things as they are are changed upon the blue guitar, and that this change leads both to brilliance and to doubt in shifting chiaroscuro, Nemerov writes a revision of the Platonic parable of the cave, recognizing yet dismissing the fact that death is the adversary and that those figures were chained. Finally, Kierkegaard's deceptively long-winded "footnote" to an earlier work (*Philosophical Fragments*) details the reasons for choosing the Savior, the absolutely original event coming out of nowhere who changes our being in the world, over the Platonic dialectic by virtue of which truth has always existed and Socrates merely midwife to its visible presence.

The music of "Unscientific Postscript" (the final poem in *The Image and the Law*) is weirdly dark, as the fusion of Kierkegaard, Stevens, and the most lyrical and melancholy side of Plato would indicate. The figures of speech are paradoxes (burning sunlight in the cave). And the poem's final five lines, however insistently they refer to the Stevens way of thought and speech, grow to a close that Stevens would never have written. But that final phrase, "with the whole instrument," is a close Yeats might have composed:

It is not to believe, the love or fear

Or their profoundest definition, death;
But fully as orchestra to accept,

Making an answer, even if lament,
In measured dance, with the whole instrument.

In general, however, the cave, the mirror, and the burning surfaces
tend to revert to the "chaste paralysis" of snow—those conservative virtues—and do not give Nemerov much room to maneuver. When he wrote
a memorial verse tribute to Paul Valéry, he was still uncertain about and
tended to force apart the questions of content and of form. The cool
elisions and evident repose of Valéry's poetry, shown in Nemerov's homage as harbor waters smooth as glass, invoke Valéry's kind of setting, his
characteristic analogies and diction, but with a muddling on Nemerov's
part. He decides that Valéry's mastery of style is not "perdurable fire,"
the rock beat against by the sea, but an exquisite, safe, and ultimately
artificial gem. It is perhaps a case of the simplistic assignment of good to
the restless ocean, and bad to the achieved elegance of glass, which leads
Nemerov to an eventual dismissal of the other poet's craft.

> Here even the ocean relaxes its incessant
> Oceanic shudders, finds an evident
> Repose where keel to keel the brilliant vessels
> Elide the shadow and the real, gliding
> Between the clearest elements of glass.
> . . . .
> But yonder in white foam Poseidon rises:
> It is a disputed field, it changes sides,
> Is turbulent, is unreflecting, deep
> And deep and deep, and boils at interruption
> Of wind or keel.
>   O valuable glass
>   . . . .
> The manners of a time, an age perhaps
> Ready to die, a classical notation
> For the harbor glass, the law against the truth.

The same fields of "The Master at a Mediterranean Port" will be disputed in Nemerov's later work, but with results of increasing subtlety of
argumentation and of attitude. In his second book, *Guide to the Ruins*
(1950), Nemerov is clearly loosening up his verse forms and giving his
attitudes more play. In *The Salt Garden* (1955), after that great exorcism
of the symbols of the blind and frozen stare, "The Scales of the Eyes," we
begin to see a greater flexibility not just in tone and attitude but in the

play of the poet's intelligence with a symbolism basically unchanged but less narrowly assertive, until in late work what might be technically inert (things like seeds and logs) are presented under the sign of wind or fire. In "A Cabinet of Seeds Displayed" these tiny "samples" may "teach / Our governors, who speak of husbandry / And think the hurricane, where power lies." The apple logs in "Firelight in Sunlight"

> unlock their sunlight
> In the many-windowed room to meet
> New sunlight falling in silvered gold
> . . . .
> O early world,
> Still Daphne of the stubborn wood
> Singing Apollo's song in light . . .

In "Seeing Things," a tree standing against the setting sun appears to be afire with a "cloud of boiling gnats,"

> Their millions doing such a steady dance
> As by the motion of the many made the one
> Shape constant and kept it so in both the forms
> I'd thought to see, the fire and the tree.

Here the image of the form continuing in the changing material is given a philosophical nudge, myriad motion making the one shape constant, chaos making shape.

Even the resistant elements of the mineral world are resurrected from stasis, by being compared to water and light, or sometimes by being placed in liquid suspension. Salt is rendered as the sodium base of blood, of semen, of the amniotic fluid in which we float till born, and of the ocean "Where the Nine Maidens still grind Hamlet's meal, / The salt and granite grain of bitter earth." Veins and arteries are accordingly described as "salt vines." Diamond, glass, and the mirror (carbon transcended, sand melted, and mercury reduced) are inserted into contexts where they shimmer, refract, flame out. Even water in its frozen forms exhibits a yearning for its liquid state:

> Not only must the skaters soon go home;
> also the hard inscription of their skates
> is scored across the open water, which long
> remembers nothing, neither wind nor wake.

The voice of *This* in "This, That & the Other: a dialogue in disregard" watches snowflakes falling on the water of a pond, "Abolished in the black and waiting water," "touching the water's face / So gently that to meet and melt are one." The voice of *That* replies that such mirroring of the flake for a brief moment above the black water reminds him of "Narcissus and his Echo, kinds / One of the other . . . Poor beauty pausing by the fountain's brim, / Is he not imaged in the snowflake's last / Moment of vanity?" The back-and-forth between *This* and *That*, between the image and the interpretation, constitutes a special cadence in Nemerov's poetry, and lends a new subtlety to his doctrine of the forms swaying through the changing materials.

Being of Three Minds

"This, That & the Other" is a combat between conflicting moods. Like all tales in which the end is contained in the beginning (Marsyas will always lose to Apollo, Jesus to Pilate), we know who will win in the real world and who will win in eternity. When *This* in his subdued and mournful way muses about the flakes abolished on the black water, the grating voice of *That* pipes in with pedantries, suggesting the mythic, epic, and scientific parallels *This* may sorely need in order to get a thought completed. Rather than exemplifying the liberal and conservative ways of viewing the world, *This* and *That* stand for two rhythms, one innocent and clear of eye yet distracted in mind, the other lathered in meanings but just missing the experience. Their voices are often separate in Nemerov's poetry. At a distance from each other, the two rhythms at which the world is approached manifest strengths they don't show in concert.

This, the believer, writes poems of gradual revelation, of the fixed stare; he is helpless, awed, possessed, and the more haunted of the two. *That,* the eternal commentator, tends to satire and, as befits the miffed citizen, is closer to the political and economic world than the lyricist, and more dependent on it. *That* studies hard (he knows several languages), watches a lot of TV, usually does his Christmas shopping late, likes long poker games, and is not above admitting the worst you can impute to him as long as it's understood the world is more absurd than he.

(There is also a sense in which the two voices over the long run of Nemerov's earlier books were thesis and antithesis, the chameleon wit coming along in the second and third volumes to bail *This* out of the frozen Cocytus of the first and second.)

The two voices also come from different epochs of the tradition; one is romantic, one not. *This* is one of the condemned dreamers, Keats, Coleridge, De Quincey, *That* a suburban Oscar Wilde, weekend Swift, or hopelessly talkative Boswell, with some of the dense lore of Empson thrown in. *That* writes "Life Cycle of the Common Man," detailing the myriad items wasted by the average American on his slovenly voyage through existence; he writes unusable instructions for the operation of unusable toys and excursions on the buffalo nickel; devises the proper grace to be said before various absurd rites (committee meetings, shopping at the supermarket); derides the critic "Who would have to rise above himself / In order to talk through his hat"; and warns that in the fray the "mild conceptualist" will get hit from either side: "The only question universals ask / Is is you is or is you ain't my baby?" He also notices that the God of being demoralized has "two hands only, which are shown / Sometimes in icons as seven because / They tremble incessantly. . . . His feet / Are really four, though, and they walk / Both widdershins and otherwise / Around him while he is standing still."

When he perorates as our public conscience, *That* may address the commencement exercises at Harvard University in a tone of sustained, derisive wrath that must have addled the proctors as much as it irritated the students. "A Relation of Art and Life," the Harvard Phi Beta Kappa poem for 1965, warns us that our shamans, "furious of mind" and weak from their crazed sojourn, have come in from the wilderness to do us in. These "savage sages," full of madness and fire, naturally need the substitute sages of the academy to interpret them, to package and market their ravings (a burning coal for every barbecue). Nemerov is talking here not only about patently false priests, wild and domestic varieties (he does not give us an easy way to see through the bad guys and side with the good). These madmen, whose "secret sayings are such / As destroy societies," are the old prophets, the Druids in Blake, who have always been just three degrees east of the truth, but who can never manage to align the image with its reflection. Once their powerful falsehoods, so full of primitive energy and deep conviction, are handed over to the folk (with the whisper, *This is just for you*), the wrong message gets around fast. Error becomes habitual. As is always the case, near-truths are harder to correct when they become the very supports of all of public life.

As the mental deities are abstracted from their objects, and passwords concocted out of the mad illuminations in the desert, even the possibility of titanic evil drops out. Instead of the grandly, one might even say professionally misguided, we find the amateur deep in the dangerous banality of drugs and boutique mysticism. In the absence of the cardinal virtues, the cardinal sins needn't work quite so hard; a folly persisted in will do the rest. In their nasty train, the massively indulged sins—sexual license, drunken disorder, "Salutary Hatred self-beshitten," "Narcosis in his kinds, / That works the doorway to the double dream / Where pose the caterpillar and the butterfly / Their contradictions to the sunshine or the shroud"—deteriorate into institutions. Rhetorically, personifications become abstractions. The priests derive "from every wisdom / Its proper doctrine,"

> from drunkenness a jail,
> From sexual license the institution of wedlock,
> From anarchy and apathy the armed services,
> Industrial development from drugged sleep,
> And from hatred the holy mystery of the law;
> Absorbing outrage into probability,
> Improving virtue from the average vice.

Finally, with Nemerov's particular venom reserved for make-believe "art" and the media, he tells us how avant-garde movies are made "And the dreams of the desert are digested in art." The sages now drive "neo-classical Cadillacs" while the young scholars we must try to imagine the poet addressing are sent on their way "elevated" by being exposed, the desire for property in their hearts and in their dreams the fiscal images of vaults beneath the corporate houses of glass

> in whose aquarian light, subdued,
> Glow golden secretaries inaccessible on stilted heels,
> And savage action paintings hanging patient on the walls.

The voice of honest indignation is the voice of God.

In contrast to the sometimes bemused, sometimes lethal humor of the commentator's voice (Palamabron and Rintrah, sweet pity and righteous wrath, two of Blake's revolutionary quarternion), the puzzled voice of the believer—the good artist *This*—rises to its larger utterance in the dramatic monologue, embodying itself in the voice of someone else: Nicodemus, the beekeeper, Cain, the woman in whalebone, Saul abandoned by Samuel and by God, Pharaoh vanquished. Spoken by a king exhausted in mind and bereft of his children by Moses' plagues, "Pharaoh's Meditation on the Exodus" (a) owes something to that earlier monologue from Pound's *Ripostes* (1912) spoken by the soul of Nikoptis:

> (a)   All the last week
> Things were bled white of meaning, and I say
> Enough! and have imposed my solitude
> On kingdom and court, so that I may have time,
> In this inner room, where I need not endure
> Daylight or darkness but am soothed by lamps,
> To think, should there be anything left to think.
> Alone, in the cool silence of the stone,
> Where only my heartbeats happen, and my thoughts
> Follow the small flame's wavering against the wall
> Until that meaningless motion is my thought,
> It may be that the world outside has stopped,
> The fountains dried up, and the brickwork broken

Under the insane silence of the sun
Centuries ago, and the whole course of the world
Shifted like sand; and I alone, the brain
In this room the skull of Egypt, am alive.

(b)   thy dead eyes
Moved not, nor ever answer my desire,
And thy light limbs, wherethrough I leapt aflame,
Burn not with me nor any saffron thing.
. . . .
I have read out the gold upon the wall,
And wearied out my thought upon the signs.
And there is no new thing in all this place.
. . . .
Have I not touched thy palms and finger-tips,
Flowed in, and through thee and about they heels?
. . . .
And no sun comes to rest me in this place,
And I am torn against the jagged dark,
And no light beats upon me, and you say
No word, day after day.

The remarkable elegiac diction of "The Tomb at Akr Çaar" inspired by that peculiarly Mediterranean and non-Christian consciousness that from time to time in Pound's poetry overcame the Browning and the Jefferson of it all, is echoed by Nemerov, but with a Senecan reserve or stop. "Thy light limbs . . . Burn not with me nor any saffron thing," the more exotic statement and the more metrically regular, may be compared with "I alone, the brain / In this room the skull of Egypt, am alive." Both excerpts depend on a similarly collapsing metaphoric series: tomb surrounding soul, soul outgrowing or enveloping body, until the speech becomes that of the chamber itself while the body in eclipse becomes too small to hold the life that is its only way to be. Yet Nikoptis's soul only affirms the saffron flame by negating it; and Pharaoh, by trying to disappear into a small flamelike clarity, fades into the greater light and shadow play of time, history, and immortality. And if theme, cultural ambience, and the habit of progressive synecdoche were insufficient to refer us from one poem to the other, the two also share the same worn classical gaiety, the blending of the metric form with the necessities of syntax, that still has spirit left for the "echo rhyme" between pure and long vowels suspended in a pattern of soft, aspirant, and vowellike consonants:

(a) *Follow* the sm*all flame's *wavering* against the *wall*
(b) *Flowed* in, and *through thee* and ab*out thy heels*

Two years after the publication of "Moses," of which "Pharaoh's Medi-tation" is the third and final section, Nemerov published "Maestria," ex-plicitly about Ezra Pound's legacy to modern literature after the smoke had cleared and only a few scholars bothered to "inspect the rusting, controversial wheels / Of the abandoned machinery":

> There remains
> A singular lucidity and sweetness, a way
> Of relating the light and the shade,
> The light spilling from fountains, the shade
> Shaken among leaves.
>   Doubtless
> It would be better to be always right, refraining
> From those millennial expectations, but strangely,
> Rising sometimes from hatred and wrong,
> The song sings itself out to the end,
> And like a running stream which purifies itself
> It leaves behind the mortality of its maker,
> Who has the skill of his art, and a trembling hand.

This is a tribute as fine and closely engaged with Pound's high elegance, his Chinese and Dorian moods, as Nemerov's verse tributes to Tate, Roethke, Yeats, Shakespeare, Herbert, and Donne are loyal to their sub-jects' subjects. In these many poems of courtesy to the tradition, the other poets' marks, the characteristic preoccupations and talismans and turns of attention, shine through rather than form the web of Nemerov's language. "Maestria" brings together sotto voce allusions to *Cathay* and to Pound's poems on the hamadryads, as well as alluding to Nemerov's own brush with the Orient. "To Lu Chi (author of the Wen Fu, or Prose Poem on the Art of Letters, A.D. 302)" (from Nemerov's 1958 collection *Mirrors and Windows*) had already initiated the theme of art's paradox-discipline, "how to hold the axe / To make its handle":

> And then you bring, by precept and example,
> Assurance that a reach of mastery,
> Some still, reed-hidden and reflective stream
> Where the heron fishes in his own image,
> Always exists.
>   . . . .
> And to the thinker, if he should ask us once
> Instead of telling us, again say nothing,
> But look into the clear and mirroring stream
> Where images remain although the water
> Passes away. Neither action nor thought,
> Only the concentration of our speech

> In fineness and in strength (your axe again),
> Till it can carry, in those other minds,
> A nobler action and a purer thought.

In these lines about the thinker taught by the silent, stream-reflected speech of the poet, which carries better action and thought, Nemerov alludes to a belief he shares with the one stated more strongly by Shelley, a belief in the ultimate strength of the powerless poet to change a world that couldn't care less about poetry itself. This is an art, wrote Nemerov in 1962, which never relinquishes

> its large claim on the world, its claim to teach the world, its prophetic claim on the ultimate realization of all possibility. For the whole business of poetry is vision, and the substance of this vision is the articulating possibilities still unknown, the concentrating what is diffuse, the bringing forth what is in darkness.

> ("The Muse's Interest")

The paradox art—those parables that are both the subject and the manner of the making—is taken up again in *Mirrors and Windows* by two neighboring poems, "Writing" and "Painting a Mountain Stream," both of which appear to have been written under the aegis of Lu Chi. In the former, a "cursive scrawl" reminds the poet of Chinese characters, which can delight even without our understanding them, and these in turn are compared to the gibberish messages of skaters "scoring their white / records in ice." Except that the messages are not nonsense:

> Being intelligible,
> these winding ways with their audacities
> and delicate hesitations, they become
> miraculous, so intimately, out there
> at the pen's point or brush's tip, do world
> and spirit wed. The small bones of the wrist
> balance against great skeletons of stars
> exactly; the blind bat surveys his way
> by echo alone. Still, the point of style
> is character. The universe induces
> a different tremor in every hand, from the
> check-forger's to that of the Emperor
> Hui Tsung, who called his own calligraphy
> the 'Slender Gold.'

The quiet, lucid, yet breathtakingly rapid accumulation of links in the metaphoric chain, from the cursive scrawl, to the Chinese ideogram, to the skater's intelligible marks that betray their glides and pirouettes and scuffed halts, to the comparison of these lessons incised on ice with the stroke of a pen or inkbrush, comes to its own halt where the small, fluid bones of the painter's wrist are seen as parts of the skeleton described (connect-the-dots fashion) by the figured constellations of stars. As in elementary astronomy manuals, a blackly inked page is "covered" by (in actuality, left blank for) a tracery of white lines supposedly resembling bears, cups, warriors, and maidens. The black ink is the void of space through which the bat in Nemerov's poem "surveys his way / by echo alone." Oddly enough, to wind up with a bat in the dark, although it may not be an immediately accessible analogy for writing, does have some logical connection with the winding intelligibility of the skater's moves. Kinesthesia, the radar by which the body knows where it is in space, links the skaters to the bat; it is only the color of the paper that is different, ice for the skater, night for the bat and for the tracery of the constellations' bare bones.

The next statement, using a pun as old as English, *still* as quiet and ever and nevertheless, encourages the latter reading: "Still, the point of style is character." "Still" may even be a quadruple pun, since the bat's radar is the echo of its high-pitched cries (hence not voiceless), and since the wrist must move the stylus from its stationary point in order to generate style or point (i.e., rendered-up meaning). The universe is then said to induce a different tremor in every hand—the cosmic skeleton sending shivers down to the local human wrist.

The different tremor in every hand brings us back to calligraphy and the elegant example of the emperor who called his script the "Slender Gold." This gemmed and enticingly alien anecdote completes the cycle of images in a splendid da capo movement, from court calligraphy back to the cursive scrawl. It is a sign of great deliberation and independence that Nemerov does not end his poem here. His remarks on Stephen Spender's poetry are apropos of this decision:

> He is a splendid phrase-maker, master of the noble gesture. . . . And I have felt that poetry, for Spender, consists not so much in composition as in what is liberated (the sublime) from composition. . . . His subjects frequently are as screens, behind which he awaits the moment for breaking rhapsodically out, and this moment is not always opportune, so that the great phrase gets little or no authority from the poem.
>
> ("A Wild Civility")

Nemerov does not desire simply to let loose the rhapsode in himself, nor are his poems mere platforms for the pretty but irrelevant saying (or, for that matter, for the true but artificially homely saying). At his best, in poems like "Writing," Nemerov with great skill prepares the ground in description and metaphor so that he can discover what the things behind the words have to say to him. Following the lines about the tremor that's different to every hand and the "Slender Gold" of Hui Tsung's script, he writes: "A nervous man / writes nervously of a nervous world, and so on." The impulse is not to debunk or undermine the validity of ice skates, bats, and dependent bones in the wrist, but to open cogitation between himself and the world; and he will not suffer a standard metaphysical conceit to mar the procedure:

> Miraculous. It is as though the world
> were a great writing. Having said so much,
> let us allow there is more to the world
> than writing: continental faults are not
> bare convoluted fissures in the brain.
> Not only must the skaters soon go home;
> also the hard inscription of their skates
> is scored across the open water, which long
> remembers nothing, neither wind or wake.

The water of the melting pond, "open" like the sea, flows out and away from us, remembering nothing, it's true, but recalling us to it nevertheless. The allusion to the fissures in the brain and the Great Divide (which are claimed to be like, not one), and the language in which the ice is seen to lapse (*scored across* mere water), suggest an association both verbal and metaphoric with the word *cortex*.[3] Denoting the bark of a tree and the rind of tissue enveloping the brain, *cortex* onomatopoetically refers to its origin as something that *splits,* and moreover, in its common meaning, bark, invites the carving of our names as, in its scientific application to the brain, it invites the inscription of meaning by the stylus of memory. Writing of signs is the most sophisticated way to put an interpretation on a thing. "Trees imagine life," says Nemerov in a late work from *The Western Approaches,* "The Thought of Trees," and one of the ways in which they do so is by referring us from themselves to other forms; specifically, the bark is hard but "nevertheless, as in the elm, reminds of water in its twisting flow."

One of Nemerov's favorite kinds of image for the form continuing in the changing material is the threshold or rind of appearance dividing water from air: the case of black sunlight that holds the pond from our gaze, the pond's pillowslip of ice, the little moon (meniscus) curving on the top of the water in a glass, the membrane of the camera lens. And of course all these thresholds resemble the eye, organ of intelligence no less than vision. The two final stanzas of "Painting a Mountain Stream" put the references to eye, threshold (cortex), and the simultaneous scoring and melting of art into a different arrangement:

> The eye travels on running water,
> out to the sky, if you let it go.
> However often you call it back
> it travels again, out to the sky.
>
> The water that seemed to stand is gone.
> The water that seemed to run is here.
> Steady the wrist, steady the eye;
> paint this rhythm, not this thing.

"This rhythm" is both the running and standing still of the stream, and the traveling of the eye out to the sky along the path the flowing water "draws." The rhythm is also the current that alternates between contemplation and commission, the circuit described by the wrist at work and at rest. The ligature in the preceding poem between the skeleton of stars and the calligrapher's wrist is collapsed again; if we think of scale and direction, the stars are the larger entity causing the hand to tremble, as here the wrist controls the tremors of the stream it "contemplates":

> Study this rhythm, not this thing.
> The brush's tip streams from the wrist
> of a living man, a dying man.
> The running water is the wrist.
>
> In the confluence of the wrist
> things and ideas ripple together,
> as in the clear lake of the eye,
> unfathomably, running remains.
>
> The eye travels on running water, etc.

We will return to these poems of tongues in trees and books in running brooks when we consider the great magisterial work in *The Western Approaches*. For the moment, I would not say that any of these poems ("The Breaking of Rainbows," "Maestria," "Painting a Mountain Stream," "Writing," or "To Lu Chi") was written either by *This* or *That*. Put in their parodic places these two voices represent two temptations not so much in evidence here. One voice wants to solve the matter right here and now and no flap from any of you. (Much of *Gnomes and Occasions* [1973], section three of *Mirrors and Windows* [1958], the "Vaudeville & Critique" section of *The Next Room of the Dream* [1962], and "The Great Society" section of *The Blue Swallows* [1967] are the handiwork of *That*.) *This* represents the temptation to wander about, muddled and unhoused, watching with utter doggedness as and until the world scrapes together a meaning. Such dilatoriness and self-absorption are not seen in the poems above. The voice or rhythm behind the five poems just discussed is more the voice of "Maia" (*Mirrors and Windows*) in which the partial attitudes of the stone-minded and the thorny-minded men are dispensed with in the closing lines of the first two stanzas: "This world is hard lines," "The world is a tangled vine." (A nervous man writes nervously.) The last two stanzas, with a nod in Yeats's direction, posit a third veil of appearance through which reality is glimpsed:

> The sun on the streaming water
> Imagines rock and branch, the moon
>   Imagines the sun,
>
> I die into these images while
> The black water and the white
>   Water race and remain.

The streaming summer water in "Maia" gives one sunny version to the light, another version to itself: that foam of stubborn black and white. "This, That & the Other" closes upon a similar resolution:

> This: The snow has stopped, the sun breaks out of cloud,
>   A golden light is drifting through the glass.
> That: A wind springs up that shatters images.
> Both: The Other is deeply meddled in this world.
>   We see no more than that the fallen light
>   Is wrinkled in and with the wrinkling wave.

Reality is the intuition of the limits that someone else is setting to the simplest scene, both further away and nearer in than is implicit in any of our versions of the boundaries of the visible, mysterious and yet self-evident at the same time.

In the "Wild Civility" essay (containing reviews of Spender, Jarrell, and Auden), Nemerov says with respect to the latter that, beyond the emotions poetry can include in its scope as subjects, from tranquillity to despair, frivolity to funk, there is a further emotion that never changes: It is always behind and in the poem no matter what the theme:

> I would hold that there is, in addition to the emotions dealt with by poetry, an emotion *of* poetry and alone proper to it, a rhythm of patterned exaltation of feelings and objects, making them dance in a different and noneditorial world, of which, despite the seriousness and sadness of its themes, the dominating traits are gaiety, energy, and control.

The meddling of the Other in this world may not always lead to the sentiment of gaiety; the black and white waters race and remain as aspects of a reality not only obstinate and unreadable, but somewhat frightening, too; a poem of the sheerest exaltation of the mind as it refines its reading of things may cast up suddenly the recognition that, whatever the elements of its "long allegory," "The anagoge is always death" ("The Sanctuary," *The Salt Garden,* 1955).

But it is not entirely true that the emotion *of* poetry, whose dominant moods are gaiety, energy, and control, is altogether separate from the control, gaiety, or energy of the subject. In *Journal of the Fictive Life* (written in 1963) Nemerov refers to a saying of Goethe's: "The attitude of belief is fertile, while the attitude of skepticism is sterile, even if one is compelled to skepticism by the age in which one lives." Goethe was speaking neither of form nor of content or the tenor of the sentiments expressed in literature, but of something between them, something like the willingness in the poet's posture, the naïveté, the enthusiasm, which can do things very different for the sophisticated soul than they do to the irrevocably or fatedly (and, no doubt, blessedly) simple soul.

Some statements of Paul Valéry, which Nemerov does not, I think, mention in his writings, support Goethe's sentence although purporting the inverse of the values assigned to skepticism and belief. Valéry, addressing the French Academy, characterizes the unique bias of the French writer as a preoccupation with form that will not establish separable scales of judgment by which to isolate "the spontaneous from that which will be considered." The spontaneous must be judged, not by its standards, but by ours. Valéry sides with classical art as against baroque art on the one hand, romantic art on the other, suggesting what we might suspect, that the two antagonists to classical perfection are allies. Classical art says: "simply give men the idea of a perfection that belongs to man." The paradoxical, if uncannily reassuring result of classical discipline is the kind of transcendence some regretted in the passing of the credulous poet: enchantment.

> And so, strict rules, and sometimes absurd, having been promulgated, and wholly artificial conventions having been established, what happened, gentlemen, and what still fills us with wonder, was that through the agency of half a dozen men of the highest order, and thanks to a few *salons,* there were born and flourished miracles of purity, of precise force and of life, those incorruptible works which make us bow, in spite of ourselves, before their divine perfection: Goddesses, they attain a degree of naturalness that is supernatural.[4]

In that stirring periodic roll (nor for nothing are the French professional patriots) Valéry promises that godhood will come from the practice of a humility, a simplicity, which is itself the height of refinement. Belief is not directed toward any deity or principle but toward the history of the fruits—the French poets' willing self-indenture to the best thoughts in the best words in the best order. The unspoken rule behind Valéry's statements is that emotions are common property; credulity and rapture belong to the same psychology that traps us all in time, whereas the emotions *of* poetry are the standards we can look up to and, by long gazing, be elevated by. Wit, satire, scurrilousness, despondency, fear are all part of what Nemerov called in *Journal of the Fictive Life* "the great human drama" to which poetry must attend, but no attitude or emotion by itself can do more than allude to the rest of the drama. And none by itself can so much as allude unless it is spoken from that further chamber where the voice we hear talking when we talk to ourselves is the voice of somebody else, "Leaping and dancing and singing, forgiving everything."

Attend to the Hands and Feet

Nemerov's poetry is respectful of particulars, and of the small laws that rest behind them. His vision is not "unique," but its exactness is of a kind peculiar to him. While it is true, as Borges says, that the image only one man could have invented is bound to be banal and to touch no one, what Nemerov writes of the folk-sayings buried in Brueghel's paintings is also true:

> We get the picture, as we say, although we miss
> The shrewd allusion to some ancient smart remark
> That would have told us what we know and never say.

His own poems delight us by those small felicities of observation of the things we know and never say, or see but never body forth in just those words. Who hasn't noticed the sinuous movements of squirrels in trees? But who else puts so well how "they flow / Heavy as waves along the bending boughs"? The same question may be asked about the humming-bird "kneeling in the air" before a flower's bell; the dead lobster on the town dump who "lifts / An empty claw in his most minatory of gestures"; the feathery fins of exotic goldfish that look "Like light in gin, / Viscous as ice first forming on a stream"; the strangely human face of the bison on the nickel, "Somewhat resembling that of Jupiter Ammon." Bath chairs on the beach in winter face the sea "in mute squadrons." The tone arm of a record player, having come to the end of a piece of music in which we had been engrossed, seems to represent or be responsible for the sudden silence; but in Nemerov's version the tone arm "cocks its head / An instant, as if listening for something / That is no longer there but might be."

The flies at the town dump are a "dynamo / Composed, by thousands, of our ancient black / Retainers." Water creates "herringbones of light /

Ebbing on the beaches," or makes a "string-bag pattern of the pebbled waves / Over the shallows of the shelving cove / In high sunlight." In a clear, spring-fed pond the water is so shallow that one can see "The numerous springs moving their mouths of sand." In "The Crossing," about butterflies gathering to migrate, the aimless look of the monarchs' massing is due to the "Brownian motion of the wind," which is one of nature's ways of getting done what it has to do, "the rise of hills / And settling of seas, the fall of leaf / Across the shoulder of the northern world." In "Threshold," when the leaf decides to go, it goes "fine as a sage . . . drifting in detachment down the road."

The last two examples, the leaf fallen across the world's northern shoulder and the leaf drifting along like an abstracted holy man, reveal perhaps more obviously the nature of many of the other closely observed particulars: They are described in metaphors. The "wave" of the squirrel running along the branch, the "mute squadrons" of the deck chairs, the "string-bag pattern" of nature's watery net, the "mouths of sand"—each says the small, observed fact in terms other and larger than itself. At the very least the practice points to the poet's minimal faith that some things in the world are connected to others. Nemerov's use of more extended metaphor suggests that his faith in connection amounts to piety, and that he will not stint the observance of mysterious rites.

One of his methods of putting particulars in a metaphoric frame (we're still outside on the temple steps) is that of contiguity. Eliot gave us the handy term objective correlative: The guilty, impassioned thing in here requires some way of becoming a visible thing out there. A poem about a woman's suicide closes with a group of red ants dragging a beetle along the path "Through the toy kingdom where nobody thinks." The statement is simple and suffused with sentiment at the same time. Another poem, "The View," shows us a man looking through a screened window at a sunny pastoral scene; the mood is one of wild desolation, even though none of the "correlatives" is anything but plainly and rather sketchily there. Although the screen dutifully frames "as in a graph / The view he has of flowers" and the blue distance does not particularly crave his participation and shadows have the standard connection with the bodies from which they are cast, the fellow is frantic with the sorrow that he fits nowhere here:

> No one will come, there's no
> Comfort, not the least
> Saving discrepancy
> In a view where every last thing
> Is rimed with its own shadow
> Exactly, and every fall
> Is once for all.[5]

The method of contiguity—of finding neutral externals full of causal significance—is particularly suited to such neurotic states as that of this
poem's protagonist.

A second method of putting the single in the path of the myriad is to
make the commonplace word refer back to its livelier origins. In a section
of "To Lu Chi" discussed above where the heron fishes in its own image
in a still, reflective stream, Nemerov writes of the "*reach* of mastery,"
concluding the verse paragraph with the certainty that, despite the conten-
tions in the world to which the poet returns, "that pure and hidden *reach*
remains." The paradox-lesson in the poem—the stillness that passes, the
stasis that moves—is further enhanced by the choice, among the possible
meanings of *reach,* of the static or *rigid* aspect, the inviolable place to
which the tensed mind then also, kinetically, *reaches.* The old pioneers
sitting useless by the dry road in "The Brief Journey West" are barraged
by temptations to lechery, the passing schoolgirls' "cold gleams of *flesh*"
soliciting in their eyes "the custom of desire." But since they are "done
with all disasters but the one," they don't respond; their indifference is of
a fierce sort, however, and the meaning of *sarcasm* as the tearing of flesh
is apt:

> Their eyes are sunk in ancient *flesh,*
> And the *sarcastic* triumph of the mind
> They now enjoy, letting their lust alone
> Who may have kin but have no longer kind.

The clever Latin infinitive *volvere,* to turn, which we find hidden in so
many English words, relates the word *volume* (the curled scroll of parch-
ment, and later, the book) to the rounded arches of a Gothic ceiling,
vault; this spatial appetite is present, of course, in a secondary meaning
of volume. Both are present in a line from the poem "To Robert Frost,"
"The leaves turn in the *volume* of the year." "Summer's Elegy" suggests
that in autumn when the butterflies are about done for, they "*regret* their
closed cocoons"; the Anglo-Saxon root is helpful, *gretan,* to weep for. In
the same poem we hear "the *terminal* sound / Of apples dropping on the
dry ground"; the etymological pressure is clear. So is the pressure of
origins in lines from poems discussed above: the savage action paintings
hanging patient on the walls, the *controversial wheels* of Pound's machinery,
Daphne of the *stubborn wood* (stubborn as stave or club). Nemerov's frequent Elizabethan turn on words like *consent, constant, custom, waste, consider, prove, proportion, gain, court, change, coin, ripe, stay,* etc., complicates
the game, since the metaphoric and punning possibilities are at once restricted by their acknowledged historical provenance and increased when
that provenance becomes another sound to strike against.

Although I don't recall that Cézanne painted a still life with dishes, apples, *and* guitars (the latter suggests Picasso), the point of "Still Life II" is an interesting description of how Cézanne, among others, used blue and black to outline and solidify the shapes; the description of the half-witted "natural man" bewildered by all these falling fruits and tilting tables is rather brilliant. *Migraine* (hemikranios, pain in one half of the head) is the punning key to his response of half-states, and to the halving of the painted things into ripe colors on one side, the "shadows of slate and sable" on the other:

> By the just rigors of an art
> That hung relation on the void,
> The natural man, for his poor part,
> Is half-embarrassed, half-annoyed,
>
> And in the slight *migraine* of form,
> Holding together every side
> Against the old atomic storm,
> His eye grows dull, and lets things slide.

A third figurative strategy, moderating the two extremes of self-conscious wordplay and resonant contiguity, is that of positing the metaphoric theme in a capsule or miniature form, and then moving out and away to the particular textures of the contributing parts. "Late Summer" tells us from the outset that it will be a comparison between "what's going on aloft" in the trees and the birth of things to come, and that this comparison is more real than, and "unaffected by, / The noise of history and the newsboy's cry." The second stanza then explores the rich possibilities of "fruits and futures" forming along the boughs—"Acorns in neat berets," "Prickly planets among the sweetgum's starry leaves"—and stanza three directs our attention to the far, forested slopes where the trees are secretly "secreting" next year,

> making news,
> Enciphering in their potencies of pulp
> The *matrix* of much that hasn't happened yet.

As the trees' destiny moves from the living mystery of their growth to their fate as newsprint paper, the poem evokes the gamut of meanings for *matrix:* the womb; the substance in which something is embedded; the cast made from the impression of that imbedded object; and finally the printer's mold from which the type is punched. The movement is thus da capo from the news-type at the end to the early cry of beginnings by the newsboy, just as the "drumming on the eardrums" of the previous poem brought us back both to the sound of the question we asked and to one of the little mysterious laws we were asking about.

We have seen the da capo movement in the return of the emperor's script to the original "cursive scrawl" in "Writing," even though we had journeyed far afield with the ice skaters, the white-boned constellations, the bat skimming the void, and the tremor in the true stylist's hand. The last verse paragraph of "Writing" also moved back to the start (skipping the first element) so that the open water bore no hard inscription of skates. The turn of mind by which Nemerov moves in many poems from particular to particular is rather like sorites; this is the next method of making metaphor we shall examine.

The sorites of similitudes is an interesting compulsion, very hard to bring off. Rather than letting all the associations float about until they are joined at the time of writing into one emblem-cluster, Nemerov has elected to coax his ideas into connecting, piece by slow piece. The "small mild Negro man with a broom" is "The Sweeper of Ways" underneath "high haughty trees." The old man's broom and its connection to the trees develops into one of these sorites; although it looks impossible to finish sweeping all those constantly falling leaves,

> the broom goes back and forth
> With a tree's patience, as though naturally
> Erasers would speak the language of pencils.

As though, in other words, the fardel of straw on the end of the broom spoke the language of the wooden stave to which it's bound, the wood like that of the trees that are growing the leaves that resume the earth and that must be swept away. Pencils then lead to the writing of thoughts (the script of leaves "stuck like emblems on the walk"). It is as though the world were a great writing:

> A thousand thoughts fall on the same blank page,
> Though the wind blows them back, they go where he
> Directs them, to the archives where disorder
> Blazes and a pale smoke becomes the sky.

When in the next verse paragraph the prayer not to be hated for being white is perfectly picked up by the broom's antennae, the theme of leaves as writings and thoughts is threaded with a slightly different twist: We are like so many souls gathered like leaves to the kindness of his task:

> we know ourselves so many thoughts
> Considered by a careful, kindly mind
> Which can do nothing, and is doing that.

We might note in passing how deftly the sweetness of the feelings the old man evokes is ordered and, as it were, cautioned by the background of semantic and metaphoric puzzling.

The Victorian beauty standing before the pier glass in "I Only Am Escaped Alone to Tell Thee" proceeds in stately fashion to become a proud Ship of Tarshish whose laced tackle can only be loosed by marriage. We arrive at the ship because the "long inaccurate glass" blurred her image and her vision: "the pictures were as troubled water." Two strands of imagery are linked in parallel sorites: The woman laced up like a ship, in whalebone, until tyrannous passion (perhaps someone else's?) undoes her is one strand; the other is the woman's vague unrest under the gas lamp before the mirror, where some shadow had its hand

> and seemed
> To hump the knuckles nervously,
> A giant crab readying to walk,
> Or a blanket moving in its sleep.

This terrible unrest, the humped shadow of passionate discontent, at last "Beat[s] at the air till the light blows out." The two strands touch by the instrument of Melville's "Epilogue" to *Moby-Dick*, where Ishmael echoes the four messengers who came to tell Job of his losses of oxen, sheep, camels, and children in catastrophes of which they were the lone survivors (I only am escaped alone to tell thee). The stanza in which the second strand meets the first involves the killing of whales "In calm beneath the troubled glass, / Until the needle drew their blood." Once blood is drawn, the proud ship, with all her bravery on, and tackle trim, sinks beneath the wounded beast:

> I see her standing in the hall,
> Where the mirror's lashed to blood and foam,
> And the black flukes of agony
> Beat at the air till the light blows out.

What one may conclude from the various ways in which Nemerov makes the particular thing visible (by likening it to other things) is roughly what we knew in other ways about his poems—that he cannot write well or interestingly unless his mind is engaged in finding the fit of language to the world. As Robert Boyers succinctly put it, "he is least afflicted by weariness when he is least submissive to things as they are in themselves, when the creative faculty is least subject to the imperatives of rational intellection."[6] The consecutiveness of reason is succeeded by the elation of apt comparison. Both tact and elegance are involved in the search for the fitting, and close attention to the Hands & Feet, to the Lineaments of the Countenances; they are all descriptive of Character. All Sublimity is founded on Minute Discriminations, Blake wrote, it is in Particulars that Wisdom consists & Happiness too.[7]

The long, interlocking, dependent statements, each of which refers to the original conception, are among Nemerov's means of achieving the sublime by way of the minute. "Figures of Thought," another poem about minutiae, also tends to call attention to the modesty of its claims in the most subtle yet minatory of gestures. Principally, however, this is a poem of the third veil through whose gay formal fabric the minute may appear as the sublime. Its subject is the small law, the "logarithmic spiral on / Sea-shell and leaf" that also rules the navigation vectors of a bomber pilot's "turn / Onto his target," the law that's also found

> in the flight of certain wall-eyed bugs
> Who cannot see to fly straight into death
> But have to cast their sidelong glance at it
> And come but cranking to the candle's flame . . .
>
> ("Figures of Thought")

The sideways indirection of those insects, which will soon enough find their directions out in death, will remind us of the lazy swarm of monarchs aloft in the Brownian motion of the wind (one of nature's ways of getting things done).

Like Yeats, Nemerov believes in the power of the unfocused frame of mind to prepare one for the most conclusive feats. You can't get there by striding straight ahead; you must subside into one of those peculiar states of distraction from which the gods will see to it that you extract the ripe, intended meaning. Fix the eye on nothing, practice a tinker shuffle, and (like the painter of the mountain stream whose brush's tip streams from the wrist—the running water is the wrist), observe the painter Michael Angelo reclined upon the scaffolding:

> With no more sound than the mice make
> His hand moves to and fro.
> *Like a long-legged fly upon the stream*
> *His mind moves upon silence.*

The subject of Nemerov's "Figures of Thought" is much more meek than Yeats's company of Caesar, Michael Angelo, and Helen of Troy; but stemming from the steepening spiral of their common forms we find warfare in the fighter pilot's turn, beauty and death in the seashell and the candle flame toward which the insect sidles, and, in the final lines, the small and thorough regulations of the works of nature and of art:

> How secret that is, and how privileged
> One feels to find the same necessity
> Ciphered in forms diverse and otherwise
> Without kinship—that is the beautiful

In Nature as in art, not obvious,
Not inaccessible, but just between.

It may diminish some our dry delight
To wonder if everything we are and do
Lies subject to some little law like that;
Hidden in nature, but not deeply so.

("Figures of Thought")

Signatures in All Things

Ein jedes Ding hat seinen Mund zur Offenbarung.
Jakob Boehme, *De Signatura Rerum* (1622)

Howard Nemerov believes, like Yeats, not only in history's slant and arbitrary angles but also in history's fatedness and massive choice. And, like Blake, not only does Nemerov attempt to rescue the sublime from the minute, but he also looks back to the time before the Fall when the serpent walked splendidly upright, the lions were man-faced, and all created things called forth their "given names." In poems like "The Loon's Cry" (*Mirrors and Windows,* 1958), Nemerov regards the world from the double (or paradox) perspective of the pieces of paradise. He stands on a spit of land between an estuary where the red sun sets and a rock-banked river over which the moon rises, regretting his alienation from the "symboled world." Not that he has abandoned symbols: He has perhaps only brought them closer to home as he points out that he "now stood but between / A swamp of fire and a reflecting rock"—a statement that refers us to the sun / fire *versus* moon / earth alternatives the poet always confronts. At the same time, in envying the fabled past when the energy in things "shone through their shapes," Nemerov reinvests that past with form and shape (its "respeaking was the poet's act"), while suggesting how such respeaking might be more perilous, more loonlike, more desolating, than the awareness of being fallen:

> [Once] sun and moon no less
> Than tree or stone or star or human face
> Were seen but as fantastic Japanese
> Lanterns are seen, sullen or gay colors
> And lines revealing the light that they conceal.
> . . . .
> I thought I understood what that cry meant,
> That its contempt was for the forms of things,
> Their doctrines, which decayed—the nouns of stones
> And adjectives of glass—not for the verb
> Which surged in power properly eternal

> Against the seawall of the solid world,
> Battering and undermining what it built,
>
> And whose respeaking was the poet's act,
> Only and always, in whatever time
> Stripped by uncertainty, despair and ruin,
> Time readying to die, unable to die
> But damned to life again, and the loon's cry.

The desperate figure damned to life again, who wants to die and cannot, appears again in the figure of Cain, about whom Nemerov has written a one-act play, and as Ahasuerus, in a poem of that title about the Wandering Jew (also known as Joseph Cartaphilus).[8] Cain and the wanderer Cartaphilus are types of insomnia, or of nightmare-ridden sleep, the limbo of the poisoned will. They belong to the frozen cities of stone about which Nemerov has so frequently written, usually, as here, under the light of the moon:

> The moon . . . went cold inside,
> Nor any strength of sun could keep its people
> Warm in their palaces of glass and stone.
> Now all its craters, mountains and still seas,
> Shining like snow and shadows on the snow,
> Orbit this world in envy and late love.

We are told in Genesis that the line of Cain created the cities of man, full of evildoing and (as Augustine is at pains to point out) generation: No one refrained from sexuality. In Nemerov's lighter moods, Cain's city is contingent, messy, and somewhat randy; in grimmer ones malicious, frozen, and damned. When the flood conveniently killed Cain's descendants, it was the descendant of Seth, Noah, who was borne to Ararat. The Christian habit of genealogy discerns a natural progression from Seth's pillars and astronomy—the city of God—to the New Jerusalem in Revelation. "Signatures in all things are," Nemerov affirms here, "and may by arts / Contemplative be found again." Perhaps these are slender clues on which to pin the massive emblems of the apocalypse, but I would like to take the argument just a bit further. If the links are false as facts about the poet's intention in "The Loon's Cry," they may nevertheless illustrate the mechanism by which things happen there.

Three verses from Revelation have a bearing on the argument. In two of them, the sea alters from that surging fluid that batters and undermines the earthly city: "And I saw as it were a sea of glass mingled with fire" (Rev. 15:2); "The first heaven and the first earth were passed away; and there was no more sea" (Rev. 21:1). Augustine puzzles over the meaning of "no more sea":

It is possible that, as prophetic diction delights in mingling figurative and real language, and thus in some sort veiling the sense, so the words "And there is no more sea" may be taken in the same sense as the previous phrase, "And the sea presented the dead which were in it" [Rev. 10:13]. For then there shall be no more of this world, no more of the surgings and restlessness of human life, and it is this which is symbolized by the *sea*.[9]

Under the aspect of God, the sea lapses from its motion and becomes the perfect work, the glass like crystal. But under the aspect of humanity, what is crystalline is dead—glass adjectives and stone nouns. In life the only mask for the eternal is the predicate of motion. The sea must remain the emblem of our hounded thought, both the only noise in which our ear can make out, from time to time, the calling of another voice, and the only motion in which fixity and power can simultaneously be seen.

The opening stanza of "The Loon's Cry" discovers the poet walking in late summer by the place where a railroad bridge divides the river from the sea. "The balanced silence centered where I stood, / The fulcrum of two poised immensities, / Which offered to be weighed at either hand." And he does weigh the immensities, river against sea, moon against sun, "God and His Lucifer's long debate, a trunk / From which, complex and clear, the episodes / Spread out their branches." As the train tracks divide in space, the loon's cry marks out in time, dividing the feeling of desolation and homelessness from the sudden premonition of being "in paradise / Again, in ignorance and emptiness / Blessed beyond all that we thought to know." Just as here the bird's mournful cry shifts the balance from desolation to beatitude, so in the poem's last stanza (coming after the one in which signatures are read in things and arts contemplative found and named again), the loon's call is strangely mixed up with another sort of clarion:

> The loon again? Or else a whistling train,
> Whose far thunders began to shake the bridge.
> And it came on, a loud bulk under smoke,
> Changing the signals on the bridge, the bright
> Rubies and emeralds, rubies and emeralds
> Signing the cold night as I turned for home,
> Hearing the train cry once more, like a loon.

It is not coincidence that the bridge cuts moon apart from sun; that Lucifer the shining debates with God (haggling over Job, Christ in the desert, and in more literary ways over Adam and Eve, Faust, Ivan, and Leverkühn); that glass opposes water (as Cain opposes Seth, false creation the true). And if it is not coincidence that "naked, hungry, cold, / We suddenly may seem in paradise," then it may not be coincidence that the red and green lights with which the sounding train signals through the cold night are recognized for "Rubies and emeralds, rubies and emeralds." As we are told by John in the third relevant verse from Revelation, the One who comes to Judgment is made of the same gems:

> One sat upon the throne. And he that sat was to look upon like jasper and carnelian; and there was a rainbow round about the throne, in sight like unto an emerald. . . . And out of the throne proceeded lightnings and thunderings and voices.
>
> (Rev. 4:3–5).

The train suggested by the still empty bridge in stanza one of "The Loon's Cry" becomes an eschatological marker as well, barreling down upon the scene with a hint of last things, final joy.

Like many of the middle-length poems of Coleridge and Wordsworth called descriptive-meditative lyrics or conversation poems, many of Nemerov's blank-verse poems tend to meander. It may take him quite a while after starting to sketch his immediate subject before the real subject of the poem works its way out, rather like a "deep syntax" emerging from the web of pleasantries. "The Pond" is such a poem, as are "The Quarry," "To Lu Chi," "The Town Dump," "Brainstorm," and "Waiting Rooms." Sometimes the inner meaning stays hidden while the outer machinery rumbles cheerfully along ("Watching Football on TV," "A Day on the Big Branch"). But there are fifteen or so blank-verse poems of the dilatory sort in which the visible yields readily and gracefully to the visionary, among them "Playing the Inventions," "The Four Ages," "Drawing Lessons," "Translation," "The Painter Dreaming in the Scholar's House," "The Sanctuary," "Painting a Mountain Stream," "The Loon's Cry," "The Mud Turtle," and the three poems to be discussed in the next section, "Boy with Book of Knowledge," "Runes," and "The Western Approaches."

A Damask Either-Sided

Knowing the secret, Nemerov writes at the end of the fifteenth rune, and keeping the secret—"it is not knowing, it is not keeping, / But being the secret hidden from yourself." A cryptic saying, but not indecipherable. "Runes" (*New Poems,* 1960) is a revision of his early plethora of symbols, a long statement devised, more precisely than "Lion & Honeycomb," to stand in place of "The Scales of the Eyes." The symbols are both simpler and fewer, and more narrative. In place of the salt vines, thickets of nerves, icy stares, white grasses, and bleeding stars (the exorbitant tropes of the earlier poem), we find running water and various kinds of seeds, which are the matrix for families and histories and stories: the egg in which the basilisk is hatching, atoms of memory, germs of empire, seeds in which time to come has tensed itself. The principal difference between the changes rung on the symbols in the two poems is that in "Runes" every symbol takes us into its future. The seed carried by the bird "Will harbor in its branches most remote / Descendants of the bird." Adam's tainted seed grew into trees from which came Aaron's rod, the tree of Jesse, and finally "The sticks and yardarms of the holy three- / masted vessel whereon the Son of Man / Hung between thieves, and came the crown of thorns, / The lance and ladder, when was shed that blood / Stained in the grain of Adam's tainted seed" ("Runes," XI).

"Runes" is also interesting because it is a deliberate attempt, perhaps the most sustained in Nemerov's *Collected Poems,* not just to follow associations through, but to think in fact of the object when that object is not only the world but also the tradition in which one thinks. (Hence, the poem's circular habits; but stories are like that). Two voyagers of the tradition, Odysseus and Conrad's Marlow, stand at either end of the journey; between them, on the variable waves of the fifteen-line stanza, one of Nemerov's favorite verse forms, flows the running sea of circumstance, the ocean of salt and blood.

Odysseus's story has two endings. In the first, black in Ithaca, he goes out with Telemachus to steal sheep, "The country squire resumes a normal life." In the other, speaking as Dante and Tennyson had him speak,

> out beyond the gates
> Of Hercules, gabbling persuasively
> About virtue and knowledge, he sails south
> To disappear from sight behind the sun;
> Drowning near blessed shores he flames in hell.
> I do not know which ending is the right one.

Nemerov knows enough about country squires, and speaks often in the poem about the banal side of existence as that is also part of the tradition in which one thinks. There are kernels and husks here, too, of course: pills and condensations, mustard seeds in lucite, cosmetic and prophylactic envelopes; and in the pinewoods, the swamps where convicts roam, the ditches where dead dogs are thrown, one sees "the buried hulls of things to come." But daily life is *in* the poem like a seed still dormant in the ground, and what Nemerov is after, I suspect, is the seed whose story surrounds its origins in much the same way Conrad's narrator described Marlow's ability to tell a tale:

> The yarns of seamen have a direct simplicity, the whole meaning of which lies within the shell of a cracked nut. But Marlow was not typical . . . and

to him the meaning of an episode was not inside like a kernel but outside, enveloping the tale which brought it out.

(*Heart of Darkness,* 1902)

The tale of Kurtz reaches outside the episodes in which it is narrated to touch those extraordinary passages at the beginning and the end of the Conrad novella where the sun sets pacifically and then luridly on the Thames. There is a "gloom to the west . . . brooding over a crowd of men," and the waters change from "the vivid flush of a short day" to evoke the "memories of men and ships it had borne. . . . What greatness had not floated on the ebb of that river into the mystery of an unknown earth! . . . The dreams of men, the seed of commonwealths, the germs of empires." In Rune XIII, in which Nemerov writes about *Heart of Darkness,* the story whose darkness is represented and framed by the sea, we encounter a sailor who leans down to the watery mirror and finds his other self, his Cain. This is Marlow finding Kurtz:

> There sailed out on the river, Conrad saw,
> The dreams of men, the seed of commonwealths,
> The germs of Empire. To the ends of the earth
> One many-veined bloodstream swayed the hulls
> Of darkness gone, of darkness still to come
> . . . .
>   its taste,
> Saline and cold, was as a mirror of
> The taste of human blood. The sailor leaned
> To lick the mirror clean, the somber and
> Immense mirror that Conrad saw, and saw
> The other self, the sacred Cain of blood
> Who would seed a commonwealth in the Land of Nod.

There are the men who come home, and the men who don't. As in the conflicting versions of Odysseus's end, sometimes those who do and don't are the same man, damned either way but in different registers. "The ground swell of all sea-returns / Muttering under history" makes the country squire poaching at night the secret sharer of the gabbling rhetor out beyond the gates of Hercules. They are two versions of the same fate, the one version the promise held out to the other. What we are not gives back to us what we are; as Nemerov elsewhere wrote, we look into the mirror and watch "with observed eyes the stranger pass." It is only a thin reflecting tissue that separates the leaning sailor from the wandering Cain; as there was something of Marlow's ethic in Kurtz's struggle with himself, so Marlow carries with him the man he saw in the jungle as if Kurtz's nightmare were the landscape he was doomed to carry on his back: one of the dark places of the earth.

When Nemerov returns in the next-to-last rune to the story of Odysseus, he casts us into the middle of things again, and we do not know whether the tapestry on which his days are counted is being woven against his return, or after that later and final departure:

> There is a threshold, that meniscus where
> The strider walks on drowning waters
> . . . .
> The water of the eye where the world walks
> Delicately, is as a needle threaded
> From the reel of a raveling stream, to stitch
> Dissolving figures in a watered cloth,
> A damask either-sided as the shroud
> Of the lord of Ithaca, labored at in light,
> Destroyed in darkness, while the spidery oars
> Carry his keel across deep mysteries
> To harbor in unfathomable mercies.

The mirror of stories and histories is either-sided. We can never know whether the other self we see is Cain or Abel, and no matter how we designate that double, we are in danger either of dying by his hand or rising up to slay. There just aren't that many plots, and when we think to prefer one role, we wind up playing the other one, too. "When the gray stranger shows up in your dream" trying to strangle you, and you waken to the mundane time that stems from yesterday, you say

> "I just got out in time." But that's not so,
> As waking from a dark to a dark you know
> That if you were for a time in mortal danger,
> And are so still, it was not from a stranger.

("Nightmare")

The nightmare is repetition, the return to the guilty place, the stopping of the frame in the middle of the action where something sinister has always been going on—the weaving of that damask of light and shadow raveling on the stream in which our future is inscribed, and on whose deeps the "spidery oars" of the small boat we sail are carrying us back to the beginning.

The title poem of Howard Nemerov's final volume in the *Collected Poems, The Western Approaches,* is also about the endless returns to the story's beginning—a beginning that is, however, an emblem of the end where "any man dissolves in Everyman," wasting away into that fog where suffering makes us general, indistinct, slightly larger than the life we had. "Beyond the Pleasure Principle" (*The Blue Swallows,* 1967) had already established the connection between the sad and horrible preparations of the dying and the telling of the story from the top:

> when his great courage
> Becomes a wish to die, there appears, so obscurely,
> Pathetically, out of the wounded torment and the play,
> A something primitive and appealing, and still dangerous,
> That crawls on bleeding hands and knees over the floor
> Toward him, and whispers as if to confess: *again, again.*

The old stories that once were waiting for us down the road have been filled out by our life, and we've done what the stories predicted we would do, although we did not know they were our stories at the time. From the vantage that looks forward, chance and possibility and variety unravel. "But looking back on life it is as if / Our Book of Changes never let us change." The "western approaches" may signify, by contrast with the eastern Book of Changes, a peculiarly western way of telling stories:[10]

> When I was young I flew past Skerryvore
> Where the Nine Maidens still grind Hamlet's meal,
> The salt and granite grain of bitter earth,
> But knew it not for twenty years or more.
> My chances past their changes now, I know
>
> How a long life grows ghostly toward the close
> As any man dissolves in Everyman
> Of whom the story, as it always did, begins
> In a far country, once upon a time,
> There lived a certain man and he had three sons . . . [*sic*]

What happens in our western way of telling stories is the absurdity that we all belong in the same tale involving fathers and mothers and children and time. This is true even of the riddling Icelandic etiology of the salt sea.[11] Hamlet's mill used to grind meal, as well as gold, peace, and happiness, but it fell into the hands of Mysingr, the Sea-King, and the maidens refused to mill gold for him and ground out salt instead. His ship sank, the mill-stone creating a great whirlpool from which come the salt of the sea and the tempests. The good king is killed by the evil one; in place of happiness there are many bitter tears; and in place of acting when we might, the law that dictates that we will never learn until too late that, as Marx said, "everything in history happens twice, once seriously and once as a parody of itself." This, too, is a realization about the child repeating the parents by mourning their deaths as our own.

Nemerov speaks of the death of his father in *Journal of the Fictive Life*. The poet's sister had written him, "He looks more like everyman than himself."[12] In speaking of sons who are in search of their fathers, Nemerov conjoins Hamlet with Telemachus (Telmah). The *Odyssey* of "Runes" and the Hamlet of "The Western Approaches," two poems I believe share the preoccupation with the story of our lives, are thus brought together in the book that is about the author's inability to write fiction, and that also explores the various degrees of truth present in the interpretations he imposes on his inner life, his dreams, and his regrets.

In the *Journal* Nemerov also makes the point, in different words, about the opposing principles of emotions *in* poetry and the emotions *of* poetry: Although the "disagreeable content" of his dreams does not decrease, his pleasure at seeing deeply into even the worst of these mirrors of the self is increased. "The greatness of the human voice, and its nobility, and its poignance, are most fully heard when it speaks of disaster, hopelessness. . . . the perfect dream, the perfect story, would be perfectly dialectical, shining with 'the light of hope out of the utmost hopelessness.'"

"Boy with Book of Knowledge" is a simpler poem than either "Runes" or "The Western Approaches." Although its subject is also the voyages one is still restless to make and the relation of youth to age, the circuit is here restricted to the life of one man. He had wanted to be a poet when he found, in the *Book of Knowledge* under the heading "Immortal Poems," the song that made him weep, "America the Beautiful." The phrase from that anthem, "from sea to shining sea," leads him in the final pair of stanzas to another meditation by the shore. This threshold gives an eastern approach on the Atlantic from the shore opposite to the Hebrides. By that habit of sorites raised almost to a method of metaphysics, what the poet will now never know becomes a mysterious library glistening in the dark like a luxury liner on the vast black water to which our infrequent lighthouses no longer shine:

> He would acknowledge all he will not know,
> The silent library brooding through the night
> With all its lights continuing to burn
>
> Insomniac, a luxury liner on what sea
> Unfathomable of ignorance, who could say?
> And poetry, as steady, still, and rare
> As the lighthouses now unmanned and obsolete
> That used to mark America's dangerous shores.

Perhaps the resolution of "Boy with Book of Knowledge" is too tender to be perfectly dialectical. But it suggests, in its elegiac mood of bewildered affirmation, a position less ironclad with respect to the eternal return of the same old story than the foregoing poems may have been made to bear. For although there are indeed only a few plots, a handful of stories that wait upon our lives, one of these plots is the one that provides for the sudden diversion, the god stepping coolly down from the catwalk, the drawing from despair, surprise. Part of our plot is described in lines of Wallace Stevens, "Out of nothing to have come on major weather / It is possible, possible, possible," and in some late prose of Nemerov: "Poetry speaks of the spirit's being compelled to renew itself, in spite of knowledge, in spite of pain, in spite of death."[13] That part of the old story that allows for a break in the story may help to decipher the lines from Rune XV:

> To watch water, to watch running water
> Is to know a secret
> . . . .
> It is a secret. Or it is not to know
> The secret, but to have it in your keeping,
> A locked box, Bluebeard's room, the deathless thing
> Which it is death to open. Knowing the secret,
> Keeping the secret—herringbones of light
> Ebbing on beaches, the huge artillary
> Of tides—it is not knowing, it is not keeping,
> But being the secret hidden from yourself.

The Footsteps of Astraea

Although I may not understand Harold Bloom's theory of the anxiety of influence well enough to claim that these lines from "Runes" either do or do not exemplify such a principle, what does seem quite clear to me is that the characteristic Wallace Stevens sound is *not* in this poem as it was in Nemerov's "Unscientific Postscript." Here, those Stevens-like statements, "It is a secret. Or it is not to know / The secret," and "it is not knowing, it is not keeping," may remind us, in the fashion of an afterthought, of "Wild Ducks, People and Distances" ("It was that they were there / That held the distances off"), "The Pure Good of Theory" ("It is never the thing but the version of the thing"), "An Ordinary Evening in New Haven" ("The barrenness that appears is an exposing. . . . It is a coming on and a coming forth"), or of "Notes Toward a Supreme Fiction":

> not to have is the beginning of desire.
> To have what is not is its ancient cycle.
> It is desire at the end of winter, when
>
> It observes the effortless weather turning blue
> . . . .

> The casual is not
> Enough. The freshness of transformation is
>
> The freshness of a world. It is our own,
> It is ourselves, the freshness of ourselves,
> And that necessity and that presentation
>
> Are rubbings of a glass in which we peer.

But I would claim that the patent similarities in syntax, and in that Stevensian sort of desultory predication, are only present in the Nemerov poem as false clues. "Runes" sounds like no one but Nemerov. Nor have most of the poems discussed just above been the sort where other poets' voices have overwhelmed Nemerov's; he has admittedly written many poems that invite identification with the work of others, but the curious fact about Nemerov's attention to the literary tradition is that, like all good poets, he has learned how to steal what he needs from his predecessors.

The comparison I forced between "Pharaoh's Meditation on the Exodus" and "The Tomb at Akr Çaar" is exemplary for the influence argument: Despite all the ammunition one can assemble, Nemerov does not generally *sound like* Pound.[14] Both Bloom and David Bromwich indicate their sense of Nemerov's similarity to Robert Frost.[15] Bromwich's essay convincingly juxtaposes passages from both. But my response is, well, yes, on paper the lines of credit are clear, but the principle of personal obstinacy is also clear, and while it may be crucial for us as critics to search out the places where the important thought of the world crosses the paths of our contemporaries, it is just as important not to miss the uniqueness, the peculiarly "owned" movement of mind, which a poet of Nemerov's dedication obstinately manifests.

The searching for debts of influence does, however, serve an important function in criticism: It gives us the negative proof. Here, for example, are two passages that illustrate how incompatibly Shelley and Nemerov respond to Dante's *Convivio* (Dissertation 2, Canzone 1). I will not indicate who wrote which, simply because there will be no question as to authorship:

> Song, I think they will be few indeed
> Who well and rightly understand your sense,
> So difficult your speech and intricate.
> Wherefore if you should come by any chance
> Among such folk so little fit to read
> As that you seem not to *communicate,*
> I'd have you take heart even at that rate,
> My latest and dear one, saying to them:
> "Look you at least how beautiful I am."

My song, I fear that thou wilt find but few
  Who fitly shall conceive thy reasoning
  Of such hard matter dost thou entertain.
Whence, if by misadventure chance should bring
Thee to base company, as chance may do,
  Quite unaware of what thou dost contain,
  I prithee comfort thy sweet self again,
My last delight; tell them that they are dull,
And bid them own that thou art beautiful.

If one can for the time being ignore the *dosts* and *prithees,* what one hears as the primary difference between the two stanzas is Shelley's far more intense attitude of connection to his song, the deeper bond of personal intercourse, which is the true spirit of dramatic monologue. Nemerov's version sounds like a meditation; he is far less comfortable with the allegory—the personhood of the song. At the same time, despite what I take to be the closer accommodation of Shelley's lines to Dante's, there's something academic about the sound; it all fits, it is spiritually "correct," but it is ingeniously imitative of the original's spirit, not profoundly like it. On the other hand, Nemerov's rendering, which lacks the enthusiasm of identification with Dante's thought, is probably the more arduous engagement. Furthermore, Nemerov's translation manages to sound like Nemerov (no *dosts,* fewer unexamined assumptions of integrity and merit for his song—the modern doubt—and then the ironic pressure of words like *communicate*), and yet, in that last line, "'Look you at least how beautiful I am,'" he captures an erotic tenderness and a completely credible sense of sudden transcendence that Shelley's lines, for all their assurance, cannot approach. Nemerov has had to go a greater distance to get at Dante, but when he comes to the end, he has surpassed Shelley. In such victories does his interest as a poet consist.

The two translations illustrate another difference between a poet of the nineteenth century and one of the twentieth. Consider the enjambment. Nemerov's is tentative and subtle; the sense is not variously drawn out in an overtly Miltonic way, although he has imported Milton's lessons to better effect than Shelley has, for he manages to preserve line integrity in every case. Shelley forces the Miltonic point, thus obviating or making too insistently frail the purer rhymes of his structure. Nemerov's rhymes are weaker, but one hears them as more powerful by virtue of the pause he has managed to build into every line-close. In other words, Nemerov can be more unobtrusive with his rhymes as visual counters, more elaborative of their dimmer grace as aural ones. This, too, is a profitable exploitation of language that Shelley doesn't attempt, choosing instead the comforts of the virtuoso with more poetic materials to hand than the poem can effectively use.

The architectonic element that Owen Barfield describes in *Poetic Diction* as "a sense of difficulties overcome—of an obstreperous medium having been masterfully subdued," is more immediately seen in the Shelley stanza. "Seen" is appropriate to the insight since, as Barfield indicates, "it is much harder to convey the *full* effect of poetry of the architectural type with the *voice*."[16] The eye is needed to take in the line and period, and since this kind of verse is more regular in number of syllables, the sight-reading of the path of the sentence provides the necessary appendix to the rigidity of the sounds, providing, that is, the slight elisions and focusing of overall stress. In the opposite kind of verse, which Barfield calls the fluid type, structure is less rigid, as are (depending how far back one goes) the number of syllables and the exigencies of strict word order. In the spirit of the dichotomy between the fluid and the fixed, Nemerov's lines, "I'd have you take heart even at that rate, / My latest and dear one, saying to them," are closer to Thomas Wyatt than to Henry Surrey.[17]

The fact that Nemerov and Shelley were both moved to translate the same passage from Dante, however, draws our attention to a realm of thought about poetry and inspiration, about moral imperatives and the emotion *of* poetry, that dictates belief—the fertile attitude, as Goethe says, especially in a world that compels one to skepticism. In the light cast by Dante on the two poets, this belief in spiritual resemblances appears to be Neoplatonic. Barfield—like Kenneth Burke, an important expositor for Nemerov, as Dante, Shakespeare, Blake, and Yeats are the crucial poets—reminds us in his Afterword to *Poetic Diction* that Neoplatonism is Platonism plus the concept of individual genius. "Unscientific Postscript" brought the two concepts together; the couplet about the measured dance that may be lament "answers" by resolving the alternatives, sudden redemption or the eternal truth in changing forms. The final stanza of "Runes" about being the secret hidden from yourself also combines both Platonic and chiliastic attitudes toward history and human action: You are the constant in a world that itself grows to something of great constancy, as well as being its unique and discontinuous, its sudden and mysterious arbiter.

The three sections of *The Western Approaches* present in dialectical form Nemerov's thought about the distance between poet and intransigent world ("The Way"), about the signatures of things ("The Ground"), and about the arts contemplative and the endless waters of creation, which give us back the world ("The Mind"). "The Way" is the world's, more specifically, the satirist's world. The frozen stare of the early work has not disappeared from Nemerov's verse, although he has learned where to place it—within a world that is not explained away by being shown for dreary, cheap, and laughable. Although the "heaven of technology" in this section's last poem, "The Backward Look," has put men on the moon to gather samples for science and to cavort about like the worst sort of American rube, the earth seen from this perspective gains a new and sadder majesty:

> Earth of the cemeteries and cloudy seas,
> Our small blue agate in the big black bag . . .

"The Ground," the second section of *The Western Approaches,* is linked to the seamless web of language and to the doctrine of signatures by the introductory epigraph from Albrecht von Haller, the eighteenth-century botanist and physician who tried to counter deism by writing on the immortality of the soul: "Nature knits up her kinds in a network, not in a chain; but men can follow only by chains because their language can't handle several things at once." In the first poem, "The Dependencies," Nemerov describes the way nighthawks, spiders, and butterflies prepare for winter; their "Change is continuous on the seamless web." We can imitate the web of nature in the chain of metaphor because, as Nemerov wrote in one of his finest long poems, "The Painter Dreaming in the Scholar's House," the world is already signed with the speech it means to speak:

> the mind relates to thinking as the eye
> Relates to light. Only because the world
> Already is a language can the painter speak
> According to his grammar of the ground.

Sometimes, as in "Figures of Thought," the grammar of his ground dictates that Nemerov read the vagaries of small laws "Hidden in nature, but not deeply so," sometimes that he read the lessons of power from "A Cabinet of Seeds Displayed," that he observe the futures forming along the boughs in "Late Summer," that the gnats enflame the tree ("Seeing Things"), or that he find the signs in which the landscape suffers its knowledge of the onset of winter as though it were a human soul: The wind goes ashen

> till one afternoon
> The cold snow cloud comes down the intervale
> Above the river on whose slow black flood
> The first few flakes come hurrying in to drown.
>
> ("Again")

In the same essay where Nemerov speaks of the spirit renewing itself in poetry despite suffering and death ("Thirteen Ways of Looking at a Skylark"), he claims that the reason we have so many ways of looking at the world is that the landscape has all our lives been teaching us how to see. Although nature shows us our doom—shows us in fact that it will be the agent of our consummation—there is nevertheless in this "quiet background of our lives" another, more benign zone of connection:

> . . . surely it has told us so much about how to be in this world, or how could we have come to know so much, feel so much within us of how to be a tree or a stone or a river? and at certain times, perhaps the darkest times, a twilight at the beginning of winter, we may feel that not we alone in it, but the landscape of itself, *knows* these things.

In the essay's ensuing quotation of "A Spell Before Winter" from *The Next Room of the Dream,* we read that during this twilight "There is a knowledge in the look of things,"

> A knowledge glimmers in the sleep of things:
> The old hills hunch before the north wind blows.

Nemerov's relation to the speaking scene is general and humble. He does not assume that the legend at the corner of this map is a message written for him alone, rather that it is visible to everyone. The signatures exist; to read them must be possible. *Ein jedes Ding hat sienen Mund zur Offenbarung:* Each and every thing has a proper language in which to express both its secrets and our own. The painter in the scholar's house is the refiner of a thought that nature shares with man:

> He is the painter of the human mind
> Finding and faithfully reflecting the mindfulness
> That is in things, and not the things themselves.

In "Seeing Things," the thought of the world moves through its many manifestations like the rivers of semblance and resemblance visible to one standing out on Sudbury Marsh "amid a hundred hidden streams / Meandering down from Concord to the sea."

But the opposite of these continuities—the promise of finality—never entirely disappears. The first few flakes hurry in to drown. The old hills hunch. "The definite announcement of an end" presents itself when

> You know the intricate dependencies
> Spreading in secret through the fabric vast
> Of heaven and earth, sending their messages
> Ciphered in chemistry to all the kinds,
> The whisper down the bloodstream: it is time.

I don't believe it is too much to claim that this same bitter tension between the cyclical procession of the seasons and the premonition of finality is as important a theme in poems like Nemerov's "The Dependencies" as it is in poems like Shelley's "The Sensitive Plant."

When in section three of *The Western Approaches* Nemerov explores the measure of poetry, the four ages, the inventions of Bach, and the thought of trees, he does so under a congruently double perspective: History reveals its ageless continuity at the same time as it introduces sudden and irremediable change. The section's epigraph from Blake is apropos of the unchanging truth: "Poetry, Painting & Music, the three powers in Man of conversing with Paradise, which the flood did not sweep away." But as Nemerov tells us in "The Four Ages," human utterance does lapse from its primitive music. Subsequently, poetry imitates in words the fading sonority of the universe. At last, only prose is left. In "The Measure of Poetry," the vowels in which primal rhythms and energies are heard achieve form by constraint, the shackles being consonants—the boundaries struck against. But at the same time as the subjection of vowel to consonant occurs historically and only once in the history of language, each poet also recapitulates the past of his speech every time he writes, by virtue of the identification Nemerov discerns between consonants and the material things, the stubborn shore, the concrete unfoldings, the local vocabulary against which the energies of all unfigured poetic ideas "enrage" themselves.

Implicit in these great final poems of Howard Nemerov as in Shelley's *Defence of Poetry* and Barfield is the Neoplatonic paradox of time. If history is a schedule of resemblances, how to account for (a) the perceived fact of diminution in the world, and (b) the feeling of crucial possibilities in the individual life? Inasmuch as Barfield's exposition has more direct analogies with Nemerov's approach, I will state the problem in his terms, although it will be clear how closely both are in tune with Shelley's *Defence*. (1) It is the balance between the poetic state and the rational ability to judge and react to that state which makes possible the composition of poetry. Nemerov's poem "Writing" and his essay "A Wild Civility" illustrate this division between poetic and rational faculties, each of which is necessary to creation. (2) The poetic and rational faculties constitute the poles between which each individual poet in the act of composition oscillates, as Nemerov suggests in the trope of heavenly frequency in his poem "Angel and Stone." (3) Historically, the perfect balance between the aesthetic and abstract principles is situated in an earlier age; according to Barfield, Shakespeare and Dante were freed for their great poetry by the emergent collateral vigor of prose as an imaginative medium.[18] Nemerov's essay "The Swaying Forme" is relevant. (4) The natural history of language is not cyclical but linear, from fluidity to fixity, poetry to prose.

We exist at a terminus. The world has become increasingly prosaic. The pertinent Nemerov texts would be "The Four Ages" and another poem from *The Western Approaches,* "Translation":

> Where is that world,
> Where did it go, in which they said those things
> And sang those things in their high halls of stone?
> . . . .
> It still may draw a tremor and a tear
> Sometimes, if only for its being gone,
> That untranslatable, translated world
> Of the Lady and the singers and the dead.

(5) Like Shelley, Barfield skirts that last issue: Despite our being late-born, sublimity is still possible because of the force of the individual's ability to make meaning. Thus the perception of redeeming spiritual force occurs at the very point where the historical sketches indicate that we have fallen from a purer consciousness, a prior period of connectedness with the world. "The Loon's Cry" is based on such a contradiction, as are "Maestria," "Playing the Inventions," "To Lu Chi," and so on.

Shelley admits that there are particularly bad periods in the history of the word when the poet must speak to the fallen mentality:

> At the approach of such a period poetry ever addresses itself to those faculties which are the last to be destroyed, and its voice is heard, like the footsteps of Astraea, departing from the world.[19]

But he then proceeds to assert the completed form behind the limited or fallen appearance. Having already quoted Bacon to explain what metaphors are ("These similitudes . . . are finely said by Lord Bacon to be 'the same footsteps of nature impressed upon the various subjects of the world,'" p. 278b), Shelley then returns to the same metaphor of the trace of the divine footfall to describe, not the last solace of men in an evil time, but poetry's eternal and changeless task:

> We are aware of evanescent visitations of thought and feeling . . . always arising unforseen and departing unbidden, but elevating and delighting beyond all expression; so that even in the desire and the regret they leave, there cannot but be pleasure, participating as it does in the nature of its object. It is as it were the interpenetration of a diviner nature through our own; but its footsteps are like those of a wind over the sea, which the coming calm erases, and whose traces remain only as on the wrinkled sand which paves it. (P. 294b)

Owen Barfield pays his respects to the presence of the divinity in the world in many similarly stirring passages. He cautions us that we may

agree with men who "logomorphically" ascribe to primitive men a simplicity, a concrete materiality in their designation of wordly things, only if
we realize that these so-called sensible objects were themselves something
more.

> Not an empty "root meaning to shine," but the same definite spiritual reality
> which was beheld on the one hand in what has since become pure human
> thinking, and on the other hand in what has since become physical light;
> not an abstract conception, but the echoing footsteps of the Goddess
> Natura—not a metaphor but a living Figure. (*Poetic Diction,* pp. 88–89)

Although the serene reality of the spirit present in things was once self-
evident, it can now be approximated only by the true poetic metaphor.
"The world, like Dionysus, is torn to pieces by pure intellect; but the poet
is Zeus; he has swallowed the heart of the world; and he can reproduce
it as a living body."

In "The Four Ages," Nemerov consciously recognizes that the footsteps of Astraea are indeed faint:

> The fourth age is, it always is, the last.
> The sentences break ranks,
>
> . . . .
> Illusion at last is over, all proclaim
> The warm humanity of common prose,
> Informative, pedestrian, and plain,
> Imperative and editorial,
> Opinionated and proud to be so,
> Delighted to explain, but not to praise.

But even in the poem's yet more lugubrious close we find traces of those
delicately impressed signatures in nature and the human soul, which poetry remembers:

> It's *de rigueur* for myths to have four ages,
>
> . . . .
> These correspondences are what remain
> Of that great age when all was counterpoint
> And no one minded that nothing mattered or meant.

Against the common certainty that the giants have passed away from the
earth, Nemerov affirms in "Playing the Inventions" the importance of
reading their instructions over again, as Bach's for the cantabile style of
playing:

> The tune's not much until it's taken up.
> O mystery of mind, that cannot know
> Except by modeling what it would know,

> Repeating accident to make it fate . . .
> . . . .
> It is a heartless business, happiness,
> It always is. Two hundred and fifty years
> Of time's wild wind that whips at the skin of that sea
> Whose waves are men, two hundred and fifty years
> Of a suffering multiplied as many times
> As there were children born to give it form
> By feeding it their bodies, minds and souls;
> And still the moment of this music is,
> Whether in merry or melancholy mode,
> A happiness implacable and austere,
> The feeling that specifically belongs
> To music when it heartlessly makes up
> The order of its lovely, lonely world
> Agreeing justice with surprise, the world
> We play forever at while keeping time.

That last stanza (again, in fifteen lines) I find nearly perfectly dialectical, happiness shining from a gutter of heartbrokenness. The singing of the sweetest songs about the saddest thought will not protect us against our suffering, but it may enhance the impersonal, steady will of the spirit to see into things. Somewhere between the disinterested dreaming of the maker in Yeats and the concerted discipline of Shelley to frame the song that knows our sorrow stands Nemerov's aesthetic, "A happiness implacable and austere."

I have not consistently differentiated those figures who have patently "influenced" Nemerov and those who seem to me most appropriate to the tradition he has worked to inherit. Perhaps this would be the place to indicate that I don't think Shelley has influenced the poetry, but rather the entire spiritual vocabulary of many modern poets. He has become already a deep part of our thought rather than specifically a part of our sound. Yeats is a different matter for Nemerov, a true mentor, and a lasting one. Blake, Shakespeare, and, more recently, Dante, are in the same pantheon. Stevens, Frost, Auden, Pound, Roethke, and Tate are fraternal forces whose techniques, vocabulary, even whose characteristic colors and symbols move here and there through Nemerov's work, but not in any persistent fashion. For that matter, Paul Valéry has probably played a more important role than any American poet in the forming of Nemerov's poetic and aesthetic thought. His "Dialogue of the Tree" (1943) informs the substance and the rhythms of "The Thought of Trees" in *The Western Approaches* just as his long poem about the graveyard at Sète informed the disputed fields of "The Master at a Mediterranean

Port," also illustrating the danger of a cool yet hyperbolic classicism that Nemerov had to reject the more vigorously as it was already a temptation in his earlier verse. Perhaps the long delicacies of Valéry's poetry have helped to subtilize Nemerov's meters as well. But the language of justice and surprise, of heartless happiness, and of the conversation with paradise, stems from a more narrowly chosen group of models, many of whom were dead by 1633:

> In the third age, without our noticing
> The music ceased to sound, and we were left
> As unaccompanied and strangely alone,
> Like actors suddenly naked in a dream.
> Yet we had words, and yet we had the word
> Of poetry, a thinner music, but
> Both subtle and sublime in its lament
> For all that was lost to all but memory.

It is a testament to the magnitude of this body of poetry that, having nearly come to what must be the present end of discussing it, I hear with some regret the clear call of poems from *The Collected Poems* which I did not treat, see images I shall not forget: the poet watching his reflection in a train window, and smiling like a Greek bearing gifts; the ominous majesty of "Departure of the Ships"; the news flash about the arrest of an angel brandishing a sword; "the high, charged carbon arc of light" of winter lighting; the description of the brain as "the transformer bathed in blood"; the accomplished sorites of "Celestial Globe," which somehow manages to move from the earth's blue sphere to Rembrandt to the *Iliad* to a Halloween pumpkin; the body's velvet and cold tiles ("Interiors"); the muse Polyhymnia's "fierce gaze and implacable small smile." But it is equally a testament to Nemerov's importance that he shows the poets to follow him one way of thinking about the modern world that will not inevitably put us in bondage to its failings. The footsteps of Astraea may sound faintly, but they do sound, they are variously impressed on real things, and she is, at last, a goddess. In the hope of such figures, Howard Nemerov has been able to bring forth out of death and irony a species of bravery, illumination, and delight.

In the last set of lectures in *Figures of Thought,* "What Was Modern Poetry?" which I first read as the "Footsteps of Astraea" section of this essay began to emerge, Howard Nemerov recognizes that there occurred something called The Great Change, and he identifies this Change (as does Paul Fussell) with World War I. At the same time he tells us that this very Great Change also occurs in every life, and has always occurred in every life: In growing up, each of us loses paradise all over again.

However, there undeniably *was* a historical change that made The Great Change of everyman particularly poignant to modern poets—the disappearance of the spirits. "Poetry was once the place where these entities did their proper work," but now "most poets shamefacedly acquiesce in the skepticism around them, careless or unaware that they are acquiescing in the destruction of their art and their vocation together."

Without knowing that Nemerov would second-guess me about the tradition I was inventing for him (although I should have known), Shelley's Astraea has seemed to be the proper figure for the passing away of magic and the poet's yearning after it. Thus Nemerov closes his homage to Richard Wilbur's "Merlin Enthralled" by speaking of the peculiarly "personal appeal" of the poem, which ends with King Arthur and Sir Gawen, after Merlin has left off dreaming about them, clopping off into a small, quaint, and one-dimensional reality. "I think," says Nemerov, "I experience this [personal] appeal whenever . . . a modern poet turns to legendary figures and themes not for decoration but in order that we shall see deeply into their present truth. When this happens, when, as here, the poet has heard the very footsteps of Astraea leaving the earth, I feel that literary criticism is scarcely to the point, and I answer with love and sorrow to his thought, as well as with that impersonal gladness, that elation, that comes when beautiful and accurate saying seems to overcome the sorrow of what is said."

This is as close to a program for modern poetry as Nemerov comes, and it is based on a religious paradox. Although poetry reflects with impersonal gladness on the sorrowful departure of the spirits, in order to mourn their passing one must believe that they exist.

The Judge Is Rue

The greatest strengths of Howard Nemerov—clarity, reserved eloquence, and bemusement—appear in the volume *Sentences* (1980) alongside the greatest flaws, lugubriousness, irritability (which often shows itself in boredom with himself or the world), personal bitterness. The last poem, called "Because You Asked About the Line Between Prose and Poetry," illustrates the boundary between the flaws and the strengths as it formulates a metaphor for another kind of boundary. It is about rain gradually turning into snow, but still acting like rain (only somehow lighter and thicker), until—there is suddenly snow flying instead of rain falling. The poem rhymes as a quatrain and a couplet and is composed in Howard Nemerov's own pentameter, an organism we recognize by the off-handed inversions of sentence order that sound at once decorous and colloquial; by his studied freedom of address and careful familiarity with old puns ("clearly flew"); and by the chill, dry precision of analogy (*gradient, aslant, random*). To these idiosyncratic marks of character, Nemerov adds the unassuming realism of the plot: You recognize only much later the poet's providence in having put something dark, living, and winged into the background.

> Sparrows were feeding in a freezing drizzle
> That while you watched turned into pieces of snow
> Riding a gradient invisible
> From silver aslant to random, white, and slow.
>
> There came a moment that you couldn't tell.
> And then they clearly flew instead of fell.

Formally, the poem is masterful, reassuring in its regularities, disturbing in its hints of chaos—those twin impulses that make up at least the necessary conditions of great verse. In Nemerov's rhymed poems, there is more activity in the final measures of the lines than in his unrhymed; the hints of chaos in "Because You Asked . . ." are whispered forth by the rhyme-dissonances between *drizzle* (the end of the fifth-foot amphibranch) and *invisible* (whose four syllables make up the two regular iambs of the fourth and fifth feet, with no supernumerary unstressed syllable at the end). Although *DRIZ*- rhymes with -*VIS*-, and although both *DRIZzle* and *inVISible* have final *l*'s, these rhyming sounds fall in different metrical places. We swallow the last two syllables of *invisible*— naturally, because the main accent falls on -*VIS*-, and, in the lines of Nemerov's in question, because we are half-consciously trying to make the metrically nonparallel words match.

This rhyming on words that are, so to speak, cross-woven metrically, and the swallowing of certain lines (which necessitates the elongation of others) are parts of a larger design in which are also woven sentence and pause. For as the words unfold forward within the abstract metrical frame, they also pick up unaligned threads of grammatical periods and endings, which then hitch back across those lines, and even back across whole stanzas. If the metaphor of fabric weaving applies to the making of verses, we must imagine either the warp as regular and the shuttle as uneven, or the warp as erratic and the voice of the shuttle as constant. The process in either case must accommodate both glide and tug, both smooth progress and lurching regress. The subject of the sentence that forms the quatrain of Nemerov's poem is "Sparrows," but the burden of the quatrain's theme is the "drizzle" that turns (for two-and-a-half lines) to "pieces of snow." A further twist is that, while "drizzle" is technically in command of the syntax for only one-half line, it is still continuing to fall through the ensuing transformations.

Because poetry moves backward and forward at once, the bit of cloth you wind up with is irregular, full of holes, yet also peculiarly complete, like a cat's cradle held in one hand by an adult and by a child in the other. Even the symmetry of the Popean couplet depends on radical asymmetries in the puns and in their disposition among parts of speech and in non-matching metrical places. In Nemerov's poem the adjectives "aslant" and "slow" do not inhabit the same semantic realm; yet for the moment of their expression, they are parallel in their doubleness: Both render both shape *and* speed. Indirectly, "silver aslant," which purports to describe a visual image, also shows us the speed with which the rain razors down, while, equally indirectly, the phrase "random, white, and slow" describes what it does not directly name by suggesting how the snow is starting to coast lethargically, scoot sideways, move anyway but straight down.

Even so bald a device as the choice of poly- over monosyllabic words in a metrical line is an indispensable means of varying speed, sentence structure, and texture. Compare the second line, "That while you watched turned into pieces of snow," with its commanding monosyllables, and the rhopalic series of polysyllables in the third line, "Riding a gradient invisible," which is softer, more rapid (because of weak secondary stresses on the last two words), more abstract, and syntactically unfinished.

In support of diction, syntax, and meter, Nemerov also employs a hovering effect, based sometimes on ambiguity, and sometimes on error. For example, one might revise his final couplet to expose the grammatical clumsiness of the final line:

> There came a moment when you scarcely knew.
> And then instead of fell they clearly flew.

But in Nemerov's couplet, with its authoritative rhyme *tell/fell*, the ungrammatical use of *fell* is largely concealed, perceived by us only as a dull after-throb. In addition to softening the awkwardness in the last line, Nemerov also invigorates the meanings in the penultimate. By using *that* instead of *when*, he divides the reference between time and quality: (1) There came a moment during which you could not tell which was which; (2) There came a moment that you couldn't tell about. Of course the poem is about not being able to pinpoint delicate change; but it is also about not being able to describe how something got itself changed from rain into snow, prose into poetry, while watcher and writer know very well what the final state has come to: "And then they clearly flew."

What clearly flew? Clearly, the pieces of snow, now soft and crowded flakes. But in the poem's updrafts are also borne aloft those feeding sparrows—not literally, rather as part of the suggestive warrant for any kind of flight. In other words (the words of the title), so is the poem launched.

Not going straight to its goal—not falling like rain—a poem imperceptibly thickens itself into its own, "other" medium out of the strikingly visible stream of prose. It crosses a line, before which it was transparent, following which it is opaque, by being *in lines,* displaying the words it holds in common with prose so that these are increasingly bracketed, thereby more choice, but also more free.

That poetry holds words in common with prose is a truth for which Howard Nemerov gives especially profound warrant in his poetry (which at his death in 1991 numbered roughly 700 pages—and these were pages of verse that possessed great variety of finish). As argued in the foregoing pages, he is a master of blank verse in the brief lyric and the middle-length poem, and has molded the unrhymed iambic pentameter line into some of the subtlest formal bodies we have. His model in this is Frost, but Nemerov is less heavily stressed and less the rural poseur. Not that Nemerov lacks his poses; on the contrary, as we have seen, he can be most irritating in his roles as watcher-of-broadcasts, man-walking-dog, suburban-stroller, visitor-of-parks. He lets the bourgeois into his satiric poetry, but he also (in less censored or censorious fashion) lets the world of solitary privilege into his lyrics. The finest poem in *Sentences,* "By Al Lebowitz's Pool," provides a protected bell jar for Nemerov's meditations on time, light, youth, distance, and correspondence. It is a superior poem, but also one that depends on our not minding the moneyed reserve of the middle classes: For even if Al Lebowitz's pool does not represent class so much as reflect season, and even if the owner himself scarcely appears, a swimming pool in St. Louis, Missouri, is undeniably part of a social order the poem disinterestedly permits. The poet observes the untouchable and undesired daughters of his host swerving like fish through the water, on which surface, on other days, float only beach balloons or a wasp. The summer wanes. The speaker usually has a drink in hand. Idly, the poet roves among these details, which seem to provide at last, in each of the poem's five sections, the hypnagogic abstraction necessary for elegy. After a late summer storm,

> The banked furnace of the sun
> With reliquary heat returns in splendor
> Diminished some with time, but splendid still.
> Beside the pool we drink, talk, and are still,
> These times of kindness mortality allows.

In such seamless weavings of the poetic traditions with his own personal tone (consider the blend in the phrases "With reliquary heat" and "The banked furnace"), Nemerov proves that the line between poetry and prose must be crossed not only by the word but also by the heart. He is a poet who, like all of us, lives in the prosaic; and he acknowledges it in order to mine it, breaking it open.

But in contrast to other masters of the typical like Frost, Auden, and Cunningham, Nemerov is not, even in his sublime poems, always able to decide what he should do with the pieces left over from the vein of prosaic feeling. His worldly poses are often double-jointed—excuses for personal pathos where we expect the satirist's probity. His jokes frequently protest their humor. Since his first poems, *The Image and the Law* (1947), his books have been peppered by gnomes too glib and constructed to be true. He tries to be playful, but sounds grim. And when he wants that grimness to be prophetic, he sounds inward and crotchety. He wants to be "bitter" as Yeats was, but has neither Yeats's formative and protective stake in the culture (perhaps no American has this), nor his obsessive delusions. Nemerov's temperament and language are not suited to displays of *saeva indignatio,* although his temperament is also such as to think it is. I do not think we hear in Nemerov that harsh transport of which J. V. Cunningham wrote in 1947 when he characterized the poetic gift:

> These the assizes: here the charge, denial,
> Proof and disproof: the poem is the trial.
> Experience is defendant, and the jury
> Peers of tradition, and the judge is fury.[20]

I suspect that Howard Nemerov desires to be viewed as a poet who can range, with indulgence, majesty, or fury, over a broad geography of subjects and moods. This is not the case. His best mood, the one that brings out the tenderest and most credible language, is that mood of pitying praise in the presence of natural law and intellectual construct. In another age, Nemerov would have been bard to the Royal Society or an enclave of Thomists. He was framed to celebrate the edifice of mind from a gargoyle's niche; he depends, that is, on a tradition of shared intellectual achievement to which he can pay orthogonal homage in the form of tears. For that is the heart of his lyricism: astrophysics, syllogism, fluid geometry, and Zeno's paradox fleshed, formal, and full of rue:

> Intent upon the target eye
> The arrow pierced a garden air
> Fragrant with flowers yellow and blue,
> It flew beside a shining hedge
> And over cobwebs jeweled with dew,
> It passed above a still black pool
> With a fountain for a heart
> Lifting its silver droplets up
> So slowly (and the flight so swift)

They stood in air before they fell
Tap tap upon the dark dripstone.
Always, while burrowing in the brain,
Always, and while the victim fell,
The hastening arrow held that still
Moment along its shining shaft.
Its feathers whistled that still air.

("In Zeno's World")

This lovely lyric is written in the same loose tetrameters Nemerov used for "The Blue Swallows" in 1967, an earlier poem about "finding again the world" by a conscious application of the mind's eye to what is (therefore) "intelligible." In the protected garden of the mind, Nemerov has made a perfect gazebo.

During a solar eclipse, the poet of *Sentences* considers how the life of one man may be charted even to its end against the rare punctuations by the moon's darkened disc across the face of the second great wanderer among the worlds:

A man may see, as I have done, but four,
In childhood two, a third in youth, and this

In likelihood my last. We stand bemused
While grass and rock darken, and stillness grows,
Until the sun and moon slide out of phase
And light returns us to the common life
That is so long to do and so soon done.

("During a Solar Eclipse")

The final monosyllabic line is a tour de force of Drab-style pathos, in the vein of Wyatt and Donne. Monosyllables serve a different function in "Insomnia I," that of blunt, noncommittal background for two more elaborate styles. If unable to sleep, you should, says Nemerov, go downstairs, have a bit to drink, read a mystery,

Then, when you know who done it, turn out the light,
And quietly in darkness, in moonlight, or snowlight
Reflective, listen to the whistling earth
In its backspin trajectory around the sun
That makes the planets sometimes retrograde
And brings the cold forgiveness of the dawn
Whose light extinguishes all stars but one.

Nemerov attaches a drag-line to the music of the spheres—the rationalist terminology of Miltonic syntax and Latinate jargon, a vocabulary canceled by the glistening Anglo-Saxon gray of the phase "cold forgiveness of the dawn" and by the uncodifiable undersong of the "whistling earth." All these features are catalyzed by the nearness of a bland, and glib, *Bürgerlichkeit*, a form of habitual shadow-self.

A final example of Nemerov's pathos-of-the-intellect is "The Makers"—a poem whose pathos in some part is owing to its recollection of Randall Jarrell's "The Emancipators" as well as to William Dunbar's "Lament for the Makaris" (all of whom, by 1508, were dead). In Nemerov's "Makers," the first poets, those nameless makers of the consciousness of interval, who made poetry and language possible, are those who felt (as immediately as the odor of a rose) that the ability to form and distinguish vowels and consonants was what made it possible to make metaphors.

> They were the first great listeners, attuned
> To interval, relationship, and scale,
> The first to say above, beneath, beyond,
> Conjurors with love, death, sleep, with bread and wine,
> Who having uttered vanished from the world
> Leaving no memory but the marvelous
> Magical elements, the breathing shapes
> And stops of breath we build our Babels of.

This is blank verse both cerebral and melodious; what moves us more than that balance—rather, what that balance calls attention to—is the very frailty of fame and the doomed circularity of poetic endeavor. The breathing shapes and stops, the vowels and consonants, are the foundations of shifting Babels whose magic is ephemeral. Although the poem can catch something of the fleet quality, feeling is already cold and fled.

Like this poem, all of Nemerov's best works are strangely sad. Encumbered with habitual self, they rise to plateaus of nostalgic obedience to the world, on which a natural, rich simplicity is flexed by mutability:

> . . . if these moments could not pass away
> They could not be, all dapple and delight.

In *Sentences* not only has Nemerov continued to accommodate himself to the literary tradition without falling back on parody; he has also in this handful of poems extended the resources of blank verse beyond what any modern practitioner, himself included, has managed to do. This extension comprises more than a mere prosodic advance; it is a rhetorical and imaginative advance. "By Al Lebowitz's Pool," "The Makers," "Monet," and "A Christmas Storm," for example, are more dazzling by virtue of their very naturalness, especially when we take into account that the last two are single, elaborated sentences, in each of which the digressive ribbons and falls of thought, with languorous, permissive grace, are drawn back into coherent movements of syntax and line. No one since Frost has done as much to move blank verse forward from where Wordsworth and Coleridge had left it. The long sentence that falls variously from clause to clause and line to line in the last verse paragraph of "By Al Lebowitz's Pool" reminds us of the feats of the romantics, but on a scale at once more thematically restricted and more spiritually daring:

> Enchanted afternoon, immune from time,
> Illusion's privilege gives me the idea that I
> Am not so much writing this verse as reading it
> Up out of water and light and shadow and leaf
> Doing the dance of their various dependencies—
> As if I might daydream my way again
> Into the world and be at one with it—
> While the shadows of harder, more unyielding things
> Edge steadily and stealthily around the pool
> To translate the revolving of the world
> About itself, the spinning ambit of the seasons
> In the simple if adamant equation of time
> Around the analemma of the sun.

This final verse paragraph, by turns reserved and gorgeous, yielding and severe, also convinces us that even a temperamental limitation, if acknowledged and persisted in, can approach transcendence.

6

Deeper Than Declared

On Seamus Heaney

I

"Was there a 'misalliance,'" asks Seamus Heaney of Robert Lowell, "between the gift and the work it was harnessed to do?"[1] To ask the question is to suggest an affirmative reply: The vivid occasion in Lowell was ever straining toward meditation, the verbal breakdowns toward a state of Horatian health (and, one could say, vice versa). Heaney's sensitivity to this "misalliance" is revealing, since he, too, the best-known poet to come out of Ireland since Yeats, hankers after a species of court dress and bardic intonation, for which almost everything in his unconscious music automatically disqualifies him. So, too, do Heaney's authentic gifts as a chronicler of the rough, marshy landscapes and family farms of Ulster ill prepare him to write the large-scale politico-religious work. Yet the misalliance is not without its hard-won triumphs.

"Station Island" is a curious poetic sequence, poignant in parts, powerful in others, but disjointed and bottled up, as if the poet could not commit himself to its deeper drift. Nor is emotion liberated by the liberal confidentiality of some of the poems. Feeling is still largely numbed with remorse, and the poems float in loose, nominal relation to one another despite Heaney's almost anxious reverence for nets and skeins of meaning. Allusions to more thoroughgoing systems of belief than his own are constantly made. Dante is present, both in the nagging background of current politics and in the variable terza rima of four of the twelve poems (the triplets of the fine poem about the young priest are near enough the terza rima norm to serve as a distant fifth); and Dante's presence is also felt in the grotesquerie of the premise that the dead masters and friends and political victims—those violently dead still bearing the marks of their deaths on their bodies—can come forward to speak with Heaney. But he does not judge, or assign his dead to circles, or give them activities that measure their sins, their expiation, or their blessedness. The afterlife is a convenient fiction, and Dante's influence a matter of shards, since his minor premise is honored, that the living may speak with the dead, but not his theism, let alone his theology.[2]

Similarly, Heaney is pursuing a series of expiatory "stations" traditionally aimed at placing the moral weaknesses of the "pilgrim" under avid, pious attack. But although this pilgrim regrets his failings, primarily those that stem from apolitical indifference or disengagement, he is not interested in examining the flawed instrument. He does not aim to school the ego, or to pacify the will. His penitential guise is almost prideful, as if to prove Johnson's dictum that "All censure of a man's self is oblique praise. It is in order to show how much he can spare."

Finally, Heaney's "Station Island" poems obsessively fasten on the idea of mortality, without seriously questioning its meaning. Whenever ultimate meaning is required, Poetry automatically steps in. Indeed, it is hygienically described, in a passage where putrefaction and decay are celebrated, as the process of cleaning out life's wounds as by the action of maggots: "another life that cleans our element." But this purifying role of verse is asserted rather than illustrated. There is some bewilderment, therefore, when we catch the notes of disembodied reverence with which the poet-pilgrim "faces into" his stations. For he does not address the redemptive function of this other ritual, either. The nearest he comes to acknowledging the purpose of the Station Island retreat occurs in the young missionary's elliptical suggestion that Heaney must be here on the island not to humble himself to God but to bid God farewell. " 'What possessed you?' " the dead priest asks the poet, his grammar twisting as his thought worms through:

> . . . all this you were clear of you walked into
> over again. And the god has, as they say, withdrawn.
>
> What are you doing, going through these motions?
> 'Unless . . . Unless . . .' Again he was short of breath
> and his whole fevered body yellowed and shook.
>
> 'Unless you are here taking the last look.'
>
> ("Station Island," IV)

Nowhere else in the sequence do we find God even nostalgically brought in. Not that the poems lack their Satanic figures. A little-known writer named William Carleton, Protestant convert, angry, bitter, blustering, is one, who undertakes the roughly stressed Anglo-Saxon attitudes familiar from Heaney's earlier volumes:

> hard-mouthed Ribbonmen and Orange bigots
> made me into the old fork-tongued turncoat
> who mucked the byre of their politics.

Another minor demon is the tinker Simon Sweeney, who first appears
with a bow-saw in his arms "held / stiffly up like a lyre," a gesture which
should betoken blessing. But he shows his truer form when he reminds
the poet of the latter's childhood fear of him in a simile that fairly shudders
with the aversion his person inspired. When

> woodsmoke sharpened air
> or ditches rustled
> you sensed my trail there
> as if it had been sprayed.

Yet in the last six stanzas of this poem, which opens the "Station Island"
suite, Heaney succumbs to the vaporous apparitions of shawled women
moving in wet fields through the rags of moisture that make up this poet's
atmospheric element. The women's chant convokes his dead in a "loosed
congregation." We lose sight of the "old Sabbath-breaker"; a last chaffing
command to " 'Stay clear of all processions!' " is Simon Sweeney's only
attempt to shed light on his encounter with the poet, whose mind he can
read. This bending of the poems' design under the weight of tangent and
digression is a particular mark of the "Station Island" poems, showing
how delicate a task of convocation Heaney has set himself.

Demonic, too, are the shadowy assassins, both Protestant and Catholic,
whose victims confront Heaney with their accusing wounds. In fact, one
might conjecture that his real demons are these self-accusations emanating
from the world where others act and die. Even his style grows demonic
in its exorbitance:

> Strange polyp floated like a huge corrupt
> Magnolia bloom, surreal as a shed breast,
> My softly awash and blanching self-disgust.

Self-disgust has a political cast, cowardice a wilting reminder of public
reticence. Unlike Lowell (a covering presence in both *Field Work* and
Station Island), Heaney declares himself wanting in one sort of "command" that Robert Lowell undeniably possessed (the unabashed manda-
rin "arrogation of his right to speak to or for an audience"), although the
lush metaphors and overripe language in Heaney announce his talent for
Lowell's second sort of "command," that over the literary tongue:

> No matter how close [Lowell] could or would bring his work to the condi-
> tion of discourse, he was always seeking to outfox if not to overwhelm the
> logic of argument by the force of image or oracle.[3]

Such a maneuver of "outfoxing" is clearly going on in the corrupt magno-
lia bloom of self-disgust in "Station Island," IX. Still, Heaney wants what

Lowell could and did take advantage of, a certified act of conscientious objection—an act, says Heaney, in which Lowell combined "public dissent with psychic liberation"[4]—an act with civic consequences, namely, a sentence. One feels by contrast that Heaney is not liberated by mere public confession. "Forgive," he asks, "my timid circumspect involvement"; "I hate how quick I was to know my place." The affairs of Ulster (the older name of Northern Ireland that encodes the indigenous heroic tradition) press upon Seamus Heaney as matters of conscience, but no more strongly than it appears they have been pressed upon him by his more engaged readers. And "Station Island" was to have been the poem where he would "be facing the North and getting shut of it."[5] Yet he draws a veil of inconclusive poignancy over the IRA killer whose whole life was lived in the context of weapons and guerrilla war. In a sleeping vision framed in elegant, moody pentameter whose unobtrusive and slant rhymes trace an equally unobtrusive sonnet pattern, Heaney sees the dead man laid out, smells the very mildew

> From the byre loft where he watched and hid
> From fields his draped coffin would raft through.
> Unquiet soul, they should have buried you
> In the bog where you threw your first hand grenade,
> Where only helicopters and curlews
> Make their maimed music, and sphagnum moss
> Could teach you its medicinal repose.
>
> ("Station Island," IX)

Would his soul thereafter begin to be healed of its rancors, absolved of its crimes? Or would the invading helicopters, their blades slapping the air, drown even the interred one in their looming modern racket? The questions can be answered only by recognizing, first, how tempered the diction is, smoothing the roughness of *helicopters* by matching its consonants with a semantically more muffled lexicon whose sounds, but not whose meanings (*unquiet, coffin, curlews*), are metallic, just as *grenade* is softened down among the aurally wet places of *bog* and *sphagnum*. Next one would note how the metaphor of ghostly palimpsest lays future over past with an air of visionary mourning; the temporal carrier is the rural landscape, where the underground soldier grew up, and held out: "the byre loft where he watched and hid / From fields his draped coffin would raft through." The uncommon verb *raft* suggests not only the watery gliding of the bier but also the kindred sluicing audible in more common past participles like *reft* (bereft) and *rift,* both of which owe something to *tearing,* especially as extended to the heart.

Finally, one should remark how the natural world ironically opens to

accept even insoluble paradoxes, burning them down to harmonies, recasting itself out of the contraries. The helicopters' cacophony is literally
subdued to the level of the curlews' cries, the bog swallows the sound of
the grenade, silence falls into the vacuum torn out by combat: " 'an am-
bush / Stillness I felt safe in settled around me.' " At times, it appears the
only constant in Heaney's world is the natural landscape, moist, overcast,
luxuriant, which lends itself to the individual's terms without infringing
on its own enormities. In the moving elegy on Barney Murphy that forms
the major part of "Station Island," V (Murphy was Heaney's schoolmas-
ter, whose school was razed to reclaim the land for farming), the old
master's asthmatic breath "rushed the air softly as scythes in his lost mead-
ows." The classical and biblical seriousness of the diction gives authority
to the kindly overlap of natural with human processes.

In a harsher style, the poor insurgent in IX speaks of his spiritual decay
in somatic terms equally magnetized by the rural milieu; his tropes go
back to Heaney's bog folk whose mummification in the peat was quite
literal:

> 'My brain dried like spread turf, my stomach
> Shrank to a cinder and tightened and cracked.
> Often I was dogs on my own track
> Of blood on wet grass that I could have licked.'

Here is an overlay of a different sort, as the thirsty, starving, bleeding
outlaw changes places with his ravenous trackers—yet another example
of nature's polymorphous sway. And in more daring elegiac fashion, the
most tawdry items of contemporary technology (car, helicopter, gun,
bomb, grenade) are subsumed by the seasonal-natural machine. In fact,
so great is the transforming energy that one could argue for this poem's
threshold achievement: The first part of "Station Island," IX can stand
with "The Tollund Man," "Funeral Rights," and "Kinship"; with the two
strong laments in *Field Work*, "The Toome Road" and "The Strand at
Lough Beg"; and, from the more recent volume, with "The First Flight"
and the superbly ironic "Sandstone Keepsake," as one of Seamus Heaney's
finest politically oriented works.

But the rest of the poem raises the specter of ambivalence on a second
front as well. The entire last half, from the third sonnet to the fifth, makes
no reference to the young warrior, but instead breaks into a medley of
dream-anguishes with three different tenors and three different styles.
First the dream shows the muddy flood of self-disgust (the polyp-breast
image, quoted earlier), which is followed by the tangential memory, still
within the dream, of an old brass trumpet Heaney found in a barn but
was too self-effacing to take ("a mystery / I shied from then for I thought

such trove beyond me"—his boyhood persona is almost too good to be true). Then the last sonnet/paragraph, strewn with self-castigations, closes with the abrupt attempt, by means of a shorthand epiphany, to haul the whole complex weight of the preceding seventy lines under a dome of shining sweetness:

> 'I hate how quick I was to know my place.
> I hate where I was born, hate everything
> That made me biddable and unforthcoming,'
> I mouthed at my half-composed face
> In the shaving mirror, like somebody
> Drunk in the bathroom during a party,
> Lulled and repelled by his own reflection.
> As if the cairnstone could defy the cairn.
> As if the eddy could reform the pool.
> As if a stone swirled under a cascade,
> Eroded and eroding in its bed,
> Could grind itself down to a different core.
> Then I thought of the tribe whose dances never fail
> For they keep dancing till they sight the deer.

To dance until something miraculous happens in the world, or until one drops, is a brave extreme to undergo, but I do not know that Heaney proposes to do this (he merely "thought of" it). Nor do I see the immediate link between the deer-invocation and the need to reform a weak character. There is a little casuistry under the attractice imagery of cascade and woodland dance, just as there is a little evasion in the stylishly flat self-confrontation in the shaving mirror, when Heaney at once mocks and approves his own chagrin. The question of responsibility is deflected, to one side determinism ("As if the cairnstone could defy the cairn"), to the other guilt ("Lulled and repelled by his own reflection").

Although they do not readily imply or support one another, the two halves of this poem do have the dim, infernal relation of photograph to negative. And perhaps what makes the young guerrilla of the first two sonnets attractive to Heaney is his complete lack of self-pity: His self-regard is of a cosmic sort, like the Croppies' of 1798: "The hillside blushed, soaked in our broken wave."[6] The two Irishmen touch by virtue of their temperamental exclusions. The barn where Heaney found the trumpet eerily reminds us of the bog where the other boy threw his first grenade, one an object of white magic and sentimentality, the other of black magic and damnation. The polyp of self-disgust that luxuriates in sexual folds in the second half is the metaphoric and stylistic and, indeed, spiritual "positive" of that dried-out brain and stomach tight as a cinder with which the poem strongly begins. It is as if action (dark, desiccated) were being opposed to thought (glistening and spongy).

But such opposites are perhaps too beguiling in their dialectical neatness; they tend to smother thought. Had Heaney *not* known his place, for example (and who knows what conditions would have conspired in such a character change?), had he been more forthcoming, less docile ("biddable"), would he have joined the IRA and eschewed poetry? What, then? He hints, I think unconvincingly, that he might have been readier to make something of his tribal knowledge, to act or to sympathize, independent of violent cadres—to dance—until he saw justice done. Although this might not have insured that justice was done, it would, the parable implies, have given him an easier conscience. Collaterally, the ambivalences that prompt such cutting of corners in the realm of self-knowledge rather mar this cumbersome second group of sonnets.

The same confrontation between beauty of thought and efficacy of deed—perfection of the work or of the life—occurs in the second half of another "Station Island" poem devoted to Heaney's cousin Colum McCartney, arbitrarily killed by Protestants. A kind youth who shied away even from the spent cartridges left by hunters, he accuses the poet of manipulating "artistic tact" until it becomes "evasion." He claims that his cousin, in his splendid elegy in *Field Work*, "The Strand at Lough Beg,"

> ' . . . whitewashed ugliness and drew
> the lovely blinds of the *Purgatorio*
> and saccharined my death with morning dew.'

The deprecatory judgment is half-hearted: It is undercut by Heaney's style. The beauty for which he has his dead cousin castigate him irrepressibly enters the rhetoric and the stately prosody of the condemnation itself. Reminiscent of Robert Lowell's dismissal of his high rhetorical mode in "The Dolphin" as mere "set-piece, set-piece," McCartney's speech in "Station Island," VIII is an attempt on the poet's part to devalue all fine speech, for it is not true grief—and yet the poet preserves the lovely language in which all such language is devalued. Then, as if to prove that he is not putting himself above his own experience, Heaney as the pilgrim lets his guard down and invites into the poem a note of whining and a flawed prosaism. When McCartney claims that even strangers showed more agitation than his cousin did, the poet replies in dialogue made doubly brittle by the recuperated grand cadences of the second pair of lines:

> 'But they were getting crisis
> first-hand, Colum, they had happened in on
> live sectarian assassination.
> I was dumb, encountering what was destined.'

Heaney countenances this patent ineptitude of emotion, and of style, in an effort to absolve himself of the finished flourish of his earlier elegy and, by "standing up for life against art, implicitly defend [] the bulk and flux of the less finished work."

Like Lowell, whom he thus describes, Heaney also has phases in which he would commit himself to the fragmentary over the finished. For anything more than fragments will falsify the brokenness and insolubility of experience—and do so in a way that amounts to complicity with the forces of repression, inactivity, and decay. (The only poem acceptable to the Left may eventually be the completely ill-written and inchoate one. Memory, tradition, and especially the literary memory, are suspect: Over a dismantled lobster in "Away from It All," another poem of postprandial funk like the "Oysters" of *Field Work*, "quotations start to rise // like rehearsed alibis.") Heaney is clearly ambivalent toward the grand modes and the traditional genres like elegy that permit breadth and sweep of utterance, because there one speaks from a stable position that can risk general statements, uphold with moderate confidence social and moral standards, relish aesthetic design, and reside in a context of literary history, hence comfortably make allusions. But like Lowell in Paul Breslin's *mot*, Heaney is also clearly "ambivalent about ambivalence."[7] For, ironically, it is the modes designed to permit the poet to say what is possible on the categorically impossible occasions (of war, death, love, awe) that now indict the writer of conservatism. "The political implications of lyric art are quite reactionary," Heaney says. "You are saying to people. 'Everything's all right.' "[8]

But even in the beginning of Seamus Heaney's own lyric art, everything was not, in this sense, all right. His poems are not straightforward heterocosms, attentive solely to their own purity of form and feeling. Even when most absorbed in the lyrical moment, he has often been impelled to thicken and adulterate the brew. To label this impulse with political motives is to ignore the long-standing urge to roughen, which early on had personal rather than chauvinist motives. Heaney has always been drawn two ways, toward high rhetoric and low, toward expansive meditation and crippled epigram, toward standard speech and dialect. His poetry grounds itself in dichotomy—which has a decidedly unbalancing effect on the verse, like that of an unpaved track on a fragile carriage—yet the unbalancing itself falls pleasingly on his ear. This is a sign of the authenticity of his divided attention, torn between the attitudes of adult reason and childlike genius, between the sounds of English and of Irish speech, the claims of tradition and the individual psychology, and, as the well-known pair of poems in *North* embodies the dichotomy, between the figures of Hercules and Antaeus.

In one of the most splendid examples of poetic criticism by any writer since Eliot, Heaney in his prose collection *Preoccupations* constructs elegant and persuasive tension-emblems to elucidate the work of his forebears and contemporaries. Yeats and Wordsworth beautifully offset one another as examples of the combative and the entranced poet. Hopkins is countered by Keats, Dylan Thomas, even Blake, as if, whatever the angle he is seen from, Hopkins cannot help sounding artificial—however seductive one finds the artifice, as Heaney admits that he does. He opposes allegory to symbol as waking to sleeping consciousness, fire and flint to oozing matrix, Christian man to natural man, Latin to Celtic thinking, and the polysyllable to the monosyllable. To this roster of paired antinomies from the pages of *Preoccupations,* we can add:

reason	*versus*	feeling
assertion		suggestion
discourse		preverbal intimation
acting out		listening in
concept		imagination
proposition		incantation
England		Ireland
adult		child
consonants		vowels
male		female
the arched back		the copious lap (of language)
disciplina		*pagus*
library		lair
literacy (intellect)		illiteracy (instinct)
Patrick		Oison
empire		local piety
flint		ooze
poem as conductor		poem as crucible
honeycomb		swarm
craft (tradition)		technique (individual)

"Poetry of any power," he writes in his essay on Irish nature poetry, "is always deeper than its declared meaning." According to the pattern of contraries above, the "declared meaning" of any work would be opposed to something like its "whispered meaning"—something hummed under the breath that makes the passage of the breath itself more touchingly apparent. For it is the gift of the undeclared and undeclarative poetic instinct to hear *how* it will say as the precondition to *what*.

Note that it is the very poet who identifies himself primarily with a fluent, feminine, preconscious, oozing, yielding mentality who is responsible for this tight trellis of opposing categories. I don't think this is unusual. Like many who live in tempo with the deeps (symbol, instinct, ooze, crucible), Heaney also thinks according to a few odd dualisms collapsed into each other like a honeycomb, with surprisingly little intellectual resistance. Although not all the left- and right-hand items match up—for example, Patrick was not English, incantation is not audition—nevertheless, Catholicism shares with Protestantism a rigor that Oison the natural man opposes: The convinced pagan recoils at the dank chill of *disciplina*. And in the context of the strong, active, masculine traits of acting-out and proposition-making, the right-hand items incantation and listening-in share the quality of receptive patience. Nor is Irish a vowel-oriented language; Heaney remarks that the Ulster accent is especially consonantal and Hopkinsian. Yet that fluidity, which the vowel requires the consonant to shape and to bound, is like the naïve and passive aspects of the national character, which the English were so ruthless in exploiting. There is no doubt that the left-hand column is construed pejoratively.

So the Englishman in Heaney, the well-read, discursive, persuasive if not imperious and form-loving poet—the one who approved the antinomies on the list, the one who makes elegies and sonnets, whose poems are sharp and edged and inter-nested with meaning—is constantly being ambushed (to his own applause) by the woodkern who is all sound irrespective of sense, whose words are runes, magical but serrated, who was just born, hence remembers the oceanic feeling that links him with the ages prior to, or ignorant of, writing.

So which self is it who writes, in "Old Pewter" (*Station Island*):

> Glimmerings are what the soul's composed of,
> Fogged-up challenges, far conscience-glitters
> and hang-dog, half-truth earnests of true love?

The theme of evanescent soul-stuff and the pileup of nonce-phrases could almost suggest Robert Browning, although the third line would then not come on us so sharply; Browning was more rangy and circumspect about his soft climaxes. Heaney has a similar way of secreting qualities, layer upon deeply embroidered layer, in the line. Now that his lines are so much longer than they were in *North,* the layering of descriptive design may sound more Victorian than it once did. Or which kind of poem is it—the poem that commands and transmits, or the poem that swarms and bubbles—in which the poet fondly relishes the mixed series that abound in *Station Island:* "Granite is jaggy, salty, punitive // and exacting"; a woman's low neckline is "inviolable and affronting"; Thomas Hardy has a "ghost life" that is "unperturbed, reliable"; morning has a "distancing, inviolate expanse"? Or consider the simply baffling reference to "sex-primed and unfurtherable moss-talk." Clearly, these packed polysyllabic clusters engage the poet, at some level, in the process of *ratio,* which lies at the root of the propositional and conceptual column. But it is as if he wished to borrow from that range of speech-acts *only* the rhythms and nuances of diction, not the words' denotative function (although obviously meaning is not altogether ignored). Perhaps Heaney is hoping to reform these polysyllables by tumbling them down the ragged cataract of his lists. Reform them, that is, from their bureaucratic flatness, undo the process by which they were first compounded—paganize them.

Unfortunately, as long as meaning clings to these polysyllables, sense will count, and the fancily involuted sound of "inanition" will not warrant its use in the recondite mixed metaphor, "between / balance and inanition," applied to "the light at the rim of the sea" in "Away from It All." On the level of *ratio,* the phrase is pedantic and obscure; on that of *inspiratio* (to coin a counterfeit etymology), it is part of some indigenous rhythm that goes on forever, deeper than what is being declared, when this poet works, and which elsewhere falls into happier synchrony with his rhetoric.

Heaney's sound has ever been hard rather than musical or melodic, just as his discursive authority had tended to extrude into density rather than strike through it. He is a poet of feelings that are the emotional counterpart to a regional dialect in speech, for he is entrained to very particular kinds of place, texture, tone, color, mood, weather, soil, and light, and able to say how their nuances relate, almost as a geologist might. The bond to his favorite locales would seem much deeper—for it seeps out everywhere—than the sympathy upheld by Auden in his "In Praise of Limestone." Heaney also sounds remarkably good-tempered in his work, despite the toughness of many poems. They are tough in their elocution, not in their sentiment. (We have seen how the reverse is true of Ted Hughes, from whom Heaney takes fire in many of his first poems.) So it is easy to see why Heaney is fired by contraries, for they provide a drama that is not inherent in his character. To the poems that otherwise tend toward exclamation and the hyperbole of repetition (the early "Churning Day," with its lavish play on the short *u* among plosive consonants, is a good example), they add the electricity of argument-with-the-self (as happens in "Blackberry-Picking," where the hard facts and the muffled antithetical claims of the couplet pull him out of the thick tangle of vegetative life toward general precept).

Thus at the same time as these dichotomous tensions are honestly come by, they do have their redolence of the lamp. Heaney's solutions to what he perceives as a basic division in his being may differ from book to book, yet the forces between which he must negotiate remain surprisingly constant, almost as if refueled and refurbished from time to time. The

"Station Island" sequence is riddled with ambivalences of theme and tone pursuant to the effort to challenge the private being in light of the public, to make the intuitive self the measure of the learned public man.

II

In the mixture of lyrics that make up the first section of *Station Island*, there are fewer poems with these ambitions. Two stand out, the perfectly modulated ironic "Sandstone Keepsake," with its faux-naïf juggling of scholarly lore reminiscent of some of Lowell's blank sonnets, and the failed but fascinating poem in a newer sweet style, "The Loaning," which is deflected from its path precisely by the obsession with contrariety discussed above.

"Sandstone Keepsake" is Heaney's most successful bourgeois political poem: It posits an entrenched invading force in a period of relative quiescence (obviously the British in Ulster), to which the protagonist responds with a powerful, even savage self-deprecation. The first four of the six quatrains describe the stone found along an estuary on whose other shore, we learn, almost in an aside, there is an internment camp. Once the lights come on there, however, the imagery in which Heaney muses about the stone in his hand becomes ever more smoky and bloody and—as if to defuse the incendiary images—literary. To begin with, rendered palpable by Heaney's exceptional descriptive skill, there is the stone itself,

> . . . a kind of chalky russet
> solidified gourd, sedimentary
> and so reliably dense and bricky
> I often clasp it and throw it from hand to hand.

The nudge there, with the color "bricky" to remind us of children punting a football in the bricky air of Lowell's public garden, backs against a heavier weight of meaning. This weight, lightened by the conversational pentameter of line 4 (with its pair of anapests), hovers over the suggestion that the narrator may yet have in him the aim and thrust of revolt. This ruddy stone, "with an underside / hint of contusion"—again suggestive of a postponed and momentarily neutralized sort of harm—was picked up before the lights came on in the camp. Once this happened, the stone began to seem infernal: Was it "A stone from Phlegethon, / bloodied on the bed of hell's hot river?" The fact that the poet's hand still smoked from the water evaporating in the cold air made him think of a fleeting reference in Dante to the heart of Prince Henry "plucked" out by Guy de Montfort in 1272 to avenge the death of his father at the hands of Edward I of England. Nations are mentioned by neither poet, but clearly hatred of the English guides Heaney's reference to Guy de Montfort's "victim's heart in its casket, long venerated" as it drips blood into the Thames.

Now the very casualness with which the final quatrains dandle these top-heavy literary allusions obtains the poet his own subtle revenge and amounts to a muted warning, for he stands there as if with that plucked-out heart in his hand:

> Anyhow, there I was with the wet red stone
> in my hand, staring across at the watch-towers
> From my own free state of image and allusion,
> swooped on, then dropped by trained binoculars:
>
> a silhouette not worth bothering about,
> out for the evening in scarf and waders
> and not about to set times wrong or right,
> stooping along, one of the venerators.

The virulence of the last two lines, which ally Heaney with those who venerated the organ of the dead English prince, is occasioned by savage emotion aware of and vexed by its own long repression. For if Heaney is one of the venerators—of empire, tradition, history, aesthetic form (and the poem *is* thwart-rhymed against a clearly avoided norm)—he scarcely honors the purely statistical might that takes him in its sights in that withering line, "swooped on, then dropped by trained binoculars." What he venerates is precisely Guy de Montfort and the impulse "to set times wrong or right," whether in history or verse. The term "venerate" is sullied by its first application to Prince Henry's bleeding heart, so the last time it appears, it is patently associated with the English, who from their watchtower control the point of view of the last stanza: In *their* eyes he is the proverbially gullible indigene in comical gear "stooping along" (in which we hear the jibe "stupid" as well). In *their* binoculars he is not worth distinguishing from all the others who have mutely borne privation, and venerated their deprivers. By his utter quiet, Heaney endorses this sinister imputation, which stings a little to the extent that it is a just profile of the outward man, and which must make any Englishman squirm, to the extent that it cannot be true of the inward. The fiery aggressive imagery of "Sandstone Keepsake" is perfectly played against the monochromatism of the terrain, the bruised, nubby stone, and the poet's depressed demeanor. These felicities that keep one another warily off-balance, coupled with a new conversational ease amounting at times to impudence, make the poem a landmark for Heaney.

"The Loaning" is a new departure as well, but its flight is clipped by old thematic tics and returns. A tangential allusiveness is at work: It is not entirely overt, yet it is not deeply imbedded in the work, either. I seem to hear the lofty suspirations of Derek Walcott's "Season of Phantasmal Peace" in the gossamer flight of the souls of all things into the limbo of lost words, and in the poet-speaker's near-levitation when he recalls the wordless communication among farming men in the summer kitchen at dusk. The verse overpowers one cumulatively, like a long daydream. The lost words

> . . . had flown there from raftered sheds and crossroads,
> from the shelter of gable ends and turned-up carts.
> I saw them streaming out of birch-white throats
> and fluttering above iron bedsteads
> until the soul would leave the body
> . . . .
> Then I knew why from the beginning
> the loaning had breathed on me, breathed even now
> in a shiver of beaded gossamers
> and the spit blood of a last few haws and rose-hips.
>
> Big voices in the womanless kitchen.
> . . . They sat on in the dark
> with the pipes red in their mouths
> . . . I closed my eyes
> to make the light motes stream behind them
> and my head went airy, my chair rode
> high and low among branches and the wind
> stirred up a rookery in the next long *Ave.*

The farm setting is pure Heaney, but the recurrence of words like the verb *stream* alerts us to affinities between the voice in "The Loaning" and other examples of this increasingly popular metaphysical-diaphanous mode indebted to the late romantics. Both the soarings and the words in which they are couched resemble the practice of Walcott and John Ashbery when they, too, work this field, even if Heaney is not a thoroughgoing convert and the poem does not pursue its insubstantial aim, as we shall see.

Even less imbedded in the text, hence much more like "lost words," are remote echoes of Patrick Kavanagh (the rural gear like the turned-up cart)[9] and Wordsworth (the breathing). Later on, some considerably more audible but no less unmoored or impermanent references to Dante appear. That Heaney's condensed translation improves that of all the other English translators of *Inferno* XIII.31–43 makes it all the more puzzling that the context does not warrant, nor does it suit, the allusions to hearing the bubbling sap of pain in the wood of the suicides (see below).

Other sources of "lost words" that find their way to Heaney's limbo are the Catholic mass (the *Introibo* from the beginning of the mass as priest and acolytes announce their approach to the altar) and W. B. Yeats (the picking carefulness with which a plain thing is sternly but a little wordily uttered: "your voice slips back into its old first place / and makes the sound your shades make there," where the plural is also a Yeatsian perturbation by particularity). And Heaney's own brash, baldly aggressive lexicon is represented in the *uvulae* of stones and the *lungs* of the hawthorn shrub. Allusion is also made to the poet's own translation of the laments of his alter ego Sweeney, in the blackbird's *volubility* (mad Sweeney had triggered their song as he crashed through the brush, "startled / by the startled woodcock / or a blackbird's sudden / volubility," *Sweeney Astray* #40).

But finally this is not a celebratory nature poem that aims to rock us on the waters of tradition fanned by the zephyrs of allusion. The third section, which begins in a continuing trance of earth song, breaks off with two uneasy verse paragraphs about torture. (The ellipsis in the middle stanza is Heaney's.)

> Stand still. You can hear
> everything going on. High-tension cables
> singing above cattle, tractors, barking dogs,
> juggernauts changing gear a mile away.
> Always the surface noise of the earth
> you didn't know you'd heard till a twig snapped
> and a blackbird's startled volubility
> stopped short.
>
>   When you are tired or terrified
> your voice slips back into its old first place
> and makes the sound your shades make there . . .
> When Dante snapped a twig in the bleeding wood
> a voice sighed out of blood that bubbled up
> like sap at the end of green sticks on a fire.
>
> At the click of a cell lock somewhere now
> the interrogator steels his *introibo,*
> the light motes blaze, a blood-red cigarette
> startles the shades, screeching and beseeching.

There "The Loaning," wrenched into a sudden grimace, abruptly ends. What happened to the clues we had picked up in the first thirty-six lines of the poem? Were we wrong to mark "The Loaning" as a bittersweet idyll of fading lives in a fading countryside? Did we overlook some stroke, some nuance of intention there, which would have primed us for the last ten lines above? Was being in limbo more desperate and canonical than we had thought? Were the dying—those with "birch-white throats"—actually the Ulster martyred?

As forecasts of horror, only two occasions flare out with more fire on subsequent and more troubled readings. One is the automatic roughness of the language describing the unhealthy color of berries in the Fall—"the spit blood of a last few haws and rose-hips"—a melodramatic detail presaged by the last poem in *North* (1975), where the stunning comet of the poet's as yet unwitnessed destiny is imagined tearing through the sky "Like a glimmer of haws and rose-hips." And the other occasion that sounds more sinister now than heretofore is the word *juggernaut* to apply to heavy machinery. But in "High Summer" and in the first "Glanmore Sonnet" in *Field Work,* farm machines far away have a soothing, almost comic sound: The country quiet in Sonnet I is "a deep no sound / Vulnerable to distant gargling tractors." Nor is the blind worship of a carnivorous deity (Jaganath; Ireland) the subject of "The Loaning," nor is the abstract notion of inevitable self-sacrifice a prominent one. Despite its pretty horrific closing tableau of interrogator and premonitory shades "screeching and beseeching," the violence is almost an accident in this gently memorious land of open meadow (*loaning*) and hedgerow. The limbo, into which lost words and resonant unspoken meanings migrate from those expiring in their beds and from the kindly taciturn farmers in their kitchen chairs, is one of retrospective pleasure and belonging. No one is being threatened or punished, no personal or cultural lack is being harshly exposed to view. And in this very mild and elegiac light the poet's reflexive swerve toward blood, steel, and malevolence appears to be unrehearsed, indefensible, yet absolutely demanded by some law of his imagination, a law by now a trifle overused.

But in a way Heaney has always rigged his poems to be violated. Recall the agricultural imagery of slicing, delving, and nicking; of piercing (to dig a well) and of plunging (to encounter the self in well water). By a quirk of association, these are conflated with images of weaving, braiding, and coalescing between laborer and land, so that an act of ostensibly violent, abrasive penetration is also one of coaxing, of restitution, of preservation, and of self-discovery. These contrary images predominate in the poems of the late 1960s. Thereafter, the people-in-the-bog poems give Heaney another way to think about digging down into the core of meaning. The exhumed mummified bodies, memorials of brutal ancient sacrifice to the Earth Mother, could also be likened to the victims of the Catholic-Protestant hatreds in Ulster, especially after 1969, at the same time as they float up from the waters of the unconscious like alter egos. Meeting the self, plunging to the interior, thus violating the unbroken

surfaces presented by water, marsh, and one's own self-esteem—all are
then implicated with corpses, guilt, and secrecy. Moreover, the bog itself
becomes human, its surface a face, its deeps like innards, its characteristic
seduction, that it can be cut into: "I love this turf-face, / its black inci-
sions." Further, and more uncanny, when pried apart the bog's face can
open its tawny lips and speak. When Heaney cuts out of the peat a turf-
spade grown over with a kind of "green fog,"

> the soft lips of the growth
> muttered and split,
> a tawny rut
> opening at my feet
> like a shed skin,
> the shaft wettish
> as I sank it upright
> and beginning to
> steam in the sun.[10]

This is poetry by someone absorbed with a kind of horror in the earth
processes, yet whose whole intellect is alert to the poetic advantage of
wettish over *wet*, and of the deep "logic" of the inner rhyme of *mutter*
with *rut*.

That said, it is equally clear that Heaney is more attracted to the sounds
and imagery of violation than he is to poetry of harmony between the
rhythms of country experience and the intoning consciousness. Consider
the use of many of the same sounds in a somewhat later poem:

> Slubbed with eddies,
> the laden silent river
> ran mud and olive into summer.

Here the impulse is to dally instead of pare; although the lines themselves
are not that much longer, the openness to ample, freighted pentameter—
"Snails in the grass, bat-squeak, the darkening trees," "Swallows mazed
from nests caked up on roof-tiles"—make the nearby briefer lines less
suffocating and the temper of the poem less manic, looser in weave.

Heaney's aversion to the mellifluous has moderated in *Field Work* and
Station Island. Here he is extending his meditative voice into new registers; he uses longer and more ambitious periods, and indulges a quality
of leisureliness that makes the narrative voice more content to meander
among its materials. "High Summer" from *Field Work* is a fine example
of the method left to itself (it was cited just above). Heaney makes only
a glancing attempt to dislodge this poem, which is about fishing and
working on hot days in France, with seismic consequence. The attempt

is so finely offhanded, the effect is more memorable than the disturbing non sequiturs in "The Loaning." "High Summer" is also a successful experiment with the staggering of strong rhymes and pause in Arnoldian fashion to round out lines of unequal lengths:

> Slubbed with eddies,
> the laden silent river
> ran mud and olive into summer.
> Swallows mazed from nests caked up on roof-tiles
> in the barn: the double doors stood open,
> the carter passed ahead of his bowed oxen.
>
> I bought the maggots in paper bags, like sweets,
> and fished at evening in the earthy heat
> and green reek of the maize.
> . . . .
> On the last day, when I was clearing up,
> on a warm ledge I found the bag of maggots
> and opened it. A black
> and throbbing swarm came riddling out
> like newsreel of a police force run amok,
> sunspotting flies in gauzy meaty flight,
> the barristers and black berets of light.

The heavily swaying pitch of the last stanza gives its own pleasure, especially when brought up against the better-behaved couplet at the end. Still, he is tempted to descriptive excess, as in the slightly ponderous verbal choices (are both *throbbing* and *riddling* doing the work they should? is the penultimate line not too rambling and approximate?), which are so much a part of Heaney's whole poetic tack. These take him far from the most interesting line. One wonders how the poet might have clarified his own shock—in the moment, and in his Irish experience—had he omitted the over-rich couplet and brooded over that newsreel image.

One answer might be the newer poem in which Heaney has taken his descriptive genius in a different direction still. Published in the 1987 volume called *The Haw Lantern*, "The Mud Vision" is his longest blank-verse poem to date. The fifty-nine lines of narration follow the middle-brow reporter's sarcastic voice as it tells of a bizarre quasi-religious vision of mud ("as if a rose-window of mud / Had invented itself out of the glittering damp"). Like the uncanny cinematic vision of Peter Weir, Heaney's universe is overlaid by one obsession:

> And then the sunsets ran murky, the wiper
> Could never entirely clean off the windscreen,
> Reservoirs tasted of silt, a light fuzz

> Accrued in the hair and eyebrows, and some
> Took to wearing a smudge on their foreheads
> To be prepared for whatever.

The coat of mud might readily be linked with Heaney's agricultural biases, as might the vocabulary of *murk, silt, fuzz,* and *smudge,* but two stylistic flourishes stand out as departures from and leavening of that language of earth and byre, the clever peeling-back of bureaucratic crust from the French word for increase, *Accrued,* and the shrugged-off colloquialism *whatever*—which, incidentally, makes secular and frivolous the wearing of the Lenten emblem of ash.

The voice throughout is wry and businesslike, not wont to indulge in moods or in the lush descriptive excursus. And under the guise of tearless, sharp, undemonstrative reportage, Heaney builds up his sparse and theatrical future-scape where (as in another kind of film, Fellini's *8½*), prelates and hopeless invalids and "menu-writers / And punks with aerosol sprays . . . and the last of the mummers," truckers and experts with "their *post factum* jabber"—all crowd into one tawdry zone, to which the mud miracle has come, and from which, by the poem's end, it will abscond. Meantime,

> A generation who had seen a sign!
> Those nights when we stood in an umber dew and smelled
> Mould in the verbena or woke to a light
> Furrow-breath on the pillow, when the talk
> Was all about who had seen it and our fear
> Was touched with a secret pride, only ourselves
> Could be adequate then to our lives. When the rainbow
> Curved flood-brown and ran like a water-rat's back
> So that drivers on the hard-shoulder switched off to watch,
> We wished it away, and yet we presumed it a test
> That would prove us beyond expectation.

At the beginning of this verse paragraph, I think we are correct in hearing echoes of the famous Nativity Sermon of Lancelot Andrewes ("Signs are taken for wonders. 'Master, we would fain see a sign,' that is a miracle.");[11] Heaney also invokes it, using a much closer (albeit displaced) paraphrase, in "The Badgers" in *Field Work*. He thinks of the badger going through backyards as the ghost of "some violent shattered boy" exploded by a bomb: "Visitations are taken for signs"—visitations by badgers, that is, taken for signs not of God but of the political unrest and unavenged ghosts incarnated in these intelligent "sturdy dirty" beasts. But in more than this one habit of allusion "The Mud Vision" pays its respects to the rhetoric of impersonal exhaustion, and to the vision of an intensely cloying and unsavory "nature," of the poem, published sixty-five years earlier, which brought the Andrewes sermon into prominence. T. S. Eliot's remarks on history, which "Gives too soon / Into weak hands, what's thought can be dispensed with" so that "Neither fear nor courage saves us," prepare the way, with their tones of quiet editorial extremity, for Heaney's view that since "our fear / Was touched with a secret pride, only ourselves / Could be adequate then to our lives," and to his "test / That would prove us beyond expectation." Similarly, Heaney's "umber dew," "mould," "Furrow-breath," and "water-rat's back," his drivers, hard-shoulders and muddy rainbow, run a stylistic and thematic course parallel to the goat coughing, the "Rocks, moss, stonecrop, iron, merds," the "peevish gutter," the "decayed house," and "windy knob" of "Geron-tion." Not to mention the rat creeping near the dull canal in "The Fire Sermon." Like Eliot, Heaney takes the poem out into the open, forcing the lyrical sensibility to operate at, or in, a pageant—whether of the bitchy international crowd (De Bailhache, Fräulein von Kulp) and the lowlife of café and boardinghouse of "Gerontion," or of paparazzi and pedants, menu-writers and casualties in "The Mud Vision."

And, like the voice we hear recurrently in T. S. Eliot's verse, Heaney's narrative consciousness is drained by weakness of will. "We had the experi-ence but missed the meaning," wrote Eliot in *Four Quartets*. We are given, says Gerontion, "What's not believed in, or if still believed, / In memory only." "We forgot that the vision was ours," writes Heaney, whose narra-tor further regrets: "What might have been founded / We dissipated in news." And here is Eliot in "Gerontion" again: "I have lost my passion: why should I need to keep it / Since what is kept must be adulterated." Eliot's vision is Christian and despairing; less despairing, Heaney's vision is agnostic but couched in Catholicized symbols. Above all, in both "Ger-ontion" and "The Mud Vision," the supernal is categorically beyond the human *from now on*. Both poems stress the apocalyptic knowledge that the present moment is the beginning of the worst of times, precipitated by something knotted and unreachable in ourselves. Eliot's awareness of this culpability seems to go deepest:

> I that was near your heart was removed therefrom
> To lose beauty in terror, terror in inquisition.

Heaney works from a tighter Audenesque base: "Our one chance to know the incomparable" is "dissipated in news" (that is, in the desire to have the power to be the lookers and interpreters for everybody else), although at last the rhetoric is obscure and coils back into a smooth little paradoxical turn:

> The clarified place
> Had retrieved neither us nor itself—except
> You could say we survived. So say that, and watch us
> Who had our chance to be mud-men, convinced and estranged,
> Figure in our own eyes for the eyes of the world.

It does not seem reasonable to wish that Heaney had the temper and the skill to take this kind of bitter vision further than he does. One could, however, wish that he would make the kind itself clearer. For "The Mud Vision" is not coherent, any more than "The Loaning" is, although it is far more integral, more ambitious, and significantly further afield of his earlier modes. Thus the poem is a sign of new terrain staked out, which means that old and rich terrain has been painfully and expensively abandoned. "The Mud Vision" is a poem that owes very little to Heaney's older working methods, those tics and tricks by which words and breath and energies got arranged. Yet by the same token neither is it one of those poems composed in backlash against the softer traits (those of the right-hand column), which we see in foreshortened, plain-style, screwed-down poems like "The Peninsula" and "For the Commander of the 'Eliza,'" or the interminably bland Frost monologues "The Wife's Tale" and "Shore Woman." Nor on the other hand is it one of those poems that chafes against the form it indentures itself to, like the twisted "Glanmore Sonnets," too large for their frames. Instead, "The Mud Vision" is a pivotal experiment in the rueful, mixed surrealist poem in which profundity of allusion, ingenuity of phrasing, crisp surprise of diction, and the drive with which syntax is stitched through the lines are of far more importance than the vision itself. It is like a hive no longer—or not yet—lived in. A style-piece that may lead to greater things.

III

In *Sweeney Astray,* however, his rendering into coherent and gripping modern English of the Middle Irish work *Buile Suibhne* (generally known as *The Madness of Sweeney* or *The Frenzy of Sweeney*), Seamus Heaney has blended style with vision at the fiercest possible temperature. Yet the major verse form he employs is the old two-stress line in the tight quatrain, which seemed exhausted in *North,* and he is girt round with pitfalls, debts, and textural and formal distractions. For this is not an original work: It diverges very little from the interpretation of the narrated events by the work's only other modern translator, J. G. O'Keeffe, in 1913.[12] The only crux where O'Keeffe and Heaney seriously differ occurs when Sweeney, a king transformed during an important battle into a skittish birdlike creature, visits his former wife Eorann. Heaney gives her some erotic dialogue that may be too blatant for her smoldering character; she wishes she and Sweeney could fly away together and then she would "swoop to pleasure you in flight." In the original—judging, that is, from O'Keeffe's literal translation—the queen merely wishes their bodies were both feathered.[13] Also, Eorann originally remarks, "though at ease am I, my body is wasted / since the day I heard of thy ruin." Robert Graves improves O'Keeffe's meaning as follows: "Though soft I lie, my body wastes / Since the day of your downfall."[14] Graves follows O'Keeffe in implying that Eorann's pining still persists; whereas Heaney suggests that her pining, once severe, is now laid by: "I am easy now, and yet I wasted / at the cruel news of your being bested." Heaney is perhaps less sympathetic to the wife of the transformed penitent: His sympathies all lie with Sweeney as the type of the artist, "displaced, guilty, assuaging himself with his utterance," as he says in the Introduction. But given the immediacy and edge with which persons and voices are brought out by Heaney, one willingly discards the quibble.

The liberties Heaney takes, here and throughout, only support the text and make more vivid the sufferings and dire rigors of Sweeney, erstwhile king of the northern half of the northern County Antrim. The brilliance of *Sweeney Astray* as a title is that it suggests the geographical element as well as the king's craziness, for Sweeney wanders long and far, virtually unprotected against the elements. It is the contrast between these facts and the familiar, comfortable room that Heaney tries to bring out in the same section in which Eorann converses with her former husband. Sweeney is all the while perched on the lintel to her room, ready to fly off at any intrusion (he is in terror of being captured and "tamed"). He sarcastically and heartbrokenly remarks his wife's remarriage, unable to remove his mind from thoughts of the bed, there in front of him, where she has found pleasure with another. The bed is *still warm* from her lover (whereas in O'Keeffe's translation Eorann was only *bound bedward* to him). Furthermore, when Sweeney regrets how little Eorann must have cared for him—

> To-day, it is readily manifest,
> thou thinkest little of thy old friend;
> warm for thee on the down of a pleasant bed,
> cold for me abroad till morn.
>
> (O'Keeffe #32)

—Heaney in his recasting wants to suggest the double torture to this driven madman, both to see the warm, beautiful woman with whom he once shared a life, knowing she is lost to him and he to her, and simultaneously to imagine her—or to refrain by brute force from imagining her—with his replacement, helplessly subjecting his mind to the details of those embraces. Consequently, Heaney's metaphors are not mere extensions of the almost unremarked tropes in O'Keeffe of clarity, warmth, and cold. Instead, he imports new tropes of *breaking* and *unmaking*, both of which take their tenor from the obsessively literal vehicle of the *bed*:

> But you have broken trust,
> unmade it like a bed—
> not mine in the dawn frost
> but yours, that he invaded.
>
> (Heaney #32)

In addition, the bed becomes the noun on which the syntax of the two halves of the stanza hinges, so that the sentence structure presses once again on the metaphoric tissue, deepening the bruise.

Although it is true to say that Seamus Heaney has done justice to the original, he has in this instance removed from the possible repertoire of the protagonist's emotions all that are soft and melancholy: Sweeney here is bitter, hectic, jealous, accusatory. Elsewhere in *Sweeney Astray,* Heaney will present Sweeney as mournfully passive where in O'Keeffe's translation he is something of a martinet (as in section #25). But in general Heaney's book does something the O'Keeffe does not: It attempts both to give us the flavor of the countryside over which Sweeney flees, and to show us a continuous consciousness reacting to hunger, pursuit by predators, loneliness, and pain from the thorns, branches, stones, and exposure to the cold. (Sweeney's feathers seem to be nominal accoutrements, and provide him no protection from the frost and wind and torrents of water that fall throughout.) Heaney's Sweeney (the trochaic rhyme amuses the translator, too) is consequently much more alert to the panoply of sensation to which his mental and bodily nakedness exposes him, just as he is more moved by the sounds and sights of other creatures. Even as the phenomena seem to take on greater density and his movements greater speed, he is more confidential toward us. The difference between the earlier version and *Sweeney Astray* is like that between a dull encrusted gemstone and its beveled and polished resplendence.

It is not just that O'Keeffe is a literal translator and Heaney an adventuresome one, though that is true: The version of O'Keeffe permits the poem to sound medieval and fragmented, for all the poignancy, even there, of the laments:

> Stumbling from withered tree-tops,
> faring through furze—deed without falsehood—
> shunning mankind, keeping company with wolves,
> racing with the red stag over the field.
>
> (O'Keeffe #61)

> Frost, ice, snow, and storm,
> forever scourging me,
> I without fire, without house,
> on the summit of Sliabh Eidneach.

(O'Keeffe #67)

Heaney elevates the poem from archeological curiosity into a text with enormous urgency:

> Alarmed out of the autumned wood,
> whipped by whins, flecked with blood,
> running wild among wolf-packs,
> shying away with the red stag.

(Heaney #61)

> Frost crystals and level ice,
> the scourging snow, the male-voiced storm
> assist at my requiem.
> My hearth grows cold, my fire dies.

(Heaney #67)

Above all, Heaney restores to the lines before us what anyone reading the O'Keeffe version realizes is a promise of electrifying keenness:

I flee before the skylarks—	The skylarks rising
'tis a stern, great race—	to their high space
I leap over the stumps	send me pitching and tripping
on the tops of the mountains.	over stumps on the moor
When the proud turtle-dove	and my hurry flushes
rises for us,	the turtle-dove.
quickly do I overtake it	I overtake it,
since my feathers have grown.	my plumage rushing,
The silly, foolish woodcock	am startled
hen it rises for me	by the startled woodcock
methinks 'tis a bitter foe,	or a blackbird's sudden
the blackbird (too) that gives	volubility.
[a cry of alarm.	
(O'Keeffe #40)	(Heaney #40)

Technically, the phenomena become the subject of the actions in Heaney, not the objects of the narrator's syntactic will. Rhetorically as well, Heaney is more deft; instead of repeating versicles, his syntax imitates surprise and swerving attention, and in place of closed stanzas, Heaney pulls the poem headlong across the open field between stanzas as Sweeney trips and crashes through branch and thorn, by turns eluding and overtaking— and being startled out of his wits (note the paralysis of the ninth line)—as other winged creatures break cover or sing complicated warnings in a mysteriously laconic landscape.

Ciaran Carson claims that Heaney's descriptive method earlier on in this section is less dramatic than the original's. Instead of directly addressing each tree in the long forest catalogue in the second person, he describes them in the third person.[15] While it is true that Heaney does opt for the descriptive rather than the exclamatory and vocative modes in many places, his prosody, syntax, and imagery *as a whole* are far more dramatic than O'Keeffe's.

O apple-tree, little apple-tree,	Ever-generous apple trees
much art thou shaken;	rain big showers when shaken;
O quicken, little berried one,	scarlet berries clot like blood
delightful is thy bloom.	on mountain rowan.
(O'Keeffe #40)	(Heaney #40)

What is lost in the third-person voice is regained in the sharpness of the landscape details and the tangibility of fluid seasonal process, fruiting like a longer-lived version of rain. In his revision of this stanza for *Sweeney Astray* (the version above appeared in his lecture on early Irish nature poetry in 1978), Heaney tightens even further the dramatic intensity of the description, adding to visible effects those of sound, as the fruit *drums down* from *clumps:*

Low-set clumps of apple trees
drum down fruit when shaken . . .

The clotting-like-blood trope, although typical of one lurid extreme of Heaney's imagination, is mindful of the emergence of berries along the outblossomed branches and of their darkening to ripeness. The O'Keeffe version contents itself with mentioning the two states separately. And when the imagery is already bloody in *Buile Suibhne*, Heaney blends function with appearance yet more skillfully:

O ash-tree, thou baleful one,	life-blood on a spear shaft
hand-weapon of a warrior.	darkens the grain of ash.

The long exhalation of the vowels in the last line, and the way they help brake the rate of our progress, suggest the labored but undemonstrative death of the men the ash spear has wounded.

Stunning above all is the role of metaphor in condensing effects of far greater poignancy and terror. The iterations of color in the picture of the wells and springs of Sweeney's lair, Glen Bolcain, for example, suggested to Heaney the kind of landscape dearest to his own heart—"bog pools lidded with innocent grass," "green, wet corners, flooded wastes, soft rushy bottoms," as he describes them in his prose memoir, "Mossbawn" (1978)—hence he transforms dark but light-reflecting well-water into wet grass:

Good its water pure-green,	Its water flashing like wet grass,
good its clean, fierce wind,	its wind so keen,
good its cress-green watercress,	its tall brooklime, its watercress
best its tall brooklime.	the greenest green.

The attribute *flashing* to link grass to water pleasantly echoes the great English bard of inland water and passive foliage, William Wordsworth, to whom the earth's surface seemed to "work like a sea," whose intimations "gleam like the flashing of a shield" as "the earth / And common face of Nature" speak to him, and who is ever alert to the habit of light to turn the reflecting surfaces of roads and the undersides of leaves and grasses into watercourses. Although Heaney is correct about the temperature of Irish nature poetry being far, far chillier than its English counterpart, his rendering of the descriptive passages of this Irish poem manifest a finely subdued sympathy with Wordsworth. And although the national nerve-fibers of this sympathy are shared by the authors of the original *Buile Suibhne,* it is Heaney who brings to them the necessary lexical and metaphoric daring that make the poem transmissible.

Heaney cuts away excess like a sculptor paring clay. According to O'Keeffe, Sweeney's green glen is "his fortress and his dwelling-place." For Heaney, it is "his ark and his Eden"—less military, but more commanding in allusive force. In his translation of Sweeney's flight from a pack of wolves, O'Keeffe is unemphatic and panoramic, showing man and beasts progressing upward as from a distance. Heaney on the other hand re-creates the desperation of being chased, trying to reach higher ground, shaking the demons off as one's feet scramble the rocky incline, only just managing to evade their jaws.

. . . wolves at their rending,	. . . the wolves behind me
I flee at the sound.	howling and rending—
They have striven to reach me,	their vapoury tongues,
coming in their swift course,	their low-slung speed
so that I fled before them	shaken off like nightmare
to the tops of the mountains.	at the foot of the slope.

The triumph that is nearly automatic in the earlier text is infinitely arduous, and still not quite achieved, in the later. In place of elevation, abasement. Clearly, Heaney's horrified interest in the wolves is the source of his passage's strength—their crouching speed, their howling, their *vapoury tongues.* He had used this haunting phrase once before, in a requiem for

the Irish wolf. Set as we might expect on a night of "sogging" rain, the
poem takes us to basalt outcrops in a wet, waste region where

> The old dens are soaking.
> The pads are lost or
> Retrieved by small vermin
>
> That glisten and scut.
> Nothing is panting, lolling,
> Vapouring. The tongue's
> Leashed in my throat.[16]

Even in this early poem, one can see at work Heaney's ability, like Crusoe,
to use everything that has come ashore with him, even if these are the
pieces of shipwreck and the evidences of extinction. It is this demon of
practicality that inspired Heaney in his meticulous work on *Sweeney
Astray,* and which continues to bear fruit in his section of Sweeney poems
in *Station Island.*

In the wake of *Sweeney Astray,* begun at least a decade previously but
brought to fruition after *Field Work,* Heaney has moved a great distance
ahead in his ability to frame a political statement, as if his greatest and
most effortless expression were to come about in the mood of release and
clarity after the translator put aside his texts. No longer a medium, but
the spokesman for his own displacements, Heaney finds it invigorating to
follow at several removes along Sweeney's *via negativa.* "The First Flight"
in *Station Island* is accordingly set in a time of "spasm," alluding to both
civil strife, and to the king's own jolt out of sanity. Despite both cata-
clysms, the quasi-Sweeney narrator still feels sufficient affinity with his
kinsmen to gauge the extent of their rifts:

> tne ties and knots running through us
> split open
> down the lines of the grain.

Instead of binding men together, their "knots" of family, tradition, affection, skill, optimism, shared grief, and immemorial allegiances have
been so tried and thwarted by dark instinct and darker circumstances that
they become their weakest spots like (and here the metaphor slides ninety
degrees from the vertical)—like the knots in wood where the cracks begin
that travel down the entire plank. Driven from the field of conflict
(Heaney moved from Ulster to Wicklow in 1972, Sweeney was driven
into madness and exile by the din of the Battle of Magh Rath), both men
revolt against their own revolts. Eager to rest somewhere and to affirm
something, both turn, with painful exhilaration, to the order and elegance

of nature, only to discover they cannot ignore the sounds of human turmoil in the distance:

> As I drew close to pebbles and berries,
> the smell of wild garlic, relearning
> the acoustic of frost
> . . . .
> my empty place [was] an excuse
> for shifts in the camp, old rehearsals
> of debts and betrayal.

Those who have ever abandoned any struggle may have observed how
little their absence, over which they so long agonized, matters to the
whole. Yet the whole still matters to them. This is why, when friend and
foe alike recognize Sweeney in the tree branches in the original poem,
and try to cajole him down, the hero is finally swayed by being told all
his family have died. Hence, the bittersweet condition Heaney calls being
"mired in attachment," a state cured not in the Irish story but in the
modern lyric by a horrible rumor, which reflects upon this poet's desire
to write meaningfully of political strife: It is as if he fed off the violence
and killings that goad him to that end:

> I was mired in attachment
> until they began to pronounce me
> a feeder off battlefields
>
> so I mastered new rungs of the air
> to survey out of reach
> their bonfires on hills, their hosting
>
> and fasting, the levies from Scotland
> as always, and the people of art
> diverting their rhythmical chants
>
> to fend off the onslaught of winds
> I would welcome and climb
> at the top of my bent.

The "people of art"—a quaint phrase for poets that shows how little
attention the Sweeney-voice can spare them—are tentative. They want
things to quiet down. Sweeney wants to challenge ferocity at its own
speed—but in the harmless realm of his own isolation. *His* art will be
to welcome the challenge of wild nature, reject the regal and domestic
constraints of his earlier life along with his nostalgia for them. His task
is ascetic, not aesthetic. Art is merely a foppish avoidance of the great
work of renunciation; it uses meagre magic to fend off the very winds
that tax, test, and ennoble the soul. Sweeney masters new rungs of the air
to climb to a different level of trial: To become *all* bird, he identifies

himself with the wordless, grim extreme of his transformation. The poem is a fascinating gloss on *Sweeney Astray* at the same time as it represents, for Seamus Heaney, a manic recoil from politics at the other extreme from the clever and wide-ranging ironies of "Sandstone Keepsake" and the grander elegiac mode of "The Toome Road" and "The Strand at Lough Beg."

In "The Master," a poem with no analogue in *Sweeney Astray,* Heaney suggests that the ascetic solution to the external challenge is either too simple for the aesthetes or too slow. It lacks the eloquence, dispatch, and dash with which, at their hands, true art has unfortunately confused itself. A poem about renewing faith in the great truths, "The Master" also implies their utter lack of emotional appeal: "nothing / arcane, just the old rules / we all had inscribed on our slates." The task of reacquaintance is therefore also one of self-reformation as the hardened ego tirelessly casts about for something to be intense upon. Instead, there are these old ciphers worn by familiarity, which the master (like another Eric Gill, the sculptor) has reinvested with *numen:*

> Each character blocked on the parchment secure
> in its volume and measure.
> Each maxim given its space.
> Like quarrymen's hammers and wedges proofed
> by intransigent service.
> Like coping stones where you rest
> in the balm of the wellspring.

Intransigence, the unwillingness to compromise, has a political cast, which illuminates the craftsmen absorbed in their skill, deaf to the demagogues. As memorial to their unbending strength, their reverence for each character in its volume, the poem gives us the carven copestone of a well such as Sweeney might have perched upon in his long insomniac ordeal, bending to drink the water that looked so much like wet grass. Heaney's evocation of that moment springs from hard looking at the stones themselves: It is as if these beautifully but simply worked things had been made long ago, like the Sweeney poem, their makers no longer near. The poignancy of the lesson to be learned is in part the loneliness it consigns all makers to, with nothing but the bare self for primary, unworked, "text," nothing but inscrutably perfect geometry on which to lay one's spirit-level.

More closely based on *Sweeney Astray,* "Sweeney's Returns" condenses the two meetings between husband and wife, and yet seems more completely Heaney's own poem than any other work so indebted in this series. It is a love poem made touching by indirection, since the wife never appears. Only her things and the signs of her orderly habits lie open to view, endlessly suggestive of a creature of charm and grace, but piercingly less than the starved returning lover had hoped to glimpse. Although the least informed by the details that announce her temper and person, the middle of the poem's three stanzas takes the reader furthest into the Sweeney figure's victorious, expectant, erotically charged arrival:

> Then when I perched on the sill
> to gaze about my coffers of absence
> I was like a scout at risk behind lines
> who raises his head in a wheatfield
> to take a first look, the throb of his breakthrough
> going on inside him unstoppably.

Eorann's bangle lying in the sun is all that spoils the fine negativity of the "coffers of absence," which her ragged husband had hoarded up in forethought. A little treasure is nearly worse than none. A little fidelity might break his stopping and starting heart. Worse even than adultery is his own "wild reflection" in the mirror greeting him across her "tucked and level bed." This frozen tableau sends the Sweeney figure back to his own wilderness, spooked, ailing, and distraught. "Sweeney's Returns" has the feeling of one of those compositions that marries the fluency of the making so warmly to the feeling of which it is born that when, like Robert Burns, the author recalls the writing, his blood must sally at the remembrance.

What is curiously missing in all but a few of the title-sequence poems in *Station Island* is to be found in a good third of the Sweeney poems. Those I have in mind are brief free-verse lyrics in a style as close to natural and uninflected by dialect or barbarous peculiarity of diction and rhythm as any Heaney has ever written ("The First Flight," "The Hermit," "The Master," "The Scribes," "In the Chestnut Tree," "Sweeney's Returns," "Holly," and "On the Road," this last a throwback to the tried and true small quatrain, but in the new pure middle-style). This quality, sometimes caught on the wing or by some minor turning, is in fact liberated by the entire work of the poem, yet indeliberately, as if by the descent of grace. It emerges in metaphors like "coffers of absence," in sudden externalizations of the self as in "my shadow over the field," in the unnerving "black pearl" of severity that pools up in the bitter scribes, and in the image of the well's moisture on a masterfully chiseled stone. Their meanings are only hinted at by the considerable literal, logical, and metrical work they do. But without that work, the flash of exhilaration would falter by which we see, along with the poet, into the depths of his unformed intuitions. These truths of technique have long been known and eloquently expounded by Seamus Heaney in his prose, but have seldom been so perfectly, and precariously, embodied in his own verse.

7

"Irreference"

On John Ashbery

Avoiding the Subject

Many nuances inhere in the conjunction between the terms *poems* and *prose,* not the least pertinent to the poetry of the last several decades being the idea that prose has *gotten itself* into the poem. What might otherwise not belong there has stolen past the censors. Robert Lowell found this stealth liberating (indeed, to it he attributes his sea change from the mode of *Mills of the Kavanaughs* to that of *Life Studies*). Randall Jarrell provides a new warrant for the introduction into postwar poetry of a prosaic or conversational emphasis alongside the ingenuousness of the child; Elizabeth Bishop extends the reach of the ingenue.

But there is an earlier tradition of prose crowding poetry, which we find in all the great modernists' work, that of Pound, Eliot, Carlos Williams, Moore, Stevens—namely, the inclusion of both rubble ("heterogeneous dreck," Auden called the matter of modern life) and extruded meditation, which on occasion takes the form of "unpoetical," quasi-philosophical thought. John Ashbery stands on the juncture between these two prosaic traditions. In fact in his later work, from the 1966 *Rivers and Mountains* onward, Ashbery has become increasingly dilatory and Jamesian. As Alan Williamson, one of his very best explicators, describes Ashbery's style, it is one in which the "anti-epiphanic" increasingly predominates, along with "the time-haunted difficulty of shifting references and overqualifications."[1] Williamson might be describing Marianne Moore as he discriminates the way in which

> The vagueness of commonplace expressions and the jargon of the inexact sciences (economics, statistics, sociology, literary criticism) bulk ever larger in Ashbery's poetic vocabulary, presumably as a way of dramatizing cognitive difficulties.
>
> [Williamson, p. 132]

One recalls T. S. Eliot's remarks in 1923 about Marianne Moore's syncretic vocabulary.[2] One recalls, too, the impulse of delighted reverence

with which Moore incorporated snippets and chunks of just such odd-
ments from the "inexact sciences" and from memoir and travelogue into
her work. Moore was not so much "dramatizing cognitive difficulties" (as
Williamson claims for Ashbery) as lowering the threshold for inclusion as
poetic matter, or permitting her enthusiasms to usher in more than had
been allowed to count before, even by so inclusive a writer as the Eliot
of *The Waste Land*. For Ashbery, too, the question of aesthetic motive is
an important one. And I am sure it is helpful to view his relation to the
heterogeneous dreck of the modern world as primarily an elegiac one. Yet
I find it so challenging to think about his work that for abstracting his
aesthetic it is for me, in a practical way, almost essential to go carefully
through a poem, testing its style, devices, and claims. The following is
just long enough to represent the many even longer poems in which his
thought effloresces, but short enough for an essay to encompass:

"The skin is broken. The hotel breakfast china
Poking ahead to the last week in August, not really
Very much at all, found the land where you began . . ."
The hills smouldered up blue that day, again
You walk five feet along the shore, and you duck   5
As a common heresy sweeps over. We can botanize
About this for centuries, and the little dazey
Blooms again in the cities. The mind
Is so hospitable, taking in everything
Like boarders, and you don't see until   10
It's all over how little there was to learn
Once the stench of knowledge has dissipated, and the trouvailles
Of every one of the senses fallen back. Really, he
Said, that insincerity of reasoning on behalf of one's
Sincere convictions, true or false in themselves   15
As the case may be, to which, if we are unwise enough
To argue at all with each other, we must be tempted
At times—do you see where it leads? To pain,
And the triumph over pain, still hidden
In these low-lying hills which rob us   20
Of all privacy, as though one were always about to meet
One's double through the chain of cigar smoke
And then it . . . happens, like an explosion in the brain,
Only it's a catastrophe on another planet to which
One has been invited, and as surely cannot refuse: 25
Pain in the cistern, in the gutters, and if we merely
Wait awhile, that denial, as though a universe of pain
Had been created just so as to deny its own existence.
But I don't set much stock in things

Beyond the weather and the certainties of living and dying: 30
The rest is optional. To praise this, blame that,
Leads one subtly away from the beginning, where
We must stay, in motion. To flash light
Into the house within, its many chambers,
Its memories and associations, upon its inscribed   35
And pictured walls, argues enough that life is various.
Life is beautiful. He who reads that
As in the window of some distant, speeding train
Knows what he wants, and what will befall.

Pinpricks of rain fall again.   40
And from across the quite wide median with its
Little white flowers, a reply is broadcast:
"Dissolve parliament. Hold new elections."
It would be deplorable if the rain also washed away
This profile at the window that moves, and moves on,   45
Knowing that it moves, and knows nothing else. It is the light
At the end of the tunnel as it might be seen
By him looking out somberly at the shower,
The picture of hope a dying man might turn away from,
Realizing that hope is something else, something concrete   50
You can't have. So, winding past certain pillars
Until you get to evening's malachite one, it becomes a vast dream
Of having that can topple governments, level towns and cities
With the pressure of sleep building up behind it.
The surge creates its own edge   55
And you must proceed this way: mornings of assent,
Indifferent noons leading to the ripple of the question
Of late afternoon projected into evening.
Arabesques and runnels are the result
Over the public address system, on the seismograph at Berkeley.   60
A little simple arithmetic tells you that to be with you
In this passage, this movement, is what the instance costs:
A sail out of some afternoon, like the clear dark blue
Eyes of Harold in Italy, beyond amazement, astonished,
Apparently not tampered with. As the rain gathers and protects   65
Its own darkness, the place in the slipcover is noticed
For the first and last time, fading like the spine
Of an adventure novel behind glass, behind the teacups.
                    (John Ashbery, "Houseboat Days")[3]

Among the many baffling and enticing poems published in the mid-
1970s that appear to resist fully intelligible response even of the pejorative
kind, John Ashbery's "Houseboat Days" may be taken as exemplary of a
new kind of contemporary poem that takes grammar far more seriously
than it takes the kind of organization of experience grammar has tradition-

ally served. Ashbery does not use the details of experience as the details of his poems. The deceptively concrete details in "Houseboat Days"—the hills, the hotel breakfast china, the cisterns, the house, the quite wide median, the shower, certain pillars, the teacups, the seismograph at Berkeley—are not incorporations of the real but signals of something else. Ashbery's mention of an adventure novel in the last line is the clearest warning, among many more murky, that we cannot expect a well-knit ending here.

At the same time, "Houseboat Days" is not the same sort of poem-about-perception as Eliot's "Preludes," "Rhapsody on a Windy Night," or "The Love Song of J. Alfred Prufrock," in which the use of fragmentary or collage detail is justified by the presence of the persona—the seeing eye. In Eliot there is still homage paid to the dramatic location of a speaker in place, whereas Ashbery is not using details as referrable to experience, although the loose bouquet of images (of traveling, staying in hotels, riding in trains, brooding and at loose ends as summer and day come to a close) might seem approximately to decorate a time and place. He is using details referrable only to literary attitudes toward carefully disparate details in such categories as travel, pain, longing, social tension, parting.

Furthermore, his expression of literary attitude, although suggestive and memorious, is not directly allusive. Thus when I mention other writers, or later suggest a range of styles from Henry James's to John Milton's, I do not pretend to uncover Ashbery's direct sources, or even claim that the poet was always aware of a "borrowing" attitude; these figures stand only as reminders of an oddly derivative use of language and argument. The same end could be reached by saying that Ashbery's details refer to other attitudes of his own but from outside the particular poem where the details themselves occur. It may also be that Ashbery's version of borrowing is subtly continuous with his patent refusal of confessional, relevant detail, and that he has deftly erased his debts in order to increase the element of chance as he lets his voice range and his syntax unravel. Rather than a Joycean pastiche of crafted imitations with conscious echoes we are meant to identify, Ashbery's allusiveness produces echoes of certain attitudes that, when closely observed, have no sharp outlines at all.

We might, for example, consider how Ashbery's poem "Houseboat Days" stylistically echoes the sensibility of Henry James.

> The mind
> Is so hospitable, taking in everything
> Like boarders, and you don't see until   10
> It's all over how little there was to learn
> Once the stench of knowledge has dissipated, and the trouvailles
> Of every one of the senses fallen back.

Now here is Henry James, the self-styled "restless analyst," on his late visit to the United States, describing the skyline of New York: "A sense of the waste of criticism, however, a sense that is almost in itself consoling, descends upon the fond critic after his vision has fixed the scene awhile in this light of its lost accessibility to some informed and benevolent despot, some power working in one great way and so that the interest of beauty should have been better saved."[4] Then in a neat little middle-class street in Boston, James wrestles with the sting if not the stench of knowledge, experiencing a momentary dizziness of the senses if not their total capitulation. He is at a loss to explain "*why* black, stale Harley Street . . . in featureless row after row, had character and depth, while what was before me fell upon my sense with the thinness of tone of a precocious child—and still more why this latter effect should have been, as it were, so insistently irritating. If there be strange ways of producing an interest, to the critical mind, there are doubtless still stranger ways of not producing one. . . ."[5] James's condemnations, however, are mild compared to Ashbery's, and his falling-back-of-the-senses usually only a momentary rest until a new explanation can be found. What one chiefly feels about James, the lumbering and delicious Victorian on this sad, solitary mission of rediscovery, is that he is remarkably game: He never relinquishes the hopeful command over meaning. In Philadelphia, he considers that it was "perverse" of him, but nevertheless an obligation,

> to take it for a working theory that the essence of almost any settled aspect of anything may be extracted by the chemistry of criticism, and may give us its right name, its formula, for convenient use. From the moment the critic finds himself sighing, to save trouble in a difficult case, that the cluster of appearances can *have* no sense, from that moment he begins, and quite consciously, to go to pieces; it being the prime business and the high honour of the painter of life always to *make* a sense—and to make it most in proportion as the immediate aspects are loose or confused. The last thing decently permitted him is to recognize incoherence—to recognize it, that is, as baffling; though of course he may present and portray it, in all richness, *for* incoherence.[6]

Ashbery's lines approximate some of James's turns of emphasis and intensification. His *so* before *hospitable;* the meager and undecorous simile, taking in everything *like boarders,* which slightly muddies the sweep of the mind's hospitality. James proceeds in the opposite direction, from *the waste of criticism* to the fact that this is *almost in itself consoling,* and from the suspicion that the scene *can* **have** *no sense* to the triumphant resolve to present it *in all richness,* **for** *incoherence.* It is as if the rhythms of James's thought demanded optimism, while those of Ashbery pressed toward the emptying out of will and interest.

Ashbery and James both move the mental process through time, Ashbery with the present participle *taking,* the present tense of *don't see* qualified to something subsequent or future by *until,* thus arriving at a more recent stage, at which knowledge becomes something past tense (*how little there was to learn*), and in which a process of surfeit, then recoil, is accomplished (*Once the stench of knowledge has dissipated*); slightly subsequent to these comes the definite completion in *then the trouvailles / Of every one of the senses fallen back,* in which we are confronted with the locked and static past that is no more in motion (as *falling* would have made it) but a finished state (*fallen*).

James carries his thought through time as well but, unlike Ashbery, moves in the direction away from the past (*stale Harley Street*) to the relative present of *what was before me* (although expressed in the "historical present" that uses the past tense in English), to the amphibious present tense of the moral, "if there be strange ways of producing an interest, . . . there are doubtless still stranger ways of not producing one." In the third of the three excerpts, James moves entirely within the present tense but with the effect of going from a primitive stage of helplessness before experience to a staunch enclosure of it. The effect is secured by the phrasing *from the moment X then Y,* a phrasing proven to have been a temporary delay with the arrival of the dénouement still in the present tense, *The last thing decently permitted him is. . . .* Thus James moves from a negative impression in a present time that soon becomes a past condition to a positive rationalization in an increasingly general and suspended present tense. Ashbery moves from the expansive present tense to the contracted future and then to the past-perfect time when conclusions are all foregone.

The use of *enough* in "Houseboat Days" has the flavor of a James intensive but, like *quite* in the following passage, it is an intensive merely next to its moorings in the flow of sense and comparison, not attached to them:

> Pinpricks of rain fall again.   40
> And from across the quite wide median with its
> Little white flowers, a reply is broadcast. . . .

In Jamesian terms, the phrase *quite wide median* would imply that, for all the limitations and flatness and unpromising thinness of the scene, the median in the road really approached to that quite wide, quite gracefully and quietly expansive, infinitely speaking sense of the European boulevard. But in Ashbery's text there is no comparative background; the median is *quite wide* in an absolute or zero-grade way and is not evidence for the placation or contradiction of any other impression. Whereas James can achieve superb condescension and, at the same time, a breezy and even languorous punctuation of rhythm—the sort of halt a butterfly makes—by pausing as he moves to take in such a detail, it will necessarily be a detail *in context,* for in his descriptions of places and styles James does set himself before things, tuning himself to the highest possible responsive pitch for taking in the accidents of experience. To be sure, he responds with a subjective vigor that makes the view systematically distorted rather than documentary; nevertheless he is *looking,* as shuddering pilgrims from Goethe to Lawrence have been supposed to do.

Ashbery can accommodate some of this Jamesian dilation and slightly haughty but genial focus on particular things, but, in the first place, Ashbery's particulars do not cohere accidentally (but completely) as the marks of views and places, and, in the second place, as indicated by the positive or even zero-grade (as in the adjective sequence from zero to positive to comparative to superlative) context for the *quite wide median,* Ashbery is not comparing one thing to another. (This claim will later be tested in light of the overt use of the language of comparison, both in similes—*the mind . . . taking in everything / Like boarders*—and in metaphors—the *house* with *its many chambers, / Its memories and associations,* in which *house* is the replacement metaphor for *life.*)

Ashbery's handling of reference is virtually to suspend reference:

> The surge creates its own edge   55
> And you must proceed this way: mornings of assent,
> Indifferent noons leading to the ripple of the question
> Of late afternoon projected into evening.
> Arabesques and runnels are the result. . . .

It is also possible to excerpt from Henry James in such a way as to produce a tone poem with structural similarities to Ashbery's: "A diffused, wasted clamour of *detonations.* . . . in the air as of a great intricate frenzied dance . . . performed on the huge watery floor. This appearance of the bold lacing-together . . . of the scattered members of the monstrous organism—lacing as by the ceaseless play of an enormous system of steam-shuttles or electric bobbins. . . ."[7] But the apparent solipsism of James's analogies becomes considerably less pressing when we supply the context—docking in New York with all its ship commerce and construction, hawsers and hammers.

On the other hand, we cannot go far enough back in the Ashbery poem for such a local context. *The surge* is related (by an obvious association not unlike James's steam-shuttles and electric bobbins) to *the pressure of sleep* in the immediately preceding line, but not subsumed under it:

> It is the light
> At the end of the tunnel as it might be seen
> By him looking out somberly at the shower,

The picture of hope a dying man might turn away from,
Realizing that hope is something else, something concrete   50
You can't have. So, winding past certain pillars
Until you get to evening's malachite one, it becomes a vast dream
Of having that can topple governments, level towns and cities
With the pressure of sleep building up behind it.
The surge creates its own edge. . . .   55

What we find as antecedent for *The surge* is the *it* that is replaced by one metaphoric term (*a vast dream / Of having*) in the play of which a subsidiary metaphor is produced (*building up* applied from *sleep* to the *vast dream*). Furthermore, *The surge,* without losing these connections, can be related even further back to the *It* equated with *the light / At the end of the tunnel* at the beginning of the previous sentence, indicating the possible use of anaphora, whereby all these *it*s would equally refer to some earlier item in common.

For example, could the *profile* in the preceding lines be the referent of these *it*s?

Pinpricks of rain fall again.   40
And from across the quite wide median with its
Little white flowers, a reply is broadcast:
"Dissolve parliament. Hold new elections."
It would be deplorable if the rain also washed away
This profile at the window that moves, and moves on,   45
Knowing that it moves, and knows nothing else. It is the light
At the end of the tunnel. . . .

It is unlikely that the profile at the window of the moving train is the referent of the *It* that is the light at the end of the tunnel; not simply because the metaphor would be jumbled (profile in train hardly equals light at the end of the tunnel through which the train moves), but also because the profile, as a still earlier passage reveals, is only one of the focal points, that of the traveler sitting by the window.

The other is the focus of a traveler who is not on the train at all but watching it go by. Also, the image of the train with its many lighted windows passing by is the by-product of association with a still earlier metaphor: life as a many-chambered house. The upshot of both the house metaphor and the train comparison is that the speaker, on one level, is aiming only to prove the *in se* indifference of, and his own indifference to, multiplicity, the pose produced that of settling on no one meaning. But on another level the speaker is creating grounds for the result that, however bland one's posture before the many-layered, there is always something fatal at the end. The fatality is prosodically supported by the "hitch" at the end of line 36 produced by a period mark we cannot take seriously:

> To praise this, blame that,
> Leads one subtly away from the beginning, where
> We must stay, in motion. To flash light
> Into the house within, its many chambers,
> Its memories and associations, upon its inscribed   35
> And pictured walls, argues enough that life is various.
> Life is beautiful. He who reads that
> As in the window of some distant, speeding train
> Knows what he wants, and what will befall.

Both images (moving through the house, the speeding train) derive from the commandment to remain *in motion*.

The central "figure" of Ashbery's "Houseboat Days," the voice that does the speaking (a relatively reduced one dramatically and apt to change places suddenly), climbs into the upper corridors of his own mind, imagining what is behind the doors but refusing to open them. He imagines the play of the torch on the experiences he could easily investigate in detail if he chose to—and chooses not to. He lets the light of intention move very rapidly across the bedsteads and china in those rooms so that these might be acknowledged without being either rejected or approved. The rapidity of this course permits him to assert neither variety nor beauty nor anything linked to a particular appetite but only rapidity, a disembodied concept seconded by another, distant movement, that of the train.

All the same, it is not entirely true that the speaker only moves from a rapid examination of the thoughts in his attic to his view of the train, its various golden decors moving past. For despite the distance of the train from the speaker, and despite the congruity between the rapid motion of the torch upon the surfaces in the house's rooms and the rapid casting of many lights from the swiftly passing windows—from *its* many chambers—still, the reference point does change. It changes from a point outside the train to one inside it, by the pull of the verb *wants*. *Life is beautiful. He who reads that* (i.e., as the man had read the blur of significances in the metaphorical house of life)—

> As in the window of some distant, speeding train
> Knows what he wants. . . .

And what he wants is not to stop for the personal and particular, not to be made to pass judgment, not to be brought up short before any trivial evidence. And lifted by the force of that desire, and because Ashbery is not writing a poem in which the train is any more substantial than the house, the speaker places himself inside the train—only to register that spooky and perhaps also comic defeat of yet another of the literary tradition's familiar grounds. For in addition to disturbing, throughout the poem, our expectations about the behavior of metaphoric and proper terms, then defeating our more general expectations of referentiality, Ashbery also jokes with our practically unconscious belief in plots—the belief that desires must provoke their deserts.

> He who reads that
> As in the window of some distant, speeding train
> Knows what he wants, and what will befall.

By making it impossible for us to say what is being likened to what, Ashbery withholds any certainty about plot and motive in their conventional forms.

One never really has the sense, in moving forward through an Ashbery poem, of having reached the most inclusive, universal statement about the motives of the poem. The lack of local connection is provisionally forgiven from the reader's sense that he will sometime soon find the "translation," the code delivered from outside the proscenium. Since the reader never does hear the code words, he returns to settle on the approximately meaningful passages, only to find that, in order to interpret these, he has to keep crawling back through the poem. The very word "referent" implies something earlier that can be retained by the reader, allusively invoked by the writer. Ashbery's referents, *this, that, the, it,* tend to be one-time only, more like "irreferents," which do not actually point to the world but only to the speaker's restless, irreverent, and preoccupied fumbling with the lexicon of pointing. Thus the momentum toward future disclosure in his poem is maintained by the disappointment of prior connection.

Ashbery's statement, that he who reads that *Life is beautiful,* "Knows what he wants, and what will befall," is an absolute statement about premonition. It does not uncover events. Hence it can be undercut by other equally absolute and contextless statements that work to cancel the knowledge gained (*that it moves . . . knows nothing else*). Perhaps the poem's sense of impending fatality—of eventfulness—was to have met precisely the failure of anything to happen and the failure of knowledge to persist for very long, or of desire focused on the future to remain in force. Then the pillars and the evening and the pressure of sleep and the toppling of governments and the surge with its own created edge will be either extensions of the uneventful defeat of eventful expectations or revisions of any motion of the straightforwardly eventful to include things that are uninterpretable (rippling questions, arabesques and runnels).

This second possibility, that "Houseboat Days" redefines the term *event*

rather than simply suggesting an existential joke about not-happening
being the real occurrence, is more in keeping with Ashbery's stubborn
refusal of sentimentality and life study. He is not, as a rule, writing self-
referential poems about the failure of the literary tradition to satisfy the
human heart. He is not criticizing the poison of drama and the frailty of
our resources for rising to the great act, or for choosing the right moment,
as Henry James did in "The Beast in the Jungle." In an Ashbery poem,
the increase in pressure toward a climax is present only as a promissory
note, seldom redeemed by dramatization. The same "promissory hovering" will need to be posited about any procedure in "Houseboat Days"
that pretends to relate one thing to another, either by cause and effect or
by the implied relation of metaphoric term to either stated or unstated
proper term (as *The surge* had no stated term that it replaced, and as the
dark *house* with light playing over it was the stated metaphoric term for
a stated proper term, *life,* but in a trope whose "real metaphor" had to
do with motion and dread).

Ashbery even invalidates his use of small, climactic grammatical promises imbedded in words like *so,* from which we expect a *that,* and in *enough*
(in *argues enough that life is various*), from which we expect not so much
a result or recoil as we expect the poem to recognize the weight, and drift,
of the relation between the sufficient *enough* and the suddenly introduced
various. That is, does *enough* mean that proof of *variety* was the demon-
strandum and that the speaker has at last found the least common denominator of it—the least active flutter of its being—which he had long
searched for? The question is not answered except in the incomplete logic
of the formulated terms, *various, argues enough.* Perhaps any Ashbery
poem does its job precisely by drawing such unsatisfied phrases to the
surface together.

Ashbery also defeats expectations vis-à-vis still grammatically related
but subtler usages. Like his adverbs, Ashbery's pronouns are often startling and hard to assign. Who is the *he* who suddenly speaks (line 13)?
What is the *it* that is *the light / At the end of the tunnel*? Who is the referent
of the pronoun *you*? In the impersonal coloration of the pronoun *you* as
a substitute for a speaking *I,* we can begin to catch the grammatical play
in which Ashbery conceals the dramatic and rhetorical force of many
poems. At the beginning of "Houseboat Days" we can blithely read *you*
as the sophisticated address of the poet to himself:

> The hills smouldered up blue that day, again
> You walk five feet along the shore, and you duck   5
> As a common heresy sweeps over.

At the end of "Houseboat Days," however, *you* (which earlier might have
meant either *one* in general or the *I* in particular) changes midway in the

line into a *you* that must be a present, second person to whom an *I* speaks.
Because of this shift in referentiality, the sentence begs the question of
who or what is *with you:*

> A little simple arithmetic tells you that to be with you
> In this passage, this movement, is what the instance costs. . . .

The plain grammatical argument could be: The cost to me of being with
you is what the instance costs. But the "values" will not stay fixed. For
example, although by itself, in terms of grade of generality, *instance* is a
less embracing concept than either *movement* or *passage,* when considered
in the framework of its full grammatical complement, *the instance* is more
abstracted from reference than *this passage* and *this movement* with their
weighty, demonstrative, specifying modifiers. Each of the demonstratively
flanked phrases is easily referred back to the temporal shifts in the previous
lines, whereas *the instance* needs the completion of the colon that follows it:

> A little simple arithmetic tells you that to be with you
> In this passage, this movement, is what the instance costs:
> A sail out of some afternoon, like the clear dark blue
> Eyes of Harold in Italy, beyond amazement, astonished,
> Apparently not tampered with.   65

If we were to continue to read a real Other for the *you,* then the cost of
the instance, brought against the *I,* should follow the colon; yet the *sail
out of some afternoon* is not a very great price for the speaker to pay,
especially since the prior goal of the voyage (the *you*) is subsumed under
the subsequent commendatory terms of the description (*clear dark blue /
Eyes*). In other words, the *you* has those eyes, and the *I* is rejoined to that
you over some distance or after being jolted by a memory.

But perhaps the *you* does not, in fact, shift into reference to a true
Other. Perhaps *you* remains the *one* that is like an *I.* The sentence will
then become troublesome at a different juncture, *what the instance costs.*
Who pays the cost? Assuming that we are dealing with *one* human figure
here, the *you* cognate with the speaker, then being with that speaker must
be what the instance itself incurs as the cost of its striving to be with *him.*
To paraphrase: To be with me is what the instance costs itself, at the
particular points of this passage and this movement just completed, and
at the following moment, which the instance generates for me: *A sail out
of some afternoon.*

Ashbery has, according to this second reading, personified a very drab
abstraction, *instance,* long enough to collect under its roof the flow of
activity during the previous verse paragraph and then let it reissue under
a different sky, Italian, point-blank, pure blue, resembling an album cover

for Berlioz. Thus *instance* is personified not in the medieval fashion whereby emotions, sins, and outcomes are portrayed in the nearest human raiment but, rather, as a suggestion that instances in the world become coherent and relevant by petitioning us—by participating in our surges and vast dreams of having. Like the train/traveler image, where the traveler is both inside looking out at the shower and outside looking in as he had looked in at the house, the speaker of Ashbery's poetry is at once world and wanderer, intention and accident. He is like the speaker of so many songs in Wallace Stevens who watches the world and is instructed by it, yet who also hears its speech flowing out of his own mouth, thus instructing it, being the world he sings.

The meaning of the general nonreferrable *it*s earlier in "Houseboat Days" is perhaps that experience collectively shared between the poet who watches and the beings who watch back. The world dreams in the poet both about him and about itself, while the poet, dreaming from the outside of the world for respite and explanation (the sort of explanation that, for a temperament shackled to realistic plot, seems most familiar and deceives the most), cannot part himself from the thing he dreams.

Let us assume that John Ashbery's poem "Houseboat Days" is not only new but also quite different from those earlier modernist poems which took mental fragmentation as theme and method—that indeed Ashbery is unique in his style of "irreference." As Donald Davie has suggested, T. S. Eliot's method of joining images and statements together in his poems is "symbolist, not syntactical," thus calling attention to the choice of inner light over outer logic—a choice that Ashbery may not need to confront in these terms. "Dislocation of syntax is the essential secret of symbolist technique," says Davie; "for even where the forms of prose syntax are retained, it does not follow that the syntax is prose syntax; for concepts may be related in formally correct syntax when the relationship between them is not really syntactical at all, but musical, when words and phrases are notes in a melody, not terms in an ordered statement."[8] We might consider the passage Davie quotes from "Little Gidding," which he later calls "a single 'image,'" the internal syntactic logic of which is irrelevant to its larger asyntactic or "musical" relationship to other image "blocs":

> There are three conditions which often look alike
> Yet differ completely, flourish in the same hedgerow:
> Attachment to self and to things and to persons, detachment
> From self and from things and from persons; and, growing between them,
>   indifference
> Which resembles the others as death resembles life,   5
> Being between two lives—unflowering, between

The live and the dead nettle. This is the use of memory:
For liberation—not less of love but expanding
Of love beyond desire, and so liberation
From the future as well as the past.[9]

What should be noted about these lines is the disjunction that occurs at
line 7, prior to which the third condition, indifference, is derogated, and
after which, in its rescue as memory, it is promulgated. But the relation
between the two parts of this passage is not so much musical as it is, quite
simply, disjunct. What holds the passage together is the somber intensity
of Eliot's pedagogic tone. Yet the pedagogy masks a severe indecision as
to the status of poignant flora; hedgerows and live nettles and dead are
idly circumstantial at first, then logically subsumed as illustrative of theme,
without ceasing to be favored as objects of feeling.

In the following passage from "Houseboat Days," we find the dilatory,
mulish "prose" of Eliot at the beginning and end, midway a momentary
obeisance to the meaningfulness of landscape, and periodically a jump-in-
the-projector tendency that far exceeds what Donald Davie discovered in
the nonsyntactical junctures of *Four Quartets*. But above all, we register
a device uncharacteristic in any form of T. S. Eliot—a disposition to
hilarity:

> Really, he
> Said, that insincerity of reasoning on behalf of one's
> Sincere convictions, true or false in themselves   15
> As the case may be, to which, if we are unwise enough
> To argue at all with each other, we must be tempted
> At times—do you see where it leads? To pain,
> And the triumph over pain, still hidden
> In these low-lying hills which rob us   20
> Of all privacy, as though one were always about to meet
> One's double through the chain of cigar smoke
> And then it . . . happens, like an explosion in the brain,
> Only it's a catastrophe on another planet to which
> One has been invited, and as surely cannot refuse: 25
> Pain in the cistern, in the gutters, and if we merely
> Wait awhile, that denial, as though a universe of pain
> Had been created just so as to deny its own existence.

There is something exorbitantly bad about Ashbery's prose *sententiae*.
The first one (lines 13–18) overtops its own strength and then breaks off
on a note of shrill and slightly batty naïveté. The second (lines 26–28)
touts a conclusion, drawn from the absurd pathetic fallacy of *Pain in the
cistern,* that mocks the paradoxicality of some mystics and existentialists
(pain created in order to deny itself). The mimesis of disjunction in the

ellipsis, *And then it . . . happens* [*sic*]; the switch to another planet; the Martian invitation one *as surely cannot refuse*—any one of these phrasings, if allowed to remain in a context of likeness, would lead to bad serious poetry. Juxtaposed in rapid succession, although no less "bad," they announce their conscious unseriousness.

Ashbery here parodies the connections he does not intend to make— between modifying and main clause; between rhetoric and outcome; between one abstraction and another (*pain, existence, denial*); between the abstract and the contingent qualities of locale (*pain* vs. *low-lying hills*); between allegorical landscape (*pain* and *the triumph over* it) and psychological landscape (the double wreathed in cigar smoke); between effect (*an explosion in the brain*) and cause (it just . . . *happens*); between one realm of discourse (the possibly literal low-lying hills, the figure seen through cigar smoke, a place that might in fact have cisterns and gutters) and another, perversely orthogonal realm (another planet, alien despite its suspiciously Jamesian manners). Finally, Ashbery parodies the connections between that part of a simile which is literal and that part which is figurative:

> . . . as though a universe of pain
> Had been created just so as to deny its own existence.

> as though one were always about to meet
> One's double. . . .

Both comparisons loosen the boundaries between figure and letter— achieve, that is, the same status as other *things* in Ashbery's poem—by having no comparative origins. The comparisons are there not to describe some other mood or event but to bring their own terms and colors—and even the abstract has its hues—into being.

The things in Ashbery's world are, as suggested earlier, objects of thought, connected not by the rank, sequence, and domain in which they might ordinarily occur in "nature" but by the easy likelihood of their occurrence to Ashbery. The key term in distinguishing Ashbery's program from the surrealists' would be the word *easy*, for the analogies of most surrealists, although just as fictitious, artificial, and peripheral as Ashbery's, lack his intent breeziness. The strain of their invention is evident in the bleakly repetitive grammar of their exhortations and in the frequently uninteresting and even predictable forcing of one noun or verb into another's place.

This sort of forcible exchange does not produce metaphor because there is no point of origin for the substitution. If a sentence has an animal subject, mechanical verb, and an emotional or human object, there is no place to look for the proper term that has generated all these exchanges. Take, for example,

> Sucking the berry's map, they curse the fired seed
> No noose can amnesty nor eyelid truncheon. . . .[10]

in which there is a human action, personified object, human subject and verb, then a mechanical past participle applied to *seed,* which generates the dependent clause with *that* understood and *seed* the object of a personified *noose* doing some forgiving and an *eyelid* using a *truncheon.* And since there is no key to the commanding term, there is no way for metaphor to work, and the sentence is, not grammatically on the lowest level, but strategically on the modest level of formed thought, nonsense. Dylan Thomas is often guilty of this sort of forced overapplication of metaphoric keys everywhere in his poems.[11] And in the work of Frank O'Hara, the surrealist program of semantic intrusion and rupture is carried forward just under the threshold of complete linguistic freedom, so that a loose sense of plot is asserted by the blocks of related matter, hilariously mixed in style:

> like someone always losing something and never knowing what.
> Always so. They were so fond of eating bread and butter and
> sugar, they were slobs, the mice used to lick the floorboards
> after they went to bed, rolling their light tails against
> the rattling marbles of granulation. Vivo! the dextrose
> those children consumed, lavished, smoked, in their knobby
> candy bars. Such pimples! such hardons! such moody loves.
> And thus they grew like giggling fir trees.[12]

But in Ashbery's minor surrealist poems, the line of consciousness running through the bleak disparities between thing and referent—disparities usually identified with surrealism—produces poetry of considerably more mystery and tact (one might consider "Sonnet," from *Some Trees* [1956], which resists almost any definition one is accustomed to accepting for the sonnet form, but in which the evocation of the old generic name is an impulse toward wistfulness, which the poem rebuffs). Still, although Ashbery resists surrealism, his details are often obtusely inappropriate. Even in "Houseboat Days," they stand in the way, or make us look too hard at the wrong elements. (The experience of reading Ashbery is that we are often "wrong.") Not that the details are irrelevant to the movement of thought he is tugging back into the poem, against the current of his own terminology, as it were; rather, it is we who may have become accustomed to a certain range of significance to be extracted from poetic detail. As Ashbery himself has commented on these conventional uses of data:

> Aping naturalness may be the first step
> Toward achieving an inner calm
> But it is the first step only, and often
> Remains a frozen gesture of welcome etched
> On the air materializing behind it,
> A convention.[13]

The convention of amassing details that, summed up, yield a portrait of an inner state is the convention that Ashbery revises. He cannot work with naturalism and accident in and for themselves, only with his own angle of refraction of their details.[14] More important, his tone is a disarming compromise between the two kinds of modernist disorientation we have mentioned, the surrealist's and the formal meditative poet's. We are probably more grateful that Ashbery has avoided the excesses of Breton than that he has deflected the applied tradition of Eliot:

> And I watched over myself and my thoughts like a nightwatchman in an
>   immense factory
> Keeping watch alone
> The circus always enchants the same tramlines
> The plaster figures have lost nothing of their expression
> They who bit the smile's fig
> I know of a drapery in a forgotten town. . . .[15]

> I met one walking, loitering and hurried
> As if blown towards me like the metal leaves. . . .[16]

In avoiding the sedulous, random variety of surrealism, Ashbery has simply found no major use for its nagging "originality," monotony of predication, and absurd replacements. But in eschewing the logic, patterning, and rhythm of the other, Ashbery has sidestepped something more central to the literary tradition than a brief period of nonsense experiment, and that is the modern legacy of measure, particularly that of blank verse.

Dissembling the Measure

The first part of this study focused on John Ashbery's styles of avoidance—the stylistic contours of his resistance to the devices of literary meaning allied with realism, plot, and verisimilitude. His syntax was seen to be mildly but crucially refractory to sense (even his pronouns produce an inconstant shimmer of possible agencies), and even when his syntax behaves, his diction and metaphors do not remain fixed. Blendings of styles and of metaphoric constructions are common, but not to the extent of surrealism: Some adherence to sequence (however whimsical) and to temperament (however preoccupied) remains in force. Although these coherences of order and temper notably resist attachment to any one style of discourse, they still rise above the poems' linguistic gargoyles and ample buffoonery in a way purely stylistic experimentation cannot.

Not only does Ashbery control his poetic maneuvers while resisting the rigors of any one stylistic medium but he also avoids the prosodic media that combine measure, interval, and euphony to reinforce semantic and rhetorical emphases. Unlike Eliot, for example, Ashbery for the most part abstains both from number and from the alternation of stressed and unstressed syllables, as if, while moving toward the prosaic in his manners, he were also moving toward prose in his rhythms. In the passage already quoted from "Little Gidding," as in the following one (from "Little Gidding," ii—the encounter with Brunetto Latini), the indirect, then the entirely direct accentual-syllabic symmetries help make Eliot's speech at once familiar and elegant; in comparison, Ashbery's speech can sound either tentative or strident.

In Eliot's hands, blank verse becomes the vessel of cool, stately, and various rhythms, of vowel progressions (like the *o* traveling, within the brief space of two lines, through *dove, tongue, below, horizon,* and *homing;* and like the modulation between *a* and *o* in *Over the asphalt where no other sound was*). Eliot's blank verse here also employs the sparing metrical relaxations provided by speech particles like *in, the, of, at,* and so on, first to supply weak stresses between strong-stressed monosyllables, then to supply the grammatical connectives an uninflected language requires, and finally to mediate between the more harsh and uneuphonious consonants, thus enabling the poet to employ the more stubborn clusters of consonants with ease. In the following Eliot passage, the rhythm of stresses in the larger verse period is mapped over the local linear rhythm (assumed to be iambic pentameter, which abstractly alternates: $|\smile- |\smile- |\smile- |\smile- |\smile- |$).

	1	2	3	4	5
In the uncertain hour before the morning		X			X
Near the ending of interminable night			X		
At the recurrent end of the unending					X
After the dark dove with the flickering tongue		X	X		
Had passed below the horizon of his homing	X		X		X
While the dead leaves still rattled on like tin		X			X
Over the asphalt where no other sound was				X	X
Between three districts whence the smoke arose		X			
I met one walking, loitering and hurried			X		
As if blown towards me like the metal leaves		X	X		
Before the urban dawn wind unresisting.[17]			X		X

By choosing words as carefully as Eliot does, yet without drawing to his choices prosodic or metric attention, Ashbery can achieve effects of accuracy on one hand, on the other ease of juncture, but without putting the achievement into *lines*:

> There ought to be room for *more* things, for a spreading out, *like*. Being immersed in the details of rock and field and slope—letting them come to you *for once,* and *then* meeting them halfway would be *so much easier—if* they took an ingenuous pride in being in one's blood. Alas, we perceive them *if at all* as those things that were meant to be put aside—costumes of the supporting actors or voice trilling at the end of a narrow enclosed street. You can do *nothing* with them. *Not even* offer to pay.
>   *It is possible* that *finally, like* coming to end of a long, *barely* perceptible rise, there is *mutual* cohesion and interaction. The *whole* scene is fixed in your mind, the music *all* present, *as though* you could see each note *as well as* hear it. I say this *because* there is an uneasiness in things *just now.* Waiting for something to be over *before* you are forced to notice it. The pollarded trees *scarcely* bucking the wind—*and yet it's* keen, *it* makes you fall over. Clabbered sky. Seasons that pass with a rush. . . . *Meanwhile* the *whole* history of probabilities is coming to life, starting in the *upper left-hand* corner, *like* a sail.[18]

It is impossible to "scan" such a prose passage. One can, at best, mark the stresses, although, as Charles O. Hartman points out, when we approach a passage in prose with the intention of hearing its stresses, we will tend to over-hear them and "increas[e] the density of accents . . . making every possible word individually luminous."[19] Thus the smoothness of surface Ashbery creates in this passage from "For John Clare" depends more on the music of the (italicized) connectives and relational words than on any adjustment of the hard and slack stresses in single words to a recurrent, additive climaxing every five measures, as in the line of blank verse.

The arena for emphasis as well as ease in the "Little Gidding" passage is more contracted, more lightly but surely circumscribed, than that of Ashbery's prose, so that in each of Eliot's lines there will be a main stress rising above the other foot stresses, sometimes mid-line, sometimes in feet 2 and 4, but seldom repeating any one pattern exactly in neighboring lines. In the Eliot, note how lines 4 and 10 illustrate the dipodal pattern of main-line stresses in the second and fourth feet, while line 5 provides its mirror image, meaningful line stresses in 1 and 3 and 5. No matter where it falls, there *will* be a central line stress somewhere in each line. This is something blank verse automatically does with and for the variable language of its many practitioners, despite the subjugation of the main-line stresses to central verse-period or -paragraph stress that we find in Shakespeare, Milton, Wordsworth, Frost, Eliot, Stevens, and Nemerov.

Even in Milton, who "invented" blank verse by showing how many different things it could do, there is always a *triple* counteraction of stresses:
word or foot stress, central line stress, and the central stress of the verse
paragraph—all at work in varying degrees over and within the logic to
which the stress placement is attuned.

This countervailing of stress is potentially present in other kinds of
utterance, even in conversation, but never so regularly; we are not mark-
edly disappointed in prose when we fail to hear the local pull of the mot
juste against the plain splendor of the central concept as other aspects of
rhythm and phrasing contribute to their placement. This description—
especially the assumption that the main stress of a verse paragraph *or* a
prose paragraph may fall on a "central concept"—makes it sound as
though the triple countervailing stress in blank verse were an instrument
of logic. This is not strictly so. The triple tension is emotional; alone the
words of the presentation and argument are logical, and even then one
must consider their order, their sound, their realm of origin (human,
inanimate, mechanical, theological).

The central period stress of any blank-verse paragraph is not always to
be found in a summation statement at the end. Sometimes the central
stress can come first, in an aside as readily as in a command, at the beginning of a passage that tapers off into examples, one of which may have a
secondary verse-paragraph stress as the capstone of the series—a detail
with more metaphoric or despairing intensity than the others. There is
no *one* way for this central period stress to work rhetorically. And yet
there *is* a logic of expectation interwoven in the technique of unrhymed
iambic pentameter that instructs the reader in a certain prosodic grammar.
For if the central period stress is once a concept and once an elegiac detail,
the reader will learn to modify his notion of "centrality." If, after a number
of variously placed line stresses occurring at words of abstraction, he
encounters a verse-paragraph stress indubitably occurring at a word of
texture, feeling, mood, here, too, the reader will be in constant process
of revising not just his understanding of the value of abstraction, as the
given passage is instructing him, but the balance of line stress to paragraph
stress, passion to abstraction, and detail to generality, in the remainder of
the poem and in his own mind as well.

It should be said that it is blank verse (in English) that raises these
dichotomies of passion and abstraction, detail and generality, in a way
few other forms do, with the exception of other "sublime" modes like the
ode and couplets arranged not in epigrams but in epics. Similarly, in
prose, as Morris Croll has shown,[20] there are some rhetorical forms that
argue the sublime—Ciceronian parallels of sound and sense—and some
that argue the predicative, personal, actively dramatic insight—what Croll

calls the *stil coupé*, with its use of intensely felt series of moments linked by emotion rather than by parallels in logic. Within these black-and-white distinctions, all kinds of blendings occur. If, for example, a writer uses details purely illustratively, he will *not* be able to turn around and center his attention on any one detail with the same one-dimensional clarity that yet points to spiritual resemblances with which a writer of the opposite kind, who makes less distinction between details and ideas, can invest either idea or detail. But this second, more object-ridden kind of writer, by the same token, cannot write hymns to the heaven and earth, either.

We could hypothesize that Ashbery uses the breadth and pacing of the sublime mode to write about kinds of perceptions that, by themselves and in combination with neighboring perceptions, are decidedly gnomic and disjoint. He secures the sweep of his statements by the vocabulary of Ciceronian parallelism and development—in "For John Clare," *at all, for once, then, more, much easier, mutual, if, not even, finally, scarcely, whole, all, as though, as well as, because, just now, before, Meanwhile, and yet, so, like*— but this vocabulary of extremely "connected" connectives, as we shall see, is actually the lever of logical disjunction or irreference.

The prose passage from "For John Clare" is no more surrealist than Ashbery's poem "Houseboat Days"; it may even sound more discursive, abrupt, predicative, and expressive (to use Josephine Miles's terminology for one of the two main modes, the "clausal"), whereas "Houseboat Days" is more descriptive (for every verb, half of them copulas or passives, at least two nouns and one adjective—proportions characteristic of the "phrasal" mode).[21] But one must also gauge the *effect* of any such array of syntactic proportions. Ashbery's poem is not "descriptive" when compared with Shakespeare's sonnet 66 or with Spenser's first *Amoretti* sonnet ("Happy ye leaues when as those lilly hands," which Josephine Miles calls "an exclamation, not an argument").[22] The crucial difference is that the two Renaissance poets use descriptive paraphrases in grammatical apposition and reduce verbs to participial adjectives, while Ashbery customarily undergirds his copulas emphatically (*It would be deplorable; The rest is optional*) or with metaphors so solid in their binary demands that the ordinary weakness of the copula-adjective or copula-noun formula is quite forgotten (*The mind is so hospitable; Arabesques and runnels are the result; It is the light / At the end of the tunnel;* or the ersatz copula "becomes" in *It becomes a vast dream / Of having*).

Ashbery's use of the participial adjective is more mobile than Shakespeare's in the sixty-sixth sonnet, perhaps because the latter's succeed one another so swiftly as states and conditions, rather than as motions; the passion is in the rhetoric whose objects are derisively frozen into compromising tableaux:

Tired with all these, for restful death I cry:
As, to behold desert a beggar born,
And needy nothing trimmed in jollity,
And purest faith unhappily forsworn,
And gilded honor shamefully misplaced,
And maiden virtue rudely strumpeted,
And right perfection wrongfully disgraced,
And strength by limping sway disablèd,
And art made tongue-tied by authority,
And folly (doctor-like) controlling skill,
And simple truth miscalled simplicity,
And captive good attending captain ill.
>Tired with all these, from these would I be gone,
>Save that, to die, I leave my love alone.

Shakespeare's method here is to throw transitive verbal weight onto the nouns and, in this way, divest the verbal constructions of their mobility. But Ashbery uses participial adjectives as if they were verbs; his *musing* in "Sonnet" ("The patience rambles on / Musing on the library's lofty holes") does not declare a meditative *state* so much as it forwards a physical movement by virtue of the word's implicit formal continuation of the verb + prepositional-adverb pair, *rambles on*. The repetition of the grammatical cluster, *rambles on / Musing on,* helps to satisfy the connection between thought and motion.

The point of this comparison is not to suggest that Ashbery is as important for the sonnet tradition, or as great a poet, as Shakespeare, but to remind us that mere tabulation of the proportions of verbs to nouns and adjectives is in itself insufficient to account for some forms of *predication* achieved in or absent from a particular poem. Shakespeare varies present-participial adjectives with past-participial adjectives for syntactic variety and not to induce a moment of imminence or, really, any other hint of the narratively temporal. Shakespeare varies the language forms, but not their temporal effects. Whereas Ashbery in "Houseboat Days" makes the present-participial adjectives, buttressed by adverbial and prepositional constructions, do the work of finite verbs:

>"The skin is broken. The hotel breakfast china
>Poking ahead to the last week in August, not really
>Very much at all, found the land where you began. . . ."

Poking subjects a brash and ugly verb (to poke) to the traditional syntax of softening (the participial -ing). But even as an ostensible adjective, *Poking* is more stubbornly active, visible, and gesticulative than the sentence's actual finite verb, *found*. In addition, the present-participial adjective's "allusion" to the present time (*Poking* rather than *Having poked*) masks the fact that the poking of the china must have preceded the breaking of the skin in the first sentence in "Houseboat Days," *The skin is broken*. When we first read the sequence, "The skin is broken. The hotel breakfast china / Poking ahead," we will, most likely, assume that the skin is first broken, and that *then* the breakfast china pokes ahead through the aperture—an aperture caused by something else. But this reading (which relates to agency—causation—by virtue of tense, and therefore syntax) is soon proven to be false. *The skin is broken* is a statement that refers to a time subsequent to the *Poking* of the china, not vice versa. Not that it is an easy matter to ponder with plausible gravity the technical quiddities of this absurdly offhand diction—a diction designed to jolly us irritably along, while quenching the underlying uncertainty about time and being.

There are in fact at least two "presents" in the poem; the one nearest to us is the dramatically immediate time of the opening and closing lines. The speaker reverts to earlier moments, occasionally drifting forward to his present consciousness again (*Pinpricks of rain; this profile; this passage; the place in the slipcover*), but the central rhythm of "Houseboat Days" is marked by the idea of a *present* from which the poem can diverge. The syntax of *Poking* is ambiguous because its tense is. It hovers between the near "present" and a subsequent one. Its ambiguity is complicated by the fact that on one reading it is purely decorative (when we assume the poking to follow the breaking of the skin), while on the other, and correct, reading, it is causal (the skin is broken *because* the china poked ahead). Thus the ungainly word *Poking* is not just another appositive added to others (*hotel, breakfast*), but an indispensable commentary on the breaking of the broken skin. Furthermore, this participial adjective is what tells us that *skin* is metaphoric (rather than literally the speaker's or someone's flesh): The skin that can be broken by the poking ahead of breakfast china at this late point in summer more closely resembles the membrane of light, memory, or consciousness than it does a tissue of the body.

Ashbery places much more weight on the connectives, adverbial intensives, adjective grades from positive to superlative, demonstratives, and tense and mood indicators, than he does on the nouns and verbs this scaffolding of grammar supports. If we were to remove all these fibers of argument from one of the "Houseboat Days" passages already discussed, we would find something like the following:

> Pinpricks of rain fall   40
> And from the wide median with its
> White flowers, a reply is broadcast:
> "Dissolve parliament. Hold elections."

> It would be [deplorable] if the rain washed away
> The profile at the window that moves on,   45
> Know[s] that it moves, [and knows nothing else].

Even at this rate, the delighted focus of conversational dread in the word *deplorable,* along with the absolute negative at the close, are nearly sufficient to reinstall the concessive command of John Ashbery over what is now an otherwise drab and portentous preamble. The full authority of this poet over the kind of emotion he is carving out of the run of experience to treat and to know is, however, indissoluble from the grammatically obtained rhythms:

> Pinpricks of rain fall *again*   40
> And from *across* the *quite* wide median with its
> *Little* white flowers, a reply is broadcast:
> "Dissolve parliament. Hold elections."
> It would be deplorable if the rain *also* washed away
> *This* profile at the window that *moves, and* moves on,   45
> Know*ing* that it moves, and knows nothing else.

The shift from the expected present-tense finite verb *Knows* to the present-participial adjective *Knowing* is the same procedure we have just witnessed at the beginning of "Houseboat Days" with the china *Poking ahead.* The phrases *moves, and moves on* were contracted in the stripped-down version to remove the eerie suspicion that either by itself would not be bona fide motion. In Ashbery's version the demonstrative *This* returns to modify the *profile* with the sense that we could be supposed to have been watching that particular profile all the while (which I doubt we were). When reinserted, the adverb *also* implies that more than what he *hadn't* been watching has, by this point, also been washed away. *Little,* although not strictly part of the concessive grammatical lyricism of this passage, was removed in my text along with other counters because its visual contribution is so much less telling than its oratorical one. As indicated earlier, *quite* with reference to *wide* implies a judgmental scale to which we are not privy. The adverb *across* in its context, *from across the quite wide median,* functions like *Little* in the feigning of specificities— here, those of geometrical placement.

Although the adverb *again* is not an intensive like *how* or *quite* or *so* or *really* or *barely* or *all,* it reintroduces the problem of reference; *again* requires an original occurrence. We may look in bewilderment through the foregoing passages of "Houseboat Days" for the (figuratively speaking) "positive case" to which this *again* forms the "comparative." It may be that the rain *once* fell *As a common heresy sweeps over* (line 6). It is Ashbery's method, however, not to need first occurrences in order to posit subsequent ones, inasmuch as he is writing about moments in themselves distinguished for quite other reasons from experience that is dull and recurrent.

To put this claim in syntactic terms: Ashbery implicitly calls forward the dailiness of his subject by using comparatives in a vacuum and (again figuratively) frequentatives, as if to subtract their prior occasions from them. The absolute occasion is so bland that no previous occasions are needed. What is important is that the day, like any other, is suddenly luminous and taut:

> Some day we will try
> To do as many things as are possible
> And perhaps we shall succeed at a handful
> Of them, but this will not have anything
> To do with what is promised today, our
> Landscape sweeping out from us to disappear
> On the horizon. Today enough of a cover burnishes
> To keep the supposition of promises together
> In one piece of surface, letting them ramble
> Back home from them so that these
> Even stronger possibilities can remain
> Whole without being tested.
>
> ["Self-Portrait in a Convex Mirror"]

Such disclaimers warrant our sense that Ashbery has found means to return to that condition in the middle of the least prepossessing day where eternity illuminates the trivial. In this light, one could reconsider the passage quoted above from "For John Clare":

> It is possible that finally, like coming to the end of a long, barely perceptible rise, there is mutual cohesion and interaction. . . . I say this because there is an uneasiness in things just now. Waiting for something to be over before you are forced to notice it. The pollarded trees scarcely bucking the wind—and yet it's keen, it makes you fall over. . . . Meanwhile the whole history of probabilities is coming to life, starting in the upper left-hand corner, like a sail.
>
> ("For John Clare")

Finally. The *barely perceptible rise. Just now. Waiting for* one thing *before* another has occurred. The trees *scarcely* doing what they are doing, *yet* in such a way that *you fall over* from it. *Meanwhile,* the deceptive epiphenomenon that is not a by-product at all—the centrifugal opening of the canvas upon the vocabulary of the sea as it *starts* to paint itself from its most human center, the motive *sail,* tacking irrelevantly from the outback of *the upper left-hand corner,* but sure to come into the real bull's eye of the private life.

Was all of this assertion, retreat, bravado, and reservation in "For John Clare" a metaphor from some other part of our experience that we would easily recognize under some other name? John Koethe believes that Ashbery is everywhere struggling with the impulse to sublimity while finding himself closed off from the Kantian sublime. What Koethe calls romantic "contestation" (by which he means the instinctive assertion of the person's importance against the echoing ache of cosmic indifference) takes an untraditional form in Ashbery, since he "does not attempt to valorize the individual self, but rather to assert the claims of [a] diffuse, impersonal subjectivity," and since his poetry is "informed throughout by an acknowledgment of its own failure" to contradict the inevitability of nonentity.[23]

As if to produce a stylistic charm against the psychological no less than the ontological pressure of despair, Ashbery has woven a dense web of particulate language with which to catch the scattershot meteors as well as the sluggish asteroids of elapsing time. This grammatical style, however, will not in and of itself serve to distinguish the form of his poetry from the form of his prose. In comparing Ashbery to Henry James earlier, as here in citing some paragraphs of his prose as texts in some fashion equivalent to his poetry, I have deliberately suspended the question of minimal norms for poetry. The suspension has had two results. First, it could be shown that Henry James thought like Ashbery, only when one removed the considerable ballast, in James, of what might be called "prose context." *The American Scene* is a travel book in which places are named, scenes described, and an itinerary followed. The "angle" of its author is consistently that of a displaced American who has become too used to the Continent. Ashbery does not depend on such a prose "location." Although he does, like James, place himself at the beginning of each adventure within a "hypothesis" of onset or imminence—although something *will* occur and nothing is without significance—still, Ashbery's goals are less parochially and nationally defined than James's. Taste and ego are not invoked as inevitably in Ashbery's work as in James's. Nor do the grammatical emphases and apparently aimless parenthetical interruptions and often ennervating habits of qualification (with which James's late style is identified) produce ambiguity or illogic—especially not when compared with Ashbery's style. James is both more straightforward in his expositions and more affirmative; he depends far less than Ashbery on the tentative particles and connectives of the language.

In the second place, to treat both Ashbery's prose and his verse as if they had a common rhythm raises the possibility that, in both forms, his typical "period" is rather long and should make us ask whether in his verse he is doing anything to *flatten* or deemphasize the ordinarily greater proportion of stresses that the verse line, by singling out passages of speech, generally creates. Further, we might wonder whether the weight

Ashbery places on connectives, intensives, demonstratives, and so forth is the same for his verse *and* his prose, that is, whether the verse line increases or reduces the accent on this substratum of his usage. Finally, this is the substratum of syntax often reserved for prose; what is the effect of transferring so much of this prose apparatus into verse? If the effect is to make Ashbery's verse more "prosaic," are the colors, details, acts, and moods modified and supported by the prose machinery made collaterally more "poetic"?

To answer some of these questions, let me suggest yet another possibility: that there is a necessary relation between the great length of the periods of thought—the long "breath" of any idea—in Ashbery and the concessive refrain of the grammatical qualifiers, which relation is used by Ashbery within the verse itself to register both the uncertainty of or in things and the absolute, reductive mode of his process of handling and presenting them. No matter how long the lines of the verses in a given poem, and to a certain extent even independent of the presence of any lineation, Ashbery still uses a great deal of what might be called atonal "fingering" to generate further discourse—words that are textureless, abstract, nondenotative. The passive voice and the fussy explicitness about tense are supportive means to Ashbery's end of making a music out of the irrelevant, derelict, and approximate.

Consider the grammatical ingredients of "Sortes Virgilianae."[24] The title, Ashbery explains, "refers to the ancient practice of fortune telling by choosing a passage from Vergil's poetry at random" (p. 95)—except that the poem mocks the very idea of future and of event, and whatever Vergilian allusion exists is veiled by the grammar of digression. I have assumed for certain phrases, some of them clichés, like *for the asking, now for a long time, it is the nature of,* and *along these lines,* the status of neutral connective tissue and therefore print them in the schema. The actual "subject" words have been indicated only by the symbols *V* (verb), *N* (noun), *V-A* (verbal adjective, i.e., participial adjectives, past and present), *V-N* (verbal nouns, or gerunds), *A* (adjective), and *ADV* (adverb).

> You have been [*V, -ing*] now for a long time and there is nothing
>   you do not [*V*].
> Perhaps something you [*V, past*] [*V, past*] you and that was very
>   frequently.
> They have [*V, past*] you to [*V*] along these lines and you have
>   [*V, past*] your own way because you [*V, past*] that
> Under their [*V-N*] was the [*N*], [*A*] as [*N*], [*V-A, -ed*] for the
>   asking.
> Then the [*N*] [*V, past*] up, [*V-A, ing*] much more than any of you   5
>   were [*V-A, -ed*] to [*V*].

It is a [A] thing how [ADV] the [N] is, almost as [ADV] as the
    [N] from a [N]
[V-A, -ed] off the [A] [N] in [N]. When you [V, present] where
    it is [V, -ing]
You have to [V] it, though at a sadly reduced [N] of [N],
Hence [N] and [N], [V-A, -ing] at the [N] of some [A] [A] [N]
    or [N].
It is the nature of these [N] to [V] each other, they [V, present]   10
    no other [N] but themselves.
Things [V, present] [ADV] out of sight, and the best is to be [V,
    passive] [ADV]
For it is [N, -ness] that [V, present], [V-A, -ing] its [A] [N] on all
    it [V, present]:
[N] [V-A, -en] in the [N] of [N], that might have been [V, pas-
    sive] in good time,
All [A] [N], all that was [V-A, -able]. These are [V-A, -ed] now,
    as the [N] in the [N] of its [N]
And can never be [V, passive] except as [A] [N] on an [V-A,   15
    -able] [N] of things,
As [N] in the [N], [V-A, -ed] from the [V-N, -ing] long before it
    was time.
Lately you've [V, past] the [A] [N] still [V, present] their [N],
    only they are [V-A, -able]
Now that [N, -ness] or [N] has [V] away. It is with us like [N]
    and [N],
The [N] upward through the [A] [V-N, -ing] and [V-N, -ing]
    into [A] [A] [N]
Like [A] [V-N, -ings], the [A] [N] of our [N], or like an [A] [N]   20
In [A] [N] for the [N], [V-A, -ing] its [A] [N] into the [N] of
    the [N].

To get a clearer idea of the place of connectives and qualifiers in his
passage from "Sortes Virgilianae," I have also provided a schema that
shows the base structure minus the code for "subject" terms.

You have been [ ] now for a long time and there is nothing you
    do not [ ].
Perhaps something you [ ] [ ] you and that was very frequently.
They have [ ] you to [ ] along these lines and you have [ ] your
    own way because you [ ] that
Under their [ ] was the [ ], [ ] as [ ], [ ] for the asking.
Then the [ ] [ ] up, [ ] much more than any of you were [ ]   5
    to [ ].
It is a [ ] thing how [ ] the [ ] is, almost as [ ] as the [ ] from
    a [ ]
[ ] off the [ ] [ ] in [ ]. When you [ ] where it is [ ]

You have to [ ] it, though at a sadly reduced [ ] of [ ],
Hence [ ] and [ ], [ ] at the [ ] of some [ ] [ ] [ ] or [ ].
It is the nature of these [ ] to [ ] each other, they [ ] no other   10
    [ ] but themselves.
Things [ ] [ ] out of sight, and the best is to be [ ] [ ]
For it is [ ] that [ ], [ ] its [ ] [ ] on all it [ ]:
[ ] [ ] in the [ ] of [ ], that might have been [ ] in good time,
All [ ] [ ], all that was [ ]. These are [ ] now, as the [ ] in the
    [ ] of its [ ]
And can never be [ ] except as [ ] [ ] on an [ ] [ ] of things,   15
As [ ] in the [ ], [ ] from the [ ] long before it was time.
Lately you've [ ] the [ ] [ ] still [ ] their [ ], only they are [ ]
Now that [ ] or [ ] has [ ] away. It is with us like [ ] and [ ],
The [ ] upward through the [ ] [ ] and [ ] into [ ] [ ] [ ]
Like [ ] [ ], the [ ] [ ] of our [ ], or like an [ ] [ ]   20
In [ ] [ ] for the [ ], [ ] its [ ] [ ] into the [ ] of the [ ].

As we found earlier in comparing their use of tenses, Henry James, in
moving from the past to the present to the general or suspended future,
describes a logical movement from negative or countercase to present
case to triumphant general case, while Ashbery describes an emotional
contraction, almost a revulsion as time moves away from the present tense
toward the future-perfect, then pluperfect outcomes. Something of the
same tense ambiguity functions in "Sortes Virgilianae" to the same end
of catastrophe, unaccountable change, and recoil as present narrows to
future. Compare the expansive present-progressive of the first line,

> You have been living now for a long time and there is nothing you do
>   not know,

with the ambiguous past tense of line 5,

> Then the sky opened up, revealing much more than any of you were
>   intended to know,

followed by a return to a moralizing present tense in lines 6–8.

> You have been living now for a long time and there is nothing you
>   do not know.
> Perhaps something you read in the newspaper influenced you and
>   that was very frequently.
> They have left you to think along these lines and you have gone your
>   own way because you guessed that
> Under their hiding was the secret, casual as breath, betrayed for the
>   asking.
> Then the sky opened up, revealing much more than any of you were   5
>   intended to know.

It is a strange thing how fast the growth is, almost as fast as the light
  from polar regions
Reflected off the arctic ice-cap in summer. When you know where it
  is heading
You have to follow it, though at a sadly reduced rate of speed,
Hence folly and idleness, raging at the confines of some miserable
  sunlit alley or court.
It is the nature of these people to embrace each other, they know no   10
  other kind but themselves.
Things pass quickly out of sight and the best is to be forgotten
  quickly
For it is wretchedness that endures, shedding its cancerous light on all
  it approaches:
Words spoken in the heat of passion, that might have been retracted
  in good time,
All good intentions, all that was arguable. These are stilled now, as
  the embrace in the hollow of its flux
And can never be revived except as perverse notations on an   15
  indisputable state of things,
As conduct in the past, vanished from the reckoning long before it
  was time.
Lately you've found the dull fevers still inflict their round, only they
  are unassimilable
Now that newness or importance has worn away. It is with us like
  day and night,
The surge upward through the grade school positioning and bursting
  into soft gray blooms
Like vacuum-cleaner sweepings, the opulent fuzz of our cage, or like   20
  an excited insect
In nervous scrimmage for the head, etching its none-too-complex
  ordinances into the matter of the day.

The past tense of line 3 ("They have left you to think along these lines
and you have gone your own way . . .") is progressive, like "You have
been living now for a long time" in line 1; but the plain past tense of line
2 is solitary and separate from these, as though the old newspaper article
were what had set the character on his road. However, this understanding
is instantly qualified in the very same line (2) by the addition of the
continued or repeated time tag *and that was very frequently*. It is as if one
said: Once you cut off your hand very frequently. There is a natural limit
to the number of times something final can be performed.

There is thus no sense Ashbery can give us that the past will have
been constituted one way, the present another, and the future, however
ominous and elusive in prospect, in still another, yet related, way. Time
does not flow to or from customary sources. Ashbery is apt to assert a

present-to-future progress in adverbs that jar against the temporal inflections they modify and to reserve the verbal element for nouns (*the growth*,
line 6; *the surge*, line 19) whose temporal aspect is rather optative than
indicative, despite the fact that both these nouns are combined with copulas in the present:

> It is a strange thing how fast the growth is . . .

> It is with us like day and night,
> The surge upward through the grade school positioning . . .

Even in passages where Ashbery returns to a beginning in the past in
order to retrace the causes for despair into their present shapes (a familiar
procedure, this going back to the past and moving again to the poem's
window on the future), the poet will instantly invalidate the present that
has been reached, by forming further "presents" to which the present we
had just reached must now play "past":

> Things pass quickly out of sight and the best is to be forgotten quickly
> For it is wretchedness that endures, shedding its cancerous light on all it
>   approaches:
> Words spoken in the heat of passion, that might have been retracted in
>   good time,
> All good intentions, all that was arguable . . .
> ["Sortes Virgilianae," lines 11–14]

But the approach to words spoken in passion is no longer situated in the
present, since the phrase is *might have been retracted*, not *might be retracted*.
No sooner is the approach of wretchedness to present events at hand than
we have been spirited backward again into the infinitely more wretched
and irrevocable world of the past.

One is easily persuaded by such movements that Ashbery is the ultimate
romanticist of the perceptual—one who, in another of Alan Williamson's
telling phrases, "attenuat[es] the individual into the thin film of his multi-
plied but conditioned responses."[25] I am also struck by the pertinence of
Williamson's conjecture, coming late and (I sense) reluctantly to this critic,
that Ashbery can be construed as controlling his poems only up to a
certain point, owing to quite a "literal mass of introjected language, preconceived ways of seeing and ordering, that interposes itself between the
mind and reality."[26] So while Ashbery manipulates, focuses, and arranges,
he is also to his own dismay the manipulator of material only accidentally
his own. Ashbery is thus unlike the Stevens he arguably follows in elegiz-
ing human consciousness, or the younger contemporaries like Pinsky who
have domesticated the Stevensian perceptual sublime: He writes poems
of detachment from affective experience without clinging to the elegiac

experience of detaching himself. (The philosopher-poet John Koethe has identified this coolness, and then proceeded to inhabit in his poems, with rigorous intellectual attention, just that domain of elegiac separation which Ashbery evades.) It is when we compare him with these others that we see just how severely in the experiential realm (for all his extrusions and highjinks) Ashbery has restricted himself. Thus the dissembling-movements of his grammar, far from being peripheral, are from another perspective the most personal elements in his style.

One line, later in "Sortes Virgilianae," shows this dissembling-movement at its simplest and most abrupt. The word *here*, like the present-tense imminence of the self-admonition in line 13, is a counter for the time of the present moment; yet as soon as the comma falls, we have traveled far away from the here and now:

> Best perhaps to fold up right here, but even that was not to be granted.

From the exhortatory intention *to fold up right here* to the long-since-foregone possibility of any such thing's occurring is quite a distance to run in one line. Ashbery runs it not once but many times in single poems, first getting on his mark, then reaching the hilltop, only to look *ahead* of him at that part of the racecourse that remains and find that it is precisely the part that has already been traversed, though in a less successful way than the momentum of his running had led him to expect.

The first temporal note in "Houseboat Days" is the return to the beginning (*the land where you began*). Then we move to a beach where the hills *smouldered up blue that day*—a landscape that could be either prior or subsequent to the discovery of the source (*where you began*). Then we traverse the present-to-the-past-perfect course of the hospitable mind that finally exhausts itself (*the trouvailles / Of every one of the senses fallen back*). Then we enter a narrative sequence where someone (*he*) *said* (past tense) that intellectual argument *leads* (present) to pain. The speaker of the poem then imperceptibly takes over from the *he* of the past to continue his logic of pain and mystery, describing the secret *still hidden* (continuous present) in the hills. Then Ashbery inserts the analogy—*as though* introducing the supplemented futurity of the subjunctive—*as though one were always about to meet;* the *always* here is the link with the mood of the continuous present, the *about* (as in the verb/adverb forms, *to be about to, to be near to, to be on the verge of*) the link with imminent futurity, and the *were* the link with the suggestive futurity of the subjunctive.

The poem proceeds temporally in this way, from the mark of onset, to a suspended, unlocated time or to a past that subtracts all human agency or to a future time that then frames itself into a present for some further future, as in the passage from "Houseboat Days" below. It begins with a

So, cutting off the previous realization from the one to follow, preparing us for something subsequent, which is here expressed in futures coming into being; *becomes* is the signal:

> So, winding past certain pillars
> Until you get to evening's malachite one, it becomes a vast dream
> Of having that can topple governments, level towns and cities
> With the pressure of sleep building up behind it.
> The surge creates its own edge   55
> And you must proceed this way: mornings of assent . . .

Here there are two areas of temporal shift. First, in the vocabulary we have been noticing: *So,* the tag of the shift from prior to subsequent; the present-participial *winding,* to which the second present-participial adjective phrase *building up* acts as a further future; *becomes,* a word like *grow* that is crucial not only for poets like Ashbery and Stevens who write about states of being that can be defined only in flux, but also, as Christine Brooke-Rose has shown, for a class of metaphor used by Donne and Yeats as well, more active in the sentence and at the same time more tentative in its analogical claim than the copula link.[27] Other Ashbery vocabulary that masks one tense beneath another is *can topple,* whose logical relation to *The surge* is that of supposition to fact; and the imperious *must proceed,* which teeters on the edge between present and future.

The second area of temporal shift in "Houseboat Days" is implicit in the background of the imagery, namely, in the semantic realm. Time is being spent between *evening's* pillar and *mornings of assent;* time is also being taken to make the arduous rising and falling gestures of the journey. First we descend (*winding past . . . until . . . evening's*), then we rise (*building up . . . The surge . . . mornings of*—and here we expect *ascent* but find instead the homonym *assent*). Also certain somatic rhythms are suggested: sleep at evening, waking at dawn.

What remain to be seen are the real measures of these temporal effects. In the absence of narrative verisimilitude, which would insure that even chaotic events followed a certain schedule even if only that of the order of perception, we must recur here to what we have discovered about Ashbery's demonstratives (*this, that, these, those*), definite articles (*the*), and impersonal pronouns (*it, they*); for like them, *Ashbery's tense markers have no referents outside themselves.* Just as the poems seem to toy with the "aura" of antecedents for phrasings that have none, so the poet may be adjusting his diction to single out the emotional coloration of certain combinations of tenses and, deeper still, the particular valence of any given tense within a certain field of vocabulary.

In the line from "Sortes Virgilianae,"

> Best perhaps to fold up right here, but even that was not to be granted,

We might measure against each other the two nodes of "substance" in the sentence: *fold up* against *was not to be granted,* the former a gentle sort of slang, the latter from an ecclesiastical or imperial context. Or we might want to gauge the "meat" of the sentence, concentrated in those two verb phrases, against the background of particles, expletives, adverbs, pronouns, negatives—all the stubborn little condiments sprinkled about the main dish. We do this to some extent anyway, but in this particular sentence we come close to the structural dynamic of Ashbery's invention by focusing on tense, so that the disparity is not so much between a drab background and an infrequently lively foreground as it is the disparity between an act about to be conceived and accomplished, and the same act, after some considerable time has passed, that never could have been completed in the first place. The play between flip and imperial tones now takes on a more ominous meaning, as if the speaker were being punished for his glibness, long after the fact.

Does this mean that the modification of verbs by tense, tense auxiliaries, and tense adverbs is the standard means in all of Ashbery's poems for organizing attention to his lines? The proportion of tense modification to modification by quality, location, and number is roughly equivalent in the twenty-one-line passage from "Sortes Virgilianae" quoted above:

Line	Tense and Rate	Quality
1	for a long time	
2	very frequently	
3		along these lines
4		for the asking
5	Then	much more than
6	how fast	
7	When	
8	at a sadly reduced rate of speed in summer	off the arctic ice-cap
11	quickly . . . quickly	out of sight
13	might have been / in good time	
14	now	in the hollow of its flux / as
15	can never be	except as
16	in the past / long before it was time	as / from the reckoning
17	Lately / still	only
18	Now . . . has worn	like day and night
19		upward through / into . . . positioning
20		Like . . . or like
21		In . . . for the head / into the matter of the day

Although there are nearly as many verbal supplements in the Quality column, consider how many of these actually reflect and extend the tense. The phrase *along these lines* (line 3) mirrors the past-into-present continuity of the verb ("They have left you to think along these lines"), while *for the asking* reinforces the abrupt switch from continuous past (in the gerund, *Under their hiding was the secret*) to completed past (in *betrayed for the asking*). The rapidity of the *growth* (line 6) and the sudden increase in insight when the clouds *opened up* (line 5) make the *much more* of revelation in the past the seed from which the present-tense *growth* emerges. In lines 7–8 distance indicates the passage of time:

> When you know where it is heading
> You have to follow it, though at a sadly reduced rate of speed.

The two *quicklys* in line 11 also mark distance and speed as versions of the time span the verbs delineate, from the present tense of *pass* where the *Things* are still visible as they disappear, to the past-participial *forgotten* of the passive infinitive, when, by implication, the things are visible no longer:

> Things pass quickly out of sight and the best is to be forgotten quickly

Consider also how much certain descriptions of the new forms taken by old things manage to reassert the emphasis on time and passage: *flux* (line 14) is counteracted by *hollow,* thus reinforcing the claim that the flow of experience—words spoken in passion and those that were not— *are stilled now.* Consonant with the stillness and the hollowness, *notations on an indisputable state of things* are nevertheless made as the minimal allowances of a future time that will revive nothing but such postmortems. This is scant comfort, needless to say. What matter if the verb posits a future only to attach to that time both a negative (*never*) and a paralysis (*an indisputable state*)? Yet it is important to recognize that Ashbery balances the present time in a sequence of time words that pull the present in both of its other directions at once—toward impossible futures and equally fruitless pasts:

> Words spoken in the heat of passion, that might have been retracted in
> good time,
> All good intentions, all that was arguable. These are stilled now, as the
> embrace in the hollow of its flux
> And can never be revived except as perverse notations on an   15
> indisputable state of things,
> As conduct in the past, vanished from the reckoning long before it was
> time.

Such a balancing of the present *now* (line 14) amounts to a redefinition of the present as a collection of the movements of the other tenses. The present, as Ashbery foregrounds it, is something that *can never be* revived in the future or save itself from having already vanished *long before it was time*. As Ashbery twists the glass of the present before him, its vistas, although they promise him space in which to move, deny him access. He uses a specialized vocabulary of tense to keep the poems moving right up to the barricades they frame for themselves:

> So the journey grew ever slower; the battlements of the city could now be discerned from afar
> But meanwhile the water was giving out and malaria had decimated their ranks and undermined their morale,
> You know the story, so that if turning back was unthinkable, so was victorious conquest of the great brazen gates.
> Best perhaps to fold up right here, but even that was not to be granted.
> Some days later . . .

["Sortes Virgilianae," lines 41–45]

Although such movement is illusory in a realistic sense, it is a flexible mode of organizing the progressive stages of the poem.

E. M. Forster long ago distinguished between the plain sequence of events in a narrative, the *story,* and the ebb and flow of meaning, memory, relation, and intensity, the *plot (Aspects of the Novel,* 1927). In Ashbery, we might say, the *story,* which is always there in any piece of writing, is self-consciously *not* that of a tale in which event succeeds event but, rather, the story of the fact that line 14 in the present is followed by line 15 in the future then by line 16 in the foregone past. The *plot* of an Ashbery poem is, then, a matter of the redistribution of these proofs by tense at different points to make different shapes of affect and consciousness. In "Sortes Virgilianae," these shapes play against one another in indirect echo: a deluge in line 5; a blinding reflection in lines 6–7; widening of a gap, lines 7–8; disappearance, line 11; light of a slow approach, line 12; a flux that is yet hollow, line 14; marginalia versus the great stasis, line 15; again disappearance, line 16; and in line 17 again the dull light of a disappearing after-time, recalling line 12; attrition (*worn away*) in line 18; an upward *surge* amid frowsy and aggravating particles, lines 19–20; then yet another disappearance at the beginning of line 21 that promises that in the near future the board will be wiped clean for another affective movement:

> Presently all will go off satisfied, leaving the millpond bare, a site for new picnics,
> As they came, naked, to explore all the possible grounds on which exchanges could be set up.

["Sortes Virgilianae," lines 21–22]

The *plot* of an Ashbery poem is a matter of the arraying of tense movements to support metaphors and images of time consciousness—a stylized and masked *durée*. The ebb and flow of the images (deluge and rapidity *versus* hollowness and contraction) produce a time consciousness based on nostalgia.

In addition, this distribution of tense markers is a crucial component of Ashbery's prosody. The pacing of these markers controls the rate of the poems' thought in the same way the "arguing" connectives (*but, yet, if*) control the rhythms in the work of a poet like John Donne. But whereas Donne is also working against a rocky pentameter line, and against a medium of characteristically knotted monosyllables, Ashbery uses neither meter, as in Donne, nor the emphatic line framing of free-verse poets like Williams, whereby word accent (as Charles O. Hartman points out) is increased at the boundaries of each line. And although Ashbery does not use a hidden (nonaural) numerical subtext as Marianne Moore does, his line ordonnance resembles hers in allowing him to impose his own prose rhythms across line boundaries judiciously chosen for their very deft avoidance of emphasis. The liminality secured by Ashbery's lines is thus neither that of the impression as framed and singled out nor that of the impression momentously broken and syncopated across line boundary. I am saying not that there is no difference between Ashbery's poetry and his prose, nor that he does not, indeed, use lineation as a means to focus our attention on what the poem is saying, but that his use of line is to call attention to other than lineated emphases—like those of tense and absconded referents—in periods of some length that *by virtue of their effortless lineation* deliberately mask the fact that they are in lines at all.

Getting us over and out of a line, and on to something else, is a description that could also be applied to Ashbery's most characteristic intellectual gesture, that of dissembling one movement in time beneath another, and to his true poetic subject, that of the intrinsic sadness of a present time in which, while it is still the present, no future is possible:

> "The skin is broken. The hotel breakfast china
> Poking ahead to the last week in August, not really
> Very much at all, found the land where you began . . ."

The posture of beginning is parodied by the quotation marks, which Ashbery insists intrude into the left margin, as if he were citing a failed version of the poem, which then stands out as the fiction to which the succeeding lines can act as "immediate" exegesis. The pose of beginning is also parodied by the temporal arrival at an end or goal that coincides with the word *began*. A feeling of futurity is obtained by the modulation from *is broken* (as if he were saying, one act has now been concluded, one barrier overcome) to the more mobile and immediate (and chaffingly comic) present-participial *Poking* with its adverbial extender *ahead,* then to the double-duty disclaimer that casually bridges the line, *not really / Very much at all,* whose temporal influence is to indicate the chance of arrival as near at hand, and to suggest that the process of getting there is not really as dramatic as *"The skin is broken"* would have led us to believe.

But at the point of this bridge, by whose operation we have also effortlessly crossed a line boundary, the future has begun to fade. In *"the land where you began . . ."* the future has now faded into the past; a course has been traversed. [*N*]*ot really / Very much at all* is the phrase that, despite having nothing specifically temporal about it, moved us partway out of the orbit in which the sentence began. The word *found* is what the enjambed phrase has prepared the way for—a past-tense verb where we would expect a continuation of the present, *finds.* Yet we accept the past tense without a murmur. A prosaic and free-floating disclaimer, *not really / Very much at all,* has been inserted not only to get us over a line boundary as well as over a shift from forward momentum toward the future into a kind of befogged stasis, but also to lead us into an abrupt arrival, a completion, without the poet having indicated what, exactly, the disclaimer modifies. What is not very much? the china? the month of August? the last week? the eternal serio-comic poking of things? We can't say. Yet the way in which Ashbery rebuffs our queries about location in time and action is not the clumsiness of someone who was trying to write a meditative-descriptive lyric and got sidetracked: These methods are the signals of the new kind of poem he *is* writing.

We said earlier that getting the reader over and out of the line and on to something else was a gesture that described Ashbery's grammar, his prosody, and his use of tense. This slipping of the frame in and out of perspective also pertains to his theme. Ashbery is an addict of the sadness of the moment. What distinguishes him from Stevens is his attempt to deal with the flat, ordinary surface of his mind; Ashbery's moments are rougher than Stevens's because he wants to secure revelation *in* the ordinary, not from it. He denies himself the great theme of meditation and denies himself the framing significance of uppercase Experience.

One could substantiate this essentially romantic view of Ashbery's motives by going back to a passage in "Houseboat Days" we have already considered in other lights. The detonations of great Experience are here, as gestures, clearing the decks for another retreat into the grim reaches of the automatic and foregone:

Pinpricks of rain fall again.   40
And from across the quite wide median with its
Little white flowers, a reply is broadcast:

"Dissolve parliament. Hold new elections."
It would be deplorable if the rain also washed away
This profile at the window that moves, and moves on,   45
Knowing that it moves, and knows nothing else. It is the light
At the end of the tunnel as it might be seen
By him looking out somberly at the shower,
The picture of hope a dying man might turn away from,
Realizing that hope is something else, something concrete   50
You can't have. So, winding past certain pillars . . .

We can focus our attention on the sentence from lines 46–51, perhaps keeping in mind that the first part of line 46 (*Knowing that it moves, and knows nothing else*) echoes by negating an earlier phrase (*Knows what he wants, and what will befall,* line 39). The new sentence that begins in line 46 (*It is the light / At the end of the tunnel*) has for referent many possible nouns (*motion, light, profile, train, rain*), but most probably the referent of the *It* is the condition of dichotomous truth for both knowing and not knowing, befalling and not befalling. *It* equals being caught in the dry bracken between clearly dramatized meanings. Now we are on the train, or at least in the neighborhood of a moving train; its motion has been established to create a context of indifferentiation of things and persons. The word *deplorable* (line 44) still sheds its chatty, moralizing, and indifferent light over the scene, masking the really deplorable, at least fantastic, hint that rain could ever wash something right out of existence—that, in fact, it has already done so (*if the rain* **also** *washed away*). The form and impact of *the light / At the end of the tunnel* is that of *deplorable*—conventional to the point of cliché, overly chipper, and a mask for a quieter phrasing that is much more sinister, *hope is something else.* The light/tunnel cliché also presents another state of imminence: the building up of the pressure of the present tense toward a future that is about to be grasped when the end of the tunnel is reached. The next phrase, *as it might be seen / By him,* although conceding nothing, does not deflect the momentum of the lines away from the thing that is about to be reached; we should, however, register its role in smoothly bridging the line boundary. As in many other Ashbery passages, the bridging of the line by the nontemporal and undramatic connective is often the process during which something temporal, not directly touched by the particular current of the bridging language, is radically shifted.

Looking back, we discover that the shift covered by the enjambment *as it might be seen / By him* intimately concerns the very words that were placed so as to evade our notice. Here the movement (between line 47 and line 49) makes the man on the train, looking somberly at the rain, into *a dying man,* and makes the light at the end of the tunnel *The picture of hope;* on both sides of the "equation," the respective terms are joined by the subjunctive *might;* the second instance (comprising *dying* and *hope*), the more daring and chancy, is slipped into place because we had chanced so little on the first instance (comprising *light* and *tunnel*). The two verbal complements, *might be seen* and *might turn away from,* revise one another's difference by their likeness, creating a case where to see is to turn away, and to turn away, to see. Superficially considered, this mutual translation of meaning is dependent on our having reached the second instance, *might turn away from;* but under the surface truth that we are indeed at a "later" point in the poem by the time we read this second *might* lies the bedrock Ashbery structure of the resultant and the subsequent.

We have been moved a great distance—a great *time*—when the train trip becomes a voyage into death and the traveler a dying man. The cliché about insight coming like light at the end of the tunnel is attached to an *It* that refers us to the mutual translation of the great knowledge of fate and happening (*befall*) by the receding knowledge of inertia (*moves*), a translation in which ignorance replaces destiny and desire; so also in lines 46–51 the contraction of time through a tunnel toward its end—that imminence of arrival at the hoped-for—is replaced by a bleak despair. The poem's words mimic this foreshortening of perspectives by turning *hope* into a thing, *something concrete,* not a view into future time. The future is now only a continuing "can't have," a reified condition in which the past is impugned as well: You could *never* have had it because hope is something concrete.

The passage closes on this cryptic saying, revising the terms in which tense and movement had been accepted. Hope is not what we have been accustomed to think it is. It is not the sort of mood that sustains the dying in its various and fitful forecasts. No, *hope is something else,* not what you need when you face a future that concerns you, but what you unknowingly have, like an extra book of matches when you don't smoke, or a bus token in a limousine. Ashbery's gesture of redefinition resembles the curve of the parable. Consider Kafka's dictum: "The Messiah will come only when he is no longer necessary." The same play between future-tense *will come* and a future-perfect time when the present-tense *is* announces a state in which the conditions for the event have receded into the past (*no longer*) is recurrent in Kafka. How or when the hoped-for disappeared it is not the work of the parable to explain: It is enough that the parable first jars us into hoping, then dismisses us into a vast and foolish regret. What Kafka does by promising a Messiah who has no saving to do is what Ashbery does in redefining hope as an object with no place in time. What makes both Messiah and hope what they really are, creations of human need, is what permits their parabolic displacement into a realm where we can have them only if we do not need them.

To glance back over the text of "Houseboat Days" is to recognize how well John Ashbery has eulogized nostalgia for the past, shown not least in the not-quite-serious sentimentality about things, the place in the slip-cover, the blue smouldering hills, "the little dazey" in the weed patch, which work their pathos against the greater abstractions of the euphonious "evening's malachite" pillar and "A sail out of some afternoon," at the same time as they shed a ghostly light on the hypothesis of death. Ashbery's diction is the more interesting in that it can contain so much reference to what is never appropriated as his "own" way of speaking—unforfended references that illuminate and then extinguish in the ominously overgrown linguistic background from which they emerge. Although style in John Ashbery's poems fends nothing off, it calls attention to the offers to do so as they are, for the time being, refused. He is in this respect one of the great poets of cliché, consenting to appear tainted by the banalities over which he broods.

8

The Cure of Poetry

On the Discipline of Word and Spirit in
Conditions of Dryness: An Essay with
Admonishments from the work of
Louise Bogan, J. M. Coetzee,
and Other Poets

Writing is ever an alternation between boredom and alertness, exhaustion and rejuvenation. When one thinks about writing, as often as not it is writing in its tributary stages, when one prepares the ground again for the germination of life. The notes that follow were gathered up to remind myself how much work of a noncompositional sort goes on in the dead lacunae after actual writing. In a sense I am also referring to writer's block and suggesting what might be done when writing seems impossible. But in another sense I am addressing the chronic challenge of poetry, that it must be about life, and the chronic dilemma of true writing, that it dies in one work and tries to be reborn in another, and that the poet also waxes and wanes. It is not simply that poetry eats one away (although this is the case). More to the point might be the reverse: that one weakens and exhausts poetry every time one succeeds in it.

The danger in finishing is that one must confront a gap in possibility. What is true in a technical sense is also true in a moral sense. The better the work—the truer to fate and experience—the emptier the maker's life without it. The now complete and self-sufficing poem departs into another sphere. In its place is the lunar landscape of forbidden matter, untouchable, unrepeatable. What has been expressed is now true only for the reader, not for the writer, who cannot keep doing the same turn. And yet the writer's whole working method is based on constancy and repetition. One walks the same path, in life, in art, until one drops. The exercises we identify with a master are the same as those of the rawest novice, but carried on for so long, in a spirit so dignified and refreshed, that all trace of unevenness, all hints of the servile, have disappeared. Except at that point, of course, the exercise has become a living poem, and a living poem must be set loose and given up. So the cycles of composition repeat themselves, on the one hand plunging the poet into revulsion at achieved form, and on the other obliging the writer, as if no such revulsion existed, to chafe the cold limbs to life with an energy of undiminished love. Haunting us when we most urgently need change is the sickness of sameness, of what haunted Keats in his "journey homeward to habitual self."

Hence my use of the term *cure*, from an interesting Latin word whose origins in a form of *quaero* suggest a ghostly intelligence that is questing and yearning, dissatisfied and ill at ease. Imbedded in the term *cura* or *care* are both experience and response, both trouble and solicitude about trouble—in other words, pains and cares, in both literal and figurative senses. But *quaero/cura* does not remain fixed in the elegiac. Something of the ponderous psychology of Rome is shown in miniature as the connotations of *cura* shift from painful anxieties, to dutifulness, thence to more public and coercive duties—governing, precise management, and upheld office—thence to elegance in style and on to a cluster of metonymies from response back to cause again, until at its furthest point from literal trouble or care, *cura* stands for the beloved object or, simply, love.

There is a feeling both eloquent and brittle conveyed by this early alternation between anguished love and nervous and obligatory painstaking. As a result, I am all the more moved by how, in English, we have narrowed and skewed its nuances in our grimly knotted word *cure*, with its inevitable local burden of disease. To feel its skeletal breath blowing over the etymologies of *cura* is to begin to see why the word *cure* might appeal. "The Cure of Poetry" would then suggest that poetry is a disease to be cleansed of; this lies at one end of my thinking. *Cure* as a warm troubling and brooding over poetry lies at the other. For a sensibility like my own—a child when the Mass was still intoned in Latin, young during the rich torment of existentialism and then the dramatic cerebrations of phenomenology—there could not be a more poignant (that is, piercing) battery of illuminations than these:

CURA

TROUBLE   CARE   PAINS
DUTY   DISCIPLINE   STYLE
OBEDIENCE   ILLNESS   LOVE[1]

I have arranged the evolutions of *cura* in a threefold matrix, a mathematical shape that permits intricate functions to be performed. If one lets the eye rove between these groupings, the sense will dawn of how much each clue snags on many others: It is revealing, for example, that *discipline* is enshrined at the center of one continuum that begins in *trouble* but ends in *love;* and of another diagonal whose origins in *pains* release the almost

unstudied gestures of *obedience,* but of a third (the middle column) in
which *care* is only rigidified into *illness.*

TROUBLE   CARE   PAINS
DUTY   **DISCIPLINE**   STYLE
OBEDIENCE   ILLNESS   LOVE

The cure or care of poetry—which means, from still another angle, the
way in which poetry exacts from us response to our own as to its cares—
this use of *cure* reminds us that, under everything that changes in literary
history, there run the great recurrences of myth, including the ages of life
and the war of self-versus-other prominent in adolescence. For here,
clearly, we find again all the great adolescent themes (which are also the
great themes of the romantic period), caught in the net of the words
for *cure:* the themes of worry, rapture, asceticism, elegance, authority,
punishment, sexuality—all webbed together under the hand of an interro-
gating consciousness who is trying, in the best Roman way, to do right.

But there is an even more stern and self-conscious way to read this
word-grid. If the love with which one is afflicted in poetry is directed
toward the reproachful beauty of the finished, self-sufficing work, rather
like the"Cruel Fayre" beloved in the Petrarchan sonnets, the idea of whom
one bears always in mind and in the contemplation of whose lofty severity one finds the intensest pleasure, the *cura* for this terminal love is the
cognate anxiety of *pains-taking*—of discipline, exercise, craft, and repetitions. In place of painful exaltations (but unimaginable apart from their
seduction) we have our pains-taking cures, a round of ritual routines and
homages and visits to the familiar shrine.

One of these returns is made bearable by leafing through language,
acknowledging the reach of time back through each word. Indeed, this is
a pious routine I have just lengthily illustrated in carrying too far the
ramifications of my title. I refer to wordplay. Specifically, the attention to
metaphor in the absence of syntax. An excellent practical exercise that
trains the mind on trope is to examine the history of words. Writers can
literally relearn their own craft by reading the dictionary. In the words
most of us use with such native, naïve fluency are buried great treasures
of image and symbol. Above all, what such perusal of the dictionary
provides is an awareness of metaphor. We see how, for centuries, matter
and spirit—or vehicle and tenor—have played a tug-of-war with our lexicon (with neither ever quite victorious). Persistently, the mutual attraction
of the figurative for the literal has kept the tenor breathing through the
vehicle, or the physical world limber with symbolic power.

Language starts in metaphor. Words begin their lives neither as abstractions divorced from the physical world nor as univocal designations of

inert items in an objective landscape, but as signals in which experience and response, immersion and meditation flicker at minute intervals. No word, as Owen Barfield points out, is "born literal," although many words have "achieved" or been reduced to a status of flat literalness, by which Barfield means they name something either physical like *heart* or immaterial like *spirit* but with no hint of their original intermittence of mixed meanings. "Just as our immaterial language has acquired its literal meanings by dropping the vehicular reference, so our material language has acquired its literalness by dropping the tenorial reference."[2] Barfield describes the unnerving way, at some point in their history, Greek *pneuma* than Latin *spiritus* ceased meaning interchangeably physical-and-spiritual. Whereas once *spiritus* and *pneuma* embraced both clusters of meaning—wind / breathing / blowing / exhalation / odor *and* life / mind / inspiration / poetic spirit—now the word *spirit* can sustain only the one limited and univocal denotation of the nonphysical and half-credible and only mistily imaginable ether. (*Pneuma*, on the other hand, has been relegated to permanent objectivity.) Barfield regrets how few people there are who can seriously believe that *spirit* means *wind*, then surprisingly says: "But what *does* it mean?" He asks the same of the

> tens of thousands of abstract nouns which daily fill the columns of our newspapers, the debating chambers of our legislatures, *progress, culture, democracy, liberality, inhibition, motivation, responsibility*—there was a time when each one of them, either itself or its progenitor in another tongue, was a vehicle referring to the concrete world of sensuous experience with a tenor of some sort peeping, or breathing, or bursting through. But now they are just 'literal' words—the sort of words we have to use when we are admonished *not* to speak in metaphors. (Pp. 52–53)

I would counter that not everyone falls into the "literal-word" trap all of the time. Poets do suspend their disbelief in the identity of *spirit* with *wind*—or they can bring themselves to participate, for certain blessed periods, in the profound and contagious truth that the wind has a nature and being quite like the voice's own. Indeed, one of the most circumspect and refined of modern poets believed that he hears his own rhythms and his own thought borne out in the wind's rumplings and the sky's planetary blaze. Any notion of fictional plot that might resemble a kaleidoscope rather than a well would rely on the same faith that, in the words of another writer, "the least things in the universe must be secret mirrors to the greatest." And again: "Every man is on earth to symbolize something he is ignorant of. . . . No one knows what he has come into this world to do, what his acts correspond to, his sentiments, his ideas."

The concept of the world and our being in it as flawed hieroglyphs of greater significations, albeit an ancient one, has seen a lively renewal in the incalculably influential work of Jorge Luis Borges (without whom, for example, Gabriel García Márquez would not be writing as he does). It is Borges who has fathomed the mysterious and life-giving truths beneath the dry, obscure, and impenetrable arcana of his library. He has elevated scholarly citations of apt texts into a curious art form—homages to others that manage to sound ineffably like Borges. (Thus far, I have quoted only the words of De Quincey and Léon Bloy as quoted by Borges in two of his meditations, although their own characters may be hard to hear under their Borgesian auras.) Here is the Argentine fabulist himself on the resemblance between words and symbols:

> What is a divine mind? . . . There is not a theologian who does not define it. I prefer an example. The steps a man takes from the day of his birth until that of his death trace in time an unimaginable figure. The Divine Mind intuitively grasps that form immediately as men do a triangle.[3]

If all temporal extension can be symbolized, if acts can have etymologies as well as words—if *wind* and *spirit* at any point still touch—perhaps it is the writer's task to extend his or her hearing of the language by recollecting how far words have already penetrated into an atmosphere of embodied spirit, into the palpably numinous. Out of such efforts can also come a different and more intimate sort of recollection, not unlike what Platonists call *anamnesis*.

Let me give an example from my own life and work. At the end of April 1987, when my daughter was one and a half, I saw almost directly overhead as I looked with her out a large window in our house—quite far up in the pale blue late afternoon sky, so that it seemed made out of paper—a slender, almost stylized aircraft. I had every reason to believe it was a real plane, and yet I was conscious that my mind had to correct itself toward that truth against the insistent impression of evanescence and unreality that meanwhile kept intruding itself. For this vessel was in the shape of a cross of silvered white that seemed in some way transparent, like the body of a May fly. At certain moments, something almost glinted from it, although the word *glint* suggests a quality too spiny and hard for this almost seraphically distant apparition. Seraphic, but fearful. I am still aware of the apprehension that looms between the image of that tiny white airplane, whose suggestions are already fearful enough—the airplane as an undeniable emblem of my daughter's soul, while in some other way presaging her future apart from me, and in some other way still my own death seen under the sign of an utter absence from her—and the more fearful sequel, as I studied the full weight of the words that came to me. For this was (I had instantly thought to call it) a *ghost ship*.

Much of poetry is given to the writer, for good or ill; even the formative or limiting language may be, as, here, the phrase *ghost ship* (which I am fairly certain I shall keep as the title of the work that has emerged from this experience).[4] And to an extent I acknowledged and could have justified the dark choice of the Germanic noun *ghost* over the more ethereal-sounding *spirit,* even if the phrase *spirit ship* has a blitheness to which I am not insensitive. But I was hardly prepared for what the *OED* had to tell me about the seemingly foregone fixing of my choice. The word *ghost,* it turns out, has a pre-Teutonic root in a word for *fury* or *anger* and is cognate with the Old Norse verb *to rage* or *to terrify* with later emergences in other Northern European languages as *wounding, tearing, pulling to pieces.* And I began in the days following this April apparition to detect the barely audible rage pouring out from the powdery innocence of sky: That airship, that condensation of rain and mica sailing above the sound barrier leaving no trail, must carry passengers paralyzed with a fury aimed at God and one another, soundlessly howling at their bereavement, their exile from the beloved earth.

Thus far have I come, still pondering the collision of eternity with death in the generated terms *ghost, rage, rend, grieve;* but I might not have maintained my interest for so long had the language I inherit not deepened itself, through no doing of my own, until I could reinterpret an experience only a knowledge of the words could have released. Without the terrified anger saturating the sky and the mind, I might have let the wistful symbol of the ghost ship drop away. Now I believe that much of the work on the poem called "Ghost Ship" amounted to obedience, not invention: obedience, that is, to the preexistent poetry of the ordinary word. To cure—to have a care for—poetry is to keep its elements, the words of our tongue, the symbols of our acts, alive—by suspicion, and by attention.

Let me suggest a second example of how the background of words electrifies their passing foreground. In a brief dramatic monologue called "Cassandra," the great American poet Louise Bogan reinterpreted her own career in light of the vehement and anguished figure of the prophetess in Greek legend. You recall that Cassandra was one of the children of King Priam of Troy, who was once approached by the god Apollo and propositioned. If she would submit to him sexually, he would give her the gift of prophecy. But after Apollo had bestowed this gift upon her, Cassandra (whose ancient motives remain inscrutable, whether in making or breaking her bargain) then reneged. Furious with the maiden, the god set out to ruin her as a living human creature no less than as a seer by insuring that all her prophetic utterances would be true, but that none would be believed. The gesture by which he ruined her prophesying is a terrible one: He spat into her mouth. The invasion of her mouth by the god's spittle of disdain is re-created by allusion in Louise Bogan's poem, and gives a deeper reverberation to Cassandra's wish to be *dumb* earth:

CASSANDRA

To me, one silly task is like another.
I bare the shambling tricks of lust and pride.
This flesh will never give a child its mother,—
Song, like a wing, tears through my breast, my side,
And madness chooses out my voice again,
Again. I am the chosen no hand saves:
The shrieking heaven lifted over men,
Not the dumb earth wherein they set their graves.[5]

The history buried in the words Bogan selects deepens the meaning of the poem. The first class of alterations is organic and overt. *Dumb* originates in an Indo-European root *dheabh*, fogged, dark, obscured. Its opposite number in the poem is the inhuman sound of ill-omened birds *shrieking* through Cassandra's helpless frame. That the dictionary tells us *shriek* is derived from a mimetic Norse word for bird-cry, and that it gives for the origin of *dumb* a visual as well as an auditory fogginess—the thickness of matter in addition to the dampened blow of sound—these facts deepen the poem at just those points where we expect deepening. In these cases, diction and drama intensify at the very time when etymology provides added sharpening. There are only two lines that are in any way encoded—line three, because of its metaphorical indirection, "This flesh will never give a child its mother," that is, my flesh will never be a mother to a child, or I will never give birth; and line six, owing to syntactical compression, "I am the chosen no hand saves," I am the chosen seer whom no hand saves; or although I am elected by a higher power, still I am raised up only in order to be tormented.

There is only one word, the verb *set* in the eighth line, which readers familiar with Bogan may hear with a little more-than-normal connotative spin, as if a gem were being *set* into a rack of golden prongs in a necklace; or as if a planet were being fearfully observed to *set*; or as if a fang were being *set* in the flesh; or, finally, as if, over the dead, some frightened and tentative action were being performed for which the word *dig* would be too bold.[6] Otherwise, none of the words begs for explication. This is even especially true of words like *silly* and *shambling*, which belong to a class of utterances almost casual and glib—words we might feel as intensives of the moods of the speaker instead of as terms of substance in themselves. *Silly* and *shambling* even exert a semantic attraction over the tonality of *dumb*, making it also part of the prophetess's bitterly dismissive self-deprecation.

But beneath the exhausted plaintiveness of Cassandra's expression, Bogan is raking over the coals of her desperate story, and for this end the crossing of etymologies furnishes parody as well as its tragic reversal. *Silly* thus plays, flickeringly, over its primary idea of a foolishness close to imbecility, a state of radical reduction in the human creature owing to Apollo's visitation as well as to the carnage at Troy. For the word can denote the feeblemindedness or senselessness that come from being dazed, as from a blow. Behind the casual or querulous put-down in the phrase "silly task" lies the fact of being stunned, turned into someone who acts in a trance of idiocy, above all someone whom the world considers "touched" or retarded.

More complex still is the attention lines two through four direct on the adjective *shambling*, which straightforwardly means awkwardly gaited. The "shambling tricks" played by "lust and pride" are ill-jointed, obvious, loosely stupid, easy to see through—and Cassandra easily sees through them; her insight is effortless. But the effortful terminology of lust, flesh, childbirth, and the parturition through breast and side, should persuade us to let a little tuck into our rereading of "shambling tricks"—enough room to peer into the other etymology also resident in the word spelled *shamble* in English, but coming from the Latin *scamnum* (footstool; counter, especially for meat; slaughterhouse; [metonymically] the place where much killing has been done; [further metonymically, often ironic] any condition of disorder, particularly in the plural, sc. "shambles"). "I bare the shambling tricks of lust and pride," says Bogan's Cassandra. The shambling$_1$, shabby, and ill-jointed tricks our appetites play on us are also unfortunately the bloody-shambling$_2$ crimes we commit in their name. Helen and Paris ask their nations to pay for their erotic devotion. Menelaus the cuckolded husband mobilizes thousands of outraged Greeks. The snit between the two most prideful and powerful Greeks, Agamemnon and Achilles, stalls the military offensive against the Trojan citadel for years. Both lust and outraged pride will nourish the single-minded revenge of Clytemnestra when Agamemnon returns to Mycenae with his human trophy, Cassandra (although I believe that Louise Bogan is imagining the prophetess at an earlier point, just after the sack of Troy, when there is nothing but carnage, death, funeral pyres, open graves). In the complete context of the works of Homer and then Sophocles, the shiftless and gawky *shambling*$_1$ necessarily also carries some flecks of blood upon

it from the accidental neighborhood of the shadow-word *shambles*₂, which
is linked to slaughter. Cassandra's term therefore connotes not merely the
inept, but also the carnal; not only the body's random indulgence but also
its mortal doom.

To support the idea of the overflow of symbolic energy from her violated body to her lesser anguishes, I would point to the way lines three
and four of Bogan's poem *fix* upon Cassandra's young body, which has no
future, and trace a hideous parody of childbirth in the Caesarean tearing of
the fetal prophecies out through her breast and womb: "This flesh will
never give a child its mother—Song, like a wing, tears through my breast,
my side. . . ." The sadness of being barren and closed to love is swallowed
up in this grotesque invasion by a bird-god Apollo who screeches pre-
scient nonsense right through her, opening her up to the torment of
feelings and knowledge that can have no issue. The distorted extremes of
Cassandra's predicament make even her most idle, secondary parenthesis
throb with disturbed, primary meanings.

This overpowering poem also moves the reader to extremes, as perhaps
all great lyrical art must, as if to persuade us that poetry's only cure—the
one concocted by its prophetic sources—is radical, a permanent alienation
from ordinary life and conventional intonations. Bogan herself unflinchingly accepted this Pythian view of poetic seizure without becoming confidential with her readers. She never gave interviews or went on the circuit.
It was enough for her to use language sparingly, with a lethal certainty
about how each word is cursed with resemblance and with the residues
of other lives and earlier meanings.

I have suggested that the poet must study words. To bring up the example
of Louise Bogan and the ethos of lyric endurance that forms the vessel
for her rare skills is to confess how much one can find to admire in her
scrupulous example, and to signal the belief that writers need to discover
models for thinking and being, and not just for saying. In this regard one
might consider also works ostensibly in prose that possess the effortless
technical concentration and transparency of poetry, alongside its ethical
seriousness. In our contemporary literary milieu, which favors the obverse
of seriousness, the novels of the South African J. M. Coetzee are exemplary. Allusive without the insularity of Borges, the encyclopedism of
Umberto Eco, or the hobbling self-consciousness of Americans like John
Barth, Thomas Pynchon, or Philip Roth, Coetzee is magisterially at home
in the literary tradition. At home, that is, in a tradition redolent of discomfort and fraught with pains and cares; familiar to his own cost with its
characteristic losses and yearnings, its millenarian fevers, its wrenching
tragedies and cruel curses, its celebrations of war, its elegies at the bier of

nocence. To be heir to the tradition of the Hebrews and Greeks is to arry the sack of Aeolus on one's back. For this tradition is not nice. It is pagan, chaotic, and unforgiving, as often as it is warm, behaved, and mild. And in his acquaintance with it Coetzee is everywhere the learned and stricken son, fully cognizant of the pain and folly of the great majority who once walked where he now walks, but baffled, too, by the old dilemmas: how to do right; how to love others; how to rescue those whom hatred drives; how to make a good death; how to pass along the truth.

What distinguishes Coetzee's most recent novel, the stunning *Age of Iron* (1990), from mere discourse about these crucial subjects is the quality of his sorrow. In this novel he has created a momentous aesthetic and human vehicle for mourning. What he mourns is at once so narrowly individual as to be delicately masked by the book, which is entirely spoken by an elderly retired professor in Cape Town who is dying of breast cancer metastasized into her bones, and who writes the words we read to be sent after her death to her beloved daughter who has left South Africa never to return; and on the other hand the object of Coetzee's mourning is aesthetically universal, despite the stubbornly localized details of conflict between Afrikaners and blacks in landscapes—whether scorched earth or mockeries of paradise—rendered with allegorical savagery.

And at the same time as Coetzee mourns, he also deeply disbelieves in the value of what is passing—almost as an ascetic might. At moments, we are startled by the apparent readiness with which he prepares to sacrifice the beauty and innocence of personal ties to a model of human change still in the making and not entirely explicit. Even as his narrator in *Age of Iron* elegizes her unquenchable love for her daughter, she peers through that net of attachments crisscrossing earth to a form of experience only dimly recognizable by the kind of decent person she is—a new form of charity more attentive to the otherness that frames the language of metamorphosis. "Read all, even this adjuration, with a cold eye," she tells her daughter (giving advice to a "you" by which we feel automatically summoned); "Let your heart not beat with mine."[7]

The profound eeriness of such an instinct of self-estrangement was earlier suggested by the narrator of Coetzee's 1986 novel *Foe:*

> We yield to a stranger's embrace, or give ourselves to the waves; for the blink of an eyelid our viligance relaxes . . . and when we awake, we have lost the direction of our lives. What are these blinks of an eyelid, against which the only defense is an eternal and inhuman wakefulness? Might they not be the cracks and chinks through which another voice, other voices, speak in our lives? By what right do we close our ears to them?[8]

So, too, the magistrate who narrates his 1980 novel *Waiting for the Barbarians* recognizes that the weave of solid reality has begun to fray as he balks at killing a ram he has left the outpost to hunt. As he stares through the emblems he and his prey comprise, he experiences a hardening and sharpening of representation over reality. He senses that he and the animal have frozen into archetypes: Either the ram will bleed to death or the aging hunter will reduce to the gesture of missing his aim. As the beast stares back at him, he perceives a stellar "configuration in which events are not themselves but stand for other things."[9] Later he acknowledges that in all the tumult as the empire arms against the shadowy barbarians—tumult he has been helpless not just to prevent but to construe as preventable—he could not quite break through to the right interpretation of the signs: "There has been something staring me in the face, and still I do not see it" (p. 155). This "something" (never made explicit) is perhaps courage—a missing act, *the* missing act, clotted with matter and fogged with unreadiness of vision. Still inchoate. Not yet part of the self.

It is thus not only the narrator of *Age of Iron,* but also the magistrate in *Waiting for the Barbarians,* the outcast Michael K in *Life and Times of Michael K* (1983), and the demented daughter of the desiccated South African heartland in Coetzee's novel *In the Heart of the Country* (1977), who are haunted by signs, apparitions, inscrutable presences. For the magistrate, these presences are the souls of the dead civilizations as well as the souls of the tortured, which saturate the air. "[Y]ou can hear them," he remarks with aggressive irony to the relentless, steely state-torturer Colonel Joll,

> you can hear them echoing forever within the second sphere. The night is best: sometimes when you have difficulty in falling asleep it is because your ears have been reached by the cries of the dead, which, like their writings, are open to many interpretations. (P. 112)

The defeated and unfinished child/spinster for whom a nightmare of incest, miscegenation, and murder overlap with the abandoned import of Africa itself in *In the Heart of the Country* carries on a fervent, one-sided conversation with creatures who hover in space. (She has decided they must be Spanish-speaking, so she patches her entreaties together in a parody of that tongue.) Before the bonfire with which she hopes to attract their attention, she shouts "ISOLADO!" then spells out with enormous stones the pitiful quest for her maker and orderer, a greater father to be her author, her authority, her authorizer: "QUIERO UN AUTR," followed by the wretchedly suggestive "FEMM—AMOR POR TU." As the broken esperanto suggests, she glimpses an existence "unmediated by words" inasmuch as words are merely sent out from one existence to another without ever conveying truth, or even clarity. "Our disease," she says of Afrikaners, of Africans, of humans generally when exiled in such an unbearable limbo, "is that we have no one to speak with, that our desires stream out of us chaotically, without aim, without response, like our words."[10] The main character in *Age of Iron,* differing in most respects from this madwoman as she does from the victimized Michael K or the middling magistrate, is nevertheless engaged as are they all in suffering the disease of South Africa—forsakenness.

I have spoken of Coetzee's vehicle of mourning. The conveyances of narrative are necessarily more ponderous, multilayered, and complex than those of a brief lyric like Bogan's "Cassandra." But as for all works of literature, narrative's logic is analogical. Thus experience in Coetzee grows comprehensible by being reflected in further experience, presence is interpreted by likeness, reality is grounded in comparison, time moves or stalls by the psychological mechanism of images. More than in most fiction works, Coetzee's vision is temporally controlled both experientially and at the level of words. By virtue of his extraordinary concentration of verbal effects, we experience the passage of time in the double way peculiar to the poem rather than the novel, whereby the social and psychological lives of human beings, broad in rhythm and variegated in pattern, are subjected to, or channeled through, the more highly specialized lens of a highly image-laden style.

   Now, one might argue that many prose stylists use images, and certainly modern writers like Virginia Woolf appear to specialize in the poetic aperçu, while James Joyce creates a texture of verbal allusiveness almost too dense to penetrate at all on the level (normally associated with prose fiction) of anecdote and event. But Coetzee would seem unusual in the balance with which he keeps the psychological and the liguistic involved. Furthermore, he does not ignore the archetypal intention of narrative, to ground the individual in history. It is a social as well as a personal grief that fuels Coetzee's extraordinary oeuvre. His profound and pervasive handling of metaphor in this new poem (*Age of Iron*) is like his contained yet brilliantly far-reaching use of allegory in *Waiting for the Barbarians* a decade ago, for in each work, emerging out of credible-seeming commonplace, the creative intelligence is saturated in a life of great extremity of conscience and understanding.

   In the new book, iron is not merely a decoration or leitmotiv: It is an emblem under which the narrator sees reality disturbed, shifted, primed to erupt. The terms appear inevitably "given" and, as it were, cooperative among the novel's participants, not just illustrations of one speaker's idiosyncrasy. The voice that speaks the book, which belongs (we learn rather far into the text) to a Mrs. E. Curren, returns again and again, in different registers, to the imagery of iron and an iron age as a means of fathoming her particular death in a country of widespread dying humanity. She compares the blacks who have perished in South Africa to iron because they will neither burn nor suffer themselves to be buried properly. She is speaking aloud to the tramp named only Mr. Vercueil who has camped out in her alley and in whom she confides:[11]

> "When I walk upon this land, this South Africa, I have a gathering feeling of walking upon black faces. They are dead but their spirit has not left them. They lie there heavy and obdurate, waiting for my feet to pass. . . . Millions of figures of pig iron floating under the skin of the earth. The age of iron waiting to return." (Pp. 125–26)

In the stricken but nominally guiltless memory of this educated and decent white woman, the painful obduracy of the blacks has seared a permanent brand, or formed there an unalterable deposit.

But "iron" also describes the quality of their stubborn lacks instead of merely commending their victimized strengths. Thus Coetzee also establishes an association in Mrs. Curren's mind between the Age of Iron and the premature relinquishment of black children by their parents to the mystique of comradeship, revolt, and early death. Mrs. Curren's maid, Florence, who says she has seen in the townships a woman on fire on whom laughing children threw more gasoline, nevertheless still approves her son Bheki's revolt against all forms of white domination—including going to school. "These are good children," she tells her employer, "they are like iron, we are proud of them." Then the narrator thinks to herself:

> Children of iron, I thought. Florence herself, too, not unlike iron. The age of iron. . . . How long, how long before the softer ages return in their cycle, the age of clay, the age of earth? . . . And I? Where is my heart in all this? My only child is thousands of miles away, safe; soon I will be smoke and ash; so what is it to me that a time has come when childhood is despised, when children school each other never to smile, never to cry, to raise fists in the air like hammers? Is it truly a time out of time, heaved up out of the earth, misbegotten, monstrous? (Pp. 50–51)

That monstrousness, those misbegotten effigies, hard and stubborn as iron, of a people who have been thrust into a mortuary realm that can neither absorb nor metamorphose them, stand in stark contrast to Mrs. Curren's images of white children, pale, moist, preskeletal grubs, mewing without articulate voices, forced into a regimented immaturity just as the black children are forced into a premature hardening of gesture and hope, amalgamated with hatred in its most unbending—and unquestioning—form.

It is never far from poetry to a consciousness of a spiritual realm. The very vehicle by which narrative and lyric are driven is one of objective counters nuanced by meaning. That is, explicit metaphors, or those implicit in the figure called metonymy, give the outer data but argue the inner truth. Metonymy may be the more important of the two figures because it is more widespread in application, allowing as it does that objects and details in the literal landscape might take on a second life. "In a narrative," Italo Calvino has claimed, "any object is always magic." For prose writers, who in general eschew the more visible tropes of verbal elegance, even one recoil from realistic technique in a realistic narrative can take on metonymic and metaphorical significance. As noted above, naming is one area of novelistic tradition in which Coetzee has decided to call realism into question by abrading the boundaries between physical and affective realms; his central characters are clearly individuals for whom the social and domestic "fitness" betokened by one's name has ceased to provide any comfort. However, like all great writers of consciousness (Chekhov, Kafka, Beckett, Proust), the stylish Coetzee is not averse to the play of local elegance—those techniques that at first appear to thicken rather than to attenuate the physically solid present.

His narrator in *Age of Iron* frequently pauses over the anagrams cast up by her life, brooding over them until her entire presence is embedded in them. One example will serve. The annual rains have come; her disease is inexorably progressing; Mrs. Curren feels increasingly helpless to ward off mold, damp, and decay. She wishes to walk once more among school children in sunshine, to hear them "laughing, giggling, smelling of clean young sweat." If she is not to be granted that dispensation, she implores that there be no surcease of gratitude:

> I write these words sitting in bed, my knees pressed together against the August cold. *Gratitude:* I write down the word and read it back. What does it mean? Before my eyes it grows dense, dark, mysterious. Then something happens. Slowly, like a pomegranate, my heart bursts with gratitude; like a fruit splitting open to reveal the seeds of love. *Gratitude, pomegranate:* sister words.[12] (Pp. 55–56)

Those unfoldings of *pomegranate* in the mind, and of an answering love in the heart, are movements that by this point in the book beckon toward all the unmentionable terrors of the physical body still in store for the narrator: Consequently one reads of those seeds, that growth and exfoliation, that bursting-open of the heart as dominantly cancerous as well as humanly generous, occurring in two dimensions of feeling at once, only the second of which is celebrated. Because torment is also implied, however, the celebration is deepened in significance. In this way, too, fate irradiates the moment, forming with it an uncanny palimpsest or moiré effect.

So even when the local actions of this ostensibly verbal figure are avoided (the convention by which, for example, *glove* metonymically stands for the *hand* that wears it, and *crown* for both the *king* and the geographical and legal extent of his *rule*), nevertheless larger metonymical habits can still remain structurally potent. For example, characters in fiction and ballads alike will often be represented by their clothes, which then become an index of virtue or charm. In this light, a *glove* might be seen as a clue to a temperament that may need covering; or it may allude to the human type that engages in rough manners or athletic or bellicose pursuits, which require that the hands be mailed; depending on the occasion, the *glove* may also represent the undressed hand that no longer wears it, with all the opportunity for privacy, eroticism, and/or revelation which these removals imply. And, really, are we not engaged here with the most profound cliché of storytelling, as of psychology, that face, posture, demeanor, body set, and somatic impression betray facts about the character's inner being? Of course, it requires a writer of true insight to see how the facts are to be seen, and to distinguish which of the various shells that surround us—body, family, state, belief—is the very one that a particular datum sees through.

Another crucial resemblance between events and representation in novels and wordplay and suggestion in poems is the constancy with which metonymy moves from without to within—it is the characteristic movement of all realism. "O my luv's like a red, red rose" employs floral softness and aroma and redness of hue to imply softness and freshness of breath and complexion, and also a hint of temperamental fire. In the primary meanings of *shambles*$_2$, the counter where meat is cut up is the outward thing that argues the inward thought: the butcher's state of soul. Blood thus points, by metonymy, to bloodthirst. Mrs. Curren's cancer represents her shame and her country's, as well as an obscurer levying of punishment. By a further extension, plot (the series of things, anecdotes, ruminations, and encounters with which a narrative is built) may be taken as metonymy for the experience undergone in purely spiritual terms.

Indeed, in Coetzee's *Age of Iron,* the narrator periodically discerns a dim, supernal tutelage imbedded in (or perhaps merely flickering about) the bald circumstance. If, as Borges urges, the "outer world is a language we humans have forgotten," the content of the message it speaks must have to do with our cognizance of another realm replete with curative reactions to our engagement with the present one. It is this shifting hope of another order—one that has been externally caused and deliberated— that impels Mrs. Curren to lean all her weight against the few contrasting clues she is "given." Twisted slightly, the idea of the dead blacks in South Africa as undegradable iron sparks a series of contrasts between the form-

ss of the well-meaning whites and the ponderous dimensions of the
aned, humorless black youths who spurn the parentage of the past.
contrast takes shape in the heaviness of iron versus the wet weakness
he grub; in the torrents of the black blood versus the trickle of "Child
owdrop's";[13] in the gravid wetness of African suffering versus the pa-
ry, dry, tissue-thinness of the Europeans' faculty of affliction. Despite
ie angelic portent, the vagrant Mr. Vercueil she sees as a dry creature
ncapable of procreation because his very semen would be "dry, dry and
brown, like pollen or like the dust of this country."

After pressing exploratively on a number of such antinomies—antinomies possible only when a work of fiction is, like this one, also a
poem—the narrator breaks through into a new order of intuition that
gathers in many of the preceding ones. (One notes that this threshold
function describes the displacements of metaphor generally.) First, she
forms a plan to set herself on fire in view of the government buildings,
giving as one reason that, being white, and being old, she would "burn
well" (however, because she is baffled by the force and meaning it would
acquire, in the end she abjures that death).[14] She also discovers (as Coetzee's magistrate does) the second order of the dead, in the form of winged
souls. Here again, the ambiguous Vercueil is the instigating figure (he
"stirs her pool," Mrs. Curren says early on):

> A dry creature, a creature of air, like those locust fairies in Shakespeare with
> their whipstock of cricket's bone, lash of spider film. Huge swarms of them
> borne out to sea on the wind, out of sight of land, tiring, settling one upon
> another upon another, resolving to drown the Atlantic by their numbers.
> Swallowed, all of them, to the last. Brittle wings on the sea floor sighing
> like a forest of leaves; dead eyes by the millions; and the crabs moving
> among them, clutching, grinding. (P. 189)

There are few prose writers capable of such delicately ravishing effects
while tracking the progress of the crabs of the cancer through a good
person's marrow. The swarms of self-extinguishing insects meanwhile co-
alesce with the myriad abandoned and helpless spirit-lives Coetzee releases
to their fate. Earlier, his narrator conflates with the life of the spineless
grub of the ruling white order the idea of winged, ineffectual apparitions
who seem to be rising from the roar of traffic (she is lying beneath an
underpass, subjecting herself to a penultimate giving-away). She is being
frisked and pried open by street children looking for something to sell:

> "Leave me alone," I said. "I am sick, you will get sick from me."
> Slowly they withdrew and, like crows, stood waiting. . . . The boys came
> closer again. I awaited the prying of their hands, not caring. The roar of
> wheels lulled me; like a grub in a hive, I was absorbed into the hum of the

spinning world. The air dense with noise. Thousands of wings passing and repassing without touching. How was there space for them all? How is there space in the skies for the souls of the departed? Because, says Marcus Aurelius, they fuse with one another; they burn and fuse and so are returned to the great cycle.

Death after death. Bee ash. (P. 158)

Taking wing from her coming death, Mrs. Curren's thoughts about insubstantial souls, ambiguous forerunners, and unfinished beings, already partly ashen, tend toward more potent and coherent metaphors of painful valediction. "Never fear," she writes to her daughter, "I will not haunt you":

> There will be no need to close the windows and seal the chimney to keep the white moth from flapping in during the night and settling on your brow or on the brow of one of the children. The moth is simply what will brush your cheek ever so lightly as you put down the last page of this letter, before it flutters off on its next journey. It is not my soul that will remain with you but the spirit of my soul, the breath, the stirring of the air about these words, the faintest of turbulence traced in the air by the ghostly passage of my pen over the paper your fingers now hold. (Pp. 129–30)

But even as Mrs. Curren embraces an idea of soul whose turbulence grows more and more faint, the illness eating at her bone and the brutal events in her country provoke in her an imagery of the opposing humor, Dantesque, infernal, raving, engorged, humiliated. The white governors squat over the country, oppressing it with their "bull testicles," urinating on the citizenry, poisoning the air with language so false the only cure is a recoil from the channels of official communication. Their executive organs, the military, function in a twilight of terrorism in a landscape pathless, comfortless, and nameless (culminating in the visionary horror of the killings of three black schoolchildren—including Florence's Bheki—at "Site C"). Thereafter, in a contrastive setting of full sunlight, grimly smiling and coldly friendly, the military invade and violate the clean habitat of the white classics professor, assassinating in Mrs. Curren's garage Bheki's friend, the truculent black schoolchild who had so threatened their regime. Locally of course, the threat was negligible. *Sub specie aeternitatis,* which is the aspect *Age of Iron* unfailingly but unpredictably casts upon all its happenings, Bheki's friend is all the former "garden boys" of South Africa—all those Mrs. Curren imagines leaning on their spades while a picture is taken of the white family at a backyard picnic in the early days. It is these myriad black presences who crowd in and roughly alter all those artificially exclusive images: "No longer does the picture show who were in the garden frame that day, but who were not there" (p. 111).

Bheki and his friend may be dead now, but because of them the logic of representation and pictorial rendering has been changed forever. Reacting to this change in the conditions of truth, the retribution of the whites is absolute. Such composite loss and violation are the more cruel for Mrs. Curren in proportion as the aggressors' motives in the paralyzed postcolonial atmosphere are superficially so bland, and in proportion as the emotion the narrator can summon, herself, toward the dead boy is at first so vexed and tenuous.

Taking on herself the mantle of utter dottiness, Mrs. Curren accuses the South African government of having caused her cancer; her shame at them all had made it grow. She realizes she is making a fool of herself—that her "protest" will convert nobody, least of all any whites in power. The narrator herself thus tempts the boundary of metonymy too far, realizing that in forcing blame back into the local, literal realm, she is hurrying her task—the task, that is, of charting through her own person the course of lovelessness. For that is the mission she finally undertakes, and not a melodramatic gesture in public: She will commit herself to a process of vast self-withdrawal and bend her will to love not only her own flesh (the daugher she refuses to summon from the great Northwest across the ocean), but primordially to love the unlovable, to love those (among the victims, be it said, *not* the oppressors) whom she cannot mentally *want to* love. Her means of loving (as only a prolonged perusal, or endurance, of Coetzee's book will prove) is to give up everything on earth.

What does Mrs. Curren realize? Or, more to the point, what does J. M. Coetzee solve in *Age of Iron*? I think it is the power of love, the real, spontaneous, overbrimming kind of love, to strengthen the soul against the coming transmigration—to strengthen one for the journey away from the familiar and beloved, away from the realm of mutable grace. The narrator speculates that what is needed in South Africa now is *not* her sort of decent outrage and offended sense of justice but some new incarnation of "heroism." By this I take her to mean not political leadership—not the odd nugget of charisma in a spectacular individual—but a lengthening out and spreading of the talent for extraordinary self-withdrawal across large numbers of people. Perhaps we must all cultivate the death-resembling faculty of self-denial; perhaps, too, Mrs. Curren cannot forestall from appropriating her entire world the death that is now inexorably claiming her body. But the talent for selflessness seems to effloresce in *Age of Iron* out of the very center of warmth and wholeness of heart, the narrator's intelligent and willing *amor matris*. Intelligent, because she permits herself no rebellion against facts, no self-flattery, no defense of entrenched cultural modes. She is immersed in the classics unpedantically—a hater of debased pedagogical bullying, which she calls "Socratic ventriloquism," and a believer in "[d]ecency: the inexplicable: the ground of all ethics. Things we do not do" (p. 187). Thus Mrs. Curren speaks for a mean, not an elite; she is a humanist and questioner, who uses the last energy she has to discover more work for her real love to perform in that other world that is too stunted and deprived to evoke pleasing affection, but too thronged with ghosts of wasted lives to ignore.

Coetzee has said that "[w]riting is not carried out in a vacuum." From the perspective of the author, the book you write is "what you are about to become, or have become, or used to be."[15] In this sense Mrs. Curren is the most sentient and sensitive of Coetzee's brilliant projections (or deflections) of himself into ostensibly alien lives. This narrator's intellectual roots, her verbal knack, not to mention her imaginative genius for reading the world are completely credible, and quite enviable. If *Foe* is Coetzee's deconstructionist masterpiece, a text preoccupied with a questioning of texts, *Age of Iron* is his most radical assertion of classical virtues, as well as being an interrogation of the boundaries the mind must cross in order to remain true to its deepest impulses (fairness, freedom, proportion, unflinching truth). For from a corollary viewpoint, the landscape of the external lives we lead—a concept which embraces those human figures en masse whose wants cannot be left out of the picture—is inescapably the landscape of the poet's inmost obligation. Instead of substituting an outward battle for an inward one in taking on the task of love, like a true poet Mr. Coetzee has brought to the threshold of comprehension a wholeness of heart that moves surely from inward to outward, complementing the pressure of being-in-the-world in the opposing direction. He would, I think, be the first to agree with a statement at first glance the obverse of the opinion quoted above:

> The artist, as one Marxian critic has pointed out, does not function in a vacuum. Neither does he function out of a vacuum. Poetry is an activity of the spirit; its roots lie deep in the subconscious nature, and it withers if that nature is denied, neglected, or negated. . . . A certain method of stilling poetic talent is to substitute an outer battle for an inner one. . . . One refusal to take up the gage thrown down by his own nature leaves the artist confused and maimed. And it is not one confrontation, but many, which must be dealt with and resolved.[16]

Thus Louise Bogan, more than half a century ago, argued for the responsibility the artist owed the true self—the true subject, as presented by one's own nature. In terms of my title, the cure of poetry, the only healing it can effect, is identical with the affliction it visits and revisits on the serious artist. As Bogan wrote in one of her most searing poems, when the inner self cowers at the task of "show[ing] outright / The bruise in the side, / The halt in the night, / And how death cried," the daemon summarily enjoins the artist to get on with it:

THE DAEMON

Must I tell again
In the words I know
For the ears of men
The flesh, the blow?

Must I show outright
The bruise in the side,
The halt in the night
And how death cried?

Must I speak to the lot
Who little bore?
It said, *Why not?*
It said, *Once more.*

(1988–90)

Conclusion: The Poet's Calling

*On a New Model of Literary
Apprenticeship*

In a response to one of my critical reviews, a letter writer some years ago made the remarkable claim—remarkable in the sense that a critic should be implicitly proscribed from speculating on the poet's psychology—that I used my "talent for analysis to spy on the author."[1] A good critic "spies" only so far as to detect whether the daemon has spoken through the writer. With Louise Bogan's injunction still in our ears, and with the searing imagining of death in Coetzee's work still palpable, arguments about the mediocre appear not only more petty but also more important to sort out according to the magisterial laws given in the greatest literature.

One of these laws is that the aesthetic mission is also a moral one. So when a defender of a novice's work calls me to task for educing false standards of moral criticism, which the writer went on to explain meant that I thought poetry "must be held politically accountable for the nature of its insights, [and] that 'perception' is not subject enough for a poem," I felt, and feel, obliged to transform the objections into the terms of a useful lesson. Yet while I took pains in my reply to remove the meaning-less modifier "politically" from the sentence, I was less certain how to put in a positive light these accusations, which were all quite true. How to persuade someone who thinks it reprehensible even to hint at such issues, that the poet and the poem alike must be held responsible for the nature of their insights, that the personality of the author as well as the flavor of the text come into play in producing a body of work, and that, indeed, "perception" with its readily plumbed empirical backdrop is hardly subject enough for a poem?

To complicate (yet also, as it turned out, to help me clarify the real differences), these objections were joined by those of another letter writer, who thought artists must be "allowed" their material, citing *Guernica* and *Howl*. One argument against unfettered exposure of the ghastly and depraved is that it depraves the exposer. I suggested that the audience was not constrained to accept the equation between dreadful and shocking matter, and aesthetic "power" (let alone aesthetic harmony). We can say: This is a decadent subject; this is a corrupt treatment; this is a marriage of the sentimental with the brutal (if these happen to be the case). We are not, in other words, sentenced to silence by the autonomy of the artist.

This view is eloquently argued in his autobiography by the poet Edwin Muir, disturbed by the perversions, castrations, and livid raging in the plays of Wedekind and Toller:

> It is curious how often the questionable is invoked by German writers when they set out with a moral purpose. The resolve to expose evil in its most squalid form may be enough to account for this; but almost invariably something sordidly inquisitive comes into the treatment as well, adding to the moral confusion. The result is that the spectator is not cleansed, but involved in the impurities he is witnessing, and the moral intention is perverted into its opposite.[2]

Indeed, this corruption where cleansing is promised is precisely what concerns me in the poems of Adrienne Rich, Sharon Olds, and Jorie Graham. Their work, more and less artful depending on the occasion, is of the nature of such visionary pornography as in these lines:

> All the
> statistics, the century's
> burned and gang-raped
> turning, lifting, a blade catching the
>   late
> light
> redeeming it, and us needing its
>   wrongest beauty . . .[3]

It is clear that such amassments of "the century's" victims are journalistic, despite the ornamental verbiage, and that the motive is a kind of civic prurience. But how to speak to the committed enthusiasts of such work? How to persuade of the wrongness of "wrongest" and of the flaccidity of "and us needing" and of the sentimentality that discovers the beautiful in the grotesque? Surely we are worlds distant from an art of which one might say that it finds the words for any situation.

I answered the letters as best I could,[4] but the feeling grew of talking to deaf ears. The problem was perhaps not one that could be resolved in a single exchange. Indeed, I began to realize that the problem was one of the gap between the typical contemporary poet's aspirations, and her intellectual and technical—especially narrative—means. I also began to believe that the solution would have to do with a new and fruitful approach to the writer's apprentice years.

Perhaps I am simplifying. For the problem is not that the contemporary poet's aspirations are excellent and the means wanting, but that the means are wanting to favor both execution and conception: Writers also need to discover in their apprenticeship some center of gravity for the taking-on of aspirations. Conceiving the mission of the poem and of poetry requires as deep a knowledge of technique and of human nature as does composing this hypothetically serious and innovative poem in response to such intentions.

Much of the poetry composed today is not merely stereotypic with regard to its style but clichéd with regard to its imaginative premise; and the clichés of feeling promote the stereotyping of the forms. This weakening codependency of clichéd feeling with, on, and against stiff execution in an empty idiom illustrates a principle the art critic Edgar Wind first articulated with respect to the mechanical reproduction of paintings in art catalogues, and the chemical cleaning of paintings to achieve what is thought by restorers to be the works' original vividness of hue. Because, says Wind, our eyes have been "sharpened to those aspects of painting and sculpture that are brought out effectively by a camera," we therefore tend to take more satisfaction in the primitive look of a painting when its colors have been "fixed" by the limitations of the photographic medium than we taken in the layered subtlety of the originals:

> Since the mechanics of stripping down a painting reverses the sequence in which it was built up, it is almost inevitable that processed pictures acquire a surface that looks machine-made, resembling the hard luminous gloss of mechanical reproductions, with brute colors in glaring juxtaposition. The satisfaction aroused by paintings reduced to that state may probably be ascribed to the fact that vision has increasingly been trained by derivative prints, which tend to over-define an image in one direction by fixing it to a mechanical scale.
>
> (Edgar Wind, *Art and Anarchy*, pp. 68–69)

What Wind describes with respect to the deterioration of the vision necessary to appreciate delicacy of color in painting could also be said of the deterioration both of the language and of the concepts necessary to appreciate the subtlety in feeling, idea, and analogy, and in the tension between the moral and sensuous gratification that enriched the poetry of the Renaissance and the eighteenth century, but which now seem obsolete if not abhorrent in the careers of contemporary poets.

At present, verse in English has, to adapt Edgar Wind's terms, been *overdefined* in the direction of perceptual and sensuous immediacy and uncensored directness, without any gradation in palette or graduation in time of response: Perception is an instantaneous good. One of the mechanisms that fix poetry to the scale of stunned immediacy is the syntax of nominalized verb and verbal adjectives, which announce great movements and perform none. Another of these mechanisms is the pursuit of colloquial presence. A poem proves authentic in proportion as it exhibits the rhetoric of a kind of un–self-conscious experiential appetite. Above all the stereotyped poem of the present cultural moment—even the poem that professes to experiment with language and syntax—to the extent that it is based on clichés of feeling, traps its writers in a circle of redundancy. But the lure of the vivid, and even the garish, is strong; cliché is only the more deeply entrenched by the illusion of "sincerity."

Vladimir Nabokov well describes these clichés of feeling (he locates them in the German ego as well as the American); to them he gives the collective name *poshlust* (to suggest the unsavory core of such assumptions as, for example, that the nuclear family is made happy by purchasing goods for one another and that size is directly proportional to value—not to mention the insidious noncommercial clichés that insist on trusting in spontaneous reactions, sharing problems, valuing the attempt more than success, believing that the old regret not being young, that beauty is somehow more correct than ugliness, that appetite is finally natural or healthy, that a certain overstuffed rondure in the female figure is desirable, and so on), and he makes clear that these clichés are the basis of advertising, even for periods before that marketplace term or the practice was widespread.[5] Whereas the true writer, like Nabokov himself, will ever work against the grain of cliché, avoiding the word's denotation, a machine-stamped rigidity of associations, rather adjusting to the shifting light-and-shadow play of experience in time.

What can be called "literal symbols" are always specific before they take on larger and possibly archetypal (that is, extensively metaphorical) significance.[6] To imagine an implement like a knife, for example, one would, like Elizabeth Bishop in her magisterial poem "Crusoe in England," instinctively avoid the implication that knives are sharp, dangerous, and ominous:

> The knife there on the shelf—
> it reeked of meaning like a crucifix.
> It lived. How many years did I
> beg it, implore it, not to break?
> I knew each nick and scratch by heart,
> the bluish blade, the broken tip,
> the lines of wood-grain on the handle . . .
>
> (*Geography III*, 1976)

The focus on the radiantly clear object (like Bishop's focus on the knife in "Crusoe in England") permits the poet to perform the writer's two tasks simultaneously—to describe the world, and to interpret it. And in order to show the general interpretation imbedded in what is literal and specific (including the literal and specific perceptual minutiae of elapsing time), it is necessary for the writer to render clearly what is near at hand. Such clarity of rendering in turn will require a sensibility that is anything but reduced to mere perceptual immediacy.

When one is in the presence of a genuinely "new" poem, one feels that it has achieved its precarious new status by adumbrating, even opening, an entire fresh volume of possible spiritual motions that are, nevertheless, recognizable, even unaccountably familiar (although the true innovation is not just the performance of a nice, familiar choreography). I believe that Eleanor Wilner's new poem "Bat Cave," 100 lines long, and as yet uncollected,[7] speaks to the same ability as does Bishop's "Crusoe"—to tread the razor's edge between archetypal manifestation and literal flatness. The immediate objects in the poem are bats hanging in myriads above virtual stalagmites of guano in a cave on the island of Bali near Denpasar. But every time the poet comes close to this or that "phenomenon," perception eloigns itself. Even as Wilner assembles the clues that indicate the ostensible subject of the poem, meaning shifts key, for the walls of the cave, on closer inspection, as they

> slanted up into a dome   5
> were beating like a wild black lung—
> it was plastered and hung with
> the pulsing bodies of bats, the organ
> music of the body's deep
> interior, alive . . .   10

And where an organ plays in a thoracic cave already somehow "sacred," an "altar" is not far to fathom, particularly owing to the rock-hard piles of white excrement, a fine contrast to their origins in that leathery, breathing, quasi-fleshlike muscle of uncanny mammals, the contrast producing a hint of greater echoings to come from this solemn, and filthy, hollow space.

Wilner is, like Bishop's persona, often a "tourist," "superior with fear" (lines 25–26), hovering as it were (she says) on the street side of a bead curtain as it trembles before a shop's suspect, dim interior (lines 27–30). Thus the voyeuristic impulse is acknowledged—and the craving for mystery and awe of the exotic that must have brought the tourists there. Accordingly, the traveling couple "thought of the caves / of Marabar" where Mrs. Moore encounters the horrible echo of cosmic emptiness in E. M. Forster's novel *A Passage to India,* and where Adela Quested believes she was raped (or almost) by the misguiding, floundering friend-to-the-English, Aziz. Interestingly, it is neither of the women, but the author

Forster whom Wilner imagines as wandering the tunnel opened in the colonial soul:

> We thought of the caves   30
> of Marabar, of a man who entered
> and never quite emerged—
> the caves' echoing black
> emptiness a tunnel in the English
> soul, where he is wandering still.   35

Through the resonant and undeniably apt recollection of another complex work of art, Wilner deepens her poem psychologically as well as historically. By comparing her own attitude to that of Forster and his characters, she is enabled to "read" the English soul—the soul of the well-meaning but protectionist colonizer, interpreter, civilizer—even as the phenomenon is held in abeyance (what *was* in the Caves of Marabar? Why/how do these tens of thousands of bats in their cave haunt and accuse the spectator?).

The multiplex echoings of the Forster novel in Eleanor Wilner's poem prepare us for a lesson that is, in a thoroughgoing sense, cultural as well as personal. Before the outing to Marabar, Forster had remarked of Adela Quested that she could not get beyond the "echoing walls" of the Indian women's civility (again, a surface assumed to be resistant and rigid transforms its substance into resilient, mysterious flesh).[8] Eleanor Wilner has remarked to me that she attempted to teach *A Passage to India* to Japanese students during her two-year stint in the 1970s in Japan, and that these students themselves appeared to her to present an echoing wall of sweet civility to her Western probing. As in the experience of teaching in Japan—like the experience, at one remove, of trying to understand Adela, Fielding, and Forster in their bafflement with India—so in the poem "Bat Cave" a clear parable of disturbance and of dissonance is in progress; the apparition of the bats in their cave can't entirely be "resolved" by the tourists' eyes—until they step across the cave's threshold (with all the nuances of transgression into an irreversible ban which that entry betokens).

Like new initiates into a frightening cult, the human couple feel "the radiant heat of pumping / veins" (lines 41–42) as they behold "the familiar / faces of this many-headed god, / benevolent" but also appetitive as the bats are released in a dark froth into the "starlit air," wheeling in "wild wide arcs / in search of fruit, the sweet bites / of mosquito" (lines 43–54). Thus far, the entry into the mystery is marked by little more than pleasant apprehension: These are warm-blooded creatures, after all, in many ways

featured like us, like us possessed with thirst. Their liberated aerial soarings appeal, just as "sweet bites" and "starlit air" carry forward their practically unconscious commendatory connotations from the work of Keats
and Shelley. But now, at the mid-point of the poem, we start to fall into
a terrible visionary world—made more horrific by the fact that it is recent
and real; I quote from the long penultimate stanza which we begin with
the clatter of the bats' bony wings still audible after they start their nightly
feeding exodus:

> while the great domes of our   55
> own kind slide open, the eye
> that watches, tracks the skies,
> and the huge doors roll slowly back
> on the hangars, the planes
> push out their noses of steel,   60
> their wings a bright alloy
> of aluminum and death, they roar
> down the runways, tear into
> the night, their heavy bodies fueled
> from sucking at the hidden   65
> veins of earth . . .

Following the emergence of the sleek phallus of fire from line 60, it takes
no more than a few lines for the bombs to begin falling on Baghdad,
whose children scream to awaken from a nightmare run on command.
The poem's third act is what Nemerov calls perfectly dialectical, the metaphysical happiness of true saying shining from the chamber of the broken
heart. The pacing of these middle lines, where the bright and heavy planes
"push out" of their shadowy hulls, is at once full of lentor and solemnity,
and electric with fascinated revulsion as the creatures of death take wing.
But what is yet more remarkable to me is that Wilner refuses to let the
poem close on her grand accusation.

   Movement after movement, Eleanor Wilner's poem resists premature
closure and easy moral positions. Just as the achieved and mysterious
analogy between creaturely and colonial appetites, which Wilner builds
in the first fifty lines of "Bat Cave," is prevented from reflecting (and
subsiding) ruefully upon itself as her head looks up from the poem she is
writing, so Wilner will not allow herself to relish, with a final stylistic
trump, even the harrowing results, in military action, of material and
global greed for the oil sucked by the aircraft out of the mother's veins
(the earth). She returns to the bat cave. She vectors in upon the homing
bats, attuned as all physics is to the shifting planets, but blind as all beings
are to their own causative role in making things happen:

```
        the bats
    circle, the clouds wheel,
    the earth turns                                          85
    pulling the dome of stars
    among the spinning trees, blurring
    the sweet globes of fruit, shaped
    exactly to desire—dizzy, we swing
    back to the cave on our stiff dark                       90
    wings . . .
```

Thus in line 89, she makes us one with *them*. Rather than political self-loathing as citizens who don't demonstrate hard enough against our vicious militaristic oil-dependent governments, we are instead provoked to question our need to be siblings of appetite, warm in our cave, "the sweet juice of papaya / drying on our jaws" (lines 91–92), pulsing with our fellows under the cave roof where

```
        we can see what was once our world
    upside down as it is
    and wonder whose altars
    those are, white,
    encrusted with shit.                                     100
```

Like the monuments to our aggressions (observatories; battlefields), the temple of the body also emits mental monsters from one end, and from the other, no matter how you turn, shit. The forthright word may not be the only one that would do, but it is the one the poem throughout has striven to find a way to use. One feels a turn of the screw as the word falls at line 100, neat, instantly hard, symmetrical, impossible to ignore.

In my estimation, Eleanor Wilner's is a superior poem of protest against all forms of (even perceptual) passivity. While lifting blame against those in high places, "Bat Cave" also implicates its speaker as a voyeur of the foreign and as a dilettante of exotic pain, and by this mechanism of complicity with a fiction of her own benightedness, the poet locates in her own habits of projection the very flaw that sentimentally sees any outpouring of the local body as holy: Indeed, whose alters *are* these, encrusted with dung? (None but ours.) She asks the question implicitly of the literary tradition as well. Who do we think we are, making and bequeathing legacies? Poetry (when it becomes too encrusted with its own wisdom—which is to say, its own ignorance) is like the men's club of commerce. And the currency of commerce, as Freud all too relentlessly reminds us, is excrement.

When I argue against prose above in "The Rhapsodic Fallacy" I argue the need for the poem like Eleanor Wilner's in which we see a new variety of response and subtlety of layering in the making of poetic works: The world grows more complex and solid, too—less a mere occasion for cleverness. It turns out that such an argument is necessarily a call for greater aesthetic honesty—a greater loyalty to the love of beauty as truth (and truth-telling)—than the stereotypic poem of almost any age evinces. More variety and truth-to-fact means greater inherent order in the writing of poetry and in conceiving the goals and ends of poems. Paradoxically, greater poetic unity demands greater complexity and openness of articulation, not stiffer univocality. The essay expresses in part a hope for a new prosodic and cognitive receptiveness to discourse in poetry so that forms other than lyric can again be pursued. It is a common call. Marjorie Perloff makes it in an essay on the avant-garde in *Formations* (Fall 1984):

> Postmodernism in poetry, I would argue, begins in the urge to return the material so rigidly excluded—political, ethical, historical, philosophical—to the domain of poetry, which is to say that the Romantic lyric [can be made to give way] to a poetry that can, once again, accommodate narrative and didacticism, the serious and the comic, verse and prose.

Now, Perloff is hardly suggesting that we should attempt a return to the eighteenth century when satire flourished alongside comic and didactic impulses; neither am I suggesting such a return. Rather, I assume as basic the need to rediscover and reinculcate the enormous musical varieties of verse (which Perloff does not emphasize), along with the many rhetorical conventions that might be combined with those musics (which she does). For even the unprepossessing conversational voice requires conventions to render its middle ranges broad and interesting. And if formal conventions bear up the meaning, conditioning and enabling it, there is nothing the least mechanical about those forms. By the same token, even explosive, impromptu free-verse conventions are mere creaking machinery in the absence of a controlling imagination.

Using terms and categories much like Perloff's toward a different end, A. D. Hope has described the middle form of verse (in which the uses of poetry mesh so provocatively with those of prose) as a form that serves

> without pretension the purposes of narration, the essay, the letter, conversation, meditation, argument, exposition, description, satire or cheerful fun. It was in this middle field that *the poets learned the exercise and management of their craft,* the maintenance and modulation of tone.
>
> ("The Discursive Mode," 1965; my emphasis)

The middle form is the area in which Hope's novice can experiment with his craft; it becomes the ground from which he can move higher if need be. Thus it differs from much of the poetry of the mid-1960s, based in what Hope calls a "profusion of startling images" (hence a poetry that obsessively soared to inflated heights); the middle mode is grounded in the same resources poetry shares with ordinary English prose "when used with inimitable aptness and animated by metre and rhyme." As Hope observes, some command of the discursive, middle style is essential for the art of modulation in any kind of poem: "On this depend proportion, harmony, connection, surprise, and the power to return without lapsing . into dullness." No long poem can exist without recourse to these skills of variety and recombination.

Despite the two-and-a-half decades that have elapsed since Hope's essay, the lyric-imagistic profusions of poets writing in English have chugged along in much the same way, although a reduction and hardening have accompanied the profusion, making the convention of sensitive free verse more dingy and inelastic than before, at once touting and masking the rhapsodic elements. As a result the middle style Hope describes, with its animation by music and invigoration by discourse, will be more appealing than ever before if, despite its conformation to and echoing of prose, it can produce poetry (even poetry like Hope's own) far more vivid and responsive to nuance and idea than the poetry under consideration in "The Rhapsodic Fallacy." Such is the case with Wilner's "Bat Cave," which achieves its harmony and surprise by the successive adoption of the arguments (some defensive) hinging on clearly defined point of view. So, too, Robert Pinsky's "At Pleasure Bay" moves beyond the mere surface of sadness by investing the lyric with historical as well as sacramental design. John Ashbery's "Fragment" takes on the appalling vantage of a figure who rejects the autonomic perceptions much the same way an insomniac resists sleep.

There is a long poem published by John Koethe in the *Gettysburg Review* (Winter 1989) that emerges from a clear background of literary indebtedness to Ashbery and to Wallace Stevens while embodying the virtues of rigorous independence. While "The Constructor" is evidently a poem about the toils of poetic inheritance, it also explores the charms that release the poet from any inherited way of thinking. In so doing, of course, it also recapitulates the revolutionary renunciations that are solidly in the romantic tradition—although Koethe's particular renunciations are tentative and exploratory. Aloofness in this poem has a curiously affectionate tinge or, rather, takes a curiously determined route through a series of self-examinations about the meaning of living in the present in which the ideas of love and responsible belonging are always prominent, even as the awareness of sentimental temptation is unremitting. In "The Constructor's" 209 lines of suspended animation before the mystery of

objectless recollection, the possibility of reduction to the banal and incomplete comes to resemble that of rescue from these conditions:

> Mustn't there be something to
> This tenderness I feel encroaching on my mind, these
> Quiet intimations of a generous, calm hour insensibly
> Approaching day by day through outwardly constricted
> Passages confused by light and air?   190

Writing of this high order has, in some ways, already resolved the romantic dilemma at the level of both feeling and word. Depth of self-knowledge
brings transcendence within reach—if not for appropriation, at least for
the purpose of scrutiny. Just as there is no irritable reaching after large
phrases, so there is, for all the pathos of the longing, no fundamental
dissatisfaction with feeling. Emotions are not disappointing. The poet
here only experiences increasingly elementary waves of doubt—expressed,
indeed, in wavelike language and long, efflorescing syntax—about the
action of time upon his perception of the future. And even here, it is not
some absolute operation he finds himself desiring through his "long,
erotic sentences," but the return of the illusion of an open horizon of
years:

> I thought I felt a moment opening like an unseen flower   125
> Only to close again, as though something had called it,
> Or as though, beneath the disaffected surface, something
> Limpid and benevolent were moving at a level of awareness
> I could not yet find; and so I let the moment slide away.

Koethe's most credible and moving achievements as a poet are those
moments when he steps over the edge of the known into what he cannot
entirely imagine—and "a different way of seeing" seems to shape itself.
Intuiting an area or space in which his experience, by analogy, might be
unfolding, he rope-dances over a precipice of uncertainty as to what exists
behind the personality: "a part that all along had / Been too close to feel
begins to breathe as it becomes / Increasingly transparent." When he reads
literary works, he wonders why, the closer he comes, the blander and less
permeable art's surfaces become. He tries to fasten on the image of a
person, prepared even to accept that persistent ghost of the self as the
sort of ordinary individual who once had hope of some higher endeavor,
but then, when he readdresses the inchoate, blent, hovering disappearance
of mind in body, that personal image full of "numinous desires" refuses
to politely disappear:

> There was this chorus of strange vapors, with a name
> Something like mine, and someone trying to get free.
> You start to see things almost mythically, in tropes   170
> And figurations taken from the languages of art—to
> See your soul as sliding out of chaos, changeable,
> Twice blessed with vagueness and a heart, the feelings
> Cumbersome and unrefined, the mood a truly human one
> Of absolute bewilderment; and floating up from that   175
> To an inanimate sublime, as though some angel said
> *Come with me,* and you woke into a featureless and
> Foolish paradise your life had gradually become; or
> From a dense, discordant memory into a perfect world
> As empty as an afterthought, and level as a line.   180

One model for the unfettered elevation of viewpoint in "The Constructor" is probably the montage—or rather, double exposure—method of the Russian modernist El Lissitzky, whose most frequently reproduced work, a self-portrait from 1924, bears this title. For this artist, unlike many of his avant-garde peers, preferred to "see through" the same photographic plate rather than to cut-and-paste images of different media. The images are soulful and haunting in a way that seems dependent on the successive intrusions of light through the prior, or continuous, surface: As metaphor and method for consciousness, luminous face and glinting cityscape come to the same upper plane almost simultaneously. Eye and avenue, post and figure, wet cobble and a steady moisture like tears settle out to the same depth, converging and confirming one another in a vision whose content is an ineffably poignant emptiness. Like the luminescent throngs of presences in El Lissitzky, the "sweet, hypnotic motions of a life" of connectedness with others of which John Koethe writes, with their "merely illusory" sense of weight and "consequence," sometimes inadvertently survive the knowledge that there is no comprehensible way for them to coexist with his awareness. Yet "[t]hey calm the days / With undirected passion," he writes at the poem's very close,

> and the nights with music,
> Hiding them at first, then gradually revealing them
> So differently—these things I thought I'd never   205
> Have—simply by vanishing together one by one, like
> Breaths, like intermittent glimpses of some incomplete,
> Imperfect gratitude. How could this quiet feeling
> Actually exist? Why do I feel so happy?

Once the personal god of overarching meanings, personal election, and stark romantic "recklessness" has departed, there remains the necessary angel of an ineradicable sense of blessedness, caught on the wing, unreasonable, unprovable, unarguable, and summoned in verse as rhetorically subtle, transparently honest, and melodious as there is to be found in any young poet now writing.

Still, of the poetry of the past two decades that attempts to reintegrate some of the virtues of prose with those of verse, for example the work of the Wintersian school and of poets in their late forties and early fifties like C. K. Williams, Anne Winters, and Frank Bidart, I would be tempted to entertain Bonnie Costello's telling maxim: "Prosaism haunts poetry at *all* its entrances."[9] Although these are all poets I admire very much, I may still regret in their work the want of the enormous *range* of energies, where style is concerned, of such paragons of rhetorical poise and visionary sophistication as Eliot, Ovid, Kafka, and Dante. Indeed, it would appear that even in much fervent and accomplished descriptive, meditative, and conversational verse today, mental and imaginative constructs are hobbled by a limited knowledge of and attention to discursive and rhetorical devices (figures of speech) and tropes (figures of thought), not to mention a flattened prosody. This latter limitation is compounded by the fact that the lineation, typography, and use of white space to control rhythm and attention too often come down, at best, to a mildly appealing visual and cognitive pattern or, at worst, to a secret (*not shared*) compositional aid.

Actually, I can think of no poet today, with the possible exception of Charles O. Hartman, who comes remotely close to the blistering mastery of syntax, rhetoric, and diction characteristic of the pyrotechnical side of John Ashbery. Ashbery is a true and dedicated genius, an inheritor of the great symbolist experiment who dazzles the senses as well as the attentive mind. He has admirably extended what poetry is capable of saying. But his ironies, apt though they may be for the times, force him into endless closed circuits and lonely sunken labyrinths, like the minotaur's. In some respects, as I have hinted in the chapter on Ashbery above, he is like the brilliant and idiosyncratic Marianne Moore, but more elusive and transparent; he is more a force unto himself. Imitating him gets many an imitator washed up, even if one or another of his stylistic tricks is accurately parodied. In this regard, I think John Koethe and Douglas Crase form a serious and innovative responsorial Ashbery school, but one that stresses the elegiac element in Ashbery's cognitive orchestration. Nevertheless, these adept and often poignant younger meditative writers show that, if imitation has any significance with regard to Ashbery, it means that his art can be imitated only from within, by following his ambiguities as well as his learning, reading voluminously and eclectically as he has read, hearkening to his mentors, looking at painting, thinking in French, brooding over the rhythms of the imagination and the drain of daily time, and taking it all so lightly there is never any hint of ponderosity.

But so one behaves with any model: One tries to reexperience the writer's sensibility, to think as and why he or she thinks. What I believe needs refreshment is the idea of such an apprenticeship. As part of a young poet's training, I would first of all encourage the apprentice to learn to discuss, which means practice in the skills that attach to the discursive mode as Hope delineates them so that a base can be learned from which to rise and range. To this end, I would also urge the study of logic, ethics, rhetoric, and metaphysics, and would highly recommend a good knowledge of European art and languages, not to mention extended periods of complete silence.

Whether or not conditions are now propitious for the recovery of such discipline as has clearly nourished the brilliant ruminations of a poet such as Koethe, surely the upholding of value in this way is preferable to the more or less explicit hisorical determinism of several of the respondents, a determinism most baldly stated by Charles Molesworth:

> Arguments like Kinzie's, with their . . . call for discursive poetry, the values of clear thought, and the responsibilities of a public rhetoric, are just whis-tlings in the dark. We get the sort of poems we deserve, and if what we all too often get is an exacerbated individual ego mired in alienation then it's because that's what history and society offer us at this juncture.

I myself am mistrustful of pieties about the social and historical conditions that legitimize the status quo. The positions taken by the extreme literary sociologists (whether the Marxist who looks back or the disciple-of-the-new who looks forward) are suspect to the extent that they posit "forces" and "waves" that bond styles to groups and periods rather than making any direct critical estimation of poetic content, its virtue or its truth. The reason "history and society offer us" the working of the ego and the tiny fireworks of perceptual romanticism instead of literature that engages on all levels is in part owing to the inertia of the institutionalized writer—what Molesworth earlier in his reply calls the "compromised pro-fessionalism" of writers' workshops (I think Bonnie Costello and Paul Breslin would both agree). As Alan Shapiro argues, the workshop syn-drome—the kind of indulgent and ahistorical poetry produced by the various schools, as well as the debasement of critical discourse that comes from the system of what might be called protective reviewing of friend by friend—can with effort be corrected. For if the workshop is part of history, so are its critics. Speaking up may change the "sort of poems we deserve," so that, at last, we may deserve better. If work is done to improve not only the discernment with which poetry is read but also the subtlety and sophistication with which poets speak, we may see not just a smarter and finer generation of poets but even a more brilliant generation of readers to appreciate and cause them.

Several respondents suggest that one should not be harsh on mediocre writers. Stephen Yenser cautions against criticizing work to which one has not surrendered oneself, to which I can only reply that it is both dangerous and fruitless to surrender oneself to sentimentality and kitsch—while, at the same time, it is important to give reasons for calling kitsch kitsch. To critics who assert that it is indelicate and wrongheaded to censure, I would again suggest that what I censure is lack of discipline and not mature aesthetic choice. Naturally, one always takes a risk in making such an estimation; one critic's censure is another's celebration. But readers can learn to estimate critics, too, and to judge their arguments by the rules of evidence, as well as by the "rules" of empathy alongside rigor. Moreover, Auden's proscription against dwelling on overboiled cabbage to the exclusion of decent cuisine is only partially relevant to contemporary letters, inasmuch as there is such a widespread belief that overboiled cabbage is delectable. The education of the palate to better and more nourishing food inevitably involves the weaning of the human subject from the food that is so familiar, so unchallenging, and so addictive. There comes a time to take the dish away and, as Melville wrote of Jonah, to appall rather than please, to court dishonor, to preach the truth to the face of falsehood.

Marjorie Perloff has a similar argument: Art is always ninety percent watery roughage; why waste one's time chewing it over? Why not, instead, offer as corrective a variety of poetry at a still further remove from the tastes that have been so clearly weakened by current practices?—which for Perloff means dismissing lyric, along with rhyme and meter, and the notion of genre, and championing the work of experimental writers who have hitherto hunted in the twilight between poetry and theory. Although she is willing to estimate and dismiss the outmoded conventions of romanticism and modernism (symbolism and pure poetry—*not* the products of Williams, Pound, or Zukofsky), her favored "language poets" are not evaluatively discriminated from each other.

Now Harold Rosenberg also thought description and clear presentation were the primary task of the critic of the new, but he suggested that one must answer the question " 'What is it?'—the question of identity . . . in such a way as to distinguish between a real novelty and a fake one," and that such an answer to the question of identity "*is itself an evaluation.*"[10] This is a distinction that cannot be maintained, however, when the *kind* of experiment is a recoil from standards, valued for itself, while the individual literary production is merely a helpful illustration of the preapproved class. Any difference between a real and a fake novelty thus disappears. So I would argue also with Bonnie Costello's defense of "process" and freely emerging forms: In order to decide that something is good, to establish a standard (even a standard vis-à-vis process), one has to be prepared to identify what is less good, to rank, to place within a hierarchy. Otherwise the real novelty will have no force.

Paul Breslin's insightful defense of "My Weariness of Epic Proportions"[11] as a "mutant pastoral" brings up a related issue having to do with the way time transforms genres like an inexorable glacier. It is Breslin's claim that, although the Simic poem is nothing more than a minor *jeu,* it can nevertheless stand in the shadow of the great debate over "poetic kinds" precisely by mimicking the turn from epic and state attitudes to pastoral and personal ones. The point is well taken. The difficulty is that one cannot study Charles Simic to learn anything one does not already know—about the possibilities in pastoral, for example. One can only study genuine attempts to reincorporate pastoral elements and attitudes into new forms of composition (Auden and Ashbery abound in examples) to get a sense of what pastoral is and has been. Then, perhaps, with this knowledge in mind, one might return to the little Simic poem and diagnose its wan demeanor.

Simic and the other poets quoted in these exchanges have recoiled from established forms to such a degree that, in Alan Shapiro's apt metaphor, they have very little left in the way of reliable conventions to perceive the world *through.* Or, as Theodore Roethke wrote to Léonie Adams at Bennington (enclosing a syllabus for a course in which he would spend two weeks on the tetrameter couplet alone): " 'Form' is regarded not as a neat mould to be filled, but rather as a sieve to catch certain kinds of material."[12] The packinghouse poem (quoted by Charles Molesworth), although forcefully defended by Stephen Yenser, has no sieve to catch much meaning in, only a funnel that directs the flow the same way at the same rate all the time—a funnel of social consciousness and pity that may at best, for the careful observer like Yenser, be seen to yield a little rust when the water is acidic.

Whether fumbling toward the first recognitions of the tribe or exploring the derivative labyrinths of temporal dilation and sequentiality, too much of the energy in contemporary poetry (whether canonical or extramural) has been spent addressing language as something alien and inscrutable—like something unearthed from a tomb whose purpose the writer no longer recognizes. Thus a compass might be tried on a loaf of bread, while an ornamental comb might be taken for some kind of calendar.

There are not only better ways to cut bread and tell time: There are better uses for these rediscovered objects that, by placing them back in a continuous perspective with the past, would irradiate their true designs as well as helping distinguish ornamental flourishes from scientific, sacramental, and even aesthetic purposes. By the same token, there are better uses for language than the enforced naïveté or blind self-referential play. To assume that language is the only telling index of its own use is at once to sanctify its abstract qualities (syntax in germ but not in use) and to posit some stereotypical "normal user" whose little impulses are dwarfed by the enormity of the expressive medium, as if language ran on automatic pilot, sweeping its user away. Furthermore, as Santayana says, "the normal, too, is pathological when it is not referred to the ideal."

Although it may be tonic for us to recall Foucault's strictures against an overfondness for the author's personality, it is neither helpful nor true to assume that the author's personality, intentions, power, and will are fictions that are inert in governing the writing of texts. I think most artists would strenuously object to Foucault's claim that " 'profundity' or 'creative' power, [the author's] intentions or the original inspiration manifested in writing" are little more than "projections . . . of our ways of handling texts."[13] However different the religious beliefs and social ease and individual forwardness of artists in time, only one kind of individual—someone intimately possessed of personality, if not with the egoism that often comes with it—ever composes poems worth saving and rereading. I have in mind the way one instinctively averts the mind from such arguments about "handling texts" in reading over again lines like these:

> This ae nighte, this ae nighte,
>   Everie nighte and alle,
> Fire and sleete and candle lighte,
>   And Christe receive thy saule.

Or these:

> O lang, lang may the ladies stand
>   Wi' their gold kems in their hair,
> Waiting for their ain dear lords,
>   For they'll see them na mair.

Or these:

> Barely a twelvemonth after
> The seven days war that put the world to sleep,
> Late in the evening the strange horses came.[14]

Denis Dutton, editor of the journal *Philosophy and Literature,* believes that questions about intention will persist in importance. We must, he says, acknowledge the value of the works to the makers of the works: To do so is not to refuse to see "the extent to which traditions, and indeed language itself, help to 'make' texts," but it might, "contra Beardsley, find a legitimate place for authorial intention in criticism, and it might, contra Barthes, set some limits on what we find worthwhile to talk about in criticism."[15]

The artist-intellectual Iris Murdoch, writing three decades ago, put the situation in terms more dire. Inasmuch as the problem is one of a limited idea of personality, so its solution has to be more internally motivated than the adoption of new skills. She suggests that the idea of sensuous immediacy is (more than simply a trend in vitiated prose or verse) a phenomenon of the social and ethical realm. Immediacy, isolation, and sincerity alike have been dictated to the modern writer by the eighteenth-century philosophical heritage that puts a "lonely self-contained individual" at the moral and cognitive center of the universe. In place of flexible concepts, we the inheritors are given implacable images, such as that of "a brave naked will surrounded by an easily comprehended empirical world."[16] To counteract this reduction, rigidification, and flattening, Murdoch recommends that we allow the incomplete: "it is through an enriching and deepening of concepts that moral progress [and imaginative vision] take[] place"; rather than a fixed shape, our sense of reality must shift about, becoming a "rich receding background" for thought and attention (20). Neither aesthetic crystal nor vapid journalism, the work of the imaginative is contingent, unpredictable, expressive; it refuses the *mere* consolations of form, while recognizing that no art can shape itself without an armature of idea.

It is something like this expressive ideal to which Julia Randall's response reflexively turns. There is no doubt that Randall speaks for many great poets when she regrets the failure of subjective vision in the nineteenth century, just as she speaks with the generations of poets in mind when, with the long, comfortable perspective of someone at home in the tradition, she admonishes: "without music poetry resigns all claim to give that pleasure which initially draws us into the magic circle of symbolic form." Julia Randall is correct: The aim is song. Contrary to Terence Diggory's careful and sympathetic response, I do not consider the mimetic attitude[17] the primordial or preoccupying one for us now, although its lessons should be learned *first* by the poets to come. In the same way, I think the pragmatic theorists' focus on the poem as something contrived with skill can guide the apprentice writer by forcing consideration of the local working, as well as the logical implication, of exempla, trope, and

ornamentation. The objective theories of art as an antiscientific hetero-
cosm or second nature that has its own weather and its own laws can
serve to reflect how every poet in every poem acts "autotelically," changing
the contours of language and of thought by compulsions intrinsic to
the work, and hence giving knowledge of objective theory a pleasantly
recollective function.

But at the deepest level, I am with Randall an upholder of the expressive theory of art. The program I have sketched with the help of A. D.
Hope and others is designed to make poetry of the highest and most
heart-piercing kind possible again, for one must learn to speak well and
leisurely again before learning what kind of song there is to sing. As the
true end and glory of art, I believe in the bias that animates the work of
Spenser, Wordsworth, Yeats, Rilke, Stevens, Bogan, and Walcott, and of
lesser-known contemporaries like William Hunt, John Koethe, and Julia
Randall herself, that all poetry originates in beauty, music, and longing,
and in something almost not namable by the waking intelligence:

THE LAST HOUR

Joy of the one who turned back,
who will do all for the beloved,
in this plateau of intoxication and pain.
Envision only the moment of turning—
will the loved one gaze back at us,
eyes lift upward and welcome us,
even our soiled hands? Blood
filling our thoughts, clouding our minds?
Will that joy be welcomed in the last hour?

In this section from the poem still in manuscript by Chicago poet William
Hunt, *One Hundred and Eleven Leaves,* which comes closer than that of
any American poet to the uncompromising interiority of Paul Célan, the
image of Orpheus and Eurydice is rewoven with the death that fills and
clouds the forward-looking consciousness. It is a reimagining as hopeless
and without redemption as anything by the name of joy can be. And yet
the saying, the singing, is carried forth on lines of great purity. Hunt is
suspended between a moment of genuine rhapsody from which song
flows, and a moment of inconsequence, hiatus, bafflement, in which all a
poet is authentically capable of telling belongs to the movements of brooding or quiet conversation in the shadow of a coming ordeal.

By such a fierce measure as that for the true rhapsode, which permits
only a handful of poets to speak with absolute gravity and transparency
of the business of the soul—by such a gauge many poets are excluded:
In this light, W. H. Auden and the frequently touching Howard Nemerov

become figures of sharp-edged dissenting demonic clarity rather to one side of the main procession of stricken souls like Paul Célan, Thomas Hardy, and Emily Dickinson, the holy cripples on the pilgrimage, and Edwin Muir, their luminous guardian with his uncanny angelic wholeness. All good lyric poets are at least slightly distorted by the task: One learns to take their queerness with their ravishing grace. What is more important is that the eloquence of the good lyric poet is to be judged only by and against the truth, in which judgment we recognize the highest function of mimesis.

I support the appeal of the British novelist Murdoch to the young writers coming along, echoing the call with which Hope, Perloff, and others address the times:

> Literature can arm us against consolation and fantasy and can help us to recover from the ailments of Romanticism. If it can be said to have a task, now, that surely is its task. But if it is to perform it, prose must recover its former glory, eloquence and discourse must return. I would connect eloquence with the attempt to speak the truth.[18]

If for "prose" we could read "poetry"—after all the greater and more embracing art—Iris Murdoch's formulation of the task facing the writer is the most accurate and fiendishly demanding of them all. For this is the call for a recuperation of stamina, variety, and valor in the work of imagination. It is the poet's calling.

Notes

Introduction

1. In this introductory meditation, female pronouns occur in place of either the male pronoun or some awkward hybrid to refer to the poet and to the sources of the basic energies of poetry. It is because I am composing these studies from the perspective of both critic and poet that I reflexively imagine the poet as "she."

2. Eavan Boland, "Outside History," *American Poetry Review* (March/April 1990). Hereafter cited as *APR*.

3. Wheelwright, *The Burning Fountain: A Study in the Language of Symbolism* (Bloomington: Indiana University Press, 1968), p. 15.

4. Allen Grossman, in the "winter conversations" in *Against Our Vanishing* [interviews conducted by Mark Halliday, 1980] (Boston: Rowantree, 1981). John Koethe also notes the prevalence of the call for the preservation of the person in Grossman's *Summa Lyrica: A Primer of Commonplaces in Speculative Poetics,* published as a special edition of the *Western Humanities Review* (Spring 1990); Koethe, "Contrary Impulses: The Tension between Poetry and Theory," *Critical Inquiry* (Autumn 1991): 74. Grossman's *Summa* and the interviews have been collected and reissued in 1992 by Johns Hopkins University Press as *The Sighted Singer: Two Works on Poetry for Readers and Writers.*

Chapter One

1. According to Edgar Wind, it was A. C. Bradley in his *Oxford Lectures on Poetry* (1909) who was the first to link Poe's denigration of the long poem to the logic of fragmentation also at work in many major romantic poems. Wind further traces the cult of the fragment through the French and German symbolists. Edgar Wind, *Art and Anarchy* (New York: Alfred A. Knopf, 1964), pp. 35–51, 150.

2. W. H. Auden would ask us to excuse the exaggeration in Poe's ideas on brevity by considering the audience to which these ideas were communicated: "Poe's condemnation of the long poem and of the didactic or true poem is essentially a demand that the poets of his time be themselves and admit that epic themes and intellectual or moral ideas did not in fact excite their poetic faculties and that what really interested them were emotions of melancholy, nostalgia, puzzled yearning, and the like that could find their proper expression in neither epic nor epigram but in lyrics of moderate length. Poe was forced to attack all long poems on principle, to be unfair, for example, to *Paradise Lost* or *An Essay on Criticism,* in order to shake the preconceived notions of poets and public that to be important a poet must write long poems and give bardic advice." Introduction to Edgar

Allen Poe, *Selected Prose, Poetry and "Eureka,"* ed. W. H. Auden (New York: Holt, Rinehart & Winston, 1950), p. xii.

3. Alec Derwent Hope, "The Discursive Mode: Reflections on the Ecology of Poetry," *The Cave and the Spring: Essays on Poetry* (Chicago: University of Chicago Press, 1965), p. 2.

4. Charles Simic, "My Weariness of Epic Proportions," *Austerities* (New York: George Braziller, 1982), p. 50.

5. Hope, p. 3.

6. Geoffrey Tillotson, "Eighteenth-Century Poetic Diction," *Essays and Studies* 25 (1939): 62.

7. The eighteenth-century view is thus closed to us, since verse was then seen as the heightening of educated conversation. See Donald Davie, *Purity of Diction in English Verse* [1952] (London: Routledge & Kegan Paul, 1967), pp. 1–28.

8. Meyer H. Abrams labels the four main schools the mimetic, pragmatic, expressive, and objective in his article on "Poetry, Theories of" in the *Princeton Encyclopedia of Poetry and Poetics,* ed. Alex Preminger, Frank J. Warnke, and O. B. Hardison, Jr. (Princeton, N.J.: Princeton University Press, 1965), pp. 640–48. Timothy Steele gives a different reason than Abrams's (and Wordsworth's) for the casting off of mimetic and pragmatic functions: ". . . by the end of the eighteenth century, Kant had given, in the system of his three critiques, philosophical legitimacy to the study of aesthetics. In the three critiques, it will be remembered, Kant divided the faculties of the mind into pure reason, practical reason, and judgment, and he identified the first of these with The True (metaphysics), the second of these with The Good and The Useful (ethics), and the third with The Beautiful (aesthetics and teleology). This division liberated art from the demands of ethical evaluation and moral purpose in much the same manner that the sciences had earlier been liberated from the weight of ecclesiastical imperatives and obsolete theory. And increasingly in the nineteenth century, one finds artists and critics contending that art is, like science, an essentially autonomous enterprise." Steele, "Sciences of Sentiment: Art as Science in the Modern Period," unpublished manuscript, p. 5. Since the writing of this essay in 1983, Timothy Steele has subsequently articulated at much greater length Kant's relation to the practice of modern poets in "Free Verse and Aestheticism," chap. 4 of *Missing Measures: Modern Poetry and the Revolt Against Meter* (Fayetteville: University of Arkansas Press, 1990), pp. 171–223.

9. Abrams, p. 644, my emphasis.

10. The terms are Gerald Bruns's, *Modern Poetry and the Idea of Language* (New Haven: Yale University Press, 1974), passim.

11. "A 1 Pound Stein," *Selected Essays of William Carlos Williams* (New York: New Directions, 1954), pp. 162, 163.

12. William Carlos Williams, "Between Walls," *Selected Poems* (New York: New Directions, 1969), p. 84.

13. See n. 2 above.

14. Indeed, Robert von Hallberg cheerfully asserts that what he calls the "Bare Style" of poets like W. S. Merwin and Mark Strand is actually further proof of the health of the audience for poetry in America; because of its ease of consump-

tion, von Hallberg implies, this poetry makes itself accessible to greater numbers. *American Poetry and Culture 1945–1980* (Cambridge, Mass.: Harvard University Press, 1985), chap. 1, "Audience, Canon," particularly pp. 10–21.

15. Linda Gregerson, "Aubade," *Fire in the Conservatory* (Port Townsend, Wash.: Dragon Gate, 1982), p. 39.

16. Catherine Rutan, "Woman in the Rain," *Georgia Review* (Spring 1981): 124.

17. See the discussion of the legacy of Stevens below, "The Romance of the Perceptual."

18. *To a Blossoming Pear Tree* (New York: Farrar, Straus & Giroux, 1977).

19. William Carlos Williams, "St. Francis Einstein of the Daffodils," *The Collected Earlier Poems of William Carlos Williams* (New York: New Directions, 1951), p. 380.

20. Gary Snyder, *Axe Handles* (San Francisco: North Point Press, 1983).

21. In *The Occasions of Poetry: Essays in Criticism and Autobiography,* by Thom Gunn (London: Faber & Faber, 1982).

22. *New York Review of Books,* 31 March 1983, p. 10.

23. Stanley Plumly, "Virginia Beach," *APR* (March/April 1980): 15.

24. The selection is from Graham's volume *Erosion* (Princeton, N.J.: Princeton University Press, 1983).

25. Chuck Rosenberg, "Landfall," *APR* (March/April 1981): 33.

26. Robert Hass, "Santa Lucia," *Praise* (New York: Ecco Press, 1979), pp. 22–23.

27. In "The Word as Such," *APR* (May/June 1984).

28. Mark Strand, "The Room," *Darker* (New York: Atheneum, 1979), p. 9. Strand and the school of "lyrical" surrealists will be studied in greater detail in "The Romance of the Perceptual" below.

29. William Logan, "Children," *Sad-Faced Men* (Boston: David R. Godine, 1982), p. 2.

30. "In Sleep," ibid., p. 3.

31. Leslie Ullmann, "The Woman at the Desk," *Natural Histories* (New Haven: Yale University Press/Yale Younger Poets, 1979), p. 25.

Chapter Two

1. *The Collected Poems of Theodore Roethke* (Garden City, N.Y.: Anchor/Doubleday, 1975), p. 3.

2. Louise Bogan, *The Blue Estuaries: Poems 1923–1968* (New York: Farrar, Straus & Giroux, 1968), p. 109.

3. Ruth Limmer, ed., *Journey Around My Room: The Autobiography of Louise Bogan* (New York: Viking, 1980); Theodore Roethke, *Straw for the Fire: From the Notebooks of Theodore Roethke 1943–1963,* ed. David Wagoner (Garden City, N.Y.: Doubleday, 1972, 1980).

4. See Elizabeth Frank, *Louise Bogan: A Portrait* (New York: Columbia University Press, 1986), p. 226.

5. Ralph J. Mills, Jr., ed., *Selected Letters of Theodore Roethke* (Seattle: University of Washington Press, 1968).

6. "Otto," *The Far Field* (1964), in *Collected Poems*, p. 216.

7. Ruth Limmer, ed., *What the Woman Lived: Selected Letters of Louise Bogan 1920–1970* (New York: Harcourt Brace Jovanovich, 1973).

8. In a parody questionnaire of 1939. *Journey Around My Room*, p. xix.

9. "For how can you compete, / Being honour bred, with one / Who, were it proved he lies, / Were neither shamed in his own / Nor in his neighbours' eyes?" *Responsibilities* (1914), in *The Collected Poems of W. B. Yeats* (New York: Macmillan, 1956), p. 107. This deft and impassioned counterpoint of syntax with line is the very opposite of Roethke's cadential end-stopping in "Open House" (and many others of his rhymed lyrics).

10. "A Note on the Scottish Ballads," in *Latitudes*, by Edwin Muir (New York: Huebsch, 1924), pp. 12–30; "Hardy and the Ballads," in *The Occasions of Poetry*, pp. 77–105.

11. This and the following two quotations are from p. 29 of "A Note on the Scottish Ballads."

12. Muir would insist that the Scottish ballads "achieve great poetry by an unconditionality which rejects, where other literatures use, the image," p. 18.

13. See Frank, pp. 268–69.

14. Ibid., pp. 252–53.

15. *What the Woman Lived*, p. 136. This letter is quoted in part by Elizabeth Frank in her discussion of "Song for a Lyre," Frank, p. 269.

16. From a journal entry; quoted in *Journey Around My Room*, p. 49.

17. Williamson, *Introspection and Contemporary Poetry* (Cambridge, Mass.: Harvard University Press, 1984).

18. See C. S. Lewis, *The Discarded Image* [1964] (Cambridge University Press, 1972), pp. 171–73.

19. "Waking Early Sunday Morning" [1965] in *Near the Ocean*, by Robert Lowell (New York: Farrar, Straus & Giroux, 1967). Later in the essay I also quote from the 1966 Farrar, Straus & Giroux combined edition of *Life Studies* (1959) and For the Union Dead (1964).

20. Lowell's autobiographical prose piece in *Life Studies*, "91 Revere Street," is apposite to the poetic pattern of bravado, exhaustion, and retreat.

21. Stephen Yenser elaborates his important corollary insight that "Waking Early Sunday Morning" develops diurnally as well, and that it parallels the progress of the morning church service. *Circle to Circle: The Poetry of Robert Lowell* (Berkeley: University of California Press, 1975), pp. 249–60.

22. "Waking Early Sunday Morning" was originally published in *The New York Review of Books*, 5 August 1965, p. 3. The madness and the china doorknobs are reminiscent of descriptions of his father in "91 Revere Street."

23. One feels again here the urge in Lowell *away* from the known toward the general. This impression is strengthened when one compares the relevant stanzas from "Waking Early Sunday Morning" to the diminutive warmth in the work of the poet he much admired, Elizabeth Bishop, whose splendid poem on Sundays

in Canada, "Cape Breton" (from *A Cold Spring*, 1955), antedates some of the details in the Lowell. Bishop's narrator is following the path of a bus (prefiguring the narrative strategy of "The Moose" in Bishop's *Geography III*, 1979):

> A small bus comes along, in up-and-down rushes,
> packed with people, even to its step.
> . . . .
> It passes the closed roadside stand, the closed schoolhouse,
> where today no flag is flying
> from the rough-adzed pole topped with a white china doorknob.
> It stops, and a man carrying a baby gets off,
> climbs over a stile, and goes down through a small steep meadow,
> which establishes its poverty in a snowfall of daisies,
> to his invisible house beside the water.

See Bishop, *The Complete Poems 1927–1979* (New York: Farrar, Straus & Giroux, 1983), p. 68. Here the things and the gestures are suffused with warmth and astonishing, even mysterious exactness (why does the *man* have the baby? how do we know the house lies below the meadow?); in Lowell, one feels, there is by contrast the precision of stereotype, and little love.

24. Marjorie Perloff is especially sensitive to this class of images. She also notes the peculiar prevalence of references to being off-balance, uncertain on one's feet, or stepping tentatively, as versions of giving up or yielding to the strong of the earth, especially in *Life Studies* and *For the Union Dead*. It's the animals and the insurance brokers who stand their ground. See the quotation above from stanza three of "Waking Early," where the smallfry are "casual, sure of foot." Perloff, *The Poetic Art of Robert Lowell* (Ithaca: Cornell University Press, 1973).

25. The rhymes of Lowell's last stanza do not keep to tetrameter couplets. Perhaps the *abba* quatrain envelope sounded more ironclad than another couplet pair, and acted for his purpose the way a couplet would at the end of a sonnet, or a tail line in terza rima. I suspect, however, that this was the only way he had to keep the orotund "monotonous sublime" for last.

26. Jerome Mazzaro's thorough examination of sources in Lowell's early verse and his assessment of the meditation-structure of his thought are hardly impugned by my addition of Augustine to the company of Sts. Ignatius and Bernard of Clairvaux. See *The Poetic Themes of Robert Lowell* (Ann Arbor: University of Michigan Press, 1965).

27. W. H. Auden, "Writing," *The Dyer's Hand and Other Essays* (New York: Vintage, 1968), p. 27.

28. Anne Sexton, *Selected Poems of Anne Sexton*, ed. Diane Wood Middlebrook and Diana Hume George (Boston: Houghton Mifflin, 1988).

29. Sandra M. Gilbert, *Blood Pressure: Poems* (New York: W. W. Norton, 1988).

30. Jim Powell, *It Was Fever That Made the World* (Chicago: University of Chicago Press, 1989).

31. John N. Morris, *A Schedule of Benefits* (New York: Atheneum, 1987).

Chapter Three

1. Like Nathaniel West, Jarrell, especially in *The Lost World* poems, tends to think of himself as coming from California (which actually he did not—rather he came from Tennessee) which is like coming from no place, or from a place that was more like a dream factory or a death factory. It is one of Jarrell's myths about himself.

2. Sven Birkerts, "Randall Jarrell," *Parnassus: Poetry in Review* (Fall 1990): 87.

3. "Children Selecting Books in a Library," *Blood for a Stranger* (New York: Harcourt, Brace & Co., 1942). Because of quotations like this one, whose revised form in *Selected Poems* (1955) strikes me as somehow bland and "off," I have decided to quote from the original volumes. The others are *Little Friend, Little Friend* (New York: Dial Press, 1945), *Losses* (New York: Harcourt, Brace & Co., 1948), *The Seven-League Crutches* (New York: Harcourt, Brace & Co., 1951). Quotations from the subsequent volumes, *The Woman at the Washington Zoo* (1960), *The Lost World* (1965), and the posthumous *New Poems* are taken from *Complete Poems* (New York: Farrar, Straus & Giroux, 1969). There is a great need for a new text of Jarrell's poems placed in chronological order with revision printed en face. Jarrell's own order for poems from the first four volumes is confusingly achronological, though his arrangement highlights some issues. William Pritchard's 1990 edition of the *Selected* (also Farrar, Straus) does not yet answer this need.

4. Identified by Suzanne Ferguson in *The Poetry of Randall Jarrell* (Baton Rouge: Louisiana State University Press, 1971), where she notes Jarrell's comments on the painting in *Art News* 56 (1957).

5. See David Kalstone, *Becoming a Poet: Elizabeth Bishop with Marianne Moore and Robert Lowell* (New York: Farrar, Straus & Giroux, 1989), p. 118.

6. Simon's review, "Randall Jarrell: Failure in Success," appeared in the *New Leader* (May 14–28, 1990): 13–17. It contains such statements as: "Most of Jarrell's poems read to me like prose outlines of a poem yet to be written–by someone else." His citations are damning, to be sure; but as I say, Jarrell should not be represented only by "The Next Day."

7. Karl Shapiro, on editing *Poetry*, in *The Little Magazine in America: A Modern Documentary History*, ed. Elliott Anderson and Mary Kinzie (New York: Pushcart Press, 1978).

8. Because there are no images of creatures at all.

9. *The Animal Family*, by Randall Jarrell, decorations by Maurice Sendak (New York: Alfred A. Knopf, 1965), pp. 171–79.

10. Bishop, in a 1966 letter about Charles Darwin. Quoted by David Kalstone, "Questions of Memory, Question of Travel" (1977), in Lloyd Schwartz and Sybil P. Estess, eds., *Elizabeth Bishop and Her Art* (Ann Arbor: University of Michigan Press, 1983), p. 6.

11. Interview with George Starbuck, *Ploughshares* 3 (1977), reprinted in Schwartz and Estess; this quotation, p. 325.

12. In this she differs from Marianne Moore, whose language bristles with alertness. T. S. Eliot noted in the *Dial* in 1923 that More had a syncretic language,

"the curious jargon produced in America by universal university education"; Moore, he said, treated satirically "that pleasantry, uneasy, solemn, or self-conscious, which inspires both the jargon of the laboratory and the slang of the comic strip." The terms Eliot notes in Moore's poems are words of art and clichés, like "fractional," "infinitesimal," and "diminished vitality," that have audible echoes in Elizabeth Bishop's work, for example, "maculate," "equinoctial," and "slight disturbances." But on the whole the jargon of pleasantry in Bishop is indebted to the medium of anecdote rather than the medium of satire. Although Bishop is as deliberate as Moore, it is not in bantering the stereotypes: Where Moore bristles, Bishop drifts.

13. Kalstone, *Becoming a Poet*, p. 122.

14. "Love Lies Sleeping," in Elizabeth Bishop, *The Complete Poems* (New York: Farrar, Straus & Giroux, 1983), p. 17

15. "Florida," *Collected Poems*, p. 32.

16. Elizabeth Bishop (with the editors of *Life*) *Brazil* (New York: Time, Inc., 1962), p. 117.

17. Indeed, even the word "cheerful" seemed talismanic. She told Anne Stevenson in 1964: "I don't like heaviness. It seems often to amount to complete self-absorption—like Mann and Wagner. I think one can be cheerful AND profound." Quoted by Lorrie Goldensohn, *Elizabeth Bishop: A Biography of a Poetry* (New York: Columbia University Press, 1991), p. 181.

18. It does appear in *The Collected Prose*, by Elizabeth Bishop, ed. Robert Giroux (New York: Farrar, Straus & Giroux, 1984).

19. "In the Village" (1953) in *Questions of Travel* (New York: Farrar, Straus & Giroux, 1965), pp. 55–56. Also in *The Collected Prose*, pp. 257–58.

20. Kalstone, "Questions of Memory, Questions of Travel," in Schwartz and Estess, p. 17.

21. David Kalstone believes this absorption to be "Wordsworthian in its evasions and circlings," *Becoming a Poet*, p. 121.

22. The "rocky breasts" of the landscape are mentioned as if quasi-maternal, and indeed Goldensohn divines a chronic link between eroticism, maternal abandonment, and willful isolation: "erotic subjects concerning the female never move very far in Bishop's work from issues of parental abandonment and the subsequent development of an uneasy and orphaned selfhood" (p. 65). What I would amend is the hint of waifish helplessness, which her poems never indulge. Instead, Bishop moves about with self-delighting composure among the compensations of her alert, and witty, imagination.

23. Of the three, Bishop is the most inventive, experimenting with end-rhyme at various intervals and for various line lengths and runovers, while Moore can almost always be relied on to run over, and Jarrell to end stop. See also Penelope Laurans's clear and sympathetic essay, " 'Old Correspondences': Prosodic Transformations in Elizabeth Bishop," in Schwartz and Estess, pp. 75–95.

24. Bonnie Costello, "The Impersonal and the Interrogative in the Poetry of Elizabeth Bishop," in Schwartz and Estess, pp. 109–32.

25. Leo Lionni, "Before Images," *Horn Book Magazine* (November/December 1984): 732; my emphasis.

26. He continues with a crucial proviso: "Obviously, because of the lightning speed of mental time, the recognition of this rudimentary stage in the evolution of images is an almost impossible undertaking." Lionni, p. 732.

27. Quoted by David Lehman, "*In Prison:* A Paradox Regained," in Schwartz and Estess, p. 65.

28. Goldensohn, p. 10.

Chapter Four

1. Miles, *Eras and Modes in English Poetry* [1957] (Westport, Conn.: Greenwood Press, 1976).

2. Wallace Stevens, "Variations on a Summer Day," from *Parts of a World* [1942], *The Collected Poems of Wallace Stevens* (New York: Alfred A. Knopf, 1954), p. 232.

3. A. R. Ammons, *Worldly Hopes* (New York: W. W. Norton, 1982).

4. Hartman, *Free Verse: An Essay on Prosody* (Princeton, N.J.: Princeton University Press, 1980). Intelligent and clear, it is the best book I know on this subject. I am indebted to his analytical method throughout the discussion of Ammons and implicitly whenever the poetic line is at issue.

5. Poets included here are Mark Strand, *The Late Hour* (New York: Atheneum, 1978); Jane Shore, *Eye Level* (Amherst: University of Massachusetts Press, 1977); Peter Everwine, *Keeping the Night* (New York: Atheneum, 1977); Barry Goldensohn, *Uncarving the Block* (Waitsfield, Vt.: Vermont Crossroads Press, 1977); Constance Urdang, *The Picnic in the Cemetery* (New York: George Braziller, 1975).

6. Paul Breslin, "How to Read the New Contemporary Poem," *American Scholar* (Summer 1978): 357–70.

7. All excerpts thus far are from *Portrait,* by Magdalena Abakanowicz (Chicago: Museum of Contemporary Art, 1982).

8. Ted Hughes, *River* (New York: Harper & Row, 1984).

9. Ted Hughes, "Learning to Think," *Poetry in the Making* (London: Faber, 1967), p. 64.

10. This is a phrase from Pablo Neruda, glossed by Ben Belitt. What he has said about one of Neruda's works, in which "the meditative life and the existential datum cohere in one reality," could as easily apply to Ted Hughes and Robert Pinsky as to himself: Neruda's ethos "epitomizes the double mind of Messianic Romanticism: the passion for the infinite and the empirical, the private fable in apocalyptic guise." *Adam's Dream: A Preface to Translation,* by Ben Belitt (New York: Grove Press, 1978), p. 103.

11. Robert Pinsky, *History of My Heart* (New York: Ecco Press, 1984); *The Want Bone* (New York: Ecco Press, 1990).

12. Robert Pinsky, *The Situation of Poetry* (Princeton, N.J.: Princeton University Press, 1976).

13. Ashbery's appearance here will be brief. But he will be given a chapter of his own later in this volume.

14. Vladimir Nabokov, *The Annotated "Lolita,"* rev. ed., ed. Alfred Appel, Jr. (New York: Vintage, 1991), p. 17.

15. In *Adam's Dream,* p. 119.

16. "On Quaking Bog," *Nowhere But Light* [1970]. All quotations from the poems are taken from Belitt's volume *Possessions: Selected Poems 1938–1985* (Boston: David R. Godine, 1986).

17. See J. C. Cooper, *An Illustrated Encyclopedia of Traditional Symbols* (London: Thames & Hudson, 1978), p. 105. Also A. C. Crombie, *Medieval and Early Modern Science,* vol. 1, *Science in the Middle Ages* (New York: Doubleday, 1959), especially the chapters on geology and the technology of the furnace; and E. J. Holmyard, *Alchemy* (Baltimore: Penguin, 1957), passim. The Old Testament Book of Job also obsessively dramatizes the extreme of physical reduction, the dung heap, locale of Job's self-scrutiny and chastisement and spur to his eventual reconciliation with God.

18. Although "bitumen" is also a painter's term for luminous gray, the contexts here and in both "The Cremation" and "On Quaking Bog" suggest a chemical precipitation into hard (bituminous) and liquid or gaseous components.

19. The other is "This Scribe, My Hand," treated at length in a monograph. See Mary Kinzie, "A Servant's Cenotaph: On Ben Belitt," *Salmagundi* (Summer 1990): 12–49.

20. Meyer Schapiro, "On a Painting of Van Gogh" [1946], in his selected papers on *Modern Art, 19th and 20th Centuries* (New York: George Braziller, 1978), pp. 87–100. These excerpts, p. 93.

Chapter Five

1. In addition to poetry, several volumes of nonfiction prose will be brought into the discussion. The volumes are: *The Collected Poems of Howard Nemerov* (Chicago: University of Chicago Press, 1977); *Poetry and Fiction: Essays* (New Brunswick, N.J.: Rutgers University Press, 1963); *Journal of the Fictive Life* (New Brunswick, N.J.: Rutgers University Press, 1965); *Reflexions on Poetry and Poetics* (New Brunswick, N.J.: Rutgers University Press, 1972); and his *Figures of Thought: Speculations on the Meaning of Poetry & Other Essays* (Boston: David Godine, 1978). The best volume of Nemerov's poetry since the *Collected,* called *Sentences* (Chicago: University of Chicago Press, 1982) is also considered. His fiction is noted in passing.

2. Two essays on Wallace Stevens, written before the critical industry adopted Stevens, rank in lucidity and range with Edmund Wilson's early and attentive exposition of *Finnegans Wake.*

3. Cf. "The Weather of the World" (*The Western Approaches,* 1975): "the atmosphere . . . The vast enfolding cortex of the globe . . . a beast / Of water and air, a shaman shifting shape."

4. "Fragment from an Inaugural Address Before the French Academy" (1927), trans. Louise Varèse, from *Selected Writings,* by Paul Valéry (New York: New Directions, 1950), p. 146.

5. Note: "rimed" is probably not a pun with whitened. Nemerov has some

spelling crotchets, among them reflexion for reflection, phantasy for fantasy, artefact for artifact, and rime for rhyme.

6. Robert Boyers, "Howard Nemerov's True Voice of Feeling," *Excursions: Selected Literary Essays* (Port Washington, N.Y.: Kennikat Press, 1977), p. 226.

7. See "Annotations to Sir Joshua Reynolds's Discourses" (1808) and "A Vision of the Last Judgement" (1810), in Geoffrey Keynes, ed., *The Complete Works of William Blake* (London and New York: Oxford University Press, 1969), pp. 453 and 611.

8. "Damned to life again, and the loon's cry" will remind us (given the company) of Coleridge's albatross and of the fact that he abandoned his prose work on the wanderings of Cain to write "The Ancient Mariner."

9. Saint Augustine, *The City of God,* trans. Marcus Dods (New York: Random House, 1950), Book XX.16, p. 735.

10. In 1978 Mr. Nemerov informed me that "the western approaches" was the RAF term for the convoy route south of Iceland, over the top of Ireland (hence past the Skerries), and down the Irish Sea.

11. See Giorgio de Santillana and Herthe von Dechend, *Hamlet's Mill: An Essay on Myth and the Frame of Time* (Boston: Gambit, 1969) for Snorri Sturluson's kenning and its connection to the end of the *Odyssey* (20.103–19) where twelve maidens grind the shepherd's meal. Chapter 6, "Amlodhi's Quern." (Tiresias's prediction about the shapely oar [*Odyssey* 11.112–37] may also be compared with the account in Saxo of Amleth's quip about the steering oar: It was a proper knife to cut the huge ham of the sea.)

12. Compare also Nemerov's poem, "Growing a Ghost" (*The Blue Swallows*).

13. *Poetry* (August 1975). Also in *Figures of Thought* (Boston: Godine, 1978).

14. Nor, despite Bloom's claims in *The Poems of Our Climate,* does Stevens sound like Whitman.

15. Respectively, in the *New Republic,* 16 November 1977, and *Georgia Review* (Winter 1976).

16. Owen Barfield, *Poetic Diction: A Study in Meaning,* rev. ed. (Middletown, Conn.: Wesleyan, 1973 [1927]), p. 96.

17. For the efforts to standardize English meters, which also flattened and demystified them, see John Thompson, *The Founding of English Metre* (New York: Columbia University Press, 1966). Nemerov's experimentation with the English line reveals his desire for a poetry that must be heard. Paul Ramsey (*Parnassus* [Spring/Summer 1976]) details the variations Nemerov introduces into the iambic-pentameter line. Attentive studies like Ramsey's can profitably be read in tandem with Vladimir Nabokov's theory of iambic variations in Russian and English verse in *Notes on Prosody and Abram Gannibal* (Princeton, N.J.: Princeton University Press/Bollingen Series, 1964).

18. Barfield, *Poetic Diction,* p. 148.

19. "A Defence of Poetry" (1821), in *Shelley's Prose,* ed. David Lee Clark (Albuquerque: University of New Mexico Press, 1954), p. 286b.

20. J. V. Cunningham, "The Judge Is Fury" (1947), in *The Exclusions of a Rhyme: Poems and Epigrams* (Chicago: Swallow Press, 1960), p. 43.

Chapter Six

1. This essay touches on the four volumes of *Poems 1965–1975* (1980), but is more closely concerned with Seamus Heaney's work between *North* (1975) and *The Haw Lantern* (1987): *Field Work* (1979), *Sweeney Astray: A Version from the Irish* (1984), and *Station Island* (1985). With one noted exception, quotations from Heaney's prose may be found in *Preoccupations: Selected Prose 1968–1978* (1980). All are published by Farrar, Straus & Giroux.

2. *Field Work* is also haunted by Dante. The two longest poems are the Dante translation called "Ugolino" and "The Strand at Lough Beg," which gives us a new "reading" of Vergil's tender washing of Dante's face with his hands dipped in dew from the grass near the inexhaustible reeds, as Heaney pictures bathing his murdered cousin in the moss strikingly pictured as "Fine as a drizzle out of a low cloud." A third poem, "An Afterwards," is parodically based on Dante (the poet's wife consigns all poets to hell). There are three further allusions in the volume; the one in "Leavings" lightly captures the whole Dantean feeling of fatedness—in the crime, the penance, and the instigating personality—as Heaney wonders how Thomas Cromwell will be punished for the crime of smashing the idols, replacing stained glass in all the chapels of England with clear panes: "Which circle does he tread, / scalding on cobbles, / each one a broken statue's head?"

3. "Lowell's Command" (1986), *The Government of the Tongue: Selected Prose 1978–1987,* by Seamus Heaney (New York: Farrar, Straus & Giroux, 1988), pp. 130–31.

4. Ibid., p. 133.

5. Frances X. Clines, interview with Seamus Heaney, *New York Times Magazine,* 13 March 1983, p. 99.

6. "Requiem for the Croppies," *Door into the Dark* (1969).

7. Breslin, "Robert Lowell: The Historical Self," in his *Psycho-Political Muse: American Poetry Since the Fifties* (Chicago: University of Chicago Press, 1987), p. 59.

8. Clines interview, p. 104.

9. Kavanagh's actual phrase appears in the first "Station Island" poem, where "tinkers camped / under a heeled-up cart."

10. "Kinship," *North* (1975).

11. Lancelot Andrewes (1555–1626), *Works* (Oxford: Oxford University Press, 1854), I, 204. Quoted in Grover Smith, *T. S. Eliot's Poetry and Plays* (Chicago: University of Chicago Press, 1956), p. 310.

12. *Buile Suibhne (The Frenzy of Sweeney), being the Adventures of Suibhne Geilt, A Middle Irish Romance,* ed. and trans. J. G. O'Keeffe (London: Irish Texts Society, 1913).

13. Heaney's liberties in translating other works are just as exotic and unmistakable, revealing his own predilections. The amendments show why he wanted to translate this work, that is, because he thinks he might almost have written it, given these salient substitutions:

In "The Digging Skeleton," he obtrudes upon the grotesque elegance of

Charles Baudelaire's diction (who wrote of *Ecorchés, muscles dépouillés,* and of the foot on the haft of the spade as *pied sanglant et nu*), the gawky Irish reference to muddy ground, "red slobland around the bones."

In "Ugolino," he takes Dante's admittedly macabre allusions to cannibalism at the close of *Inferno* and metaphorizes in his own direction: A head of meat and bones is "some spattered carnal melon"; the brain is "the sweet fruit of the brain"; Ugolino devouring Ruggieri in Hell is "monstrously at rut." Late in the poem, as if a tiny gasket had blown in an overtaxed machine, Heaney turns the condescending reference to Pisa (as a blot of shame on the region where *si* is spoken) into an echoic orgy: "Pisa, your sounds are like a hiss / Sizzling in our country's grassy language."

14. Robert Graves, *The White Goddess: A Historical Grammar of Poetic Myth,* rev. ed. (New York: Farrar, Straus & Giroux, 1966), p. 452.

15. Ciaran Carson, "*Sweeney Astray:* Escaping from Limbo," in Tony Curtis, ed., *The Art of Seamus Heaney* (Chester Spring, Pa.: Dufour Editions, 1985), p. 145. The Curtis anthology is noteworthy for several fine essays, including Carson's, one by Dick Davis on *Door into the Dark,* and a landmark piece by Philip Hobsbaum on *Wintering Out.* This volume is also valuable for reprinting all the manuscript drafts of the poem "North," which illustrate not only Heaney's considerable technical skill—which is to say, his self-knowledge and self-control as a craftsman as he discards dead wood and relineates the verses for a livelier and more supple effect—but also his list toward the discursive: He tries over and over to find a place to insert the adjective "moral" into the "cascade of light," which art's long winter begrudges the poet. Finally he gives up, content to indicate that, well before the moral faculty grows thirsty, even romantic notions of poetic afflatus evade one's reach: "Expect aurora borealis / in the long foray of your art / but no cascade of light."

16. "Midnight," *Wintering Out* (1972).

Chapter Seven

1. Williamson, *Introspection and Contemporary Poetry,* p. 132.

2. See above, Chap. 3, "A New Sweetness: Randall Jarrell and Elizabeth Bishop," pp. 316–17, n. 17.

3. John Ashbery, "Houseboat Days," in his *Houseboat Days* (New York: Penguin, 1977), pp. 38–40.

4. Henry James, *The American Scene* (1907), ed. Leon Edel (reprint, Bloomington: Indiana University Press, 1968), pp. 140–41.

5. Ibid., p. 248.

6. Ibid., p. 273.

7. Ibid., p. 75.

8. Donald Davie, *Purity of Diction in English Verse* (1952; reprint, London: Routledge & Kegan Paul, 1967), p. 96.

9. *The Complete Poems and Plays of T. S. Eliot* (London: Faber & Faber, 1969), p. 195, quoted in Davie (pp. 92–93, n. 27).

10. "Anglo-American Chainpoem," the lines in question by John Hastings and Parker Tyler, in *English and American Surrealist Poetry,* ed. Edward B. Germain (New York: Penguin, 1978), p. 160.

11. See Christine Brooke-Rose, *A Grammar of Metaphor* (London: Secker & Warburg, 1958), pp. 320–23.

12. Frank O'Hara, "Blocks," in Germain, p. 206.

13. John Ashbery, "Self-Portrait in a Convex Mirror," in his *Self-Portrait in a Convex Mirror* (1975; reprint, New York: Penguin, 1976), p. 82.

14. It is fairly clear that, unlike Marianne Moore, John Ashbery is not in the constant process of creating a sensibility that, for all its quirks, is continuous with itself. In the same way, unlike Stevens and Eliot, Ashbery is not imbedded in the self who generates the specifics with which his own poems engage. John Koethe has suggested that Ashbery adopts something closer to a metaphysical than a psychological ego—the latter being Cartesian, the former a variant of the Kantian transcendental subject modified through Wittgenstein. In place of those confidential poetic voices that present the reader with an experiential realm "to which the poet has a privileged means of introspective access," there are in Ashbery "the extreme . . . dislocations . . . that make it impossible to read [his poems] as an autobiographical record of the experiences of a time-bound, self-identical Cartesian ego," and along with these, we have the evidence of "his subject's characteristic impulse to identify or produce an adequate representation of itself while simultaneously distancing itself from every such image, which all become 'other' as soon as they become concrete or clear enough." See Koethe's essay "The Metaphysical Subject of John Ashbery's Poetry," in David Lehman, ed., *Beyond Amazement: New Essays on John Ashbery* (Ithaca: Cornell University Press, 1980), pp. 87–100; these excerpts, pp. 96–97. I would conjecture that the surrealist mode for Koethe would fall somewhere in the middle between dependence on a personal voice and the use of a transcendental subject's voice. This "middle," in fact, is where he locates the sensibility of Frank O'Hara, immersed in perceptions but averse to the illusion of a *self* (pp. 94–95, 97–99).

15. André Breton, "The Spectral Attitudes," in Germain, pp. 117–18.

16. *The Complete Poems and Plays of T. S. Eliot,* p. 193.

17. "Little Gidding," ii, ibid.

18. John Ashbery, "For John Clare," in his *The Double Dream of Spring* (1970; reprint, New York: Ecco Press, 1976), pp. 35–36; my emphasis.

19. Hartman, *Free Verse: An Essay on Prosody,* p. 56.

20. Morris Croll, "The Baroque Style in Prose" (1929), in his *"Attic" and Baroque Prose Style* (Princeton, N.J.: Princeton University Press, 1969), pp. 207–33.

21. Miles, *Eras and Modes in English Poetry,* pp. 2–19.

22. Ibid., p. 16.

23. John Koethe, "The Absence of a Noble Presence," *Verse* (Spring 1991): 26.

24. John Ashbery, "Sortes Virgilianae," in *The Double Dream of Spring,* pp. 74–75.

25. Williamson, p. 140.
26. Ibid.
27. Christine Brooke-Rose, *A Grammar of Metaphor*, pp. 123–31.

Chapter Eight

1. Based on the entry under *cura* in *The White Latin Dictionary*, by John T. White [1928] (Chicago: Follett, 1955), p. 160a.

2. Owen Barfield, "The Meaning of the Word 'Literal,'" in *Metaphor and Symbol: Proceedings of the Twelfth Symposium of the Colston Research Society, University of Bristol*, ed. L. C. Knights and Basil Cottle (London: Butterworths Scientific Publications, 1960), pp. 48–63. This excerpt, p. 55.

3. "The Mirror of Enigmas," in Donald A. Yates and James E. Irby, eds. & trans., *Labyrinths*, by Jorge Luis Borges (New York: New Directions, 1962). p. 212.

4. A version of "Ghost Ship" has appeared in *TriQuarterly* 83 (Winter 1991/ 92): 107–13.

5. From Bogan's 1929 collection *Dark Summer*, collected in *The Blue Estuaries: Poems 1923–1968*, p. 33.

6. It is the second and third of these meanings that collaborate in the second and final stanza of Bogan's poem "When at Last." In this uncollected and undated work, a period of disentangling clarity seems to have succeeded the heat of more savage feeling, but in place of unalloyed relief there ensue shutting-in and petrifaction:

WHEN AT LAST

When at last we can love what we will not touch;
Know what we need not be;
Hum over to ourselves the tune made by the massed instruments
As the shell hums the sea;

Then come the long days without the terrible hour,
And the long nights of rest.
Then the true fruit, from the exhausted flower
Sets, in the breast.

The "true fruit sets" like an extinguishing comet, never to surge forth in a blossom of flame again.

That the third of the meanings is also hovering over the primary, planetary setting is corroborated by a 1959 journal entry about looking back on sexual passion:

When it is over, you say to yourself: "Never possibly can I feel that way again." It is like a wild beast in the heart, that turns its prey over slowly, seeking the soft places, the tender places between bone and bone, the yielding muscle and soft flesh, wherein the teeth may sink. . . . The dead yet living victim is turned; the eater seeks slowly, passionately, the next place in which to *set its fang*. The wounds are made but do not bleed. (My emphasis)

Both poem and prose appear in *Journey Around My Room: The Autobiography of Louise Bogan,* pp. 68, 130.

7. J. M. Coetzee, *Age of Iron* (New York: Random House, 1990), p. 113.

8. J. M. Coetzee, *Foe* [1986] (London: Penguin, 1987), p. 30.

9. J. M. Coetzee, *Waiting for the Barbarians* [1980] (Harmondsworth: Penguin, 1982), p. 34.

10. J. M. Coetzee, *In the Heart of the Country* [1977] (Harmondsworth: Penguin, 1982), pp. 130, 134, 135.

11. As will have become apparent, Coetzee assigns names to his people only grudgingly, as if they deterred the emergence of true selves from the chrysalis of contingency. Any commentary like mine inevitably misgives the flavor of the book by the frequent necessity of calling the speaker by her married surname (we never learn her given name, nor does her beloved daughter have any name at all). But Coetzee's suppression of true names takes on an added dimension in *Age of Iron,* in part political, in part mystical. In keeping with her suspicion that "Vercueil" may have been sent as her angelic psychopomp, to lead her out of life, the narrator speculates that this already rickety invention of syllables is probably not his real name; at least it is only a partial one, truncated by formality (the "Mr."). Furthermore, the woman in domestic service to Mrs. Curren, known as "Florence" (who has no surname), has for years concealed her son Bheki's true name (he had for twelve years been known to her as "Digby"), and even now she presents her two baby daughters to the whites under the allegorical masks of "Hope" and "Beauty." The native names (like "Guguletu") are as disturbing in their evocation of an uncharted second world as is the erasure of all individuality by certain authoritarian designations (Florence's relatives live in a village called only "Site C").

12. The narrator of *Age of Iron,* which is at once the longest and most eloquent of Coetzee's novels, and the one with the greatest urgency and sense of terseness, is a word-child: She hungers for words, she hungers for the comfort in their meanings that her intelligence is glancingly able to provide, while also haunted by the meanings that disappear behind their meanings. She ponders the analogies between like sounds, also between the words for experiences that have become inextricably plaited at this new threshold of nightmare on painkillers. Thus the drug "diconal" and the battlefield from *War and Peace* about which she dreams, "Borodino," become anagrammatic in a ghostly sense. She educes false linkages, like the two above, and an earlier one, in which she informs Vercueil that "charity" derives "from the Latin word for heart." Then she admits to her daughter and to herself that this was "A lie: charity, *caritas,* has nothing to do with the heart. . . . Care: the true root or charity. I look for him to care, and he does not. Because he is beyond caring. Beyond caring and beyond care" (22). Strictly speaking, of course, *caritas* derives from the word for *dear one, carus.* On the other hand, *to care* comes from the Anglo-Saxon *cearin,* to sorrow, grieve, or worry for.

13. Mrs. Curren is here numb from trying to hold the skin closed over a black

child's severely gashed forehead, and recalling a day when her daughter had to have a cut dressed at the hospital.

14. Coetzee does not even need to mention the fact that self-immolation is the most haunting modern image of political dissent. One can still see the flames around the rigid figure of the seated Buddhist monk in Vietnam.

15. See the *Current Biography Yearbook* (New York: H. W. Wilson, 1987), p. 106a.

16. Harold E. Stearns, ed., *America Now: An Inquiry into Civilization in the United States by Thirty-Six Americans* (New York: Charles Scribner's Sons, 1938), pp. 82–83. Quoted by Ruth Limmer in *Journey Around My Room*, p. 62.

Conclusion

1. This exchange of letters appears in *APR* (May/June 1984): 37–38.

2. Muir, *An Autobiography* (London: Hogarth Press, 1954), p. 221.

3. Jorie Graham, "Updraft," *Erosion*, p. 62. See also "The Rhapsodic Fallacy," above, especially pp. 18–21. Considerations of Adrienne Rich and Sharon Olds appear in my essays, "Weeds in Tar" (*APR* [May/June 1985]) and "Idiom and Error" (*APR* [July/August 1984)], respectively.

4. In the same issue of *APR* (May/June 1984).

5. See Nabokov's study, *Gogol* (New York: New Directions, 1944), pp. 63–74.

6. The phrase "literal symbol" was coined by Christine Brooke-Rose in *A Grammar of Metaphor*. Her examples are from Yeats—tower, stare's nest, ditch—objects that are themselves in a deeply localized way before (but as a precondition for) their emergence as archetypes of thought, transient effort, and the sordidness of human fate. See chaps. 1 and 2 on "Simple Replacement" metaphors, passim, also pp. 29–30, 67, and 315–17.

7. Eleanor Wilner, "Bat Cave," revised manuscript version of "Return to Bali," *Calyx* (Summer 1991). The poem is forthcoming (from the University of Chicago Press) in Wilner's fourth volume, *Otherwise*.

8. E. M. Forster, *A Passage to India* (New York: Harcourt, Brace & World, 1952 [1924]).

9. Bonnie Costello's comment, along with responses by Marjorie Perloff, Julia Randall, Alan Shapiro, Paul Breslin, and Stephen Yenser to "The Rhapsodic Fallacy" as it originally appeared in *Salmagundi* (Fall 1984), appeared in *Salmagundi* (Summer 1985). Responses by Terrence Diggory and Charles Molesworth appeared in the Fall 1984 issue along with the essay.

10. Harold Rosenberg, *The Tradition of the New* (New York: McGraw-Hill, 1960), in Preface, n.p.

11. By Charles Simic. See above, "The Rhapsodic Fallacy."

12. *Selected Letters of Theodore Roethke*, p. 104.

13. Michel Foucault, "What Is an Author?" [1969], in *Language, Counter-Memory, Practice: Selected Essays and Interviews*, by Michel Foucault, ed. D. F.

Bouchard (Ithaca: Cornell University Press, 1977), pp. 113–38. These references, p. 127.

14. The first two excerpts are from the anonymous ballads "This ae nighte" and "Sir Patrick Spens," and the third from "The Horses" (1956), by Edwin Muir.

15. Denis Dutton, "Why Intentionalism Won't Go Away," in *Literature and the Question of Philosophy,* ed. Anthony J. Cascardi (Baltimore: Johns Hopkins University Press, 1987), pp. 207–8.

16. Iris Murdoch, "Against Dryness: A Polemical Sketch," *Encounter 16* (1961): 16–20. These citations are on pp. 18, 19.

17. See "The Rhapsodic Fallacy," p. 4, and the note on M. H. Abrams and the four theories of poetry, p. 312 above.

18. Murdoch, "Against Dryness," p. 20.

Index